W9-DFT-845

POLITICAL DYNAMICS

OF

CONSTITUTIONAL LAW

Third Edition

By

Louis Fisher
Senior Specialist in Separation of Powers
Congressional Research Service
The Library of Congress

Neal Devins
Goodrich Professor of Law
Marshall-Wythe School of Law
College of William and Mary

AMERICAN CASEBOOK SERIES®

WEST
GROUP

ST. PAUL, MINN., 2001

West Group has created this publication to provide you with accurate and authoritative information concerning the subject matter covered. However, this publication was not necessarily prepared by persons licensed to practice law in a particular jurisdiction. West Group is not engaged in rendering legal or other professional advice, and this publication is not a substitute for the advice of an attorney. If you require legal or other expert advice, you should seek the services of a competent attorney or other professional.

American Casebook Series, and the West Group symbol
are registered trademarks used herein under license.

COPYRIGHT © 2001 By WEST GROUP
    610 Opperman Drive
    P.O. Box 64526
    St. Paul, MN 55164–0526
    1–800–328–9352

All rights reserved
Printed in the United States of America

ISBN 0–314–24230–9

 *TEXT IS PRINTED ON 10% POST CONSUMER RECYCLED PAPER*

*To The College of William
and Mary for intellectual
stimulation*

*

PREFACE

Constitutional decisionmaking cannot be traced solely to the efforts of nine Justices, or a majority of nine. Other parts of government both interpret the Constitution and influence the judiciary. Volleys between the elected branches and the courts take place on a regular basis. Unfortunately, this creative and healthy exchange is largely overlooked in the literature on constitutional law. The consequence, as noted by Professor Michael Reisman of the Yale Law School, is that there is no "comprehensive course on constitutional law in any meaningful sense in American law schools." W. Michael Reisman, International Incidents: Introduction to a New Genre in the Study of International Law, 10 Yale J. Int'l L. 1, 8 n.13 (1984).

This state of affairs is regrettable. Courses in constitutional law and the judicial process offer a rare opportunity for students to learn both about governmental operations and the workings of three-branch interpretation. A book highlighting the interchange between the courts and the elected branches will help correct this deficiency.

The purpose of this book is to expose students to a broad array of materials that bear directly on constitutional law—materials not covered in traditional constitutional law casebooks. These materials include excerpts from congressional sources (legislative debates, hearings, committee reports, and court filings), White House sources (presidential signing statements, executive orders, and White House/departmental communications), Department of Justice sources (Attorney General opinions, Solicitor General briefs, and internal departmental memoranda), Supreme Court sources (oral arguments, correspondence between Justices, and case conferences), interest group activities (briefs, position papers, party platforms), academic research (studies on implementation of judicial decisions, as well as studies of litigants and attorneys involved in landmark cases), and executive, legislative, and judicial activities at the state level.

These materials will allow the student to understand the process of lawmaking and oversight in Congress, the stages of decisionmaking within agencies, and the preparation of documents for a court challenge. Effective participation in constitutional and administrative law requires a sophisticated understanding of the operations in all three branches.

Conventional constitutional law casebooks omit these materials. Aside from incompletely describing the shaping of constitutional values, these omissions are unfortunate for several reasons. First, the constitutional law class is enlivened by the introduction of nonjudicial material. Students are better equipped and more willing to discuss constitutional doctrine when it is played against the larger backdrop of political pressures welling within and outside the government.

Second, the inclusion of nonjudicial materials is much more than an intellectual exercise. Irrespective of whether students ever participate in constitutional litigation, exposure to legislative and executive documents is critical for a quality legal education. The typical law school curriculum, however, does not mandate coverage of such materials. This book fills a void in the traditional legal education.

Third, a good attorney must be able to function in every sector: judicial, legislative, and executive (state as well as federal). If an attorney finds one avenue closed, others may be available. Thus, Nathan Lewin represented Captain Goldman on the yarmulke case. Goldman v. Weinberger, 475 U.S. 503 (1986). First he tried to convince the Air Force to change its regulation to permit Goldman to wear his yarmulke indoors while on duty. Losing that effort, Lewis took the issue to federal district court and the U.S. Supreme Court, failing once again. On a final round, he turned to Congress to seek legislation directing the Air Force to change the restrictive regulation. His last move proved to be the winning one.

The dilemma faced by law professors is understandable. To make room for new cases, textbooks in constitutional law give short shrift to nonjudicial activities or ignore them altogether. The result is a truncated view of how law develops. Our book is designed to supplement the traditional textbook in constitutional law. The detailed case studies in this book—each illustrated with documents—will allow the student to understand the deficiencies of court-centered analyses and to appreciate the richness of more comprehensive perspectives.

Table of Abbreviations

In all documents and readings, footnotes have been deleted. For citations in the introductory essays and some of the readings, standard reference works are abbreviated as follows:

Annals of Cong.	Annals of Congress. Volumes of congressional debates of Congress from 1789 to 1824.
C.F.R.	Code of Federal Regulations. Agency rules, regulations, and orders currently in effect.
Cong. Globe	Congressional Globe. Volumes of congressional debates from 1833 to 1873.
Cong. Rec.	Congressional Record. Volumes of congressional debates from 1873 to present.
Elliot	Jonathan Elliot, ed., The Debates in the Several State Conventions, on the Adoption of the Federal Constitution (5 vols., Washington, D.C., 1836-1845).
Fed. Reg.	Federal Register. Includes presidential proclamations, executive orders, and agency regulations.
Farrand	Max Farrand, ed., The Records of the Federal Convention of 1787 (4 Vols., New Haven: Yale University Press, 1937).
Landmark Briefs	Landmark Briefs and Arguments of the Supreme Court of the United States: Constitutional Law. G. Gunther & G. Casper, eds. University Publications of America.
Pub. Papers	Public Papers of the Presidents, published annually by the Government Printing Office.
Richardson	James D. Richardson, ed., A Compilation of the Messages and Papers of the Presidents (20 vols., New York: Bureau of National Literature, 1897-1925).
Stat.	United States Statutes at Large.
Weekly Comp. Pres. Doc.	Weekly Compilation of Presidential Documents, published each week by the Government Printing Office since 1965.

Appreciation

The initial book proposal was reviewed by several scholars who provided careful critiques. We appreciate the insights of Erwin Chemerinsky, Jesse Choper, Larry Evans, John H. Garvey, Michael Gerhardt, Chuck Hobson, Yale Kamisar, Charles Koch, Thomas R. McCoy, Robert Nagel, Peter Shane, and Ron Wright. We have also benefitted from conversations with faculty who adopted the book, including Ann Althouse, Bill Banks, Bob Katzmann, Andy Koppelman, Jessica Korn, Andrew Kull, William Ross, and Laura Tartakoff. We value their support and enthusiasm for studying constitutional law as the product of nonjudicial as well as judicial forces. Special thanks are also owed to Cheryl Keller and Tim Sullivan for their support and encouragement. Michael Strine very generously gave us a number of key documents from the Carter Library that we relied on in analyzing the *Garcia* case in Chapter 3.

Several students at the William and Mary School of Law read the draft chapters and offered important substantive and stylistic suggestions for both editions of this book. They did cite-checking and proof-reading for all the documents and performed a variety of research tasks in locating and analyzing documentary materials. In particular, we want to thank Ro Carlton, Katherine Ennis, Keith Finch, Elizabeth Hallock, Robert Juelke, Mary Kay Korb, Susan Korzick, Dan Pringle, Nick Procaccini, Chris Shea, Jan Starkweather, Josh Stump, Mary Thrower, Wendy Watson, Krista Weber, and Jarrell Wright.

The word processing for this edition was performed ably by Della Harris at the William and Mary School of Law. For her patience and expertise we are deeply in debt.

Finally, we would like to thank West Publishing's Tom Berreman, Doug Powell, Pam Siege, and Pat Sparks. Their willingness to sign onto this project as well as their advice and encouragement have been appreciated.

About the Authors

Louis Fisher is Senior Specialist in Separation of Powers at the Congressional Research Service of the Library of Congress. He has testified before congressional committees on such constitutional issues as the balanced budget amendment, covert funding, the legislative veto, the item veto, the pocket veto, executive privilege, recess appointments, presidential reorganization authority, and the Gramm-Rudman Act. He served as research director of the House Iran-Contra Committee in 1987 and wrote major sections of the final report. His publications include more than 260 articles in edited books, law reviews, political science journals, magazines, and newspapers. His books include *Congressional Abdication on War and Spending* (Texas A&M University Press, 2000); *American Constitutional Law* (3d ed., Carolina Academic Press, 1999); *Presidential War Power* (University Press of Kansas, 1995); *Encyclopedia of the American Presidency*, with Leonard W. Levy (4 vols., Simon & Schuster, 1994); *Constitutional Conflicts between Congress and the President* (4th ed., University Press of Kansas, 1997); *Constitutional Dialogues* (Princeton University Press, 1988); *The Politics of Shared Power* (4th ed., Texas A&M University Press, 1998); *The Constitution between Friends* (St. Martin's, 1978); *Presidential Spending Power* (Princeton University Press, 1975); and *President and Congress* (The Free Press, 1972). Professor Fisher is a graduate of the College of William and Mary (B.S. 1956) and the New School for Social Research (Ph.D. 1967).

Neal Devins is a professor of law and lecturer in government at the College of William and Mary. Professor Devins previously served as Assistant General Counsel, U.S. Commission on Civil Rights (1984-87) and as Project Director, Vanderbilt Institute for Public Policies Studies (1982-84). He is the author of *Shaping Constitutional Values: The Supreme Court, Elected Government, and the Abortion Dispute* (Johns Hopkins University Press, 1996), editor of *Government Lawyering* (Law and Contemporary Problems, 1998), co-editor of *Redefining Equality* (Oxford University Press, 1998), editor of *Elected Branch Influences in Constitutional Decisionmaking* (Law and Contemporary Problems, 1993), and editor of *Public Values, Private Schools* (Stanford Series on Education and Public Policy, 1989). He is the author of numerous articles on constitutional, civil rights, and education topics. His work has appeared in *The Public Interest, Commonweal, The ABA Journal, The Stanford Law Review, The Columbia Law Review, The Michigan Law Review, The California Law Review, The Virginia Law Review, The University of Pennsylvania Law Review, The Texas Law Review, The Duke Law Journal, The UCLA Law Review, The Georgetown Law Journal*, and several other journals and magazines. Professor Devins is also the author of op-eds appearing in *The Wall Street Journal, The New York Times, The Washington Post, The Christian Science Monitor, The Chicago Tribune*, and several other newspapers. He has testified before Congress on budget reform and separation of powers. Professor Devins is a graduate of Georgetown University (A.B. 1978) and Vanderbilt Law School (J.D. 1982).

ACKNOWLEDGMENTS

We would like to thank the authors and copyright holders of the following works, who permitted their inclusion in this book:

Robert H. Bork, Neutral Principles and Some First Amendment Problems, 47 Indiana Law Journal 1 (1971 by the Trustees of Indiana University. Reprinted by permission.)

John H. Chafee, Congress Should Remedy the Court's Decision, Washington Post, June 7, 1991. Copyright (c) The Washington Post. Reprinted with permission.

Walter Dellinger and H. Jefferson Powell, The Constitutionality of the Bank Bill: The Attorney General's First Constitutional Law Opinions. Originally published in 44 Duke Law Journal 110, 122, 127, 130, Copyright 1994, The Duke Law Journal. All Rights Reserved.

Charles Fried, Order and Law. Copyright (c)1991 by Charles Fried. Reprinted by permission of Simon & Schuster.

Paul Gewirtz, Congress, As Well As Courts, Must Make Constitutional Law, Hartford Courant, July 24, 1988. Reprinted by permission.

Barry Goldwater, The Gay Ban: Just Plain Un-American, Washington Post, June 10, 1993. (c)1993 The Washington Post. Reprinted with permission.

Lani Guinier, Voting Rights and Democratic Theory—Where Do We Go From Here?, in Controversies in Minority Voting: The Voting Rights Act in Perspective, 283, 289-90 (Bernard Grofman & Chandler Davidson eds., 1992). Reprinted by permission of The Brookings Institute.

Peter Irons, The Courage of Their Convictions. Reprinted by permission of Peter Irons, Professor of Political Science, University of California, San Diego.

Robert H. Jackson, A Presidential Legal Opinion, 66 Harvard Law Review 1353 (1953). Copyright (c)1953 by the Harvard Law Review Association.

John C. Jefferies, Jr., Justice Lewis F. Powell, Jr. Copyright (c)1994 by John C. Jeffries, Jr. Reprinted by permission of the author.

Anthony Lewis, Law or Power?, The New York Times, October 27, 1986. Copyright (c)1986 by The New York Times Company. Reprinted by permission.

Edwin Meese, The Law of the Constitution, 61 Tulane Law Review 979 (1987). Reprinted by permission of Tulane Law Review.

Ronald Reagan, Abortion and the Conscience of the Nation (1984). Reprinted with permission.

William H. Rehnquist, The Supreme Court. Copyright (c)1987 by William H. Rehnquist. Reprinted by permission of the author.

Laurence H. Silberman, The Road to Racial Quotas, The Wall Street Journal, August 11, 1977. Copyright (c)1977 by Laurence H. Silberman. Reprinted by permission of the author.

Earl Warren, The Bill of Rights and the Military, 37 New York University Law Review 181, 182, 191-93 (1962). Reprinted with permission of New York University Law Review.

Pete Wilson, Equal Rights, Not Special Privileges, The Los Angeles Times, June 1, 1995. Copyright (c)1995 Pete Wilson. Reprinted with permission.

TABLE OF CONTENTS

Chapter 1. Constitutional Politics 1

Principal cases discussed: Marbury v. Madison (1803), Dred Scott v. Sandford (1857); Cooper v. Aaron (1958)

Chapter 2. Judicial Authority 23

Principal cases discussed: Marbury v. Madison (1803), McCulloch v. Maryland (1819), Ex Parte McCardle (1868), Bob Jones University v. United States (1983), Allen v. Wright (1984), Powell v. McCormack (1969)

Chapter 3. Federalism 61

Principal cases discussed: Hammer v. Dagenhart (1918), Child Labor Tax Case (1922), United States v. Darby (1941), The Civil Rights Cases (1883), Heart of Atlanta Motel v. United States (1964), Katzenbach v. McClung (1964), National League of Cities v. Usery (1976), Garcia v. San Antonio Metropolitan Transit Authority (1985), New York v. United States (1992), United States v. Lopez (1995), Boerne v. Flores (1997), United States v. Morrison (2000)

Chapter 4. Separation of Powers: Domestic Conflicts . 105

Chapter 5. The War Power and Covert Actions 153

Chapter 6. Privacy 181

Chapter 7. Gay Rights 219

Chapter 8. Race 243

Principal cases discussed: Bradwell v. State (1883), Muller v. Oregon (1908), Frontiero v. Richardson (1973), Rostker v. Goldberg (1981)

TABLE OF CASES

CONSTITUTIONAL POLITICS

The complex and pervasive interactions among the branches of government in making constitutional law are largely unknown to students. They are taught that the courts are the dominant if not exclusive interpreters of the Constitution. Beginning with *Marbury* v. *Madison* (1803), students learn that judges are the "final arbiters" of the meaning of the Constitution, that all issues of constitutional moment percolate upwards to the Court for resolution, and that nonjudicial actors sit passively awaiting the Court's judgment.

This picture is highly simplistic. Even a general understanding of American legal history does not support the view that courts are the predominant force in shaping the Constitution. Court judgments are regularly overturned by constitutional amendments, congressional statutes, state actions, and shifting social and political attitudes. Judges are merely one of many authoritative actors in the complicated process of constitutional change.

To be effective in this complex environment, the student of law needs to understand the various arenas that affect constitutional values. A defeat in the courts does not necessarily end the struggle for constitutional rights and liberties. It may only mark a momentary setback, stimulating the attorney and client to pursue their interests in the legislature, an executive agency, in the states and in the public media. When the courts close one door, others remain open. To this extent, it can be said that a court ruling is "final" only when society accepts it as well-reasoned and persuasive. Otherwise, the search for constitutional values continues.

I. PARTICIPANTS AND PROCESSES

Constitutions draw their life from a variety of forces that operate outside the courts: ideas, customs, social pressures, and the constant dialogue that takes place among political institutions. Just as the judiciary leaves its mark on society, so does society drive the agenda and decisions of the courts. Justice Cardozo reminded us that the "great tides and currents which engulf the rest of men do not turn aside in their course and pass the judges by." Benjamin N. Cardozo, The Nature of the Judicial Process 168 (1921). *[handwritten: judicial attitudes]*

To safeguard their institutional position, courts must make accommodations with social pressures and public opinion. At times they take the lead, but the historical record demonstrates that the judiciary often accepts the political boundaries of its times. Attempts to defy those boundaries and invalidate the policies of elected leaders create substantial risks for the legitimacy and effectiveness of the judicial system. Abstract legal analysis is tempered by a sense of pragmatism and statesmanship among judges.

Of course, constitutional interpretations by the courts are not simply mirror images of contemporary values. If that were true, there would be no need for a constitution or for courts to decide constitutional decisions. All constitutional questions could be left with legislative bodies, as is the case in such countries as England and Holland. By contrast, federal courts in the United States play an important function in deliberating on constitutional questions and deciding the constitutional powers of Congress, the President, executive agencies, and the states. But courts are not the sole participants in the process of shaping and declaring constitutional values. They share that task with other political institutions at both the national and the state level.

A. Congress

Congress performs a crucial role in constitutional analysis at many stages: enacting laws that balance various constitutional values, investigating constitutional violations by legislators and executive officials, and intervening in court cases. Bills are subjected to constitutional analysis by members, committee staff, and such legislative agencies as the Congressional Research Service of the Library of Congress. Outside experts are invited to testify at congressional hearings on constitutional questions. Constitutional questions are regularly analyzed in committee reports and during floor debate.

Throughout the legislative process, Congress invokes its powers to decide constitutional issues. It uses its power of the purse to add restrictive riders and provisos to appropriations bills, thereby controlling the executive branch on constitutional issues and announcing to private citizens the limits of their constitutional rights (such as access to public funds to finance abortions). Legislation is introduced to strip the federal courts (including the Supreme Court) of jurisdiction to hear a case. Legislation may also be introduced to reverse a court ruling that interprets a statute. Through this process, called statutory reversal, Congress may overturn judicial decisions on issues of constitutional moment, including racial and gender discrimination. In 1991, Congress passed a civil rights bill that overturned or modified nine Supreme Court rulings, five of them from 1989, two from 1991, and one each from 1986 and 1987. Moreover, Congress passes constitutional amendments and sends them to the states for ratification, all part of a process that results in overturning Supreme Court decisions.

Congress may respond to a Supreme Court decision by reenacting a statute that the Court struck down. For example, Congress strongly disagreed with the Court's 1918 ruling that the commerce power could not be used to regulate child labor. Hammer v. Dagenhart, 247 U.S. 251 (1918). Twenty years later, after the Court's composition had changed, Congress again based child labor legislation on the commerce clause—legislation that a unanimous Court upheld! United States v. Darby, 312 U.S. 100 (1941). Another way Congress expresses its disapproval of a Supreme Court decision is to protect rights that the Court is unwilling to protect. For example, Congress passed legislation in 1980 to prohibit third-party searches of newspapers, despite the Court's approval of such searches two years before. Zurcher v. Stanford Daily, 436 U.S. 547 (1978). For Congress, this legislation was necessary because the Supreme Court's decision had "thrown into doubt" "a longstanding principle of constitutional jurisprudence." 126 Cong. Rec. 26562 (1980) (statement of Rep. Kastenmeier).

Congressional responses to Supreme Court decisions are not always hostile. Sometimes Congress affirmatively assists in the implementation of a Court decision. For example, in response to Southern resistance to the school segregation decision, Congress took bold steps to make *Brown* v. *Board of Education* (1954) a reality. In 1964, it prohibited segregated systems from receiving federal aid and authorized the Department of Justice to file desegregation lawsuits. These federal efforts proved critical in ending dual school systems. More actual desegregation took place the year after these legislative programs took effect than in the decade following *Brown*.

The appointment of federal judges offers Congress another opportunity to exert its influence on constitutional law. The Senate, during the confirmation process, not only examines the judicial temperament and competence of nominees but inquires into their judicial philosophy as well. If Senators are uncomfortable about the legal doctrines of a nominee, they may reject the person and require the President to send forth another name.

Congress may present its constitutional viewpoints directly to the judiciary. Although Congress initially relied on the Attorney General and the Justice Department to defend congressional interests in court, Congress always retained the prerogative to represent itself directly. In *Myers* v. *United States*, 272 U.S. 52 (1926), which concerned the President's power to remove executive officials, the Supreme Court invited Senator George Wharton Pepper (R-Pa.) to present an amicus curiae (friend of the court) brief and participate in oral argument. Other courts have invited the House of Representatives and the Senate to submit briefs on pending cases.

Individual members of Congress may take constitutional issues directly to the courts for resolution. When President Nixon used the "pocket veto" during a brief Christmas recess in 1972, Senator Edward M. Kennedy (D-Mass.) went to court as a litigant and successfully argued that Nixon's action violated the Constitution. Kennedy v. Sampson, 364 F.Supp. 1075 (D.D.C. 1973), aff'd, Kennedy v. Sampson, 511 F.2d 430 (D.C. Cir. 1974).

On most occasions, members of Congress who take constitutional issues to the courts are told by judges that they lack standing to sue, that the issue is not ripe for adjudication, or that the matter is a "political question" to be resolved by Congress and the President. Judges conclude that few of these cases are genuine cases or controversies between Congress and the President. Instead, they generally represent the failure of one faction of legislators to convince a majority to work its will against the President. Judges basically advise the faction to return to the legislative branch and build a majority. E.g., Crockett v. Reagan, 558 F.Supp. 893 (D.D.C. 1982), aff'd, 720 F.2d 1355 (D.C. Cir. 1983), cert. denied, 467 U.S. 1251 (1984).

In recent decades, members of Congress have created legislative institutions to defend congressional interests in court. The Justice Department sometimes refused to defend the constitutionality of certain statutes, either because they threatened presidential powers or because they invaded constitutional rights. In some situations the Justice Department agreed to defend congressional interests in the district and appellate courts, only to withdraw its representation of Congress when the case reached the Supreme Court. S. Rep. No. 170, 95th Cong., 1st Sess. 11-12 (1977).

To safeguard its institutional prerogatives, the Senate established an Office of Senate Legal Counsel in 1978 to defend the Senate or a committee, subcommittee, member, office, or employee of the Senate. The Senate Legal Counsel may also intervene or appear as amicus curiae in cases involving legislative powers and responsibilities. The House General Counsel handles litigation that involves members, House officers, and staff. Senate and House counsel frequently file briefs and participate in oral argument before the courts.

B. The Executive Branch

Executive power in constitutional decisionmaking is extraordinarily broad. The executive nominates Supreme Court Justices, recommends legislation and constitutional amendments, exercises the veto power, promulgates regulations, and delivers speeches. In each of these ways, the executive interprets the Constitution and shapes constitutional values.

The Constitution guarantees the executive a large role in legislative decisionmaking, requiring the President to recommend measures judged necessary and expedient. The executive has made frequent use of this power, sending proposals to Congress on busing, abortion, flag burning, and school prayer.

Presidents wield the veto power in part to protect the prerogatives of their office and to prevent Congress from passing laws they consider unconstitutional. For example, President George Bush helped maintain strict abortion funding restrictions by successfully vetoing five bills that allowed some federal funding of abortion. Even the threat of a veto is often sufficient reason for Congress to revise or remove contested language in a bill. In cases where the Supreme Court upholds the constitutionality of a federal statute and that statute is later revived or reauthorized by Congress, the President may exercise his own independent judgment and veto the bill on constitutional grounds.

The power of the President to nominate federal judges is a potent tool for redirecting judicial doctrines. Although executive officials deny that they use a "litmus test" to screen potential nominees on their views concerning abortion and other key issues, enough is known in advance about an individual's views before even extending an invitation. Of course an individual, once on the bench, has lifetime tenure and can decide cases antagonistic to the President who originally made the nomination. Presidents are known to express deep disappointment in the conduct of their selections. Nevertheless, the power of appointment can transform the judiciary. President Franklin D. Roosevelt was able, over time, to convert the Supreme Court from a conservative institution to one that was more liberally inclined. Similarly, successive appointments by Presidents Nixon, Reagan, and Bush helped convert the liberal Supreme Court of the Earl Warren era into the conservative Rehnquist Court. Appointments by President Bill Clinton have moved the Court in a more moderate direction.

Through their speeches and use of the "bully pulpit," Presidents may radically change the course of constitutional law. President Franklin D. Roosevelt confronted the Court's views on the commerce power and proposed that the number of Justices be increased so that he could "pack" the Court with nominees sympathetic to his policies. President Ronald Reagan pressed his case against abortion and mobilized opposition to the Court's decision in *Roe* v. *Wade* (1973).

Executive agencies wield enormous power through the process of issuing rules and regulations. Although rulemaking is supposed to implement congressional intent, there is sufficient ambiguity in many statutes for executive officials to push in one direction or another depending on their constitutional beliefs. Congress can challenge these agency interpretations by adopting restrictive riders. Agency rules may also be contested in court, although recent Supreme Court decisions severely limit such challenges. For example, in *Rust* v. *Sullivan* the Court refused to overturn Reagan administration regulations prohibiting federally funded abortion counseling, ruling that substantial deference is owed to executive interpretations. 500 U.S. 173 (1991). Because of the deference given to executive interpretations, however, pro-choice President Clinton was able to order a rewriting of Reagan's regulation.

The Judiciary Act of 1789 established an Attorney General to prosecute and conduct all suits in the Supreme Court concerning the federal government. He represented the interests of Congress as well as the President. The Attorney General functioned as a part-time official for many years. It was not until 1870 that Congress established the Department of Justice. The Attorney General and the Office of Legal Counsel issue important opinions on constitutional matters and also testify before Congress on constitutional questions.

The Solicitor General, created in 1870 to assist the Attorney General, is now primarily responsible for representing the federal government in court. The Solicitor General conducts (or assigns and supervises) Supreme Court cases, including appeals, petitions for certiorari, and the preparation of briefs and arguments. He authorizes or declines to authorize appeals by the federal government to appellate courts, thus controlling the appellate interests of federal agencies. The Solicitor General also authorizes the filing of amicus briefs by the government in all appellate courts.

In 1978, Congress created a mechanism for the appointment of a Special Prosecutor (later called Independent Counsel) to investigate high-level officials in the executive branch. In the wake of the Watergate affair, Congress concluded that the executive branch lacked the necessary independence to investigate allegations of crime and wrongdoing in the high echelons of the administration. In *Morrison* v. *Olson*, 487 U.S. 654 (1988), the Supreme Court upheld the constitutionality of the independent counsel. Legislation in 1994 reauthorized the independent counsel, but in 1999 Congress decided not to renew it.

C. Private Interests

Private organizations sometimes pursue their interests through the regular legislative process, through the executive branch, or through the courts. When one arena is blocked, they test another. The political branches were largely unreceptive to civil rights during the first half of this century, forcing such organizations as the National Association for the Advancement of Colored People (NAACP) to turn to the judiciary for redress of their grievances. As the Court has acknowledged, litigation is not merely a technique for resolving private differences. It is a form of political expression and association. In re Primus, 436 U.S. 412, 428 (1978); NAACP v. Button, 371 U.S. 415, 429-30 (1963).

The heavy resort to litigation by private organizations in the 1940s and 1950s produced fundamental changes in the amicus curiae brief. Previously these briefs permitted third parties, without a direct interest in a case, to bring certain facts to the attention of judges and thereby minimize error in the courts. Eventually the amicus brief became a sharp instrument for advancing the special interests of private groups. The amicus brief progressed "from neutrality to partisanship, from friendship to advocacy." Samuel Krislov, The Amicus Brief: From Friendship to Advocacy, 72 Yale L. J. 694 (1963).

Although many private organizations thought that their interests would be better served through the courts in the 1950s and 1960s, they began to alter their strategy as the judiciary became more conservative as a result of appointments by Presidents Nixon, Ford, Reagan, and Bush. These organizations now often turn to Congress for the protection of their interests. On June 27, 1991, the National Abortion Rights Action League (NARAL) sent a "Supreme Court Alert" to its membership, calling attention to the abortion restrictions being enacted by statute in the states and by regulation in the Bush administration. NARAL, which had previously pursued its interests in court, now stated: "Clearly Congress is our Court of Last Resort. All hope of protecting our constitutional right to choose depends upon our elected representatives in Congress responding to the will of the American people." The American Civil Liberties Union (ACLU), which has used litigation heavily to advance its interests, now said: "Congress is increasingly asked to look at these [constitutional] issues because there is nobody else. It is now the court of last resort." W. John Moore, In Whose Court?, Nat'l J., October 5, 1991, at 2400.

When Congress seems too oriented toward liberal causes, conservative organizations will seek legal change through the courts or executive agencies. Over time, conservatives and liberals change their methods and tactics. In the 1930s, conservatives championed the courts as the necessary defenders of liberty against congressional and presidential pressures. Liberals accused the courts of actively pursuing their agenda at the cost of democratic institutions. A few decades later, liberals and conservatives switched sides. Liberals were now pleased with the leadership of the courts, especially during the Earl Warren years, while conservatives appealed to Congress and the President to curb judicial excesses.

D. Independent State Action

So much attention is directed to decisions of the federal courts that we forget that the states, through their constitutions and statutes, can make constitutional determinations that are wholly at variance with rulings from the U.S. Supreme Court. Instead of a hierarchical system, with each legal issue percolating up to the Supreme Court for a decision that will be applied uniformly across the country, the process is much more pluralistic and decentralized.

The federal Constitution provides only a minimum, or a floor, for the protection of individual rights. State governments remain free to grant greater rights to their citizens. As noted by the U.S. Supreme Court, each state has the "sovereign right to adopt in its own Constitution individual liberties more expansive than those conferred by the Federal Constitution." PruneYard Shopping Center v. Robins, 447 U.S. 74, 81 (1980).   State courts frequently exercise this authority, playing a leadership role on the exclusionary rule, freedom of speech, freedom of religion, equal educational opportunity, and privacy.

State courts must make clear that their rulings rest exclusively on the constitution and laws of the state. If state courts base their decisions on "bona fide separate, adequate and independent grounds," the U.S. Supreme Court will not undertake a review. Michigan v. Long, 463 U.S. 1032 (1983).   Under those conditions, the "final word" on state constitutional law rests with the states, not the U.S. Supreme Court.

Exemplifying the many ways state constitutions provide broader protection than the federal Constitution are state court rulings on abortion. State court involvement here is not surprising: ten state constitutions contain explicit privacy provisions and several others contain clauses that have been interpreted to protect the right to privacy. Before *Roe* v. *Wade*, many state courts struck down abortion prohibitions. State courts have remained active. Following the Supreme Court's 1980 approval of federal abortion funding bans, state courts in Massachusetts, California, New Jersey, Oregon, Connecticut, and Michigan ruled that indigent women were nevertheless guaranteed the right to a state-funded abortion. For example, the New Jersey Supreme Court proclaimed that "[a]lthough the state constitution may encompass a smaller universe than the federal constitution, our constellation of rights may be more complete." Right to Choose v. Byrne, 450 A.2d 925, 931 (N.J. 1982). Similarly, the California Court of Appeals declared its state constitution a "document of *independent* force" providing privacy protections "broader" than the federal Constitution. American Academy of Pediatrics v. Van de Kamp, 263 Cal. Rptr. 46, 49, 51 (1989) (original emphasis).

Holdings such as these are likely to become increasingly commonplace. The Rehnquist Court's reluctance to expand constitutional protections has already resulted in interest groups turning their attention to state courts and state legislatures. The ongoing flurry of activity in state government and state courts on the abortion question therefore is more than a harbinger of things to come; it is proof positive of the fundamental role played by the states in shaping constitutional values.

E. Conclusion

The view that constitutional truth derives solely from nine individuals (or a majority of them) sitting on the Supreme Court is overly parochial and ultimately shortsighted. Congress, the White House, government agencies, interest groups, the general public, and the states all play critical interdependent roles in shaping constitutional values. As noted by Ruth Bader Ginsburg a year before her appointment to the Supreme Court, judges "play an interdependent part in our democracy. They do not alone shape legal doctrine but . . . they participate in a dialogue with other organs of government, and with the people as well." Ruth Bader Ginsburg, Speaking in a Judicial Voice, 67 N.Y.U.L. Rev. 1185, 1198 (1992).

II. THREE-BRANCH INTERPRETATION

Beginning with Chief Justice Marshall's declaration in *Marbury v. Madison* that it is "emphatically the province and duty of the judicial department to say what the law is," the Supreme Court regularly insists that it alone delivers the "final word" on the meaning of the Constitution. According to a 1958 decision, *Marbury* "declared the basic principle that the federal judiciary is supreme in the exposition of the law of the Constitution." Cooper v. Aaron, 358 U.S. 1, 18. The Court reasserted this principle in 1962: "Deciding whether a matter has in any measure been committed by the Constitution to another branch of government, or whether action of that branch exceeds whatever authority has been committed, is itself a delicate exercise in constitutional interpretation, and is a responsibility of this Court as ultimate interpreter of the Constitution." Baker v. Carr, 369 U.S. 186, 211. The notion that the Court is the ultimate interpreter of the Constitution was repeated in *Powell v. McCormack*, 395 U.S. 486, 549 (1969).

In a memorable aphorism, Justice Jackson claimed that decisions by the Supreme Court "are not final because we are infallible, but we are infallible only because we are final." Brown v. Allen, 344 U.S. 443, 540 (1953). Yet the historical record provides overwhelming evidence that the Court is neither final nor infallible. The Court is the ultimate interpreter in a particular case, but not always the larger issue of which that case is a part.

Under the doctrine of "coordinate construction," the elected branches have both the authority and the competence to engage in constitutional interpretation. They participate before the courts decide and they participate afterwards as well. The process is circular, turning back on itself again and again until society is satisfied with the outcome.

All public officers—executive, legislative, and judicial—are required by Article VI, Clause 3 of the U.S. Constitution "to support this Constitution." That obligation is supplemented by federal law, under which executive and legislative officials "solemnly swear (or affirm) . . . [to] support and defend the Constitution of the United States against all enemies, foreign and domestic; . . . bear true faith and allegiance to the same; . . . take this obligation freely, without any mental reservation or purpose of evasion; and . . . well and faithfully discharge the duties [of their office]." 5 U.S.C. §3331 (1994).

To fulfill that oath of office, members of Congress and their staffs study the constitutionality of a bill while it is being drafted, considered in committee, and debated on the floor. Executive officials apply their constitutional knowledge at each stage of the legislative process. When the bill is finally presented to the President, staff in the White House, the Justice Department, the Office of Management and Budget, and other executive agencies carefully review the bill for possible constitutional problems.

A. Establishing Precedents

In the early decades of our Republic, constitutional analysis was by necessity dominated by Congress and the President. The Supreme Court had handed down few decisions on constitutional law, giving practically no guidance for the many complex constitutional issues that perplexed legislators and executive officials. In 1789, Congress had to decide whether the President possessed an implied power to remove executive officials. Some members of Congress suggested that the issue might be better handled by the courts. James Madison disagreed, seeing no need to defer to the judiciary. There was no reason why Congress should not "expound the Constitution, so far as it relates to the division of power between the President and the Senate." 1 Annals of Cong. 439. It was just as important to Congress "that the Constitution should be preserved entire. It is our duty, so far as it depends upon us, to take care that the powers of the Constitution be preserved entire to every department of Government." Id.

Passage of the Alien and Sedition Acts in 1798 sparked a fierce debate about constitutional values. Opponents focused particularly on the sedition law, which prohibited citizens from criticizing their own government. The dominant agencies in this battle were Congress and the President. When Thomas Jefferson took office as President in 1801, he considered the Sedition Act a "nullity" and pardoned every person prosecuted under it (document 1). Congress used its power of the purse to reimburse anyone fined under the Act, expressing its own views about the unconstitutionality of the statute (document 2). Over a century later the Supreme Court acknowledged that the Sedition Act had been struck down not by a court of law but by "the court of history." New York Times Co. v. Sullivan, 376 U.S. 254, 276 (1964).

Jefferson believed that the three branches must be "co-ordinate, and independent of each other." Decisions by one branch, including judicial interpretations of constitutional issues, were to be given "no control to another branch." 11 Writings of Thomas Jefferson 213-14 (Albert Ellery Bergh ed. 1904). Each branch of government "has an equal right to decide for itself what is the meaning of the Constitution in the cases submitted to its action; and especially, where it is to act ultimately and without appeal." 15 Writings of Thomas Jefferson 214 (Albert Ellery Bergh ed. 1904).

In 1832, President Andrew Jackson announced his own theory of coordinate construction when he vetoed a bill that would have rechartered the Bank of the United States. Many urged Jackson to sign the bill, advising him that the issue was "settled" because the Bank had already been upheld by the Supreme Court in *McCulloch v. Maryland* (1819) and previous Congresses and Presidents had accepted the constitutionality of the Bank. Jackson rejected such arguments. Regardless of what others had decided in the past, even on the precise question now before him, Jackson felt totally free to reach his own independent judgment (document 3).

Another insight into three-branch interpretation comes from the bitter struggle over slavery. Opposition to slavery came from the public, not from judicial, legislative, or executive actions. Individual Americans, although untutored in the fine points of constitutional law, viewed slavery as repugnant to fundamental political and ethical principles, especially those embedded in the Declaration of Independence. The pivotal antislavery documents were private writings and speeches, not court decisions or legislative statutes.

For decades, Congress tried to maintain a balance between free states and slave states. The Missouri Compromise Act of 1820 admitted Missouri as a slave state but prohibited slavery in future states north of the 36° 30' line. With the Compromise Act of 1850 and the Kansas-Nebraska Act of 1854, the political branches seemed unable to resolve the issue and appeared to punt the question to the courts. James Buchanan, elected President in 1856, wanted to mention the subject of slavery in his inaugural address, but was uncertain of the Court's plans to decide a pending case. Justices Catron and Grier wrote to him that the Court was indeed ready to decide the matter, and that Buchanan should say that in his address (document 4). Buchanan then assured the country that the divisive issue of slavery was before the Court where it would be "speedily and finally settled" (document 5). Two days later the Court issued *Dred Scott v. Sandford*, propelling the nation toward civil war.

Throughout 1858, Stephen Douglas and Abraham Lincoln debated the finality of *Dred Scott*. Douglas insisted that the decision was the law of the land and should be obeyed. Lincoln agreed that he would not disturb the case as it related to the particular litigants, but refused to accept the Court's major holding that blacks could not be citizens and that Congress could not prohibit slavery in the territories. Lincoln regarded the Court as a coequal, not a superior, branch of government (document 6). In his inaugural address of 1861, Lincoln denied that constitutional questions could be settled solely by the Supreme Court. If public policy on "vital questions affecting the whole people is to be irrevocably fixed" by the Court, "the people will have ceased to be their own rulers." 7 A Compilation of the Messages and Papers of the Presidents 3210-11 (James D. Richardson ed. 1897-1925).

Dred Scott was eventually overturned by the Civil War Amendments (ratified from 1865 to 1870), but long before that time it was effectively eviscerated by legislative and executive actions. Acting through the regular legislative process, Congress passed a bill to prohibit slavery in the territories. 12 Stat. 432, c.111 (1862). In that same year, Attorney General Bates issued an opinion in which he concluded that blacks had been citizens in the past and could be in the future. 10 Op. Att'y Gen. 382 (1862).

B. Contemporary Debates

In 1986, Attorney General Edwin Meese III sent shock waves across the country by challenging the last-word dogma. In a speech delivered at Tulane University, he distinguished between the Constitution and constitutional law. He referred to the first as fundamental law, capable of change solely by constitutional amendment, while the second represents only the body of law developed by the Supreme Court. He quoted from constitutional historian Charles Warren that "however the Court may interpret the provisions of the Constitution, it is still the Constitution which is the law, not the decisions of the Court" (document 7).

Meese was careful in explaining that Warren did not mean that Supreme Court decisions lack the character of law, and that the decisions bind the parties to the case and require the executive branch to enforce the decisions. However, the decisions do not "establish a 'supreme Law of the Land' that is binding on all persons and parts of government, henceforth and forevermore." Obviously that is so, for otherwise the Court could never reverse itself, which it does with some regularity.

Although Meese had added these qualifiers to his general thesis, the speech triggered an avalanche of criticism. A journalist accused Meese of dropping a "jurisprudential stink bomb" that showed disrespect for the Court. Michael Kinsley, Meese's Stink Bomb, Wash. Post, October 29,1986, at A19. Constitutional scholars predicted "enormous chaos" if Meese's view ever prevailed. Howard Kurtz, Meese's View on Court Rulings Assailed, Defended, Wash. Post, October 24, 1986, at. A12. Professor Laurence Tribe of the Harvard Law School warned that Meese's position "represents a grave threat to the rule of law." Stuart Taylor, Liberties Union Denounces Meese; The N.Y. Times, October 24, 1986, at A17. Anthony Lewis of *The New York Times* stated that the speech invited anarchy (document 8).

In response to this criticism, Meese offered to clarify his position. He said again that Supreme Court decisions have general applicability and that they bind the parties in the case at hand. A Court decision is binding precedent on lower federal courts as well as state courts. He agreed with Lincoln that such decisions are "entitled to very high respect and consideration in all parallel cases" by the other departments of government, both federal and state. Arguments from prudence, the need for stability in the law, and respect for the judiciary "will and should persuade officials of these other institutions to abide by a decision of the Court." However, Meese continued to hold to the view that "only the Constitution is our paramount law, not what the three branches say about it." Edwin Meese, III, The Tulane Speech: What I Meant, 61 Tulane L. Rev. 1003-07 (1987).

This controversy over Meese seemed to prompt Senators to use the nomination of Supreme Court Justices as a forum for defending judicial supremacy. The question of whether the Court has the "last word" on constitutional issues added spice to three confirmation hearings for Supreme Court Justices in 1986 and 1987.

In 1986, when Justice William Rehnquist appeared before the Senate Judiciary Committee as nominee for Chief Justice, Senator Arlen Specter inquired about the "binding precedent" of *Marbury*. He asked Rehnquist whether the Court "is the final arbiter, the final decision-maker of what the Constitution means." Rehnquist replied disarmingly: "Unquestionably." Specter pursued the point. If the Court ruled on a legal issue, would the

President and Congress "have a responsibility to observe the decisions of the Supreme Court of the United States on a constitutional matter?" Rehnquist replied: "Yes, I think they do." Nomination of Justice William Hubbs Rehnquist: Hearings Before the Senate Comm. on the Judiciary, 99th Cong., 2d Sess. 186 (1986).

A different impression emerged later in 1986 when Judge Antonin Scalia appeared before the Senate Judiciary Committee as nominee for Associate Justice. Unlike Rehnquist, Scalia was reluctant to discuss the scope of *Marbury*. Chairman Strom Thurmond put this question: "Do you agree that *Marbury* requires the President and Congress to always adhere to the Court's interpretation of the Constitution?" Acknowledging that the case was one of the "great pillars of American law," Scalia refused to say that "in no instance can either of the other branches call into question the action of the Supreme Court." Significantly, he declined to make the Court the exclusive, final authority on constitutional questions. Nomination of Judge Antonin Scalia: Hearings Before the Senate Comm. on the Judiciary, 99th Cong., 2d Sess. 187 (1986).

Even more significant were the nomination hearings for Judge Anthony Kennedy in 1987. Senator Specter was concerned about a speech Kennedy had given in 1982 while serving as a federal appellate judge for the Ninth Circuit. Kennedy had stated in that speech: "As I have pointed out, the Constitution, in some of its most critical aspects, is what the political branches of the government have made it, whether the judiciary approves or not." Kennedy engaged in a dialogue with Specter to explain his position. Kennedy said that in such areas as separation of powers, the office of the presidency, the commerce clause, and federalism, the meaning of the Constitution depends largely on the judgments of the executive and legislative branches, not the Court. Although he agreed that Supreme Court decisions are the law of the land and must be obeyed, he was "somewhat reluctant to say that in all circumstances each legislator is immediately bound by the full circumstances of a Supreme Court decree." Nomination of Anthony M. Kennedy to be Associate Justice of the Supreme Court of the United States: Hearings Before the Senate Comm. on the Judiciary, 100th Cong., 1st Seas. 222 (1987). In a colloquy with Specter, Kennedy went on to explain why the political branches should not defer to every Court decision (document 9). During her confirmation hearings in 1993 to be an Associate Justice of the Supreme Court, Ruth Bader Ginsburg also spoke about the delicate and interdependent relationship of the Court to the elected branches and to the public (document 10).

C. Conclusion

"Judicial supremacy" has been a useful rallying cry at certain junctures of our constitutional history, including the Little Rock confrontation in 1958 and the Watergate crisis in 1974. Governor Orval Faubus of Arkansas defied three court orders calling for the integration of the Little Rock Central High School. President Nixon threatened to ignore any court order requiring him to release documents related to the Watergate scandal. Unanimous decisions by the Supreme Court contributed to political stability in Little Rock and the surrender by President Nixon of incriminating tapes. Nevertheless, the importance of those decisions lay more in political utility than in legal doctrines. The two cases by themselves failed to advance either the cause of desegregation or the definition of executive privilege. Clarifications in both areas have had to come through the regular political process.

The power of judicial review carries with it the risk of legislative policymaking by the courts. Justices of the Supreme Court regularly caution their colleagues about the dangers of judicial activism. Justice Stone observed that courts "are not the only agency of government that must be assumed to have capacity to govern." United States v., Butler, 297 U.S. 1, 87 (1936) (dissenting opinion). Court decisions are always subject to scrutiny by the elected branches and the people. Chief Justice Taney once noted that an opinion by the Supreme Court "upon the construction of the Constitution is always open to discussion when it is supposed to have been founded on error, and that its judicial authority should hereafter depend altogether on the force of the reasoning by which it is supported." The Passenger Cases, 48 U.S. 283, 470 (1849) (dissenting opinion).

Just because the Court issues its judgment does not mean that we must suspend ours. The courts are an important element, but not the only element, in maintaining a constitutional order. That task is necessarily shared with Congress, the President, the states, and the general public. The specific case studies in this book underscore the political dynamics that accompany the development of constitutional law.

DOCUMENTS

1. Jefferson's Response to Sedition Act

Source: 11 The Writings of Thomas Jefferson 43-44, 50-51 (Albert Ellery Bergh ed. 1904)

[Letter to Mrs. John Adams, July 22, 1804]:

. . . I discharged every person under punishment or prosecution under the sedition law, because I considered, and now consider, that law to he a nullity, as absolute and as palpable as if Congress had ordered us to fall down and worship a golden image; and that it was as much my duty to arrest its execution in every stage, as it would have been to have rescued from the fiery furnace those who should have been cast into it for refusing to worship the image. It was accordingly done in every instance, without asking what the offenders had done, or against whom they had offended, but whether the pains they were suffering were inflicted under the pretended sedition law. . . .

[Letter to Mrs. John Adams, September 11, 1804]:

You seem to think it devolved on the judges to decide on the validity of the sedition law. But nothing in the Constitution has given them a right to decide for the Executive, more than to the Executive to decide for them. Both magistrates are equally independent in the sphere of action assigned to them. The judges, believing the law constitutional, had a right to pass a sentence of fine and imprisonment; because the power was placed in their hands by the Constitution. But the executive, believing the law to be unconstitutional, were bound to remit the execution of it; because that power has been confided to them by the Constitution. That instrument meant that its co-ordinate branches should be checks on each other. But the opinion which gives to the judges the right to decide what laws are constitutional, and what not, not only for themselves in their own sphere of action, but for the legislature and executive also, in their spheres, would make the judiciary a despotic branch.

2. Congress Reimburses Persons Fined for Violating the Sedition Act

Source: H.R. Rep. No. 86,
26th Cong., 1st Sess. (1840)

That in the month of October, 1798, the late Matthew Lyon, the father of the petitioners, at the circuit court held at Rutland, in the State of Vermont, was in-dicted and found guilty of having printed and published what was alleged to be a libel against Mr. John Adams, the then President of the United States. . . .

Upon this indictment Matthew Lyon was convicted, and sentenced by the court to be imprisoned for four months; to pay a fine of one thousand dollars, and the costs of the prosecution, taxed at sixty dollars and ninety-six cents; and to stand committed until the fine and costs were paid: which were paid, as appears by the exemplification of the record of the said trial and proceedings, now in the archives of this House.

The committee are of opinion that the law above recited was unconstitutional, null, and void, passed under a mistaken exercise of undelegated power, and that the mistake ought to be corrected by returning the fine so obtained, with interest thereon, to the legal representatives of Matthew Lyon.

The committee do not deem it necessary to discuss at length the character of that law, or to assign all the reasons, however demonstrative, that have induced the conviction of its unconstitutionality. No question connected with the liberty of the press ever excited a more universal and intense interest—ever received so acute, able, long-continued, and elaborate investigation—was ever more generally understood, or so conclusively settled by the concurring opinions of all parties, after the heated political contests of the day had passed away. All that now remains to be done by the representatives of a people who condemned this act of their agents as unauthorized, and transcending their grant of power, to place beyond question, doubt, or cavil, that mandate of the constitution prohibiting Congress from abridging the liberty of the press, and to discharge an honest, just, moral, and honorable obligation, is to refund from the Treasury the fine thus illegally and wrongfully obtained from one of their citizens: for which purpose the committee herewith report a bill.

[The statute reimbursing the legal heirs and representatives of Matthew Lyon appears at 6 Stat. 802 (1840).]

3. Jackson's Veto of U.S. Bank

Source: 3 A Compilation of
the Messages and Papers
of the Presidents 1144-45
(James D. Richardson ed.
1897-1925)

It is maintained by the advocates of the bank that its constitutionality in all its features ought to be considered as settled by precedent and by the decision of the Supreme Court. To this conclusion I can not assent. Mere precedent is a dangerous source of authority, and should not be regarded as deciding questions of constitutional power except where the acquiescence of the people and the States can be considered as well settled. So far from this being the case on this subject, an argument against the bank might be based on precedent. One Congress, in 1791, decided in favor of a bank; another, in 1811, decided against it. One Congress, in 1815, decided against a bank; another, in 1816, decided in its favor. Prior to the present Congress, therefore, the precedents drawn from that source were equal. . . .

If the opinion of the Supreme Court covered the whole ground of this act, it ought not to control the coordinate authorities of this Government. The Congress, the Executive, and the Court must each for itself be guided by its own opinion of the Constitution. Each public officer who takes an oath to support the Constitution swears that he will support it as he understands it, and not as it is understood by others. It is as much the duty of the House of Representatives, of the Senate, and of the President to decide upon the constitutionality of any bill or resolution which may be presented to them for passage or approval as it is of the supreme judges when it may be brought before them for judicial decision. The opinion of the judges has no more authority over Congress than the opinion of Congress has over the judges, and on that point the President is independent of both. The authority of the Supreme Court must not, therefore, be permitted to control the Congress or the Executive when acting in their legislative capacities, but to have only

such influence as the force of their reasoning may deserve.

4. Supreme Court Justices Advise President Buchanan on Inaugural Address

Source: 10 John Basset Moore,
The Works of James Buchanan
106-08 (1910)

Thursday, Feby. 19th [1857].
MY DEAR SIR:
The Dred Scott case has been before the Judges several times since last Saturday, and I think you may safely say in your Inaugural,
"That the question involving the constitutionality of the Missouri Compromise line is presented to the appropriate tribunal to decide; to wit, to the Supreme Court of the United States. It is due to its high and independent character to suppose that it will decide & settle a controversy which has so long and seriously agitated the country, and which *must* ultimately be decided by the Supreme Court of the United States. And until the case now before it, (on two arguments) presenting the direct question, is disposed of, I would deem it improper to express any opinion on the subject."
A majority of my Brethren will be forced up to this point by two dissentients.
Will you drop Grier a line, saying how necessary it is—& how good the opportunity is, to settle the agitation by an affirmative decision of the Supreme Court, the one way or the other. . . .
Sincerely yr. frd.
J. CATRON.
Washington, Feby. 23d 1857.
MR. DEAR SIR:

Your letter came to hand this morning. I have taken the liberty to shew it in confidence to our mutual friends Judge Wayne and the Chief Justice. We fully appreciate and concur in your views as to the desirableness at this time of having an expression of the opinion of the court on this troublesome question. With their concurrence, I will give you in confidence the history of the case before us, with the probable result. . . .

. . . There will therefore be six if not *seven* (perhaps Nelson will remain neutral) who will decide the compromise law of 1820 to be of *non-effect*. But the opinions will not be delivered before Friday the 6th of March. We will not let any others of our brethren know any thing about *the cause of our anxiety* to produce this result, and though contrary to our usual practice, we have thought due to you to state to you in candor & confidence the real state of the matter.

Very Truly Yours

D. GRIER.

A difference of opinion has arisen in regard to the point of time when the people of a Territory shall decide this question for themselves.

This is, happily, a matter of but little practical importance. Besides, it is a judicial question, which legitimately belongs to the Supreme Court of the United States, before whom it is now pending, and will, it is understood, be speedily and finally settled. To their decision, in common with all good citizens, I shall cheerfully submit, whatever this may be. . . .

---

5. Buchanan's Inaugural Address

Source: 7 A Compilation of the
Messages and Papers of the
Presidents 2962 (James D. Richardson
ed. 1897-1925)

We have recently passed through a Presidential contest in which the passions of our fellow-citizens were excited to the highest degree by questions of deep and vital importance; but when the people proclaimed their will the tempest at once subsided and all was calm.

The voice of the majority, speaking in the manner prescribed by the Constitution, was heard, and instant submission followed. Our own country could alone have exhibited so grand and striking a spectacle of the capacity of man for self-government.

What a happy conception, then, was it for Congress to apply this simple rule, that the will of the majority shall govern, to the settlement of the question of domestic slavery in the Territories! Congress is neither "to legislate slavery into any Territory or State nor to exclude it therefrom, but to leave the people thereof perfectly free to form and regulate their domestic institutions in their own way, subject only to the Constitution of the United States."

As a natural consequence, Congress has also prescribed that when the Territory of Kansas shall be admitted as a State it "shall be received into the Union with or without slavery, as their constitution may prescribe at the time of their admission."

6. Lincoln's Critique of *Dred Scott*

Source: 2 The Collected Works of
Abraham Lincoln 516, 518,
519-20 (Roy P. Basler ed. 1953)

Now, as to the Dred Scott decision; for upon that [Stephen Douglas] makes his last point at me. He boldly takes ground in favor of that decision.

This is one-half the onslaught, and one-third of the entire plan of the campaign. I am opposed to that decision in a certain sense, but not in the sense which he puts on it. I say that in so far as it decided in favor of Dred Scott's master and against Dred Scott and his family, I do not propose to disturb or resist the decision.

I never have proposed to do any such thing. I think, that in respect for judicial authority, my humble history would not suffer in a comparison with that of Judge Douglas. He would have the citizen conform his vote to that decision; the Member of Congress, his; the President, his use of the veto power. He would make it a rule of political action for the people and all the departments of the government. I would not. By resisting it as a political rule, I disturb no right of property, create no disorder, excite no mobs.

. . .

He says this Dred Scott case is a very small matter at most—that it has no practical effect; that at best, or rather, I suppose, at worst, it is but an abstraction. I submit that the proposition that the thing which determines whether a man is free or a slave, is rather concrete than abstract. I think you would conclude that it was, if your liberty depended upon it, and so would Judge Douglas if his liberty depended upon it. . . .

One more thing. Last night Judge Douglas tormented himself with horrors about my disposition to make negroes perfectly equal with white men in social and political relations. He did not stop to show that I have said any such thing, or that it legitimately follows from any thing I have said, but he rushes on with his assertions. I adhere to the Declaration of Independence. If Judge Douglas and his friends are not willing to stand by it, let them come up and amend it. Let them make it read that all men are created equal except negroes. Let us have it decided, whether the Declaration of Independence, in this blessed year of 1858, shall be thus amended. In his construction of the Declaration last year he said it only meant that Americans in America were equal to Englishmen in England. Then, when I pointed out to him that by that rule he excludes the Germans, the Irish, the Portuguese, and all the other people who have come amongst us since the Revolution, he reconstructs his construction. In his last speech he tells us it meant Europeans.

.   .   .

My declarations upon this subject of negro slavery may be misrepresented; but can not be misunderstood. I have said that I do not understand the Declaration to mean that all men were created equal in all respects. They are not our equal in color; but I suppose that it does mean to declare that all men are equal in some respects; they are equal in their right to "life, liberty, and the pursuit of happiness." Certainly the negro is not our equal in color-perhaps not in many other respects; still, in the right to put into his mouth the bread that his own hands have earned, he is the equal of every other man, white or black. In pointing out that more has been given you, you can not be justified in taking away the little which has been given him. All I ask for the negro is that if you do not like him, let him alone. If God gave him but little, that little let him enjoy.

7. Meese's Tulane Speech

Source: Edwin Meese, III, The Law of the Constitution, 61 Tulane L. Rev. 981-83, 985-86 (1987)

Since becoming Attorney General, I have had the pleasure to speak about the Constitution on several occasions. . . . Tonight I would like . . . to consider a distinction that is essential to maintaining our limited form of government. This is the necessary distinction between the Constitution and constitutional law. The two are not synonymous. What, then, is this distinction?

The Constitution is—to put it simply but one hopes not simplistically—the Constitution. It is a document of our most fundamental law. It begins "We the People of the United States, in Order to form a more perfect Union. . ." and ends up, some 6,000 words later, with the twenty-sixth amendment. It creates the institutions of our government, it enumerates the powers those institutions may wield, and it cordons off certain areas into which government may not enter. . . .

Constitutional law, on the other hand, is that body of law that has resulted from the Supreme Court's adjudications involving disputes over constitutional provisions or doctrines. To put it a bit more simply, constitutional law is what the Supreme Court says about the Constitution in its decisions resolving the cases and controversies that come before it .

. . . The answers the Court gives are very important to the stability of the law so necessary for good government. Yet as constitutional historian Charles Warren once noted, what's most important to remember is that "[h]owever the Court may interpret the provisions of the Constitution, it is still the Constitution which is the law and not the decision of the Court."

By this, of course, Charles Warren did not mean that a constitutional decision by the

Supreme Court lacks the character of law. Obviously it does have binding quality; it binds the parties in a case and also the executive branch for whatever enforcement is necessary. But such a decision does not establish a supreme law of the land that is binding on all persons and parts of government henceforth and forevermore.

This point should seem so obvious as not to need elaboration. Consider its necessity in particular reference to the Court's own work. The Supreme Court would face quite a dilemma if its own constitutional decisions really were the supreme law of the land, binding on all persons and governmental entities, including the Court itself, for then the Court would not be able to change its mind. It could not overrule itself in a constitutional case. Yet we know that the Court has done so on numerous occasions. . . .

[Meese summarizes the Lincoln-Douglas debates over *Dred Scott* and the support it lends to the freedom of citizens and the political branches to express opposition to court decisions.]

Once we understand the distinction between constitutional law and the Constitution, once we see that constitutional decisions need not be seen as the last words in constitutional construction, once we comprehend that these decisions do not necessarily determine future public policy, once we see all of this, we can grasp a correlative point: constitutional interpretation is not the business of the Court only, but also properly the business of all branches of government.

The Supreme Court, then, is not the only interpreter of the Constitution. Each of the three coordinate branches of government created and empowered by the Constitution—the executive and legislative no less than the judicial—has a duty to interpret the Constitution in the performance of its official functions. In fact, every official takes an oath precisely to that effect.

Judicial review of congressional and executive actions for their constitutionality has played a major role throughout our political history. The exercise of this power produces constitutional law. In this task even the courts themselves have on occasion been

tempted to think that the law of their decisions is on a par with the Constitution.

Some thirty years ago, in the midst of great racial turmoil, our highest Court seemed to succumb to this very temptation. . . .

In this case, *Cooper v. Aaron*, in dictum, the Court characterized one of its constitutional decisions as nothing less than "the supreme law of the land." Obviously constitutional decisions are binding on the parties to a case; but the implication of the dictum that everyone should accept constitutional decisions uncritically, that they are judgments from which there is no appeal, was astonishing; the language recalled what Stephen Douglas said about *Dred Scott*. In one fell swoop, the Court seemed to reduce the Constitution to the status of ordinary constitutional law, and to equate the judge with the lawgiver. Such logic assumes, as Charles Evans Hughes once quipped, that the Constitution is "what the judges say it is." The logic of the dictum in *Cooper v. Aaron* was, and is, at war with the Constitution, at war with the basic principles of democratic government, and at war with the very meaning of the rule of law.

---

8. Anthony Lewis Responds to Tulane Speech

Source: Law or Power?,
N.Y. Times,
Oct. 27, 1986, at A23

In speech after speech Attorney General Meese has been calling for radical changes in our view of the Constitution. . . . He is making a calculated assault on the idea of law in this country: on the role of judges as the balance wheel in the American system. And that has to be taken extremely seriously.

The far-reaching character of Mr. Meese's campaign was made evident by the case he chose to illustrate his argument that Supreme Court decisions are not the supreme law of the land. That was the Court's 1958 decision in the Little Rock school case, Cooper v. Aaron.

Remember what happened in Little Rock. Central High School, under a court order to desegregate, agreed to admit nine black children. But the Governor of Arkansas, Orval Faubus, posted National Guard units at the school and declared it "off limits" to the black children. He asserted that he was not bound by the Supreme Court's school segregation decision.

. . . The Supreme Court rejected the idea that a state could stir up violence and then use it as an excuse to escape constitutional obligations. . . . It said that ever since Marbury v. Madison in 1803 Americans had accepted the principle that the judiciary was "supreme in its exposition of the law of the Constitution."

Of course it is true that Presidents and the rest of us can criticize the Supreme Court. We can urge the Court to overrule its own constitutional decisions, as it has often done.

But unless and until a decision is overruled, it is the law. To argue otherwise—to argue that no one owes respect to a Supreme Court decision unless he was actually a party to the case—is to invite anarchy. That was the argument made by Governor Faubus in the Little Rock case. And that was the case on which Attorney General Meese relied.

The extremity of the argument drew a grave warning this past weekend from the new president of Yale, Mr. Meese's alma mater. Benno Schmidt Jr., himself a noted constitutional scholar, said Mr. Meese was on a "disastrous" course, speaking as "a man of power, not a man of law."

---

9. Judge Anthony Kennedy Testifies on Three-Branch Interpretation

Source: Nomination of Anthony M. Kennedy to be Associate Justice of the Supreme Court of the United States: Hearings Before the Senate Comm. on the Judiciary, 100th Cong., 1st Sess. 222-23 (1987)

Senator [Arlen] SPECTER [R-Pa.]. Well, this is a very important subject. And I want to refer you to a comment which was made by Attorney General Meese in a speech last year at Tulane, and ask for your reaction to it.

He said this: But as constitutional historian Charles Warren once noted, what is most important to remember is that, however the Court may interpret the provisions of the Constitution, it is still the Constitution which is the law, not the decisions of the Court.

Do you agree with that?

Judge [Anthony M.] KENNEDY. Well, I am not sure—I am not sure I read that entire speech. But if we can just take it as a question, whether or not I agree that the decisions of the Supreme Court are or are not the law of the land. They are the law of the land, and they must be obeyed.

I am somewhat reluctant to say that in all circumstances each legislator is immediately bound by the full consequences of a Supreme Court decree.

Senator SPECTER. Why not?

Judge KENNEDY. Well, as I have indicated before, the Constitution doesn't work very well if there is not a high degree of voluntary compliance, and, in the school desegregation cases, I think, it was not permissible for any school board to refuse to implement Brown v. Board of Education immediately.

On the other hand, without specifying what the situations are, I can think of instances, or I can accept the proposition that a chief executive or a Congress might not accept as doctrine the law of the Supreme Court.

Senator SPECTER. Well, how can that be if the Supreme Court is to have the final word?

Judge KENNEDY. Well, suppose that the Supreme Court of the United States tomorrow morning in a sudden, unexpected development were to overrule in New York Times v. Sullivan. Newspapers no longer have protection under the libel laws. Could you, as a legislator, say I think that decision is constitutionally wrong and I want to have legislation to change it? I think you could. And I think you should.

Senator SPECTER. Well, there could be legislation—

Judge KENNEDY. And I think you could make that judgment as a constitutional matter.

Senator SPECTER. Well, there could be legislation in the hypothetical you suggest which would give the newspapers immunity for certain categories of writings.

Judge KENNEDY. But I think you could stand up on the floor of the U.S. Senate and say I am introducing this legislation because in my view the Supreme Court of the United States is 180 degrees wrong under the Constitution. And I think you would be fulfilling your duty if you said that.

Senator SPECTER. Well, you can always say it, but the issue is whether or not I would comply with it.

Judge KENNEDY. Well, I am just indicating that it doesn't seem to me that just because the Supreme Court has said it legislators cannot attempt to affect its decision in legitimate ways.

---

10. Judge Ruth Bader Ginsburg Testifies on Judicial Interdependence

Source: Nomination of Ruth Bader Ginsburg, to be Associate Justice of the Supreme Court of the United States: Hearings Before the Senate Comm. on the Judiciary, 103d Cong., 1st Sess. 50, 125, 141-42 (1993)

Judge GINSBURG. . . .

Supreme Court Justices are guardians of the great charter that has served as our Nation's fundamental instrument of government for over 200 years. It is the oldest written constitution still in force in the world. But the Justices do not guard constitutional rights alone. Courts share that profound responsibility with Congress, the President, the States, and the people. Constant realization of a more perfect Union, the Constitution's aspiration, requires the widest, broadest, deepest participation on matters of government and government policy.

One of the world's greatest jurists, Judge Learned Hand, said . . . that the spirit of liberty that imbues our Constitution must lie first and foremost in the hearts of the men and women who compose this great Nation. Judge Hand defined that spirit, in a way I fully embrace, as. one which is not too sure that it is right, and so seeks to understand the minds of other men and women and to weigh the interests of others alongside its own without bias. . . .

. . . It would be one solution, wouldn't it, to appoint Platonic guardians who would rule wisely for all [of] us. But then we wouldn't have a democracy, would we?

We cherish living in a democracy, and we know that this Constitution did not create a tricameral system. Judges must be mindful of their place in our constitutional order; they must always remember that we live in a democracy that can be destroyed if judges take it upon themselves to rule as Platonic guardians.

. . .

Senator [Strom] THURMOND [R-S.C.]. Judge Ginsburg, it is my firm belief that the responsibility of the Congress is to make the laws. The executive branch is to execute the laws, and the role of the judiciary is to interpret the laws. Clearly, there are times when the responsibilities of the three branches of government will overlap.

. . .

. . . James Madison, in the 47th Federalist, has argued that the preservation of liberty requires that the three great departments should be separate and distinct. . . . [W]hen do you believe it is appropriate for the Federal courts, including the Supreme Court, to engage in what would traditionally be considered a legislative activity?

. . .

Judge GINSBURG. I think James Madison had it absolutely right. He explained that ours is a system of separate branches of Government, but . . . each branch is given by the Constitution a little space in the other's territory. We see that in operation today. The judiciary is separate and independent, but I can't be a Federal judge unless you, the legislators, advise and consent. You make the laws, but the President can veto laws that you pass.

Senator THURMOND. Of course, we can override him, you know.

Judge GINSBURG. Yes, but only by a supermajority. So the Constitution has divided government, but it also has checks and balances, and it makes each branch a little dependent on the other.

2

JUDICIAL AUTHORITY

Before the judiciary can act, it must have jurisdiction. This chapter is about internal and external constraints on jurisdiction. Is Article III a ceiling *or* may Congress add to the Supreme Court's original jurisdiction? Is Article III a floor *or* may Congress subtract from the jurisdictional authority of either the Supreme Court or the lower federal courts? Does the Article III specification that the judicial power be limited to "cases" and "controversies" caution against judicial review of elected government? Finally, are there inherent limits on judicial authority beyond Article III itself?

These questions will be considered through five separate investigations. The first section examines the Court's formal establishment of judicial review in *Marbury* v. *Madison* (1803). Section II examines another landmark case in constitutional law, *McCulloch* v. *Maryland* (1819), and draws from it insights into three-branch interpretation. Section III considers congressional efforts to prevent Supreme Court review of abortion, busing, and school prayer. Section IV evaluates the tugs and pulls between threshold justiciability decisions and elected branch conduct with regard to tax breaks for discriminatory private schools. Finally, Section V assesses Congress' challenge of the Warren Court in *Powell* v. *McCormack* (1969) and, with it, the Court's reluctance to invoke the political question doctrine.

Two principal lessons flow from this chapter. First, Court jurisdictional determinations are part and parcel of a case's political context. Indeed, often the Supreme Court's desire to protect itself from elected branch domination seems the driving force in its jurisdictional decisionmaking. Similarly, the Court often fashions jurisdictional doctrines to avoid costly collisions either with Congress or the executive. Second, both elected government and the courts view jurisdiction as sacrosanct. Elected government appears unwilling to challenge unpopular judicial decisions by stripping the Court of jurisdictional authority. On the other hand, judges recognize that the doctrine of "judicial supremacy," if pushed indiscriminately, can weaken the independence and integrity of the courts.

I. JUDICIAL REVIEW

The intersection between politics and constitutional decisionmaking lies at the heart of *Marbury* v. *Madison*, 5 U.S. (1 Cranch) 137 (1803), a case concerning the propriety of Secretary of State James Madison's refusal to deliver a Justice of the Peace commission to William Marbury.

In holding for the first time that a section of an act of Congress was
unconstitutional, Chief Justice John Marshall's assertion that it is
"emphatically the province and duty of the judicial department to say what
the law is" stands as *the* beacon of Supreme Court authority. By
establishing judicial review, that is, the judiciary's power to declare an act
of Congress, the President, or state government unconstitutional, *Marbury*
is the inevitable point of departure in the study of constitutional law.

When decided, however, the Court's justification for judicial review
was hardly noticed. Instead, the controversy surrounding *Marbury*
centered on Marshall's assertions that a conscientious executive branch
would have delivered to Marbury his commission and that a mandamus
directed against the Secretary of State is a proper remedy. That the
Supreme Court ruled an act of Congress unconstitutional played a small
role in Marshall's depiction of the case as among the most important
decided during his tenure as Chief Justice. 6 The Papers of John Marshall
160-164 (Charles Hobson ed. 1990). As Justice Samuel Chase's 1802
letter to John Marshall suggests (document 1), the grounds for judicial
review were well established before *Marbury*. Prior to its decision in
Marbury, for example, the Supreme Court spoke of the "general opinion"
that it could declare an act of Congress unconstitutional. Cooper v.
Telfair, 4 Dall. 14, 19 (1800).

State ratifying conventions and the Federalist Papers also reveal that
judicial review was generally accepted—at least against state legislative
action—at the time of *Marbury*. At the Virginia ratifying convention,
John Marshall anticipated that unconstitutional legislative acts would be
struck down by the federal judiciary. 3 The Debates in the Several State
Conventions, on the Adoption of the Federal Constitution 553 (Jonathan
Elliot ed. 1888). Likewise, Oliver Ellsworth, at the Connecticut ratifying
convention, said he expected federal judges to void any legislative acts
that were contrary to the Constitution. 2 Elliot 196. Finally, at the
Pennsylvania ratification convention, James Wilson argued that the
legislature would be "kept within its prescribed bounds" by the judiciary.
Id. at 445.

The Federalist Papers likewise support judicial review. In Federalist
No. 80, Alexander Hamilton said that "[t]hirteen independent courts of
final jurisdiction over the same causes, arising upon the same laws, is a
hydra in government from which nothing but contradiction and confusion
can proceed." The Federalist 500 (Benjamin Fletcher Wright ed. 1961).
This passage justifies judicial review directed against the states, not
against the coequal branches of Congress and the President. However, it
was also generally argued that a countermajoritarian check was needed to
combat legislative excess at any level, state or national. That check was
to be the judiciary. Indeed, Hamilton's Federalist No. 78 contends that
"the courts were designed to be an intermediate body between the people

and the legislature, in order, among other things, to keep the latter within the limits assigned to their authority" (document 2). The arguments in Federalist No. 78 were later borrowed by John Marshall to buttress his *Marbury* opinion.

Marshall's legal reasoning was hardly novel, even if judicial review against Congress and the President was hotly debated at the time of the decision. *Marbury*, while unremarkable as a matter of constitutional interpretation, still proved to be Marshall's coup de grace. As Chief Justice Warren Burger put it:

> It does not disparage John Marshall's greatness as a judge or a statesman to say that when he wrote the opinion in *Marbury* he was doing little more than declaring what was widely accepted by so many of the best legal minds of his day—at least when they could divorce politics from reason! If it had not come in *Marbury*, it would have come later, but John Marshall was not a man to wait for perfect opportunities if a plausible one offered itself. It had to be said, and *Marbury* was the fortuitous circumstance that made it possible to establish this great principle early in our history. Presidential Address to the Bentham Club, University College, London, England (Feb. 1, 1972).

A. The Politics of *Marbury*

Marbury's claim that Madison wrongly withheld his commission did not call into question any of the Constitution's majestic provisions. *Marbury*, instead, addressed the constitutionality of § 13 of the Judiciary Act of 1789, which empowered the Supreme Court to issue writs of mandamus "in cases warranted by the principles and usages of law, to any courts appointed, or persons holding office, under the authority of the United States." 1 Stat. 73, 81 (1789). Relying on § 13, Marbury brought his claim against Madison directly to the Supreme Court, as an exercise of the Court's original jurisdiction. Chief Justice Marshall, while acknowledging the merits of Marbury's claim, ruled that the Court was without jurisdiction to issue the mandamus. Marshall concluded that § 13 did indeed expand the Court's original jurisdiction *but* that Article III forbade such legislative action.

Marshall deliberately chose the *Marbury* case to establish judicial review. To understand that choice and his opinion structure in *Marbury*, proper consideration must be given to the historical background and the political influences originating in the legislative and executive branches. Marbury's eleventh hour appointment was part of Federalist party efforts to transform the judiciary into a Federalist stronghold in the wake of John

Adams' defeat by Thomas Jefferson (document 3). Through the Judiciary Act of 1801, the lame duck Federalist Congress and President Adams created a host of new judicial offices and then rushed through the appointments and confirmations of Federalist judicial appointees. Federalists viewed the Judiciary Act as a bulwark against their political opponents; Jeffersonians (forerunners of the Democratic Party), saw the Act as a partisan effort to subvert their well-earned victory in 1800. Consequently, once in office, they made repeal of the Act their first order of business and repealed it in 1802.

Marbury thus became a symbol of the political battle between Federalists and Jeffersonians, with the principal warriors being Federalist John Marshall (who as Secretary of State under Adams had neglected to deliver Marbury's commission and, then, as Chief Justice was set to rule on the legal significance of his negligence) and President Thomas Jefferson (who refused to deliver Marbury's commission). Marshall and Jefferson, although both Virginians and distant cousins, also viewed Marbury as a personal battle. In reference to Jefferson, Marshall stated that "I have never thought him a particularly wise, sound and practical statesman" and "[h]is foreign prejudices seem to me totally to unfit him for the chief magistracy of a nation which can not indulge those prejudices without sustaining deep & permanent injury." Donald Dewey, Marshall v. Jefferson: The Political Background of Marbury v. Madison 36, 41 (1970). Conversely, Jefferson commented on Marshall's "lax lounging manners" and his "profound hypocrisy." Id. at 37.

This antagonism between Federalists and Jeffersonians is also revealed in congressional action pertinent to Marbury v. Madison. After Marbury filed suit, Chief Justice Marshall issued a "show cause" order to President Jefferson requesting reasons why a mandamus forcing the delivery of the commissions should not be issued to Secretary of State Madison. Jeffersonians in Congress thought this "show cause" order outrageous, with Senator John Breckenridge labelling it "the most daring attack which the annals of Federalism have yet exhibited." Walter Murphy, James Fleming & William Harris, II, American Constitutional Interpretation 203 (1986). This displeasure was concretely expressed in the Congress' cancellation of the 1802 Supreme Court term (to prevent, in part, the Federalist Court from considering Marbury) and in pitched legislative debates about the propriety of judicial review (document 4).

Congress also entered the Marbury fray when the Senate was asked by Marbury to assist him in demonstrating that he was duly confirmed. Specifically, Marbury asked the Senate to turn over its proceedings relating to his nomination and appointment. In debating this request, Jeffersonians and Federalists squared off on whether the motion's success spelled doom for the executive or whether its failure would eviscerate the judiciary. Typifying this debate, Jeffersonian Robert Wright called the motion "an audacious attempt to pry into Executive Secrets" whereas Federalist James Hillhouse argued that the denial of Marbury's request "would be considered an arbitrary, tyrannical act." Not surprisingly, the Jeffersonian Senate defeated the motion by a 15-13 vote. 12 Annals of Cong. 34-50 (1803).

These high level squabblings make clear that *Marbury* was political drama at its best. Surprisingly, however, one side was not represented before the Court. President Jefferson, viewing *Marbury* as a Federalist powergrab, directed Madison to ignore the "show cause" order thereby forcing the Court to decide the case without the benefit of executive arguments. This opprobrium of the *Marbury* proceedings, among other things, convinced Marshall that Jefferson would ignore any mandamus that the Court might order. Furthermore, as Supreme Court Justice Harold Burton recognized, "if the Court asserted such power over the Legislative and Executive Branches of the Government, this assertion would provide Congress with the necessary basis for the impeachment of the offending Justices and for their removal from office." Harold H. Burton, The Cornerstone of Constitutional Law: The Extraordinary Case of *Marbury* v. *Madison*, 36 A.B.A.J. 805, 807 (1950). Marshall took the impeachment threat seriously, writing that it would be better for the elected branches to reverse a Court opinion by statute than to impeach Supreme Court Justices.[1] For Marshall: "A reversal of those legal opinions deemed unsound by the legislature would certainly better comport with the mildness of our character than a removal of the Judge who has rendered them unknowing of his fault" (document 5).

Marshall's challenge, therefore, was to craft an opinion that would both support judicial power over the elected branches (to prevent the Court and, with it, the Federalists from appearing impotent) and avoid a head-to-head confrontation between the judiciary and the executive (a battle that the Court would lose so badly that it would become impotent). The solution, as suggested in Chief Justice Warren Burger's examination of *Marbury* (document 6), was Marshall's peculiar sequencing of discussion on the merits and jurisdiction in *Marbury*. Through this sequencing, the administration won the case in spite of the Court's assertions that the executive's conduct was unlawful and amenable to a court order.

---

[1]Marshall's fear of impeachment was well founded. In the spring of 1801, two Federalist judges instructed a district attorney to prosecute a newspaper that had published an attack on the judiciary. Viewing this episode as evidence that Federalists were engaged in a national conspiracy, the Jeffersonians launched a counterattack. Federalist district judge John Pickering was impeached and removed, and action against Justice Chase of the Supreme Court was begun. Indeed, there was even talk of removing Marshall. See Jerry W. Knudson, The Jeffersonian Assault on the Federalist Judiciary, 1802-1805: Political Forces and Press Reaction, 14 Am. J. Leg. Hist. 55 (1970).

President Jefferson was not especially pleased by Chief Justice Marshall's reasoning but—since he technically won the case—he could do little to counteract. Consequently, although he considered the most controversial features of *Marbury* "obiter dictum", he never sought retaliation. Another explanation for Jefferson's mild reaction is that he supported coordinate constitutional interpretation, which empowers each branch to actively interpret the Constitution for itself (document 7).

Chief Justice Marshall's tactics in *Marbury* are but one example of his efforts to protect the Federalist judiciary from hostile Jeffersonians. Immediately after *Marbury*, Marshall staved off a likely assault on the courts by upholding the constitutionality of the repeal of the 1801 Judiciary Act. Stuart v. Laird, 5 U.S. (1 Cranch) 299 (1803). Since the Judiciary Act and its repeal symbolized Federalist-Jeffersonian antagonism, the Court's action here deflected Congress' plans to impeach Federalist judges.

John Marshall's status, in the words of Chief Justice Earl Warren, as *the* "expounder of the Constitution" and *Marbury* v. *Madison*'s fame as *the* landmark decision of the U.S. Supreme Court are both well deserved. Earl Warren, Chief Justice Marshall: The Expounder of the Constitution, 41 A.B.A.J. 687 (1955). This recognition, however, derives from the political practicality of Marshall and his opinion in *Marbury*, not the brilliance of Marshall's erudition of the justifications for judicial review. Moreover, it is significant that Marshall never again declared an act of Congress unconstitutional, although he remained on the Court until 1835. Instead, he regularly *upheld* statutes that expanded congressional power.

DOCUMENTS

1. Justice Chase Recognizes Necessity of Judicial Review Before *Marbury* Decision

Source: Letter from Samuel Chase to John Marshall, Apr. 24, 1802, reprinted in 6 The Papers of John Marshall 109, 112 (Charles Hobson ed. 1990)

My dear Sir

. . . The Constitution of the United States is certainly a *limited* Constitution; because (in Art. 1 § 9.) it *expressly prohibits* Congress from making *certain enumerated Laws*; and also from doing certain specified Acts, in *many* cases; and it is very evident that these restrictions on the *Legislative* power of Congress would be entirely nugatory, and merely waste paper, if there exists no power, under the Constitution, to declare Acts made, *contrary to these express prohibitions*, null and void. It is equally clear that the *limitations* of the power of Congress can only be preserved by the *Judicial* power. There can be no other rational, peaceable and secure barrier against violations of the Constitution by the Legislature, or against encroachments by it on the Executive, or on the *Judiciary* branches of our Government. It is provided by the Constitution (Art 6. § 2) that the Constitution of the United States shall be the *supreme* law of the Land; and *by the Oath of Office* prescribed by the statute (24th. September 1789) all Judges engage to discharge and perform all their duties, as Judges, *agreeably to the Constitution.* Further, all Judges, by the Constitution (Art 6 § 3) are required to bind themselves, by Oath, to *support* the Constitution of the United States. This engagement, in my judgement, obliges every Judge (or other taker thereof) not to do any *affirmative* act to contravene, or render ineffectual, any of the provisions in the Constitution. It has been the uniform opinion (until very lately) that the Supreme Court possess the power, and that they are bound in duty, to declare acts of Congress, or of any of the States, contrary to the Constitution, *void*: and the Judges of the Supreme Court have *separately* given such opinion. . . .

---

2. Alexander Hamilton Defends Judicial Review

Source: The Federalist No. 78, at 489-93 (Benjamin Wright ed. 1961)

Whoever attentively considers the different departments of power must perceive, that, in a government in which they are separated from each other, the judiciary, from the nature of its functions, will always be the least dangerous to the political rights of the Constitution; because it will be least in a capacity to annoy or injure them. The Executive not only dispenses the honors, but holds the sword of the community. The legislature not only commands the purse, but prescribes the rules by which the duties and rights of every citizen are to be regulated. The judiciary, on the contrary, has no influence over either the sword or the purse; no direction either of the strength or of the wealth of the society; and can take no active resolution whatever. It may truly be said to have neither FORCE nor WILL, but merely judgment; and must ultimately depend upon the aid of the executive arm even for the efficacy of its judgments.

Some perplexity respecting the rights of the courts to pronounce legislative acts void because contrary to the constitution, has arisen from an imagination that the doctrine would imply a superiority of the judiciary to the legislative power. It is urged that the authority which can declare the acts of another void must necessarily be superior to the one whose acts may be declared void. As this doctrine is of great importance in all the American constitutions, a brief discussion of the ground on which it rests cannot be unacceptable.

There is no position which depends on clearer principles, than that every act of a delegated authority, contrary to the tenor of the commission under which it is exercised, is void. No legislative act, therefore, contrary to the Constitution, can be valid. To deny this would be to affirm that the deputy is greater than his principal; that the servant is above his master; that the representatives of the people are superior to the people themselves; that men acting by virtue of powers may do not only what their powers do not authorize, but what they forbid.

. . . The interpretation of the laws is the proper and peculiar province of the courts. A constitution is, in fact, and must be regarded by the judges, as a fundamental law. It therefore belongs to them to ascertain its meaning, as well as the meaning of any particular act proceeding from the legislative body. If there should happen to be an irreconcilable variance between the two, that which has the superior obligation and validity ought, of course, to be preferred; or, in other words, the Constitution ought to be preferred to the statute, the intention of the people to the intention of their agents.

Nor does this conclusion by any means suppose a superiority of the judicial to the legislative power. It only supposes that the power of the people is superior to both; and that where the will of the legislature, declared in its statutes, stands in opposition to that of the people, declared in the Constitution, the judges ought to be governed by the latter rather than the former. They ought to regulate their decisions by the fundamental laws, rather than by those which are not fundamental.

3. The Marbury Appointment

Source: Sarah Randolph,
The Domestic Life of Thomas
Jefferson 307-08 (1858)

Just at the close of Adams' administration a law was hurried through Congress by the Federalists, increasing the number of United States courts throughout the States. At that time, twelve o'clock on the night of the 3d of March was the magical hour when one administration passed out and the other came in. The law was passed at such a late hour that, though the appointments for the new judgeships created by it, had been previously selected, yet the commissions had not been issued from the Department of State. Chief Justice Marshall, who was then acting as Secretary of State, was busily engaged filling out these commissions, that the offices might be filled with Federal appointees, while the outgoing administration was still in power. The whole proceeding was known to Jefferson. He considered the law unconstitutional and acted in the premises with his usual boldness and decision. Having chosen Levi Lincoln as his Attorney-General, he gave him his watch and ordered him to go at midnight and take possession of the State Department, and not allow a single paper to be removed from it after that hour.

Mr. Lincoln accordingly entered Judge Marshall's office at the appointed hour. "I have been ordered by Mr. Jefferson," he said to the Judge, "to take possession of this office and its papers." "Why, Mr. Jefferson has not yet qualified," exclaimed the astonished Chief Justice. "Mr. Jefferson considers himself in the light of an executor bound to take charge of the papers of the government until he is duly qualified," was the reply. "But it is not yet twelve o'clock," said Judge Marshall, taking out his watch. Mr. Lincoln, pulling out his watch and showing it to him, said, "This is the President's watch and rules the hour."

4. Senate Debates Repeal of the 1801 Judiciary Act

Sources: 11 Annals of Congress
32, 38, 89, 179-180, 661 (1802)

Mr. [Jonathan] MASON [Fed-Mass.]. . . .

. . .

[T]he people, in forming their Constitution, meant to make the judges as independent of the Legislature as of the Executive. Because 'he duties which they have to perform, call upon them to expound not only the laws, but the Constitution also; in which is involved the power of checking the Legislature in case it should pass any laws in violation of the Constitution. . . .

Mr. [Gouvernour] MORRIS [Fed-N.Y.]. . . .

[T]he people of America . . . vested in the judges a check intended to be efficient—a check of the first necessity, to prevent an invasion of the Constitution by unconstitutional laws—a check which might prevent any faction from intimidating or annihilating the tribunals themselves.

. . . I know this doctrine [of judicial review] is unpleasant; I know it is more popular to appeal to public opinion—that equivocal, transient being, which exists nowhere and everywhere. But if ever the occasion calls for it, I trust the Supreme Court will not neglect doing the great mischief of saving this Constitution, which can be done much better by their deliberations than by resorting to what are called revolutionary measures.

. . .

[W]here [do] the judges [get] their pretended power of deciding on the constitutionality of laws? . . . I answer, they derived that power from authority higher than this Constitution. They derive it from the constitution of man, from the nature of things, from the necessary progress of human affairs. . . . The decision of the Supreme Court is, and, of necessity, must be final. . . .

. . .

Mr. [John] BRECKENRIDGE [D-Ky.]. . . .

. . . Is it not truly astonishing that the Constitution, in its abundant care to define the powers of each department, should have omitted so important a power as that of the courts to nullify all the acts of Congress, which, in their opinion, were contrary to the Constitution?

. . .

To make the Constitution a practical system, this pretended power of the courts to annul the laws of Congress cannot possibly exist. My idea of the subject . . . is, that the Constitution intended a separation of the powers vested in the three great departments, giving to each exclusive authority on the subjects committed to it. That these departments are co-ordinate, to resolve each within the sphere of their own orbits, without being responsible for their own motion, and are not to direct or control the course of others.

Mr. [John] RANDOLPH [D-Va.]. . . .

. . .

. . . The decision of a Constitutional question must rest somewhere. Shall it be confided to men immediately responsible to the people, or to those who are irresponsible? . . . To me it appears that the power which has the right of passing, without appeal, on the validity of your laws, is your sovereign. . . .

---

5. Marshall Suggests that Congress Could Overturn the Court by Statute

Source: 3 Albert J. Beveridge, The Life of John Marshall 177 (1919)

[Letter from John Marshall to Samuel Chase, January 23, 1805.]

Admitting it to be true that on legal principles Colo. Taylors testimony was admissible, it certainly constitutes a very extraordinary ground for an impeachment. According to the ancient doctrine a jury finding a verdict against the law of the case was liable to an attaint; & the amount of the present doctrine seems to be that a Judge giving a legal opinion contrary to the opinion of the legislature is liable to impeachment.

As, for convenience & humanity the old doctrine of attaint has yielded to the silent, moderate but not less operative influence of new trials, I think the modern doctrine of impeachment should yield to an appellate jurisdiction in the legislature. A reversal of those legal opinions deemed unsound by the legislature would certainly better comport with the mildness of our character than [would] a removal of the Judge who has rendered them unknowing of his fault.

---

6. Chief Justice Warren Burger Depicts *Marbury* as a Political Decision

Source: Presidential Address to the Bentham Club, University College, London, England (Feb. 1, 1972), reprinted in Views From the Bench 7, 12-14 (Mark W. Cannon & David M. O'Brien eds. 1985)

From the day Jefferson took office as President on 4 March 1801, those who were even slightly aware of his hostility toward the Supreme Court, the Federal Judicial Branch as a whole, and John Marshall in particular, could sense that these events foreshadowed a collision of two strong men who had quite different views as to how the United States could best fulfill its destiny.

Underlying the impending conflict was a very fundamental difference between the Federalist belief that a strong national government was the key to the future of the new nation and the opposing belief of the Jeffersonian radical Republicans who feared all centralized power and wanted to keep the states the strong and indeed the dominant political power. . . .

. . .

The minor office of Justice of the Peace was hardly worth a lawsuit, but Marbury was a spunky fellow and he sought a direct mandamus in the Supreme Court against Madison, Jefferson's Secretary of State . . .

. . . If mandamus issued and Jefferson's Administration ignored it—as was likely—the first confrontation between court and Executive would be lost—and all of it over a Justice of the Peace commission! The court could stand hard blows, but not ridicule, and the ale houses would rock with hilarious laughter. . . .

But if, as no one had even remotely suspected up to that time, Congress could not vest original jurisdiction in the Supreme Court in any cases except those specifically recited in Article III, then the court could say, "Yes, Marbury was duly confirmed"; and "Yes, the Commission was duly signed and sealed"; and "Yes, this court may examine into the manner in which the Executive conducts its own affairs"; and "Yes, delivery is a purely ministerial act," and "Yes, it is shameful that the new administration will not perform the simple, ministerial act of delivery"; but the court could also say, "However, this court has no power under the Constitution to entertain any original action except those specified in Article III, and hence section 13 of the Judiciary Act of 1789 purporting to give the Supreme Court such authority is invalid and, sadly, this action to compel the Executive to do its duty cannot be entertained here as an original action."

And this is precisely what Marshall persuaded the court to do in a straight-faced, long-winded opinion that exhaustively, and exhaustingly, explored every possible alternative. . . .

Jefferson's Secretary of State, Madison, had won the battle; Marbury, the Federalist, had lost, and the real war, the great war over the supremacy of the Supreme Court in constitutional adjudication, had been won by Marshall—and by the United States.

[Concerning *Marbury*]

[Although], [t]he Court determined at once, that being an original process, they had no cognizance of it; . . . the Chief Justice went on to lay down what the law would be, had they jurisdiction of the case, to wit: that they should command the delivery. The object was clearly to instruct any other court having the jurisdiction, what they should do if Marbury should apply to them. Besides the impropriety of this gratuitous interference, could anything exceed the perversion of law? . . . Yet this case of Marbury and Madison is continually cited by bench and bar, as if it were settled law, without any animadversion on its being merely an *obiter* dissertation of the Chief Justice.

. . . I have long wished for a proper occasion to have the gratuitous opinion in Marbury v. Madison brought before the public, and denounced as not law. . . .

[Concerning the Judiciary]

The great object of my fear is the federal judiciary. That body, like gravity, ever advance, gaining ground step by step, and holding what it gains, is ingulfing insidiously the special governments into the jaws of that which feeds them.

[If the Supreme Court is the ultimate arbiter,] [t]he constitution . . . is a mere thing of wax in the hands of the judiciary, which they may twist and shape into any form they please.

---

7. Jefferson's Views On *Marbury* And Judicial Power

Sources: 15 The Writings of Thomas Jefferson 447-48 (Albert Bergh ed. 1904); 11 Bergh 215; 10 The Writings of Thomas Jefferson 189 (Paul Ford ed. 1899); 15 Bergh 213

II. McCULLOCH v. MARYLAND

Just as Marshall's decision in *Marbury v. Madison* is fundamental in understanding the source and scope of judicial power, so does his opinion in *McCulloch v. Maryland*, 17 U.S. (4 Wheat.) 316 (1819), illuminate the basic choices and methods available to a court in interpreting a constitution. Moreover, *McCulloch* is a vivid example of Congress, the President, and executive officials contributing to three-branch interpretation. The political branches performed all of the constitutional analysis, to be blessed later by the Court

A. Creating a Bank by Implied Power

A central constitutional question in *McCulloch* was whether Congress could establish a national bank in the absence of express authority in the Constitution. Is the Constitution only one of "enumerated powers," with specific powers identified and clearly marked out for government, or are there, in fact, implied powers for each of the three branches?

That identical issue had arisen under the Articles of Confederation, when the Continental Congress debated whether to establish a national bank. Robert Morris, Superintendent of Finance (the forerunner of the Secretary of the Treasury), offered a plan to create a national bank. After committee consideration and legislative debate it was decided that it would be proper and advantageous to do so. 20 Journals of the Continental Congress, 1774-1789, 519, 530-31, 542, 545-48. Nine states supported the plan, one state (Massachusetts) voted against it, and one state (Pennsylvania) was divided.

Of the four delegates from Virginia, James Madison was the only one to vote against the bank. He appeared to have misgivings because there was no express authority provided in the Articles of Confederation for a national bank. 9 The Writings of James Madison 419-21 (Gaillard Hunt ed.); 4 The Papers of James Madison 18-19, 21 n.7 (William T. Hutchison & William M. E. Rachal eds.). After the Articles of Confederation had been replaced by the U.S. Constitution, Madison would offer the same argument in opposition to a national bank in 1791.

The issue of a national bank was debated at the constitutional convention in 1787. In the section in Article I regarding the power of Congress to establish post offices and post roads, Benjamin Franklin moved to add the words "a power to provide for cutting canals where deemed "to grant charters of incorporation where the interest of the U.S. might require & the legislative provisions of individual States may be incompetent." Rufus King of Massachusetts objected that the states "will be prejudiced and divided into parties by it," and that in Philadelphia and New York the power to grant charters of incorporation "will be referred to the establishment of a Bank, which has been a subject of contention in those Cities. In other places it will be referred to mercantile monopolies." James Wilson did not agree with King that a national bank "would excite the prejudices & parties apprehended. As to mercantile monopolies they are already included in the power to regulate trade." George Mason thought it better to limit the power to the single case of canals, noting that he was "afraid of monopolies of every sort, which he did not think were by any means already implied by the Constitution as supposed by Mr. Wilson." The motion was modified to admit a distinct question limited to the case of canals, but the motion fell with only three states in favor and eight opposed. Other proposals, including Madison's, were discarded with the same vote. 2 Farrand 615-16.

B. Congressional Action in 1791

In response to a request from the House of Representatives, Secretary of the Treasury Alexander Hamilton prepared a report on the establishment of a national bank. He submitted the report on December 13, 1790, and both in general outline and in specific detail he strongly endorsed the bank. 2 Annals of Cong. 2082-2112. Both Houses considered Hamilton's proposal early the next year. Much of the legislative debate concerned the constitutional authority available to Congress to act in this area. The Constitution did not expressly authorize Congress to establish a national bank. Was that authority somehow implied in the structure and operation of government?

The Senate acted first on the bill to incorporate subscribers to the bank. A motion to delete a section that prohibited the establishment of any other national bank during the continuation of the corporation was soundly defeated, 18 to 5. 2 Annals of Cong. 1791 (Jan. 20, 1791).

The bill was taken up in the House on January 31. Apparently with few legislators on the floor, it was "read in paragraphs; and no amendments being offered" was reported to the House for final consideration. 2 Annals of Cong. 1935. That meant that when members began debate the following day, there was no opportunity to offer amendments except by recommitting the bill to committee. Id. at 1940. During the debate on recommittal, several constitutional objections were raised (document 1). The first motion to recommit lost on a vote of 23 to 34, the second by a vote of 21 to 38.

Madison, who voted both times for recommittal, debated at length the substance and constitutionality of the bank bill. On policy grounds, he listed the advantages and disadvantages of banks. He then focused on constitutional considerations, asking whether the power of establishing an incorporated bank was among the powers vested in Congress by the Constitution. On that ground he adhered to a strict interpretation of the Constitution, arguing that it was not a general grant of power but rather an itemization of particular powers with the balance of power left in the hands of the states and challenged by other legislators. Fisher Ames of Massachusetts argued: "If the power to raise armies had not been expressed in the enumeration of the powers of Congress, it would be implied from other parts of the Constitution." Otherwise, he noted, the country could be invaded with no constitutional power to resist. 2 Annals of Cong. 1955. Theodore Sedgwick, also of Massachusetts, reminded the House that two years earlier Madison had convinced a majority of members that the President had the power to remove executive officials, even though that power is not specifically stated in the Constitution. Id. at 1960.

In the course of the debate, George Jackson read several passages from *The Federalist*, claiming that they supported his contention that the bill was unconstitutional. Id. at 1941. Elias Boudinot disputed that interpretation, charging Jackson with selecting some passages while ignoring others nearby that reached the opposite conclusion. The particular essay in dispute was Federalist No. 44, written by Madison, who devoted the essay to an examination of the Necessary and Proper Clause. Madison suggested that the framers of the Constitution could have attempted "a positive enumeration of the powers comprehended under the general terms 'necessary and proper' [and] they might have attempted a negative enumeration of them, by specifying the powers excepted from the general definition." As Boudinot pointed out, two paragraphs after posing the question, Madison repudiates the doctrine of enumerated powers:

> Had the convention attempted a positive enumeration of the powers necessary and proper for carrying their other powers into effect, the attempt would have involved a complete digest of laws on every subject to which the Constitution relates; accommodated too, not only to the existing state of things, but to all the possible changes which futurity may produce; for in every new application of a general power, the *particular powers*, which are the means of attaining the *object* of the general power, must always necessarily vary with that object, and be often properly varied whilst the object remains the same. The Federalist 321 (Benjamin Wright ed. 1961); cited by Boudinot at 2 Annals of Cong. 1977.

Boudinot did not read Madison's comment, two paragraphs later, that even if the Constitution had omitted a Necessary and Proper Clause it would have been implied: "Had the Constitution been silent on this head, there can be no doubt that all the particular powers requisite as means of executing the general powers would have resulted to the government, by unavoidable implication. No axiom is more clearly established in law, or in reason, than that wherever the end is required, the means are authorized; wherever a general power to do a thing is given, every particular power necessary for doing it is included." The Federalist 321-22 (Benjamin Wright ed. 1961). Delegates might also have mentioned that if the framers wanted to say "absolutely Necessary and Proper" they knew how to do it. Art. I, Sec. 10, para. 2, provides that no state shall, without the consent of Congress, "lay any Imposts or Duties on Imports or Exports, except what may be absolutely necessary for executing it's [sic] inspection Laws." After extensive debate, the House voted 39 to 20 in favor of the bank. Madison was the most prominent member in the opposition. 2 Annals of Cong. 2012 (1791).

C. Executive Consideration

After the two Houses had passed legislation creating a national bank, President Washington asked Cabinet members to comment on the constitutionality of the bill. Attorney General Edmund Randolph and Secretary of State Thomas Jefferson concluded that Congress lacked the constitutional power to grant a corporate charter for a national bank. Secretary of the Treasury Hamilton prepared a detailed analysis, defending the power of Congress to act in this area.

Jefferson advised Washington that the Tenth Amendment meant that all powers not *expressly* delegated to the federal government were reserved to the states or to the people. Jefferson cautioned: "To take a simple step beyond the boundaries thus specially drawn around the powers of Congress, is to take possession of a boundless feild [sic] of power, no longer susceptible of any definition." 19 The Papers of Thomas Jefferson 276 (Julian P. Boyd ed. 1974). But the legislative history of the Tenth Amendment makes it clear that members of the First Congress gave consideration to the phrase "expressly delegated" and deliberately rejected the qualifier "expressly" on the ground that there "must necessarily be admitted powers by implication, unless the Constitution descended to recound every minutiae." 1 Annals of Cong. 761 (August 18, 1789). With regard to the Necessary and Proper Clause, Jefferson argued that the powers enumerated for Congress in the Constitution "can all be carried into execution without a bank. A bank therefore is not *necessary*, and consequently not authorized by this phrase." 19 The Papers of Thomas Jefferson 278.

Randolph, like Madison, had a personal history with the bank, but, unlike Madison's opposition of the bank in 1781, Randolph had drafted the bill that enabled the Constitutional Congress to charter the Bank of North America. He was, moreover, the author of a committee report to

Congress in 1781 that regarded a national bank as essential. Walter Dellinger and H. Jefferson Powell, The Constitutionality of the Bank Bill: The Attorney General's First Constitutional Law Opinions, 44 Duke L.J. 110, 115 (1994). A decade later, however, Randolph held strong reservations about the constitutionality of a national bank. He denied that the 1781 action was a valid precedent and he rejected the argument that a bank could be justified either on the basis of implied powers or under the Necessary and Proper Clause (document 3).

The third constitutional opinion submitted to President Washington was by Hamilton, who had the benefit of first reading the analyses by Jefferson and Randolph before starting his own inquiry. Having drafted the bank bill, he was hardly in a position to view the matter with detachment and objectivity, but all the major players, including Madison, Jefferson and Randolph, had well-formed attachments and predilections. Hamilton, conceding at the outset his personal involvement with the bill, argued forcefully that the doctrines advanced by Jefferson and Randolph "would be fatal to the just & indispensible authority of the United States" (document 4). Having digested the three constitutional opinions, Washington signed the bank bill. 1 Stat. 191 (1791).

D. Conclusion

The banks's twenty-year life lapsed in 1811, at which point Congress decided against extending the charter. Five years later Congress reversed course and established the Second Bank of the United States. 3 Stat. 266 (1816). It was this second statute that was challenged in *McCulloch*. Hamilton's interpretation of implied powers, sovereignty, and the Necessary and Proper Clause would now be borrowed wholesale by Chief Justice John Marshall when he wrote for the Court in a unanimous opinion upholding the power of Congress to establish a bank.

McCulloch precipitated a rancorous debate about the scope of national power. Anonymous articles (probably written by William Brockenbrough, a state judge from Virginia) ripped the decision for undermining states' rights. Marshall, working through his colleague Justice Bushrod Washington, responded with a number of anonymous rebuttals (signed "A Friend of the Constitution"). Judge Spencer Roane of the Virginia Court of Appeals, also writing under a pseudonym, joined in the attack on *McCulloch* and Marshall responded to those articles as well (again signing them "A Friend of the Constitution"). Gerald Gunther, ed., John Marshall's Defense of *McCulloch v. Maryland* (1969).

The controversy about the U.S. Bank continued into the 1830s, when President Andrew Jackson waged a personal war against the Bank. Congress tried to renew the Bank in 1832, but Jackson vetoed the bill on the ground that it granted monopoly and exclusive privileges to the rich at the expense of the poor. Although previous Congresses and Presidents had regarded the Bank as constitutional, and despite the Court's ruling in *McCulloch*, Jackson vetoed the bill partly on his own judgment that the Bank was unconstitutional. He insisted that "Congress, the Executive, and the Court, must each for itself be guided by its own opinion of the Constitution," and that precedent has been accepted ever since. In exercising the veto power, Presidents take into account earlier constitutional interpretations of Congress and the judiciary but then exercise their own independent judgment.

DOCUMENTS

1. House Members Debate Bank on Constitutional Grounds

Source: 2 Annals of Cong.
1940-41 (1791)

Mr. [George] JACKSON [Va.] said, he was in favor of the motion for a recommitment; but not for the reasons offered by the gentleman from South Carolina. He was opposed to the principle of the bill altogether. He then adverted to the situation of the United States, and observed, that it was so different from that of Great Britain, at the time the Bank was established in that country, that no reason in favor of the institution can be deduced from thence. He adverted to the arguments arising from the facility which Banks afford of anticipating the public resources in cases of emergency. This idea of anticipations he reprobated, as tending to involve the country in debt, and an endless labyrinth of perplexities. This plan of a National Bank, said he, is calculated to benefit a small part of the United States, the mercantile interest only; the farmers, the yeomanry, will derive no advantage from it; as the bank bills will not circulate to the extremities of the Union. . . . He urged the unconstitutionality of the plan; called it a monopoly; such a one as contravenes the spirit of the Constitution; a monopoly of a very extraordinary nature; a monopoly of the public moneys for the benefit of the corporation to be created. . . .

Mr. [John] LAURENCE [spelled "Lawrence" in debate] [N.Y.] . . . noticed the constitutional objections of Mr. JACKSON, and said, the Government of the United States is vested by the Constitution with a power of borrowing money; and in pursuance of this idea, they have a right to create a capital, by which they may, with greater facility, carry the power of borrowing on any emergency into effect. Under the late Confederation, the Pennsylvania Bank, called the Bank of North America, was instituted. He presumed that it will not be controverted, that the present Government is vested with powers equal to those of the late Confederation. He said that he had no doubt its operation would benefit, not only the centre, but the extremities also of the Union.

2. Madison Analyzes Constitutionality of Bank

Source: 2 Annals of Cong.
1945-46 (1791)

In making these remarks on the merits of the bill, he had reserved to himself the right to deny the authority of Congress to pass it. He had entertained this opinion from the date of the Constitution. His impression might, perhaps, be the stronger because he well recollected that a power to grant charters of incorporation had been proposed in the General Convention and rejected. [As noted in the text, the debate and vote at the constitutional convention was more oblique and opaque on the bank question than Madison suggests.]

Is the power of establishing an incorporated Bank among the powers vested by the Constitution in the Legislature of the United States? This is the question to be examined.

After some general remarks on the limitations of all political power, he took notice of the peculiar manner in which the Federal Government is limited. It is not a general grant, out of which particular powers are expected; it is a grant of particular powers only, leaving the general mass in other hands. So it had been understood by its friends and its foes, and so it was to be interpreted.

As preliminaries to a right interpretation, he laid down the following rules:

An interpretation that destroys the very characteristic of the Government cannot be just.

Where a meaning is clear the consequences, whatever they may be, are to be admitted—where doubtful, it is fairly triable by its consequences.

In controverted cases, the meaning of the parties to the instrument, if to be collected by reasonable evidence, is a proper guide.

Contemporary and concurrent expositions are a reasonable evidence of the meaning of the parties.

In admitting or rejecting a constructive authority, not only the degree of its incidentality to an express authority is to be regarded, but the degree of its importance also; since on the will depend the probability or improbability of its being left to construction.

Reviewing the Constitution with an eye to these positions, it was not possible to discover in it the power to incorporate a Bank.

3. Randolph Finds the Bank Bill Unconstitutional

Source: Walter Dellinger and H. Jefferson Powell, The Constitutionality of the Bank Bill: The Attorney General's First Constitutional Law Opinions, 44 Duke L.J. 110, 122, 127, 130 (1994)

The Attorney General of the United States in obedience to the order of the President of the United States has had under consideration the bill, entitled "An Act to incorporate the Subscribers to the Bank of the United States," and reports on it, in point of constitutionality, as follows:

It must be acknowledged that, if any part of the bill does either encounter the Constitution or is not warranted by it, the clause of incorporation is the only one.

. . .

That the power of creating corporations is not *expressly* given to the Congress, is obvious.

If it can be exercised by them, it must be:

1st. because the nature of the federal government implies;
or

2d. because it is involved in some of the specified powers of legislation; or

3. because it is necessary and proper to carry into execution some of the specified powers:

1. To be implied in the nature of the federal government would beget a doctrine so indefinite, as to grasp every power.

Governments having no *written* constitution may perhaps claim a latitude of power not always easy to be determined. Those which have written constitutions are circumscribed by a just interpretation of the words contained in them. . . .

[Randolph examines the argument that certain specified powers of Congress—the power to lay and collect taxes, to borrow money, regulate commerce, etc.—are sufficient grounds for establishing a national bank. He rejects such arguments, turning next to the Necessary and Proper Clause.]

The general qualities of the federal government, independent of the Constitution and the specified powers, being thus insufficient to uphold the incorporation of a bank, we come to the last enquiry, which has been already anticipated, whether it be sanctified by the power to make all laws which shall be necessary and proper for carrying into execution the powers vested by the Constitution. To be necessary is to be incidental, or in other words may be denominated the natural means of executing a power.

The phrase, "and proper," if it has any meaning, does not enlarge the powers of Congress, but rather restricts them. For no power is to be assumed under the general clause, but such as is not only necessary and proper, or perhaps expedient also. But as the friends to the bill ought not to claim any advantage from this clause, so ought not the enemies to it, to quote the clause as having a restrictive effect: both ought to consider it as among the surplusage which as often proceeds from inattention as caution.

However, let it be propounded as an eternal question to those who build new powers on this clause, whether the latitude of construction which they arrogate will not terminate in an unlimited power in Congress?

In every respect therefore under which the attorney general can view the act, so far as it incorporates the Bank, he is bound to declare his opinion to be against its constitutionality.

.   .   .

5. It has been also pretended, that even the infirm old Congress incorporated a bank; and can a less power be presumed to be vested in the federal government which has been formed to remedy their weakness? This argument is so indefinite, the time of the incorporation was so pressing, and the states had such an unlimited command over Congress and their acts, that the public acquiescence ought not to be the basis of such a power under the present circumstances.

---

4. Hamilton Defends the Bank's Constitutionality

Source: 8 The Papers of Alexander Hamilton 97-103, 107 (Harold C. Syrett ed. 1965)

The Secretary of the Treasury having perused with attention the papers containing the opinions of the Secretary of State and Attorney General concerning the constitutionality of the bill for establishing a National Bank proceeds according to the order of the President to submit the reasons which have induced him to entertain a different opinion.

It will naturally have been anticipated that, in performing this task he would feel uncommon solicitude. Personal considerations alone arising from the reflection that the measure originated with him would be sufficient to produce it: The sense that he has manifested of the great importance of such an institution to the successful administration of the department under his particular care; and an expectation of serious ill consequences to result from the failure of the measure, do not permit him to be without anxiety on public accounts. But the chief solicitude arises from a firm persuasion, that principles of construction like those espoused by the Secretary of State and the Attorney General would be fatal to the just & indispensable authority of the United States.

In entering upon the argument it ought to be premised, that the objections of the Secretary of State and Attorney General are founded on a general denial of the authority of the United States to erect corporations. The latter indeed expressly admits, that if there by any thing in the bill which is not warranted by the constitution it is the clause of incorporation.

This general & indisputable principle puts at once an end to the *abstract* question—Whether the United States have power to *erect a corporation*? That is to say, to give a *legal* or *artificial capacity* to one or more persons, distinct from the natural. For it is unquestionably incident to *sovereign power* to erect corporations, and consequently to *that* of the United States, in *relation to the objects* intrusted to the management of the government. The difference is this—where the authority of government is general, it can create corporations in *all cases*; where it is confined to certain branches of legislation, it can create corporations only in those cases.

. . .

The first of these arguments [against the power of the government to erect corporations] is, that the foundation of the constitution is laid on this ground "that all powers not delegated to the United States by the Constitution nor prohibited to it by the States are reserved to the States or to the people", whence it is meant to be inferred, that congress can in no case exercise any power not included in those enumerated in the constitution. And it is affirmed that the power of erecting a corporation is not included in any of the enumerated powers.

The main proposition here laid down, in its true signification is not to be questioned. It is nothing more than a consequence of this republican maxim, that all government is a delegation of power. But how much is delegated in each case, is a question of fact to be made out by fair reasoning & construction upon the particular provisions of the constitution—taking as guides the general principles & general ends of government.

It is not denied that there are *implied*, as well as *express* powers, and that the former are as effectively delegated as the latter. . . .

Then it follows, that as a power of erecting a corporation may as well be *implied* as any other thing; it may as well be employed as an *instrument* or *mean* of carrying into execution any of the specified powers, as any other instrument or mean whatever. The only question must be, in this as in every other case, whether the mean to be employed, or in this instance the corporation to be erected, has a natural relation to any of the acknowledged objects or lawful ends of

the government. Thus a corporation may not be erected by congress, for superintending the police of the city of Philadelphia because they are not authorised to *regulate* the *police* of that city; but one may be erected in relation to the collection of the taxes, or to the trade with foreign countries, or to trade between the States, or with the Indian Tribes, because it is the province of the federal government to regulate those objects & because it is incident to a general *sovereign* or *legislative power* to *regulate* a thing, to employ all the means which relate to its regulation to the *best & greatest advantage*.

. . .

[Hamilton rejects the interpretation of the Necessary and Proper Clause advanced by Jefferson and Randolph.] it is certain that neither the grammatical, nor popular sense of the term requires that construction. According to both, *necessary* often means no more than *needful, requisite, incidental, useful,* or *conducive to*. It is common mode of expression to say, that it is *necessary* for a government or a person to do thing or that thing, when nothing more is intended or understood, than that the interests of the government or person require, or will be promoted, by the doing of this or that thing. The imagination can be at no loss for exemplification of the use of the word in this sense.

. . . To understand the word as the Secretary of State does, would be to depart from its obvious & popular sense, and to give it a *restrictive* operation; an idea never before entertained. It would be to give it the same force as if the word *absolutely* or *indispensably* had been prefixed to it.

. . .

[Hamilton asks: How do we determine what is constitutional?] This criterion is the *end* to which the measure relates as a mean. If the end be clearly comprehended within any of the specified powers, & if the measure have an obvious relation to that end, and is not forbidden by any particular provision of the constitution—it may safety be deemed to come within the compass of the national authority.

III. COURT STRIPPING

Article III of the Constitution recognizes a direct link between judicial power and politics. Under Section 1, the power to "ordain and establish" lower federal courts rests with Congress. Moreover, Section 2 makes the Supreme Court's appellate jurisdiction subject to "such exceptions" and "such regulations as the Congress shall make." Unlike judicial review, which the Court uses to expand its own power, court stripping concerns external political forces curtailing judicial power.

This section will examine the constitutional and political boundaries of elected branch efforts to curb the judiciary. The focus here is on "court stripping" proposals that prohibit the Supreme Court and/or lower federal courts from either resolving specified disputes or issuing specified remedies. For example, may Congress prohibit the Supreme Court from using busing remedies or deciding challenges to state laws that outlaw abortions or mandate school prayer?

Court stripping proposals typically seek to reinstate majoritarian preferences in the wake of unpopular Supreme Court decisions. Congressional efforts to protect Reconstruction legislation from the Chase Court and attempts to strip the Warren Court of jurisdiction in the wake of "pro-communist," "pro-criminal" decisions exemplify these proposals. This section highlights efforts that began in the late 1970's to challenge judicial rulings on school prayer, school busing, and abortion.

A. Constitutional Background

The leading case for empowering Congress to withdraw appellate jurisdiction from the Supreme Court is *Ex Parte McCardle*, 74 U.S. (7 Wall.) 506 (1868), a case concerning Congress' 1868 repeal of a statute granting the Court jurisdiction to review habeas corpus actions. William McCardle, a Mississippi newspaper editor arrested for publishing articles that incited "insurrection, disorder, and violence," had filed a habeas corpus motion pursuant to an 1867 statute that authorized the granting of relief by the federal courts to anyone illegally held in custody by either the state or federal government. The statute, moreover, authorized Supreme Court review of lower court habeas judgments.

Congress, fearing that the Supreme Court would use *McCardle* to find the Reconstruction military government in the South unconstitutional, repealed the statute. The 1868 repeal was more than a simple court stripping measure, however. The Supreme Court had already heard oral arguments in *McCardle*. In explaining Congress' power to alter Court jurisdiction in a case already before the Court, Republican Senator William Stewart of Nevada argued: "The Supreme Court has no power to interfere with the question of reconstruction. . . . [It] only has power to decide cases, and it must receive the law from the lawmaking power." Cong. Globe, 40th Cong., 2d Sess. 2118 (1868).

President Andrew Johnson objected to the timing of the repeal, vetoing the bill five days before the Senate was to begin its impeachment trial of him for alleged obstruction of Reconstruction. While broadly declaring that "any person restrained of his or her liberty in violation of the Constitution" must have "the right of appeal to the highest judicial authority," Johnson ultimately grounded his veto on the fact that *McCardle* was already before the Court (document 1). Congress overrode his veto by large margins. Surprisingly, neither Johnson nor Democrats in Congress objected to the bill on the principle that it was constitutionally improper for the Congress to limit the Court's appellate jurisdiction.

In a unanimous opinion upholding the repeal statute, Chief Justice Chase stated that the Court was "not at liberty to inquire into the motives of the legislature. We can only examine into its power under the Constitution; and the power to make exceptions to the appellate jurisdiction of this court is given by express words." McCardle, 74 U.S. (7 Wall.) at 514. Three years later, however, the Supreme Court ruled in *United States v. Klein* that Congress may not dictate substantive outcomes by removing Supreme Court jurisdiction. 80 U.S. (13 Wall.) 128 (1871). Asking rhetorically whether Congress "may prescribe rules of decision to the Judicial Department . . . in cases pending before it?" the Court answered that "Congress has inadvertently passed the limit which separates the legislative from the judicial power." Id. at 146-47.

Klein and *McCardle*, by embracing conflicting views of congressional authority over Supreme Court jurisdiction, leave the question of political controls over Court jurisdiction in a shadowy realm. Consequently, the debate over such congressional controls is principally about policy and political prudence, not constitutionality.

B. The Politics of Court Stripping

Prior to 1953, Congress did not see its jurisdictional power as a mechanism to statutorily undermine unpopular Supreme Court rulings. When jurisdiction was limited, such as in the Reconstruction Era, it was a preemptive strike to protect legislative priorities by foreclosing judicial action. The Warren Court changed all that. By playing an affirmative countermajoritarian role, the Warren Court seemed quite willing to overturn the legislative apple cart and open itself to political reprisals. From 1953 to 1968, over 60 bills were introduced in Congress to limit the jurisdiction of the federal courts over school desegregation, national security, criminal confessions, and a variety of subjects.

Typical of these efforts is Senator William Jenner's response to Supreme Court decisions protecting the First Amendment rights of communists. Outraged by these decisions, Jenner introduced a bill to withhold the Supreme Court's appellate jurisdiction on these and related matters. S. 2646, 85th Cong., 1st Sess. (1957). In defending his proposal, Jenner regarded the withholding of jurisdiction as a more effective check than the "slow and uncertain" route of constitutional amendment. Limitation of Appellate Jurisdiction of the U.S. Supreme Court: Hearings on S. 2646 Before the Subcomm. to Investigate the Administration of the Internal Security Act and Other Internal Security Laws of the Senate Comm. on the Judiciary, 85th Cong., 1st Sess. 22 (1957). Attorney General William Rogers, however, found the bill a dangerous threat to judicial autonomy. For Rogers: "The natural consequences of such an enactment is that the courts would operate under the constant apprehension that if they rendered unpopular decisions, jurisdiction would be further curtailed." Id. at 574. Jenner answered Rogers' charge, claiming that, rather than "threaten[ing] the independence of the judiciary," his bill "threaten[s] the imbalance which has been created by decisions of the Supreme Court in recent years. It threatens the power to legislate which the Supreme Court has arrogated to itself during those years." 104 Cong. Rec. 4423 (1958). The Jenner proposal and other proposals of this era were eventually defeated, but not without stirring up substantial debate as to the scope and meaning of the Article III exceptions clause.

The proliferation of court stripping proposals during the Warren era is not surprising. For similar reasons, it is not surprising that in the late 1970s a second wave of court stripping proposals attacking the Burger Court emerged. With decisions like *Roe* v. *Wade* (abortion) and *Swann* v. *Charlotte-Mecklenburg Bd. of Educ.* (busing), the Burger Court continued what the Warren Court began, namely, a transformation of the federal judiciary. Conservatives in Congress and the Reagan administration expressed dissatisfaction with this increasingly intrusive judicial role. Reagan's Attorney General, William French Smith, rebuked the judiciary, explaining that "[n]ot only are unelected jurists with life tenure less attuned to the popular will than regularly elected officials, but judicial policy making also is inevitably inadequate or imperfect policy making." William French Smith, Urging Judicial Restraint, 68 A.B.A.J. 59, 60 (1982). The question remained whether this dissatisfaction would translate into administration support of court stripping measures.

Some conservatives, despite their displeasure with the Supreme Court, nonetheless oppose court stripping proposals. For example, warning that there is no principled way to distinguish appropriate from inappropriate limits on jurisdiction, Senator Barry Goldwater (R-Ariz.) argued that "judicial excesses" should not be met with "legislative excesses" (document 2). Other conservatives, however, are not troubled by such risks. For example, Senator Jesse Helms (R-N.C.), in answering arguments that the appropriate way to respond to Court rulings is through a constitutional amendment, bluntly put it: "[T]here is more than one way to skin a cat, and there is more than one way for Congress to provide a check on arrogant Supreme Court Justices who routinely distort the Constitution to suit their own [n]otions of public policy." 130 Cong. Rec. 5919 (1984).

C. School Prayer

The tenor of recent court stripping battles is exemplified by the so-called "Helms amendment," where the constitutionality and propriety of court stripping were examined by both Congress and the White House. The Helms amendment refers to congressional efforts (from 1978 to 1984) to return state-sponsored prayer to the public schools. Specifically, the Helms amendment would deny jurisdiction to the Supreme Court and lower federal courts in "any case arising out of any . . . State statute, ordinance, rule, or regulation, which relates to voluntary prayers in public schools and public buildings." S. 450, 96th Cong., 1st Sess. (1979). Although never approved by both Houses of Congress, the Senate's passage of the amendment in 1979 triggered a floodgate of political maneuvering and academic commentary.

Senator Max Baucus (D-Mont.) warned against the onslaught of court stripping proposals, cautioning that such proposals are "inconsistent with the goals of stability [and] certainty in our judicial system." 128 Cong. Rec. 4432-33 (1982). Moreover, he observed that an unintended consequence of preventing Supreme Court reconsideration is to freeze in place disfavored precedents. Id. On the other side, Senator Helms—emphasizing the difficulty of utilizing the amendment process—defended his proposal as the only effective check available to the Congress to counteract judicial transgressions. When pressed by Senator Baucus on the propriety of constitutional rights being denied by a simple majority, Senator Helms noted that the Constitution may well grant such a power to Congress (document 3).

The question of the constitutionality of the Helms amendment was considered initially by the Carter administration and then by the Reagan administration. The Carter administration had little difficulty in concluding that the amendment was unconstitutional, arguing that it threatened the unity and supremacy of the Constitution. The Reagan administration proved more ambivalent toward the Helms Amendment. Although willing to defend the bill in court, Attorney General William French Smith reminded Congress that "[t]he remedy for judicial overreaching . . . is not to restrict the Supreme Court's jurisdiction over those cases which are central to the core functions of the Court in our system of government." Nomination of Edwin Meese III: Hearings Before the Senate Comm. On the Judiciary, 98th Cong. 2d Sess. 197 (1984).

The administration's decision here is in accord with the American legal community which, in the wake of the nearly successful "Helms amendment," spoke as one in voicing opposition to jurisdiction-stripping measures. For example, the Conference of Chief Justices of State Courts argued that jurisdiction-stripping measures could result in fifty distinct and unreviewable interpretations of federal constitutional protections. (document 4).

D. Alternatives to Court Stripping

Congress has access to other mechanisms, in addition to its Article III powers, that effectively strip the court of its authority either to hear a case or to issue a remedy. Section 5 of the Fourteenth Amendment, which empowers Congress to "enforce by appropriate legislation" the equality guarantee, has been advanced as a source of legislative authority to prohibit court-ordered busing. President Nixon in 1972 and Senator J. Bennett Johnston (D-La.) in 1981 both advanced antibusing proposals grounded in Section 5. Neither proposal was enacted.

By adopting explicit language in statutes, Congress may preclude judicial review of agency actions. Thus, legislation in 1885 stated that decisions by the accounting officers of the Treasury Department regarding claims for property were to be treated as final determinations "and shall never thereafter be reopened or considered." A unanimous Court held that the statute conferred exclusive and final jurisdiction on the Treasury Department and that federal courts had no power to exercise judicial review over the agency's judgment. United States v. Babcock, 250 U.S. 328 (1919). Decisions by the Veterans Administrator on "all questions of law and fact" affecting veteran's benefits "shall be final and conclusive and may not be reviewed by any other official or by any court . . ." 38 U.S.C. 211(a) (1994). The Court accepts the prohibition of judicial review on these questions of benefits or claims, providing there is no constitutional issue. Johnson v. Robison, 415 U.S. 361, 366-367 (1974). Legislation in 1988 subjected certain actions by the Veterans Administration (now the Department of Veterans Affairs) to judicial review. 102 Stat. 4105 (1988).

The Administrative Procedure Act prohibits judicial review over agency action "committed to agency discretion by law." 5 U.S.C. 701(a)(2) (1994). In a case challenging the Defense Base Closure and Realignment Act of 1990, which established a commission to recommend the closing of unnecessary military bases, a unanimous Court concluded that "[w]here a statute, such as the 1990 Act, commits decisionmaking to the discretion of the President, judicial review of the President's action is not available." Dalton v. Specter, 511 U.S. 462, 477 (1996). An amendment by Senator Arlen Specter to subject base closures to judicial review was rejected a month later. 140 Cong. Rec. 14078-90.

Congress' Article I, Section 9 appropriations powers have also been used as a mechanism to advance court stripping objectives. In 1980 and again in 1981, Congress gave serious consideration to the so-called Helms-Collins amendment which would have prohibited the Department of Justice from expending funds "to bring or maintain any sort of action to require directly or indirectly the transportation of any student to a school other than the school which is nearest the student's home. . . ." 127 Cong. Rec. 12468 (1981).

President Carter vetoed the bill, castigating Congress for intruding into executive prosecutorial discretion authority. Pub. Papers, 1980-81 (III), at 2809. This concern was echoed by the Reagan administration when "Helms-Collins" was debated in 1981. The Reagan administration, although opposed to mandatory busing, concluded that Helms-Collins is "unnecessary and may inhibit the [administration's] ability to present and advocate remedies which may be less intrusive and burdensome than those being urged on a court by other litigants." 6 Op. Off. Legal Counsel 1, 3-4 (1982).

Another, albeit peculiar, alternative to Article III court stripping is a constitutional amendment divesting the Court of some power. This technique was advanced in April 1990, when Senator John Danforth (R-Mo.) sought the adoption of a constitutional amendment providing that federal courts lack the power to direct the "imposition of taxes." This measure, proposed in response to the Supreme Court's approval of court-ordered taxation in *Missouri* v. *Jenkins*, 495 U.S. 33 (1990), was phrased in the form of a constitutional amendment to demonstrate that elected government's control of the taxing power is a "fundamental premise" of American government. 136 Cong. Rec. 8183 (1990). There was no action on this amendment.

E. Conclusion

Congress' power to alter the jurisdiction of the federal courts, especially the Supreme Court, raises profound questions about the judiciary's status as a coequal branch. That Congress has not exercised its exceptions power since Reconstruction reveals that court stripping is ultimately a disfavored mechanism of checking judicial excess. Nonetheless, the potential reach of this power and the near enactment of the Helms' school prayer amendment cautions against the judiciary straying too far or too often from elected branch preferences.

DOCUMENTS

1. Andrew Johnson Vetoes Court-Stripping Measure

Source: 6 A Compilation of the Messages and Papers of the Presidents 3844-46 (J. Richardson ed. 1897)

To the Senate of the United States:

I cannot give my assent to [this] measure. . .

The bill not only prohibits the adjudication by the Supreme Court of cases in which appeals may hereafter be taken, but interdicts its jurisdiction on appeals which have already been made to that high judicial body. If, therefore, it should become law, it will by its retroactive operation wrest from the citizen a remedy which he enjoyed at the time of his appeal. It will thus operate most harshly upon those who believe that justice has been denied them in the inferior courts.

The legislation proposed . . . is not in harmony with the spirit and intention of the Constitution. It cannot fail to affect most injuriously the just equipoise of our system of Government, for it establishes a precedent which, if followed, may eventually sweep away every check on arbitrary and unconstitutional legislation. Thus far during the existence of the Government the Supreme Court of the United States has been viewed by the people as the true expounder of their Constitution, and in the most violent party conflicts its judgments and decrees have always been sought and deferred to with confidence and respect. In public estimation it combines judicial wisdom and impartiality in a greater degree than any other authority known to the Constitution, and any act which may be construed into or mistaken for an attempt to prevent or evade its decision on a question which affects the liberty of the citizens and agitates the country can not fail to be attended with unpropitious consequences. . . .

2. Senator Barry Goldwater Opposes Court-Stripping

Source: 128 Cong. Rec. 4458-59 (1982)

Mr. [Barry] GOLDWATER [R-Ariz.]. [R]ecently I expressed my concern about proposals that would interfere with Federal court independence. These measures would put limits on judicial consideration of social issues, particularly busing, abortion, and prayer.

I happen to believe the Federal courts have wrongly decided these subjects. I am strongly opposed to the breakup of neighborhood schools. I think the unborn baby is entitled to some legal protection. And I believe schoolchildren should be allowed a few moments of voluntary prayer.

In my view, the Supreme Court has erred. But we should not meet judicial excesses with legislative excesses.

As vacancies occur, we can confirm Federal judges who believe in judicial restraint. We can amend the Constitution. We can use the power of the purse to deny Federal money for activities we disapprove, such as abortions. But to make a frontal assault on the independence of the courts is a dangerous blow to the foundations of a free society.

It is contrary to the will of the framers. It is destructive of the federal system. And it will result in the reverse outcome of what the Court's critics wish.

What particularly troubles me about trying to override constitutional decisions of the Supreme Court by a simple bill is that I see no limit to the practice. There is no clear and coherent standard to define why we shall control the court in one area but not another. The only criteria seems to be that whenever a momentary majority can be brought together in disagreement with a judicial action, it is fitting to control the Federal courts.

Now it is busing and abortion and prayer. But what will be next? Will a majority lay hold of Congress who puts all actions of the Internal Revenue Service beyond judicial scrutiny? Might opponents of private schools muster sufficient support to deny a challenge in Federal court to confiscatory taxes which may be levied on church schools?

3. Helms Defends Court-Stripping

Source: 131 Cong. Rec. 23174-76 (1985)

Mr. [Jesse] HELMS [R-N.C.].

. . .

What I am proposing is not a constitutional amendment. It is not "court stripping" as is so often charged. It is simply the implementation of article III of the Constitution of the United States. I am sure the Senator is familiar with that. Article III of the Constitution provides the Congress of the United States with the authority, and I think the duty, to limit the jurisdiction of the Supreme Court and/or the other Federal courts when in the judgment of the Congress of the United States the Supreme Court has exceeded its purview. . . .

. . .

As is well known, the constitutional amendment process was intentionally set up to be difficult. The normal procedure is for a two-thirds vote in both Houses of Congress followed by ratification by three-quarters of the State legislatures. . . .

If, however, Congress relegates itself solely to the amendment process to correct judicial errors and usurpations, then the very difficulty of the amendment process will be used to protect, not the constitutional text, but distortions of it. Thus, in the face of usurping Federal judges, the amendment process would serve to subvert the Constitution rather than to preserve it.

4. State Chief Justices Repudiate Jurisdiction Withdrawal Proposals

Source: 128 Cong. Rec. 689 (1982)

. . . [T]he Conference of Chief Justices, without regard to the merits of constitutional issues involved, expresses its concern about the impact of [proposed court stripping] bills on state courts and views them as a hazardous experiment with the vulnerable fabric of the nation's judicial systems, arriving at this position for the following reasons, among others:

A. These proposed statutes give the appearance of proceeding from the premise that state court judges will not honor their oath to obey the United States Constitution, nor their obligations to give full force to controlling Supreme Court precedents;

B. If those proposed statutes are enacted, the current holdings of those Supreme Court decisions targeted by this legislation will remain the unchangeable law of the land, absent constitutional amendments, beyond the reach of the United States Supreme Court or state supreme courts to alter or overrule.

C. State court litigation constantly presents new situations testing the boundaries of federal constitutional rights. Without the unifying function of United States Supreme Court review, there inevitably will be divergence in state court decisions, and thus the United States Constitution could mean something different in each of the fifty states;

D. Confusion will exist as to whether and how federal acts will be enforced in state courts and, if enforced, how states may properly act against federal officers;

E. The proposed statutes would render uncertain how the state courts could declare a federal law violative of the federal Constitution and whether Congress would need to wait for a majority of the state courts to so rule before conceding an act was unconstitutional;

F.   The added burden of litigation engendered by the proposed acts would seriously add to the already heavy caseload in state courts;

Now, therefore, be it *Resolved*, That the Conference of Chief Justices expresses its serious concerns relating to the above legislation, approves the report of the Conference's Subcommittee of the Committee on State-Federal Relations, and directs its officers to transmit that report, together with this resolution, to appropriate members of Congress.

IV. JUSTICIABILITY

Article III of the Constitution informs us that "the judicial power" extends to "cases" or "controversies." By limiting court participation to concrete disputes, the case-or-controversy requirement guards against abstract judicial declarations of policy. Towards this end, the Court insists that litigants have standing and that their claims be presented in an adversary context.

A litigant who lacks standing or does not present her case in an adversarial setting is denied access to the courts. In other words, the fact that a litigant's substantive arguments are correct may not be enough. This section, by examining the evolution of federal policy governing the tax-exempt status of racially discriminatory private schools, uncovers the critical role that justiciability plays in defining the Court's role in government.

A. Tax-Exempt Policy for Racially Discriminatory Private Schools

After *Brown v. Board of Education*, IRS tax-exemption policy became a major civil rights issue. As the pace of court-ordered school desegregation quickened in the late 1960s, thousands of white students in the South flooded into private schools. Newly-formed private schools mushroomed in southern states, many of them organized for the express purpose of providing white students a segregated education.

Prior to 1970, the Internal Revenue Service (IRS) granted exemptions to schools regardless of their racial admissions policies or practices. That practice was predicated on a "plain meaning" interpretation of Internal Revenue Code language providing that institutions organized for educational purposes would be tax-exempt. I.R.C. §501(c)(3) (1954). Recognizing the high political costs of granting tax breaks to racist schools, the Nixon administration reversed the IRS policy as "no longer legally justif[iable]."

In 1978, a nationwide class action lawsuit filed by Inez Wright, a black parent, and her teenage daughter challenged the adequacy of IRS enforcement of this nondiscrimination requirement. Wright, however, could not prove that a change in IRS policy would prompt private schools to change their admissions practices. And without such proof, there was reason to question whether the IRS could have harmed Wright. But the Carter IRS did not question Wright's standing. Instead, it proposed—consistent with plaintiff's demands—a more exacting tax-exemption procedure which would have denied tax-exempt status to private schools that had an insignificant number of minority students. This proposal sparked an overwhelmingly negative public response. 150,000 letters—principally from Christian fundamentalists who viewed the proposal as a threat to their schools—poured into the IRS. Critics within Congress joined the outcry. More significant, Congress prevented the implementation of the proposed IRS plan by denying any funds to the Service to enforce the proposed policy. 93 Stat. 559, 562 (1979).

The Carter IRS controversy was not lost on candidate Ronald Reagan. In an appeal to the growing voting block of Christian fundamentalists (whose schools would have been adversely affected by the Carter proposal), the 1980 Republican Party Platform stated that "[w]e will halt the unconstitutional regulatory vendetta launched by Mr. Carter's IRS Commissioner against independent schools." 1980 Republican Party Platform, reprinted in 36 Cong. Q. Almanac 63-B (1980). The battleground in which the Reagan administration sought to implement this campaign pledge became centered around Bob Jones University, a school which prohibited interracial dating as a matter of religious conviction.

In 1976, the IRS had revoked Bob Jones University's tax-exempt status. The university challenged the revocation both on statutory and First Amendment freedom of religion grounds. The lawsuit worked its way up to the Supreme Court where certiorari was granted in October 1981. At that time, the Reagan administration defended the Nixon policy. In an unexpected reversal, however, the Treasury Department announced on January 8, 1982, that the IRS would no longer deny tax-exempt status to discriminatory institutions. On the same day, the Justice Department petitioned the Supreme Court to vacate the case as moot.

Administration staff members warned Attorney General William French Smith of the backlash of such a dramatic policy reversal. Specifically, with government lawyers seeking to dismiss the *Wright* litigation on standing grounds (document 1), aides in the Justice Department feared that the administration's petition to vacate *Bob Jones* might well lead to a defeat in the *Wright* litigation (document 2). For these staffers, the granting of tax breaks to racist schools would prompt the Court to grant standing in *Wright* in order to judicially mandate the nondiscrimination policy. In so doing, the standing to sue barrier would be lowered and government regulation would be increasingly subject to judicial scrutiny.

The Reagan Administration ignored such warnings and proceeded with the policy announcement, provoking a barrage of criticism from newspapers and civil rights groups. In the wake of this attack, President Reagan sent legislation to Congress that would have prohibited the granting of tax exemptions to racially discriminatory organizations. Congress, however, threw the issue back at the administration and urged officials to "find a way out of the impasse," either by admitting error or discovering a legal theory that would allow the Supreme Court to settle the case (document 3).

A solution materialized on February 18, 1982, when the D.C. Circuit enjoined the administration from issuing any new tax exemption rulings pending the outcome of the *Wright* litigation. Since this court order prevented the administration from restoring Bob Jones' tax-exempt status, the Justice Department withdrew its mootness petition and requested the Court to appoint a "counsel adversary" to defend the 1970 policy. The Court complied with the government's unorthodox request and appointed William T. Coleman, Jr., to argue the "government's side" in these cases, thus permitting the case to proceed despite its apparent lack of adverseness.

B. The Politics of Justiciability

The Court's decision to hear *Bob Jones* made political sense. It took pressure off both the Congress (which did not want to enact legislation) and the President (who did not want to reverse his policy or implement an unpopular policy). Moreover, the Court lifted a burden from its own shoulders. Its refusal to hear the case would have transformed the *Wright* litigation into a referendum over the 1970 non-discrimination policy and thereby exponentially increased the stakes of *Wright*. As Justice Cardozo suggested long ago: "[W]hen the social needs demand one settlement rather than another, there are times when we must bend symmetry, ignore history and sacrifice custom in the pursuit of other and larger ends." Benjamin N. Cardozo, The Nature of the Judicial Process 65 (1921).

In May 1983, the Supreme Court ruled that racially discriminatory schools are statutorily prohibited from receiving federal tax-exempt status. Bob Jones Univ. v. United States, 461 U.S. 574 (1983). The Court held that tax-exempt institutions' operations must not be "contrary to a fundamental public policy" and that "there can no longer be any doubt that racial discrimination in education violates deeply and widely accepted views of elementary justice." Id. at 592. With respect to the enforcement of this nondiscrimination mandate, the Court recognized "very broad authority" in the IRS to interpret the laws. Id. at 596.

The resolution of *Bob Jones University* did not settle the *Wright* litigation, for black parents in *Wright* sought the judicial imposition of Carter-like standards. Unlike *Bob Jones University*, where the judiciary winked at case or controversy limitations, the Supreme Court ruled here that the black parents lacked standing. Allen v. Wright, 468 U.S. 737 (1984). In language strikingly similar to the Department of Justice brief (document 1), the Court emphasized its "properly limited [role] in a democratic society," id. at 750, that "[plaintiffs'] approach would have the federal courts [assume Congress' role] as virtually continuing monitors of the wisdom and soundness of Executive action," id. at 760, and that "the idea of separation of powers . . . counsels against recognizing standing in [such] a case." Id. at 761.

The Court had good reason to sidestep *Wright*. *Bob Jones'* recognition of broad IRS discretion to administer the tax code strongly suggests that civil rights plaintiffs would not have prevailed on the merits. In other words, a decision granting standing would have unnecessarily prolonged this divisive controversy, created tensions between the judiciary and elected government, and ultimately resulted in an anti-civil rights ruling on the merits.

DOCUMENTS

1. Department of Justice Urges Dismissal of *Wright*

Source: Petition of the United States for a Writ of Certiorari at 18-21, Regan v. Wright, 468 U.S. 737 (1984) (No. 81-970)

The broad authority that Congress has given the Secretary of the Treasury and the Commissioner of Internal Revenue over the administration of the tax laws shows that it did not intend the courts to entertain suits of this kind. To adjudicate respondents' generalized claims, a broad-scale inquiry into the enforcement practices of the Internal Revenue Service, as well as into the racial policies of an indefinite number of private schools, would be required. The role respondents would assume and have the court assume, "as virtually continuing monitors of the wisdom and soundness of Executive action," belongs to Congress in the exercise of its oversight function over the operation, administration, and effects of the internal revenue system and to the President, who, along with the Treasury officials, is required to "take Care that the Laws be faithfully executed." Absent an assertion of concrete and remedial injury directly attributable to unlawful government action, the judiciary should not assume the "amorphous [task of] general supervision of the operations of government. . . ."

Of course, we do not suggest that policies of the Internal Revenue Service should be immune from public inquiry and examination. The broad tax policy questions raised by respondents' suit are properly a matter for public debate. However, the appropriate forum for such a debate concerning the correctness of Treasury policy is in the Congress . . . and not in the courts.

"Any other conclusion would mean that the Founding Fathers intended to set up something in the nature of an Athenian democracy or a New England town meeting to oversee the conduct of the National Government by means of lawsuits in federal courts."

---

2. Justice Department Staff Warn About Effect of Concession in *Bob Jones*

Source: Administration's Change in Federal Policy Regarding the Tax Status of Racially Discriminatory Private Schools: Hearing Before the House Comm. On Ways and Means, 97th Congress 2d Sess. 535-37 (1982)

To: Edward C. Schmultz,
        Deputy Attorney General
From: John F. Murray, Deputy Assistant
        Attorney General, Tax Division

[T]he Tax Division fears that concession of the *Bob Jones* and *Goldsboro* cases at the Supreme Court level will have a substantial adverse effect on our position on standing to sue. The basis for that fear cannot be demonstrated syllogistically or by conventional logical analysis. On the other hand, the belief that we would be worse off is based upon the perceptions of experienced litigators as to judicial attitude and behavior, and, as such, merits consideration.

For more than ten years, the Tax Division has opposed, on grounds of lack of standing, numerous efforts of plaintiffs describing themselves as taxpayers, or otherwise interested parties, to obtain injunctive orders directing the Secretary of the Treasury and the Commissioner of Internal Revenue to administer some one or more provisions of the Internal Revenue Code not in accordance with current practice but in accord with their particular desires. . . .

Should *Bob Jones* and *Goldsboro* be disposed of without decision, *Wright v. Regan*, would remain. . . . [Consequently]

should the Supreme Court grant certiorari in *Wright v. Regan*, we would have the standing question presented to a Court fully aware of the statutory and constitutional questions in the background and aware that more than details of administration are involved. Indeed, in our petition for certiorari in *Wright v. Regan*, though the question presented is limited to the standing issue, we have referred to the substantive position taken in *Goldsboro* and *Bob Jones*.

In sum, we believe that disposing of *Bob Jones* and *Goldsboro* without decision on the merits would simply postpone disposition of the issue there until *Wright v. Regan* finally is decided, and that our standing position meanwhile would be placed at hazard in an extremely unfavorable context.

---

3. Congress Urges Administration To Let Court Resolve Tax Exemption Issue

Source: Administration's Change in Federal Policy Regarding the Tax Status of Racially Discriminatory Private Schools: Hearings Before the House Comm. On Ways and Means, 97th Congress, 2d Sess. 193-94

Mr. [James] MARTIN [R-N.C.]. . . .
One of our earlier witnesses made a suggestion that it would have been more prudent to allow the Supreme Court to go ahead and consider issues of religious discrimination, racial discrimination. I wondered what would be wrong with your going forward with the case, temporarily withholding the tax exemption from Bob Jones University and/or the Goldsboro Schools in order for the Supreme Court to reach its final determination; and related to that, why could you not go for it and present to the Supreme Court your determination to root out and punish racial discrimination as well as your reservation about the legal basis for doing so?
Mr. [William Bradford] REYNOLDS [Assistant Attorney General]. Congressman,

that would certainly be our preference. We would like to do that. There is a problem and that is that when we reached the decision as a matter of law, the position that we would have to assert in the Supreme Court was the one that was indicated on January the 8th. That left the case in a posture where there were no longer two litigants that were involved in a controversy because we would then be taking the side on the legal issue that was similar to the side that was being advanced by Bob Jones University and Goldsboro Schools, as far as the statutory authority question. The court has said any number of times that it will not render advisory opinions where there is no case or controversy before it. . . .

Mr. MARTIN. It is not possible for you to argue what you regard to be valid points on both sides? With regard to racial discrimination and with regard to the case law that the gentleman from New York was discussing and the other with regard to the legal basis?

. . .

[Mr. REYNOLDS] In order for the Court to hear the case in a controversial setting, I guess that what the Court would have to do is to allow the NAACP—and I believe the NAACP has requested—allow it to intervene and argue the case on the other side. But that would then require, I think, in terms of our jurisprudence, that you ignore the fact that there are not two litigants in the Court that are in controversy and it would require the Court to render an advisory opinion. I think that is something the Supreme Court has indicated it will not do.

V. POLITICAL QUESTIONS

Are there circumstances where it is inappropriate for the judiciary to review the constitutionality of elected branch conduct? *Marbury* v. *Madison* speaks of "[q]uestions, in their nature political," which "can never be made in this court." 5 U.S. (1 Cranch) 137, 170 (1803). Yet, were the judiciary to rule every case of a political character a nonjusticiable political question, the judicial power would be a nullity.

In 1962 the Supreme Court identified criteria to judge whether a matter is a political question. Baker v. Carr, 369 U.S. 186 (1962). One of these criteria, textual commitment to another branch, demands independent constitutional analysis for the very question of whether an issue has been textually committed requires judicial interpretation. Other criteria set forth in *Baker* v. *Carr* are pragmatic concerns of varying degrees, e.g., "unusual need for unquestioning adherence to a political decision already made," "the potentiality of embarrassment from multifarious pronouncements." Id. at 217.

The question remains whether and when a court should avoid a judicial decision by claiming that it is institutionally incapable of speaking to the substantive claims presented. This section examines this question through the lens of *Powell v. McCormack*, 395 U.S. 486 (1969).

A. Congress Tests the Constitutionality of Excluding a Member

Adam Clayton Powell, a flamboyant black Democrat from New York's 18th Congressional District, was one of the most controversial political figures of his day. A member of Congress for twenty-two years and Chairman of the House Education and Labor Committee, Powell had been re-elected once again by his 450,000 constituents by a three-to-one majority in the 1966 election. However, rumors had been circulating in the press that Powell was misallocating public funds and unlawfully abusing the privileges of his office. In addition, he was being held in criminal contempt of New York state courts in connection with a defamation suit against him.

When Powell was reelected, there was a growing sentiment among members of the Congress, responding to intense public pressure, that Powell should not be allowed to serve his term. Several Congressmen argued that it was within Congress's Article 1, Section 5 power to refuse to seat Powell for any reason it saw fit, including moral character. Other members feared that the exclusion of Powell would risk an almost certain clash with the courts.

On March 1, 1967, Emanuel Celler (D-N.Y.) introduced House Resolution 278, recommending that Powell be seated and then publicly censured and fined. 113 Cong. Rec. 4997 (1967). Most members, however, disagreed with this cautious approach. For them, fear of retaliation by the courts was irrelevant: "[S]ince when should action in this House be predicated on fear of what the Supreme Court may or may not do?" queried Representative Samuel Devine (R-Ohio). Id. at 5012. Furthermore, many House members were confident that disputes concerning the internal affairs of Congress, such as decisions over membership, constituted political questions and were thus immune from judicial scrutiny. As Representative Clarence Long (D-Md.) remarked: "The courts [under the political question doctrine] will not handle questions inherently in the power of other coordinate branches at the same level of Government." Id. at 5001.

House Resolution 278 failed by a vote of 202-222. Id. at 5020. An amendment by Representative Curtis, which required Powell to stand aside while the oath of office was administered to the other members-elect of the 90th Congress, passed by an overwhelming majority vote of 307-116. Id. at 5037-5038.

B. The Supreme Court's Decision

Congress's decision not to seat Powell was a direct challenge to the Supreme Court. Rather than avoid an interbranch squabble by adopting

H. Res. 278, the House boldly proclaimed ultimate constitutional authority over the seating of its members. This confrontational strategy is also underscored by the House's litigation strategy in the Powell dispute. Citing separation of powers doctrine, the House claimed "exclusive power" over the seating of members. Indeed, the House claimed that its decisions here, "whether right or wrong, must command the same respect from the other branches as do the decisions of this Court". 68 Landmark Briefs at 724. House counsel Bruce Bromley was similarly unyielding at oral argument, insisting that the Court was without authority to restrain House action, regardless of how audacious or unconstitutional (document 1).

It was in this setting, with Congress thumbing its nose at the Court, that Chief Justice Earl Warren composed the *Powell v. McCormack* opinion. Deciding to fight fire with fire, Warren used *Powell* as an opportunity to issue a stern rebuke to the House. Depicting the Court as "the *ultimate* interpreter of the Constitution," Warren reasoned that it must sometimes disagree with the constitutional interpretations of another branch. 395 U.S. at 549. His decision did just that; holding that Congress' authority under Section 5 of Article I extended no further than Section 2 age, citizenship, and residency requirements, the Court found Congress' exclusion of Powell unconstitutional. 395 U.S. at 550.

In Congress, reaction to Warren's opinion ranged from disgruntlement to defiance. The leaders of both parties viewed the decision as an impermissible intrusion into the internal affairs of Congress. Representative John Rarick (D-La.), himself a former judge, termed the *Powell* ruling "a law school model of judicial impropriety," 115 Cong. Rec. 16198 (1969), and fumed: "If this House is to bow to court orders controlling the conduct of its internal business—the separation of powers—the Constitution itself is dead." Id. at 15824. Republican Floor Leader Gerald Ford (R-Mich.) characterized the opinion as "an unfortunate transgression of the court on another branch of the Federal government." Wash. Post, June 17, 1969, at A8, col. 4. Representative William Colmer (D-Miss.), chairman of the House Rules Committee, invoked the infamous words of President Andrew Jackson: "John Marshall has made his decision. Now let him enforce it." Id. at 15823. Bruce Bromley seemed drawn to that strategy. In a letter to Judge George L. Hart, Jr., he hinted that the House would engage in the ultimate act of defiance: disobedience (document 2).

In the week following the announcement of the *Powell* opinion, House and Senate Joint Resolutions were introduced to curb the power of the federal judiciary, even to the point of denying courts any jurisdiction over disputes between an individual Member of the House of Representatives and the House itself. 115 Cong. Rec. 15858, 16197-98 (1969). Proponents of these measures complained of "the trend toward [an] all-powerful" Supreme Court and urged the Congress to "affirm its sovereignty as a coequal and coordinate branch." Statements by Rep. William Nichols (D-Ala.) and Rep. John Flynt (D-Ga.); 115 Cong. Rec. 15858, 16198 (1969). Although none of this legislation was ultimately successful, it reflects the rebellious mood in both Houses of Congress in the wake of *Powell*.

C. Conclusion

Powell was much more than a defense of judicial independence. Issued just one week before Earl Warren stepped down, the decision was his last important act as Chief Justice. For this reason, *Powell* appears both a swan song and a benchmark of the Warren era. By limiting the political question doctrine, *Powell* reveals a willingness—characteristic of the Warren Court—for the judiciary to actively check elected government.

Powell, however, should not be deemed a relic of another judicial era. Political question cases suggest there are inherent limits on the judicial power and therefore inevitably raise concerns about the Court's status as coequal branch. As such, the Court, not surprisingly, is reluctant to say that some matters are simply best left to elected government. Only on rare occasions in recent decades has the Supreme Court explicitly invoked the political question doctrine to hold an issue nonjusticiable. Gilligan v. Morgan, 413 U.S. 1 (1973) (federal courts cannot evaluate the training of National Guard units because Article I, Section 8 of the Constitution commits such supervision to Congress); Nixon v. United States, 506 U.S. 224 (1993) (Senate has exclusive power under Article 1, Section 6 to conduct impeachment trials).

DOCUMENTS

1. The House Urges the Supreme Court to Validate Powell's Exclusion

Source: 68 Landmark Briefs 928-29, 930, 933, 934-35

MR. [Bruce] BROMLEY [Counsel for the House of Representatives]: [T]his is an action against the Members of the House, questioning their action in their official capacity. . . . It is our view that this Court does not have the power to entertain this action against the Members, any more than it would have the power to order the Members to pass or repeal a statute.

THE COURT: Supposing [Powell] had been excluded because of his race in a formal resolution. Would you say that he would have any judicial remedy?

MR. BROMLEY: I should say, sir, in answer to that question, that the action of the House would be clearly unconstitutional.

THE COURT: And would he have judicial remedy?

MR. BROMLEY: As I read the speech or debate clause, he would not, sir.

So, our position is that what the House did in this matter was for the House, and the House alone, to decide; and its action should not and is not subject to judicial review. . . .

THE COURT: . . . To put an extreme case: Do you find that if the Congress had expelled

Mr. Powell, saying, "Well, we will lay aside a majority vote required for exclusion and the two-thirds vote for expulsion. We'll just take a general consensus and expel him." Would you say that was nonjusticiable?

MR. BROMLEY: I think so. Of course, it was improper and unconstitutional.

THE COURT: No relief?

MR. BROMLEY: No relief, because the power to judge, which includes the power to judge erroneously, has been confided to the House.

THE COURT: Oh, then the Court has no jurisdiction to draw the line?

MR. BROMLEY: Except in cases of utter perversion, sir.

THE COURT: And in response to Justice Black, I take it an exclusion solely on the grounds of race would not be within the category of utter perversion, as you see it?

MR. BROMLEY: In my opinion it would not, sir, although clearly unconstitutional, clearly improper. . . .

THE COURT: Well, what could be more—Judge Bromley, what could be more "perverse" than that?

[Laughter]

MR. BROMLEY: Well, a great many things.

THE COURT: For instance?

MR. BROMLEY: Seizing the President and dragging him into the well of the House under a resolution that he be beheaded.

[Laughter]

---

2. The House Questions the Authority of the Court in a Letter to Judge George L. Hart, Jr.

Source: McKay, Comments on *Powell v. McCormack*, 17 UCLA L. Rev. 117, 126-29 nn. 42-44 (1969)

[The Supreme Court decision provided only declaratory relief, and left the ultimate issues, including disbursement of back pay, to the lower court for resolution. Judge Hart requested letters from the parties suggesting ways in which the Court's order could be implemented, but later dismissed the claim for back pay.]

August 18, 1969

Dear Judge Hart:

We are instructed by our clients to advise Your Honor that the House, with all due respect, does not agree with the decision of the Supreme Court in this matter. The House believes that the decision and mandate of that Court constitute an unwarranted action inconsistent with the separation of powers provided by the Constitution. . . .

As to the desirability of any further proceedings, it is our clients' position that Mr. Powell is not entitled to any further relief in this action, and that the action should be dismissed. . . . [I]n view of the position of the House with respect to the Supreme Court's decision and mandate, as described above, I am not able to state what action the House might take with respect to any order which any court might direct against its officer-agents. . . .

Respectfully yours,
Bruce Bromley

August 20, 1969

Dear Judge Hart:

. . . The overwhelming public interest in the reaffirmation of principle that the rule of law demands compliance by all, regardless of their station, with the decisions of the highest court of the law now requires that the resolution of questions raised in the [August 18] letter of counsel for the defendants not be protracted or delayed. This is no ordinary law suit. In its present posture, it now touches upon the most fundamental concept upon which the Republic rests—namely whether the rule of law applies to all or is to be invoked only when poor and powerless citizens are involved. The constitutional liberties of all of us depend upon the acceptance of the rule of law by every organ of government, no matter how exalted in status.

Respectfully submitted,
Arthur Kinoy
Rutgers University, School of Law

Herbert O. Reid
Howard University, School of Law

August 21, 1969

Dear Judge Hart:

.   .   .

[In response to plaintiffs' attorney's August 20 letter, we] submit that it is not inadmissible, or in derogation of the rule of law, for one branch of the Government to call attention to the principle of separation of powers with its attendant system of checks and balances which is designed to insure that no one branch becomes dominant. . . .

Respectfully submitted,
Bruce Bromley

[Judge Hart dismissed the claim for back pay.]

3

FEDERALISM

The meaning of federalism has been shaped more by Congress and the President than by the Supreme Court. The two political branches affect the distribution of power between states and the national government whenever they decide the extent to which the federal government shall exercise its spending power, the taxing power, and the Commerce Clause in directing state activities. Throughout most of the nineteenth century the Court functioned basically as a yea-saying branch, lending its legitimacy to the constitutional judgments already reached by Congress and the President through the regular legislative process.

However, toward the end of the nineteenth century and for several decades into the twentieth, federal and state courts struck down legislative efforts to regulate economic conditions. Policies adopted by the elected branches were regularly invalidated by the courts. It was during this period of "substantive due process" that the political branches tried to curb the judiciary, culminating in the court-packing plan presented by President Franklin D. Roosevelt in 1937. By adding new Justices to the Court, he hoped to eliminate the Court as an obstacle to his national economic programs.

Although that plan backfired and resulted in a resounding legislative defeat for Roosevelt, the "Revolution of 1937" precipitated the resignation of conservative Justices from the Court. Within a few years, Roosevelt had a solid majority on the Court to sustain his New Deal measures, especially the interpretations of the Commerce Clause advanced by Congress and the executive branch.

Section I of this chapter focuses on congressional efforts to use the powers of commerce and tax to regulate child labor in the states. The Supreme Court invalidated two statutes passed by Congress in 1916 and 1919, but Congress continued to press for reforms in this area. Eventually it legislated again on child labor, in 1938, and this time the congressional will prevailed.

These legislative struggles are closely related to Roosevelt's court-packing plan. Although his proposal was decisively defeated, the confrontation with the Court—coupled with legislation that offered full pay to Justices who wanted to retire—gave Roosevelt the opportunity to put new Justices on the Court. It was this new Court that upheld the child-labor legislation of 1938. That story is presented in Section II of this chapter.

Section III concentrates on President Kennedy's proposal in 1963 to guarantee blacks equal access to public accommodations. A key element in that fight was the administration's interpretation of the Commerce Clause. Previous legislation on public accommodations, grounded on the Fourteenth Amendment, had been declared unconstitutional by the Supreme Court.

Section IV begins with the Court's announcement in *National League of Cities* v. *Usery* (1976) that the principle of federalism establishes strict limits on the power of Congress to regulate economic matters in the states. That doctrine was emphatically rejected nine years later in *Garcia* v. *San Antonio Metro. Transit Auth.* (1985). The latter case recognized that the meaning and application of federalism lay almost exclusively with Congress and the political process.

Section V reviews federalism in the 1990s, with the Supreme Court much more active in policing the boundaries between the national government and the states. The revival of federalism began with Ronald Reagan's election in1980, setting the stage for Court rulings that limited what Congress may do under the Commerce Clause and breathed new life into the Tenth and Eleventh Amendments.

Section VI analyzes a major collision between Congress and the Court: the enactment of the Religious Freedom Restoration Act of 1993, which reversed a 1990 Court decision, and the Court's action in 1997 to invalidate the statute. Congress is now considering legislative language that can survive judicial scrutiny.

I. CHILD LABOR CASES

Congress passed legislation in 1916 to prevent the products of child labor from being shipped interstate, basing the statute squarely on the national power to regulate commerce. No producer, manufacturer, or dealer could ship or deliver for shipment in interstate or foreign commerce any article produced by children within specified age ranges. In reviewing the proposed legislation, the House Labor Committee concluded that "the entire problem has become an interstate problem rather than a problem of isolated States and is a problem which must be faced and solved only by a power stronger than any State." H.R. Rep. No. 46 (Part 1), 64th Cong., 1st Sess. 7 (1916). Based on the record developed during its hearings, the committee maintained that the bill was constitutional and in accord with recent Supreme Court rulings that permitted Congress to use the Commerce Clause to regulate public health and morals. The report also identified the constitutional issue that would become a sticking point: whether Congress could regulate goods only at the end of their interstate journey or also at an earlier point when they were first produced in a state (document 1).

A. The Court Invalidates the Statute

In 1918, the Supreme Court held the statute unconstitutional. Divided 5 to 4, the Court argued that the production and manufacture of goods are not commerce and may not be controlled by Congress. According to the Court, the statute attempted to give the national government control over questions of the police power that are reserved to the states. In his dissent, Justice Holmes stated: "The act does not meddle with anything belonging to the States. They may regulate their internal affairs and their domestic commerce as they like. But when they seek to send their products across the state line they are no longer within their rights." Hammer v. Dagenhart, 247 U.S. 251, 281 (1918).

Within a matter of days, members of Congress confronted the Court by introducing new measures to regulate child labor. 56 Cong. Rec. 8341 (1918). One of the ideas that took hold was to rely on the taxing power. An excise tax would be levied on the net profits of persons employing child labor within prohibited ages. Id. at 11560.

Senator Robert L. Owen (D-Okla.) proposed stronger medicine by reintroducing the child labor bill, again based solely on the Commerce Clause, and adding a section that would strip the courts of jurisdiction to hear future cases on the issue. His bill provided: "Any executive or judicial officer who in his official capacity denies the constitutionality of this act shall ipso facto vacate his office." 56 Cong. Rec. 7432 (1918). Owen questioned at length the Court's authority to announce the last word on constitutional issues (document 2).

Senator Thomas Hardwick (D-Ga.) believed that the Court's decision settled the issue and Congress had no authority to reopen it. He further argued that Congress should not attempt to do indirectly through the taxing power what it had been forbidden to do under the Commerce Clause. 57 Cong. Rec. 609-10 (1918). However, a leading conservative Senator at that time, Henry Cabot Lodge (R-Mass.), denied that there was anything inappropriate about Congress making another legislative attempt (document 3). The child-labor amendment to the tax bill passed the Senate by a large margin (50-12) and was accepted by the House. 57 Cong. Rec. 621, 3035 (1919). The bill imposed an excise tax of ten percent on the net profits from the sale or disposition of any product from a mine, quarry, mill, cannery, workshop, factory, or manufacturing establishment that depended on child labor. 40 Stat. 1138 (1919).

B. The Second Invalidation

A federal district court in North Carolina declared the excise tax unconstitutional. When the issue was taken to the Supreme Court, Solicitor General James M. Beck prepared a brief that defended the tax.

Of special interest is the section in which Beck cautioned the Court to exercise political prudence when reviewing, and possibly overturning, the considered efforts of its coequal branches, Congress and the President (document 4). The Court struck down the child-labor tax by an 8-1 majority, holding that Congress had passed not a tax but rather a means to prohibit and to regulate. It was not a tax but a "mere penalty." *Child Labor Tax Case*, 259 U.S. 20 (1922).

Congress responded to this second setback by passing a constitutional amendment in 1924 to give it the power to regulate child labor. However, it could never attract three-fourths of the states to ratify the amendment. Part of the problem may have been the language of the amendment, which gave Congress the power to regulate "the labor" of persons under 18 years of age. Some critics interpreted that as authority for Congress to regulate the labor of a child on his parent's farm. Note, *What Is the Status of the Child Labor Amendment?*, 26 Geo. L.J. 107, 108 (1937).

C. Try, Try Again

By 1937, only twenty-eight of the necessary thirty-six states had ratified the amendment. Congress returned to the Commerce Clause in 1938 when it included a child-labor provision in the Fair Labor Standards Act of 1938. The prohibition on child labor did not apply to children employed in agriculture, motion pictures, or theatrical productions. H.R. Rep. No. 2738, 75th Cong., 3d Sess. 8-9 (1938).

Thus, Congress had decided to return to the very constitutional power that had been denied by the Court in 1918: the Commerce Power. This may appear to be a brusque confrontation with a coequal branch, but the Court of 1938 was in the process of change. Because of new appointments that year and the next few years, the Court would be more receptive to legislative efforts to regulate child labor. When the statute reached the Supreme Court, it was upheld unanimously. *United States v. Darby*, 312 U.S. 100 (1941). Congress had finally prevailed in its efforts to eliminate the evils of child labor.

D. Conclusion

Although it took the Court more than twenty years, it decided to return to the doctrines of Chief Justice Marshall who gave broad support to the power of Congress to regulate commerce. Congress refused to accept the narrow judicial construction adopted by the Court in the child labor cases. Congress persevered and won. The Court later admitted that "the history of judicial limitation of congressional power over commerce, when exercised affirmatively, had been more largely one of retreat than of ultimate victory." Prudential Ins. Co. v. Benjamin, 328 U.S. 408, 415 (1946).

DOCUMENTS

1. House Labor Committee Defends Constitutionality of Child Labor Bill

Source: H.R. Rep. No. 46 (Part 1), 64th Cong., 1st Sess. 13-14 (1916)

The constitutional problem involved in this bill has received the careful attention of the committee, who have invited a full discussion of this phase of the proposed legislation. Needless to say, however, your committee did this, not with a view to arrogate to themselves the duty of passing judgment upon a problem of constitutional law, but rather with a view of provoking discussion and of informing themselves and Congress as to the general attitude upon this problem of experts familiar with the authorities and the trend of judicial thought.

. . .

For the purpose of this report, it will be sufficient to say that, so far as the opinion of your committee is entitled to any weight, the proposed bill falls properly within the power granted to Congress to regulate commerce among the States, and that such seems to be the strongly prevailing view among students of constitutional law.

In considering this phase of the bill, the committee has been strongly impressed by what may properly be termed the broadening view of the powers of Congress under the interstate commerce clause, a view emphasized in a number of recent cases decided by the Supreme Court of the United States, particularly those cases bearing upon the lottery act, the food and drugs act, and the white-slave act.

The question of the constitutionality of the bill was ably argued before the committee. Ex-Gov. W. W. Kitchin, of North Carolina, representing the Southern cotton manufacturers, and Mr. J. A. Emery, representing the board of directors of the National Association of Manufacturers, argued against the constitutionality of the bill, and Prof. Thomas I. Parkinson, director of the legislative drafting research department of Columbia University, New York City, argued for the constitutionality of the bill. . . .

We conceive that the heart of Mr. Parkinson's argument [which we endorse] is contained in the following excerpt:

". . . The Supreme Court of the United States has upheld the lotteries legislation, it has upheld the congressional legislation forbidding transportation of prostitutes, the Mann White Slave Act. In neither case was there any purpose of protecting commerce itself, or the instrumentalities of commerce. Those two acts were both upheld by the Supreme Court because the court held that the power to regulate commerce included the power to regulate it in the interest of the public safety, the public health, the public morals, and the public welfare. . . ."

2. Senator Owen Confronts the Supreme Court

Source: 56 Cong. Rec. 7431-33 (1918)

Mr. [Robert L.] OWEN [D-Okla.]. . . .

Mr. President, I have just submitted to the Senate a bill to prevent interstate commerce in the products of child labor.

This is the same bill which was passed on September 1, 1916, whose constitutionality was denied by five members of the Supreme Court of the United States on Monday last.

. . .

I add a new section 7, as follows:

"The constitutionality of this act having been declared by the competent authority of Congress and of the President of the United States at the time of its passage shall only be questioned thereafter by the Congress itself and the people of the United States in their sovereign capacity as voters. Any executive or judicial officer who in his official capacity denies the constitutionality of this act shall ipso facto vacate his office. No judge of an inferior Federal court shall permit the question of the constitutionality of this act to be raised in the court over which he presides, and the United States Supreme Court shall have no appellate power to pass upon such questions."

. . . .

One man has nullified the opinion, the matured public opinion, of the country, as expressed by Congress, and has overruled both Houses of Congress and the President of the United States and four members of the Supreme Court, and has established as a judicial decree that every Member of the Senate and every Member of the House voting for the act and the President of the United States violated the Constitution of the United States, which they severally lifted up their hands before Almighty God and swore to observe.

This act of the Supreme Court is not intended as a personal affront to the Members of the House, to the Senators, and to the President of the United States approving the act by charging that they have severally violated the Constitution of the United States. These learned justices who have declared this act of Congress unconstitutional have merely followed the unwarranted, the unjust, and unsound precedent set by John Marshall in the petty case of Marbury against Madison, when he had the temerity to exercise the veto over Congress as the first judge on the bench to declare an act of Congress unconstitutional. John Marshall's decision was absolutely wrong and contrary to the history and spirit of the law, and was a piece of judicial usurpation which was not followed by the Supreme Court of the United States in a single case for 50 years until the fatal case of Dred Scott, when that honorable Supreme Court declared slavery a constitutional national right and the Missouri Compromise as unconstitutional, void, and of no effect.

The deadly consequences which followed that unwise decision had to be remedied on the field of battle by the armed forces of the majority in four years of blood and tears of the American people. . . .

. . . .

It is said by some that the judges are much more learned and wiser than Congress in construing the Constitution. I can not concede this whimsical notion. They are not more learned; they are not wiser; they are not more patriotic; and what is the fatal weakness if they make their mistakes there is no adequate means of correcting their judicial errors, while if Congress should err the people have an immediate redress; they can change the House of Representatives almost immediately and can change two-thirds of the Senate within four years, while the judges are appointed for life and are removable only by impeachment.

---

3. Senator Henry Cabot Lodge Supports Another Legislative Effort

Source: 57 Cong. Rec. 611 (1918)

Mr. [Henry Cabot] LODGE [R-Mass.].

. . . I have been very deeply interested in the question of child labor for a great many years. I introduced the first bill here for the protection of child labor in the District of Columbia, and I have always sought for legislation on that subject.

I am not going to argue the details. It is a great evil. The States have had ample and abundant opportunity to deal with it themselves. Most of the States have; some have not. I think it is something that ought to be ended.

Congress passed the bill for that purpose by a large majority. That form of legislation has been held unconstitutional by the Supreme Court, and therefore it would seem to me that our only resort is to the taxing power. I am no fonder of resorting to that power for this purpose than anyone else, but the Government of the United States has resorted to it in more than one case. In the lottery cases it was not a taxing power, but exclusion from the mails, but the court dwelt on the justification of the action of Congress very largely on account of the ethical question involved, that the lottery was against public policy. We used it in the oleomargarine cases. We used in the bank cases. . . .

It so happened that some years ago I carried through a bill, which became a law, to exterminate by the use of the taxing power the manufacture of white phosphorus matches, which produced hideous diseases among the workers. The bill failed in one Congress and passed in the next. I think the constitutionality of that law has never been questioned.

---

4. Solicitor General Beck Defends Constitutionality of Child-Labor Tax

Source: Brief on Behalf of Appellants and Plaintiff in Error, Bailey v. Drexel Furniture Co., U.S. Supreme Court, October Term, 1921; 21 Landmark Briefs 52, 59-60

. . . The impression is general—and I believe that it is a mischievous one—that the judiciary has an unlimited power to nullify a law if its incidental effect is in excess of the governmental sphere of the enacting body. Our whole constitutional jurisprudence, with respect to the dual power over commerce, shows that this is not the fact.

Moreover, there is a large field of political action, into which the judiciary may not enter. It is the sphere of action which may be described as that of political discretion. The motives and objectives of an exercise of a delegated power are always matters of political discretion.

. . .

The belief that the judiciary is fully empowered to sit in judgment upon the motives or objectives of other branches of the Government is a mischievous one, in that it so lowers the sense of constitutional morality among the people that neither in the legislative branch of the Government nor among the people is there as strong a purpose as formerly to maintain their constitutional form of Government.

Let this Court clearly say that in this broad field of political discretion there is no revisory power in the Judiciary, and that the remedy must lie in the people, then, if there be any longer a sufficient sense of constitutional morality in this country, the people will themselves protect their Constitution.

The erroneous idea that this court is the sole guardian and protector of our constitutional form of government has inevitably led to an impairment, both with the people and with their representatives, of what may be called the constitutional conscience.

. . . The prevalent disposition seems to be to ignore constitutional questions by shifting them to the Supreme Court, in the belief that that court will exercise the full powers of revision, which I have tried to show the Framers of the Constitution did not intend this court to have. The result may be an exaltation of this court, as a tribunal of extraordinary power; but, in the matter of constitutionalism, it inevitably leads to an impairment of the powers and duties of Congress and, above all, to the impairment of the popular conscience; for, in the last analysis, the Constitution will last in substance as long as the people believe in it and are willing to struggle for it.

II. PACKING AND UNPACKING THE COURT

After the Supreme Court struck down a number of major New Deal statutes intended to ease the Great Depression, President Franklin D. Roosevelt attacked the conservative orientation of the Court. Especially controversial was the Court's decision in *Schechter* in 1935, declaring invalid the National Industrial Recovery Act (NIRA), which invoked the Commerce Clause to create industrial codes to regulate economic activities. Schechter Corp. v. United States, 295 U.S. 495 (1935). The Court held the statute unconstitutional in part because Congress had failed to set forth adequate standards to guide the executive branch, but Roosevelt knew that the question of delegation was less important than the Court's narrow definition of the Commerce Clause. He lashed out at the Court for taking the country back to the "horse-and-buggy" days (document 1).

A. The Court-Packing Plan

Roosevelt was reelected in 1936 by an overwhelming margin. This decisive victory appeared to bolster his confidence in confronting the unelected Court, but his annual message to Congress on January 6, 1937, gave no hint of an impending attack on the judiciary. His message included only a modest appeal to the Court to reconsider its doctrines and support the administration's program: "Means must be found to adapt our legal forms and our judicial interpretation to the actual present national needs of the largest progressive democracy in the modern world." 5 Public Papers and Addresses of Franklin D. Roosevelt (1936 volume), at 639-40.

A month later, however, he unveiled his radical plan to "reorganize" the federal judiciary. Claiming that the Supreme Court was unable to function effectively, he proposed that for every Justice over 70 years of age, he be empowered to appoint an additional Justice until the number of Supreme Court Justices reached fifteen. He wanted similar powers to appoint judges in the appellate and trial courts. Roosevelt suggested that his basic motivation was to improve the efficiency of the courts, rather than promote the New Deal. The problem was one of "aged or infirm judges" (document 2).

On March 9, 1937, Roosevelt revealed his true goals. In a "fireside chat" to the nation, he described the national government as "a three horse team" of Congress, the President, and the courts. Two of the horses "are pulling in unison; the third is not." Roosevelt accused the Supreme Court of acting "as a policy-making body" by invalidating federal and state statutes. The problem was no longer mere inefficiency. What Roosevelt wanted, he finally admitted, was a "liberal-minded Judiciary" (document 3).

Later that month, on March 21, Chief Justice Hughes released a letter to Senator Burton K. Wheeler (D-Mont.), explaining that the Court "is fully abreast of its work." This remarkable letter helped discredit Roosevelt's bill. It demonstrated that the Court was not overworked or in need of additional Justices. It helped spotlight Roosevelt's political agenda (document 4).

On June 7, the Senate Judiciary Committee reported the bill adversely, recommending that it not pass. Probably at no time in history has a presidential proposal been so savaged in a congressional report. The committee exposed the real purpose of the bill: to use force against the judiciary. Using blunt and forceful language, the committee ripped the proposal with such thoroughness that no President in the future would be tempted to offer it again (document 5).

B. The Retirement Bill

Although the Senate repudiated Roosevelt's judicial reorganization bill, Congress completed action on a bill to provide full pay for Supreme Court Justices who retired. Congress had passed legislation in 1869 authorizing a lifetime salary for federal judges who resigned after serving at least ten years and who had reached the age of seventy. 16 Stat. 45, § 5 (1869). By resigning from office, judges could no longer perform judicial duties.

In 1919, Congress gave federal judges at age 70 and with ten years of service the option of *retiring*, allowing judges to perform judicial duties assigned by the Chief Justice or the senior circuit judge. Retirement offered financial benefits. Judges who resigned received the salary payable at the time of resignation, but that salary was not protected by the constitutional provision prohibiting any diminution of salary. Judges who retired retained that constitutional protection and were eligible for salary increases voted by Congress. For some reason, the 1919 statute specifically excluded Justices of the Supreme Court ("any judge other than a justice of the Supreme Court"). 40 Stat. 1157, § 6 (1919).

The House Judiciary Committee reported legislation in 1935 to give Justices of the Supreme Court the same option of retiring, permitting them to discharge judicial duties in any circuit assigned by the Chief Justice. H.R. Rep. No. 212, 74th Cong., 1st Sess. (1935). The bill failed on a vote of 144 to 210 and was reintroduced in 1937. The House Judiciary Committee reported the measure precisely one day before Roosevelt's bombshell message on judicial reorganization. H.R. Rep. No. 176, 75th Cong., 1st Sess. (1937). The retirement bill sailed through both Houses and was enacted on March 1. 50 Stat. 24 (1937).

After a decent interval, Justice Van Devanter wrote to President Roosevelt on May 18, announcing his retirement as of June 2 to take advantage of the new statute. Roosevelt, with his first chance to alter the Court, picked Senator Hugo Black. On January 5, 1938, Justice Sutherland wrote to Roosevelt announcing his intention to retire as of January 18. As Sutherland's replacement, Roosevelt named Solicitor General Stanley Reed. Justice Cardozo died on July 9, 1938, giving Roosevelt the opportunity to nominate a close friend, Felix Frankfurter. Justice Brandeis retired on February 13, 1939, and was replaced by William O. Douglas, who had served in the Roosevelt administration as chairman of the Securities and Exchange Commission. Justice Butler died on November 16, 1939. Frank Murphy, who filled several positions in the Roosevelt administration, including Attorney General, took Butler's place.

C. Conclusion

Thus, after going four and half years without naming anyone to the Court, within a little over two years Roosevelt appointed five close associates, two because of deaths on the Court, three because of the inducements offered by the retirement bill. Roosevelt later looked back at the court-packing fight and concluded that he had lost that particular battle but won the war. Writing in 1941, he expressed satisfaction with the outcome despite the shellacking he took on the court-packing proposal (document 6).

One of the conservative Justices who rethought his position on the Commerce Clause was Owen Roberts, who began to alter his economic philosophy in 1934 and by 1937 was supplying key votes to sustain New Deal measures. After leaving the Court he explained the force of public opinion that beat against the Court: "Looking back, it is difficult to see how the Court could have resisted the popular urge for uniform standards throughout the country—for what in effect was a unified economy." Owen Roberts, Jr., The Court and the Constitution 61 (1951).

DOCUMENTS

1. President Roosevelt Objects to the Interpretation of the Commerce Clause in *Schechter*

Source: 4 Public Papers and Addresses of Franklin D. Roosevelt (1935 volume), at 205, 208-10, 220-21

Now, coming down to the decision [Schechter Corp. v. United States] itself. What are the implications? For the benefit of those of you who haven't read it through I think I can put it this way: the implications of this decision are much more important than almost certainly any decision of my lifetime or yours, more important than any decision probably since the Dred Scott case, because they bring the country as a whole up against a very practical question. . . .

. . . . .

. . . [T]he Court in this decision, at least by dictum—and remember that dictum is not always followed in the future—has gone back to the old Knight case in 1885 [United States v. E.C. Knight Co., 156 U.S. 1 (1895),] which in fact limited any application of interstate commerce to goods in transit—nothing else!

Since 1885 the Court in various decisions has enlarged on the definition of interstate commerce—railroad cases, coal cases and so forth and so on. It was clearly the opinion of the Congress before this decision and the opinion of various attorneys-general, regardless of party, that the words "interstate commerce" applied not only to an actual shipment of goods but also to a great many other things that affected interstate commerce. . . .

The whole tendency over these years has been to view the interstate commerce clause in the light of present-day civilization. The country was in the horse-and-buggy age when that clause was written and if you go back to the debates on the Federal Constitution you will find in 1787 that one of the impelling motives for putting in that clause was this: There wasn't much interstate commerce at all—probably 80 or 90 percent of the human beings in the thirteen original States were completely self-supporting within their own communities.

In other words, the whole picture was a different one when the interstate commerce clause was put into the Constitution from what it is now. Since that time, because of the improvement in transportation, because of the fact that, as we know, what happens in one State has a good deal of influence on the people in another State, we have developed an entirely different philosophy.

The prosperity of the farmer does have an effect today on the manufacturer in Pittsburgh. The prosperity of the clothing worker in the city of New York has an effect on the prosperity of the farmer in Wisconsin, and so it goes. We are interdependent—we are tied in together. . . .

The implication, largely because of what we call obiter dicta in this opinion, the implication of this opinion is that we have gone back, that the Supreme Court will no longer take into consideration anything that indirectly may affect interstate commerce. That hereafter they will decide the only thing in interstate commerce over which they can permit the exercise of Federal jurisdiction is goods in transit plus, perhaps, a very small number of transactions which would directly affect goods in transit.

You see the implications of the decision. . . . We have been relegated to the horse-and-buggy definition of interstate commerce.

---

2. Roosevelt Announces His Court Packing Plan

Source: 6 Public Papers and Addresses of Franklin D. Roosevelt (1937 volume), at 51-52, 53-55

I have recently called the attention of the Congress to the clear need for a comprehensive program to reorganize the administrative machinery of the Executive Branch of our Government. I now make a similar recommendation to the Congress in regard to the Judicial Branch of the Government, in order that it also may function in accord with modern necessities.

The Judiciary has often found itself handicapped by insufficient personnel with which to meet a growing and more complex business. . . .

In almost every decade since 1789, changes have been made by the Congress whereby the numbers of judges and the duties of judges in federal courts have been altered in one way or another. The Supreme Court was established with six members in 1789; it was reduced to five in 1801; it was increased to seven in 1807; it was increased to nine in 1837; it was increased to ten in 1863; it was reduced to seven in 1866; it was increased to nine in 1869.

The simple fact is that today a new need for legislative action arises because the personnel of the Federal Judiciary is insufficient to meet the business before them. A growing body of our citizens complain of the complexities, the delays, and the expense of litigation in United States Courts.

A part of the problem of obtaining a sufficient number of judges to dispose of cases is the capacity of the judges themselves. This brings forward the question of aged or infirm judges—a subject of delicacy and yet one which requires frank discussion.

Modern complexities call also for a constant infusion of new blood in the courts, just as it is needed in executive functions of the Government and in private business. A lowered mental or physical vigor leads men to avoid an examination of complicated and changed conditions. Little by little, new facts become blurred through old glasses fitted, as it were, for the needs of another generation; older men, assuming that the scene is the same as it was in the past, cease to explore or inquire into the present or the future.

We have recognized this truth in the civil service of the nation and of many states by compelling retirement on pay at the age of seventy. We have recognized it in the Army and Navy by retiring officers at the age of sixty-four. A number of states have recognized it by providing in their constitutions for compulsory retirement of aged judges.

. . . A constant and systematic addition of younger blood will vitalize the courts and better equip them to recognize and apply the essential concepts of justice in the light of the needs and the facts of an ever-changing world.

---

3. Roosevelt Reveals His Real Purpose

Source: 6 Public Papers and Addresses of Franklin D. Roosevelt (1937 volume), at 123-28

Last Thursday I described the American form of Government as a three horse team provided by the Constitution to the American people so that their field might be plowed. The three horses are, of course, the three branches of government—the Congress, the Executive and the Courts. Two of the horses are pulling in unison today; the third is not.

. . . [S]ince the rise of the modern movement for social and economic progress through legislation, the Court has more and more often and more and more boldly asserted a power to veto laws passed by the Congress and State Legislatures in complete disregard of this original limitation.

In the last four years the sound rule of giving statutes the benefit of all reasonable doubt has been cast aside. The Court has been acting not as a judicial body, but as a policy-making body.

The Court in addition to the proper use of its judicial functions has improperly set itself up as a third House of the Congress—a super-legislature, as one of the justices has called it—reading into the Constitution words and implications which are not there, and which were never intended to be there.

We have, therefore, reached the point as a Nation where we must take action to save the Constitution from the Court and the Court from itself. We must find a way to take an appeal from the Supreme Court to the Constitution itself. We want a Supreme Court which will do justice under the Constitution—not over it. In our Courts we want a government of law and not of men.

. . . [W]e must have Judges who will bring to the Courts a present-day sense of the Constitution—Judges who will retain in the Courts the judicial functions of a court, and reject the legislative powers which the courts have today assumed.

[My] plan has two chief purposes. By bringing into the judicial system a steady and continuing stream of new and younger blood, I hope, first, to make the administration of all Federal justice speedier and, therefore, less costly; secondly, to bring to the decision of social and economic problems younger men who have had personal experience and contact with modern facts and circumstances under which average men have to live and work. This plan will save our national Constitution from hardening of the judicial arteries.

If by that phrase "packing the Court" it is charged that I wish to place on the bench spineless puppets who would disregard the law and would decide specific cases as I wished them to be decided, I make this answer: that no President fit for his office would appoint, and no Senate of honorable men fit for their office would confirm, that kind of appointees to the Supreme Court.

But if by that phrase the charge is made that I would appoint and the Senate would confirm Justices worthy to sit beside present members of the Court who understand those modern conditions, that I will appoint Justices who will not undertake to override the judgment of the Congress on legislative policy, that I will appoint Justices who will act as Justices and not as legislators—if the appointment of such Justices can be called "packing the Courts," then I say that I and with me the vast majority of the American people favor doing just that thing—now.

4. Chief Justice Hughes Reports That the Court Is Not Behind In Its Work

Source: S. Rep. No. 711,
75th Cong., 1st Sess.
38-40 (1937)

MY DEAR SENATOR WHEELER: In response to your inquiries, I have the honor to present the following statement with respect to the work of the Supreme Court:

1. The Supreme Court is fully abreast of its work. When we rose on March 15 (for the present recess) we had heard argument in cases in which certiorari had been granted only 4 weeks before—February 15.

During the current term, . . . we have heard argument on the merits in 150 cases (180 numbers) and we have 28 cases (30 numbers) awaiting argument. We shall be able to hear all these cases, and such others as may come up for argument, before our adjournment for the term. There is no congestion of cases upon our calendar.

[Justice Hughes prepared a table showing statistics for the terms 1930-32 and for 1933-35, indicating the cases pending, disposed of, and remaining on the docket. There had been no increase in the latter.]

   . . .

7. An increase in the number of Justices of the Supreme Court, apart from any question of policy, which I do not discuss, would not promote the efficiency of the Court. It is believed tht it would impair that efficiency so long as the Court acts as a unit. There would be more judges to hear, more judges to confer, more judges to discuss, more judges to be convinced and to decide. . . .

I understand that it has been suggested that with more Justices the Court could hear cases in divisions. It is believed that such a plan would be impracticable. A large proportion of the cases we hear are important and a decision by a part of the Court would be unsatisfactory.

I may also call attention to the provisions of article III, section 1, of the Constitution that the judicial power of the United States shall be vested "in one Supreme Court" and in such inferior courts as the Congress may from time to time ordain and establish. The Constitution does not appear to authorize two or more Supreme Courts or two or more parts of a supreme court functioning in effect as separate courts.

   . . .

> I have the honor to remain,
> Respectfully yours,
> CHARLES E. HUGHES,
> *Chief Justice of the United States.*

5. The Senate Judiciary Committee Rejects Roosevelt's Proposal

Source: S. Rep. No. 711,
75th Cong., 1st Sess.
3, 8, 14, 23 (1937)

THE ARGUMENT

The committee recommends that the measure be rejected for the following primary reasons:

I. The bill does not accomplish any one of the objectives for which it was originally offered.

II. It applies force to the judiciary and in its initial and ultimate effect would undermine the independence of the courts.

III. It violates all precedents in the history of our Government and would in itself be a dangerous precedent for the future.

IV. The theory of the bill is in direct violation of the spirit of the American Constitution and its employment would permit alteration of the Constitution without the people's consent or approval; it undermines the protection our constitutional system gives to minorities and is subversive of the rights of individuals.

V. It tends to centralize the Federal district judiciary by the power of assigning judges from one district to another at will.

VI. It tends to expand political control over the judicial department by adding to the powers of the legislative and executive departments respecting the judiciary.

   . . .

THE BILL APPLIES FORCE TO THE JUDICIARY

The answer is clear. It applies force to the judiciary. It is an attempt to impose upon the courts a course of action, a line of decision which, without that force, without that imposition, the judiciary might not adopt.

Can there be any doubt that this is the purpose of the bill? Increasing the personnel is not the object of this measure: infusing young blood is not the object; for if either one of these purposes had been in the minds of the proponents, the drafters would not have written the following clause to be found on page 2, lines 1 to 4, inclusive:

"*Provided*, That no additional judge shall be appointed hereunder if the judge who is of retirement age dies, resigns, or retires prior to the nomination of such additional judge."

This is the first time in the history of our country that a proposal to alter the decisions of the court by enlarging its personnel has been so boldly made. Let us meet it. Let us now set a salutary precedent that will never be disregarded by any succeeding Congress, declare tht we would rather have an independent Court, a fearless Court, a Court that will dare to announce its honest opinions in what it believes to be the defense of the liberties of the people, than a Court that, out of fear or sense of obligation to the appointing power, or factional passion, approves any measure we may enact. We are not the judges of the judges. We are not above the Constitution.

Even if every charge brought against the so-called "reactionary" members of this Court be true, it is far better that we await orderly but inevitable change of personnel than that we impatiently overwhelm them with new members. . . .

SUMMARY

We recommend the rejection of this bill as a needless, futile, and utterly dangerous abandonment of constitutional principle.

It was presented to the Congress in a most intricate form and for reasons that obscured its real purpose.

It is a measure which should be so emphatically rejected that its parallel will never again be presented to the free representatives of the free people of America.

6. Roosevelt Reflects on Court-Packing Battle

Source: 6 Public Papers and Addresses of Franklin D. Roosevelt (1937 vol.), at lviii, lxiii, lxvi [signed by Roosevelt June 3, 1941]

By June, 1936, the Congressional program, which had pulled the nation out of despair, had been fairly completely undermined. What was worse, the language and temper of the decisions indicated little hope for the future. Apparently Marshall's conception of our Constitution as a flexible instrument—adequate for all times, and therefore, able to adjust itself as the new needs of new generations arose—had been repudiated. Apparently the physical conditions of 1787 in farming, labor, manufacturing, mining, industry, and finance were still to be yardsticks of legal power for dealing with the wholly different world of one hundred and fifty years later. . . .

. . . I was convinced that an amendment was wholly unnecessary to meet the situation. I knew that the Constitution was not to blame, and that the Supreme Court as an institution was not to blame. The only trouble was with some of the human beings then on the Court. Need I add here, parenthetically, that later judicial history has proven that all these assumptions were absolutely correct?

Events happened in the midst of the fight to becloud the chief issue. There was, first, the retirement of Justice Van Devanter in June, 1937. Some have said that it was strategically timed; but of course that is incapable of proof at the present time. There came, then, the death of Senator Robinson, the Senate Democratic leader of the members in favor of the [court-packing] plan.

But the startling fact which did more than anything else to bring about the defeat of the plan in the halls of the Congress, was a clear-cut victory on the bench of the Court for the objectives of the fight. The Court yielded. The Court changed. The Court began to interpret the Constitution instead of torturing it. It was still the same Court, with the same justices. No new appointments had been made. And yet, beginning shortly after the message of February 5, 1937, what a change!

Whether this change came as a result of the election returns of 1936, whether it came as a result of my message, whether it came as a result of public discussion during the course of the fight, or a combination of all these—

those are important questions for the later historians of the period. These need not be discussed here.

I feel convinced, however, that the change would never have come, unless this frontal attack had been made upon the philosophy of the majority of the Court. . . .

III. EQUAL ACCOMMODATIONS

Federalism was at issue in 1875 and 1964 when Congress passed legislation to guarantee blacks equal access to public accommodations. Although blacks were citizens as a result of the Civil War Amendments, in many states they were denied access to theaters, restaurants, inns, and other public facilities. The first statute, grounded principally on the Fourteenth Amendment, was declared unconstitutional by the Supreme Court in 1883. The Civil Rights Cases, 109 U.S. 3 (1883). When Congress passed similar legislation in 1964, it based the statute on both the Fourteenth Amendment and the Commerce Clause. This time the Court unanimously upheld the legislation.

A. Legislation in 1875

Congress passed a bill in 1875 "to protect all citizens in their civil and legal rights." In part, the statute finally gave legal force to the Declaration of Independence by stating in the preamble: "Whereas, it is essential to just government we recognize the equality of all men before the law . . . ." All persons within the United States were now entitled "to the full and equal enjoyment of the accommodations, advantages, facilities, and privileges of inns, public conveyances on land and water, theaters, and other places of public amusement . . . ." 18 Stat. 335 (1875).

The statute did not identify the part of the Constitution that empowered Congress to act. The Thirteenth Amendment abolished slavery and it could have been argued that any denial of equal accommodation was a "badge of slavery." The Fourteenth Amendment prohibited states from abridging the privileges or immunities of citizens, from depriving persons of life, liberty, or property without due process of law, or denying any person the equal protection of the laws. This amendment provided grounds for acting against states that denied equal accommodation, and might have been a basis for acting as well against private citizens.

During debate on the bill, sponsors spoke forcefully for the bill because of "illogical, unjust, ungentlemanly, and foolish prejudice," and appeared to rely almost entirely on the Fourteenth Amendment. 3 Cong. Rec. 979-80 (1875) (Rep. Hale); id. at 1791 (Sen. Thurman); id. at 1792 (Sen. Boutwell). Members referred frequently to the protection of privileges and immunities which appears both in Section 2 of Article IV and in Section 1 of the Fourteenth Amendment (document 1). The Commerce Clause was not seriously promoted as a source of authority. Id. at 1861 (Sen. Carpenter). Although the Commerce Clause was rarely mentioned during the legislative debate, it was cited along with the Civil War Amendments in Attorney General Devens' brief to the Supreme Court defending the constitutionality of the 1875 statute (document 2).

B. Invalidation by the Court

The statute of 1875 was declared unconstitutional by the Supreme Court in the *Civil Rights Cases* (1883). The Court stated that "no one will contend that the power to pass [the law] was contained in the Constitution" before the adoption the Civil War Amendments. 109 U.S. 3, 10 (1883). Nor did the Court find adequate support in the Thirteenth or Fourteenth Amendments. Section 5 of the Fourteenth Amendment empowered Congress "to enforce, by appropriate legislation, the provisions of this title," but the Court decided that Section 5 empowered Congress only to enforce the prohibitions placed upon the states. Congress could regulate only "state action," not actions by the private parties who operated inns and hotels, railroads and other public conveyances, theaters, and other places of public amusement. The Court also denied that the exclusion of blacks from public accommodations represented a badge of slavery subject to regulation under the Thirteenth Amendment.

The Court hinted that Congress might have had some leverage through the Commerce Clause, especially with regard to transportation from one state to another: "And whether Congress, in the exercise of its power to regulate commerce amongst the several States, might or might not pass a law regulating rights in public conveyances passing from one State to another, is also a question which is not now before us, as the sections in question are not conceived in any such view." Id. at 19.

C. The Civil Rights Act of 1964

There the matter lay for eighty years until 1963, when President John F. Kennedy advocated equal access for blacks to public accommodations. In subsequent messages, Kennedy spoke with greater urgency in view of a series of violent demonstrations that had wracked the South. He also spoke with greater specificity about the public accommodations title and cited the Commerce Clause and the Fourteenth Amendment as constitutional authorities (document 3).

A month later his brother, Attorney General Robert F. Kennedy, testified before the Senate Commerce Committee and presented the administration's legal reasoning behind the public accommodations title. He explained that Congress had two constitutional authorities to enact the title: the Commerce Clause and the Fourteenth Amendment. Although the *Civil Rights Cases* of 1883 had rejected the latter and was still "good law," Kennedy believed that the contemporary Court would uphold the power of Congress under the Fourteenth Amendment. Still, he said that the administration relied primarily on the Commerce Clause (document 4).

By offering the Court two constitutional arguments, the administration wanted to avoid a full-scale confrontation with the judiciary. When the Senate Commerce Committee reported the bill, it argued forcefully that the Commerce Clause provided adequate constitutional authority for congressional action. S. Rep. No. 872, 88th Cong., 2d Sess. 12-14 (1964).

The public accommodations title was upheld in two unanimous opinions by the Supreme Court. The first case involved a large motel in Atlanta, Georgia, that served interstate travelers. The Court concluded that Congress had "ample power" under the Commerce Clause and "we have therefore not considered the other grounds relied upon." That was "not to say that the [Fourteenth Amendment] was not adequate, a question upon which we do not pass, but merely that since the commerce power is sufficient for our decision here we have considered it alone." Heart of Atlanta Motel v. United States, 379 U.S. 241, 250 (1964).

The second case concerned a restaurant in Birmingham, Alabama that served local white customers inside and provided a take-out window for blacks. The food it prepared was obtained from interstate commerce and therefore within the reach of the Commerce Clause. The statute specifically covers restaurants where "a substantial portion" of the food served "has moved in commerce." Katzenbach v. McClung, 379 U.S. 294 (1964).

D. Conclusion

On this fundamental issue of giving blacks equal access to public accommodations, the guardians of minority rights and constitutional liberties were the political branches, not the courts. Congressional persistence and ingenuity for nearly a century finally triumphed over judicial obstacles. Significantly, majoritarian branches driven by majoritarian pressures took the lead in defending the constitutional rights of minority citizens. In this contemporary drama courts were passive bystanders, offering mechanical approval for the creative initiative of Congress and the President.

DOCUMENTS

1. Debate on 1875 Bill

Source: 3 Cong.
Rec. 939-40 (1875)

Mr. [Benjamin] BUTLER [R-Mass.]. . . . I cannot understand how there can be a class of American citizens, entitled to all the privileges and immunities of American citizens, who can be, or ought to be, deprived of any privilege or immunity or right that appertains to any American citizens.

It seems to me wholly illogical, as I know it to be wholly unjust and wrong. The colored men are either American citizens or they are not. The Constitution, for good or for evil, for right or for wrong, has made them American citizens; and the moment they were clothed with that attribute of citizenship they stood on a political and legal equality with every other citizen, be he whom he may. And I repel and repudiate the idea that there is any intention by the provisions of any one of these bills to make any social equality. That is simply an argument to the prejudice.

Social equality is not effected or affected by law. It can only come from the voluntary will of each person. Each man can in spite of the law, and does in spite of the law, choose his own associates.

But it is said we put them into the cars. The men that are put into the cars and the women that are put into the cars I trust are not my associates. There are many white men and white women whom I should prefer not to associate with who have a right to ride in the cars. That is not a question of society at all; it is a question of a common right in a public conveyance.

And so in regard to places of amusement, in regard to theaters. I do not understand that a theater is a social gathering. I do not understand that men gather there for society, except the society they choose to make each for himself. So in regard to inns. Inns or taverns are for all classes of people; and every man, high and low, rich and poor, learned or ignorant, clean or dirty, has a right to go into an inn and have such accommodations exactly as he will pay for, and no other and no different; and there can be no discrimination made in that regard by law. . . .

. . . The bill is necessary because there is an illogical, unjust, ungentlemanly, and foolish prejudice upon this matter. There is not a white man [in] the South that would not associate with the negro—all that is required by this bill—if that negro were his servant. He would eat with him, suckle from her, play with her or him as children, be together with them in every way, provided they were slaves. There never has been an objection to such as association. But the moment that you elevate this black man to citizenship from a slave, then immediately he becomes offensive. That is why I say that this prejudice is foolish, unjust, illogical, and ungentlemanly.

2. Attorney General Devens Cites Commerce Power

Source: Brief for the
United States, Civil Rights
Cases, Term, 1879;
8 Landmark Briefs 314-15

Inns are provided for the accommodation of travelers; for those passing from place to place. They are essential instrumentalities of commerce . . . which it was the province of the United States to regulate even prior to the recent amendment to the Constitution.

The relation of innkeepers to the State differs from that of a man engaged in the more common avocations of life. The former is required to furnish the accommodations of his inn to all well-behaved comers who are prepared to pay the customary regular price.

This business and that of conducting a theatre are carried on under a license from the State, through the intermediate agency of municipal authority, which is part of the machinery of the State, being delegated to this extent with the power of the State. This is because the business to be carried on is quasi public in its nature, and for the general accommodation of the people.

For this reason Congress has the right to prohibit any discrimination against persons applying for admission to an inn or theatre based upon race, color, or previous condition of servitude.

The early amendments to the Constitution were added further to limit the Federal power. The last three [the Thirteenth, Fourteenth, and Fifteenth], the result of bitter, costly experience, were intended to enlarge that power. Such enlargement must necessarily be pro tanto a diminution of, or an encroachment upon, the power previously exercised by the State. These amendments also interfered, for the first time, with the relation borne by the citizen to his State, and with those institutions and regulations of a (so called) domestic character.

---

3. President Kennedy Provides Constitutional Arguments for Public Accommodations Statute

Source: Pub. Papers, 1963, at 485-87

Events of recent weeks have again underlined how deeply our Negro citizens resent the injustice of being arbitrarily denied equal access to those facilities and accommodations which are otherwise open to the general public. That is a daily insult which has no place in a country proud of its heritage—the heritage of the melting-pot, of equal rights, of one Nation and one people. No one has been barred on account of his race from fighting or dying for America—there are no "white" or "colored" signs on the foxholes or graveyards of battle. Surely, in 1963, 100 years after Emancipation, it should not be necessary for any American citizen to demonstrate in the streets for the opportunity to stop at a hotel, or to eat at a lunch counter in the very department store in which he is shopping, or to enter a motion picture house, on the same terms as any other customer.

. . . [F]urther Federal action is needed now to secure the right of all citizens to the full enjoyment of all facilities which are open to the general public.

Such legislation is clearly consistent with the Constitution and with our concepts of both human rights and property rights. The argument that such measures constitute an unconstitutional interference with property rights has consistently been rejected by the courts in upholding laws on zoning, collective bargaining, minimum wages, smoke control and countless other measures designed to make certain that the use of private property is consistent with the public interest. While the legal situations are not parallel, it is interesting to note that Abraham Lincoln, in issuing the Emancipation Proclamation 100 years ago, was also accused of violating the property rights of slave-owners. Indeed, there is an age-old saying that "property has its duties as well as its rights"; and no property owner who holds those premises for the purpose of serving at a profit the American public at large can claim any inherent right to exclude a part of the public on grounds of race or color. Just as the law requires common carriers to serve equally all who wish their services, so it can require public accommodations to accommodate equally all segments of the general public. Both human rights and property rights are foundations of our society—and both will flourish as the result of this measure.

In a society which is increasingly mobile and in an economy which is increasingly interdependent, business establishments which serve the public—such as hotels, restaurants, theatres, stores and others —serve not only the members of their immediate communities but travelers from other States and visitors from abroad. Their goods come from all over the Nation. This participation in the flow of interstate commerce has given these business establishments both increased prosperity and an increased responsibility to provide equal access and service to all citizens.

. . . .

Clearly the Federal Government has both the power and the obligation to eliminate these discriminatory practices: first, because they adversely affect the national economy and the flow of interstate commerce; and secondly, because Congress has been specifically empowered under the Fourteenth Amendment to enact legislation making certain that no State law permits or sanctions the unequal protection or treatment of any of its citizens.

---

4. Attorney General Kennedy Testifies Before the Senate Commerce Committee

Source: Civil Rights—Public Accommodations: Hearings Before the Senate Comm. on Commerce, 88th Cong., 1st Sess. 23, 26, 28, 90 (1963)

The constitutional authority of Congress to enact this law is derived from the commerce clause and the 14th amendment, but our primary reliance is on the commerce clause.

The list of public accommodations covered—hotels and motels, retail stores, restaurants, theaters, and motion picture houses demonstrates that each has a direct and intimate relation to the movement of persons and goods across State lines . . .

In addition to the commerce clause, we rely on Congress' power under the 14th amendment, to prohibit the denial to equal protection of the laws to any person. The 14th amendment also provides that Congress may enforce this provision of appropriate legislation.

We recognize that in 1883 the Supreme Court held in the *Civil Rights Cases* (109 U.S. 3), Congress did not have power under the 14th amendment to prohibit discrimination in privately owned places of public accommodation, and that Congress' power under that amendment is only over discrimination accomplished by the action of a State.

But in 80 years, much of the force of that decision has disappeared. State regulation of private business has increased. State relationships with business have become more varied and complex, and views of what action may be attributed to the State have changed.

There are a number of recent cases in which the Federal courts have held that private decisions to discriminate may be attributed to the State for purposes of the 14th amendment. Consequently, if the Supreme Court were now asked to pass upon the constitutionality of a public accommodations law based on the 14th amendment, it might well uphold the law.

However, the 1883 decision has not been overruled and remains the law of the land. It is for this reason that we rely primarily on the commerce clause.

. . .

I would say that there are a number of my colleagues who feel that if this act was based just on the 14th amendment we might very well have some difficulty on its constitutionality.

We base this on the commerce clause which I think makes it clearly constitutional. In my personal judgment, basing it on the 14th amendment would also be constitutional.

. . .

I think that we come into Congress, we go to the Senate and the House of Representatives with an extra burden if we are advocating a bill which the Supreme Court has specifically declared is unconstitutional.

If it is determined that everybody who was in favor of this bill in Congress was all clear in his own mind that the 1883 decision would be overruled by the Supreme court and was no longer the law of the land, then I would be glad to base it on the 14th amendment. I think that there are many who have legitimate questions in their minds.

There cannot be any legitimate question about the commerce clause. That is clearly constitutional. . . .

IV. FROM *NATIONAL LEAGUE* TO *GARCIA*

In *National League of Cities v. Usery* (1976), the Supreme Court divided 5 to 4 in striking down a congressional statute that extended federal wage-and-hour provisions to almost all state employees. The decision claimed that the statute threatened the independent existence of states. Nine years later, the Court reversed itself in *Garcia v. San Antonio Metropolitan Transit Authority* (1985), again by a 5-4 vote. *Garcia* announced that the protection of federalism depends largely on the political process operating within Congress. During the 1990s, the Court has once again revisited this issue, casting doubt on *Garcia* through a string of 5-4 decisions. But before it can revive the 1976 ruling, the Justices would have to discover a doctrine of federalism that is more intelligible and workable. *National League* proved to be too abstract and vague for federal judges to apply.

A. Fair Labor Standards Act

The Fair Labor Standards Act of 1938 expressly exempted all states and their political divisions from the federal minimum wage and overtime provisions. In 1966, Congress extended federal minimum wages and overtime pay to state-operated hospitals and schools. Two years later the Court decided that Congress had a rational basis for the legislation, citing the effect on interstate competition and the avoidance of labor disputes and strikes. Maryland v. Wirtz, 392 U.S. 183 (1968).

President Nixon's election in 1968 signalled a renewed interest in state sovereignty. His address to the nation on August 8, 1969, described the basic tenets of a "New Federalism in which power, funds, and responsibility will flow from Washington to the States and to the people." Pub. Papers, 1969, at 638. Several other messages to Congress underscored the need to focus power at the level where it could be best exercised.

In 1973, Congress passed legislation extending minimum wage and maximum hour provisions to cover almost all employees of states and their political subdivisions. President Nixon vetoed the bill, largely out of concern for the bill's inflationary impact. He also objected on grounds of federalism, calling the bill "an unwarranted interference with State prerogatives." Pub. Papers, 1973, at 749. Congress persisted by reintroducing and passing the bill the following year, compromising with Nixon by stretching out the minimum wage increases but still applying them to state and local government. Satisfied by the stretch-out feature, Nixon signed this bill. 88 Stat. 58 (1974).

Nixon's nominees to the Supreme Court—Warren Burger, Harry A. Blackmun, Lewis F. Powell, Jr., and William H. Rehnquist—brought to the Court a greater sensitivity to states' rights, jeopardizing both *Wirtz* and the 1974 amendments. *Wirtz* took a shot across the bow in 1975 when the Court noted that the Tenth Amendment prohibited Congress from exercising power "in a fashion that impairs the States' integrity or their ability to function effectively in a federal system." Fry v. United States, 427 U.S. 542, 547 n.7 (1975).

B. 1974 Amendments Invalidated

The National League of Cities brought an action for a declaratory judgment that the 1974 amendments were unconstitutional. *National League* was argued twice before the Supreme Court: April 16, 1975, and March 2, 1976. During the second argument, Justice Powell made it clear that the Court was looking down the road with some anxiety, wondering if it upheld the 1974 amendments what limits remained on congressional exercise of the Commerce Power (document 1).

These fears prevailed. In an opinion written by Justice Rehnquist, the 1974 amendments were invalidated because they "directly displace the States' freedom to structure integral operations in areas of traditional governmental functions. . . ." National League of Cities v. Usery, 426 U.S. 833, 852 (1976). The Court attempted to distinguish between traditional and nontraditional functions, but its rough cut gave meager guidance to lower court judges, legislators, and administrators. It listed these functions as traditional and exempt from congressional control through the commerce power: schools and hospitals, fire protection, police protection, sanitation, public health, and parks and recreation.

For the first time in four decades the Court had invalidated a statute passed by Congress pursuant to the Commerce Clause. Four Justices dissented: Stevens, Brennan, White and Marshall. Blackmun's concurrence supplied the fifth vote needed for Rehnquist's majority. Blackmun admitted that he was "not untroubled by certain possible implications of the Court's opinion." Id. at 856.

In the years following *National League*, the Court's bifurcation between traditional and nontraditional governmental functions could not be applied with confidence or consistency either in the lower courts or in the Supreme Court itself. Lower courts frequently found a function to be "traditional" and thus within the area of state sovereignty. Repeatedly, the Court would reverse these decisions and call the function nontraditional and beyond the protection of *National League*.

For example, in 1980 a federal district court concluded that land use regulation for surface coal mining represented a "traditional governmental function" reserved to the states under *National League*. A unanimous Supreme Court rejected the district court's argument by holding that

National League applied to "states as states" and not to the private business operations at issue in this case. Hodel v. Virginia Surface Mining & Recl. Assn., 452 U.S. 264 (1981).

Two years later, the Court reversed a federal district court ruling that the federal Age Discrimination in Employment Act violated the Tenth Amendment theory articulated in *National League*. Justice Brennan spoke for a 5-4 Court. EEOC v. Wyoming, 460 U.S. 226 (1983). Significantly, 'Justice Blackmun contributed the fifth vote needed for Brennan's majority. Many legal interpreters concluded that there was little life remaining in *National League*.

C. *National League* Is Overruled

One of the curious facts about *National League* is that when the Supreme Court remanded the case to a three-judge district court, instead of the district court determining the difference between traditional and nontraditional functions, it asked the Department of Labor (DOL) to identify nontraditional state functions. DOL published a "final interpretation" in December 1979 listing nontraditional governmental functions that were subject to federal minimum wage and overtime provisions. On its own initiative, it also listed traditional functions. In addition to those mentioned in *National League*, DOL suggested only two others: libraries and museums (document 2).

Included in DOL's list of nontraditional functions was "local mass transit systems." William T. Coleman, Jr., representing the interests of the American Public Transit Association, wrote to Secretary of Transportation Neil Goldschmidt on April 15, 1980, protesting DOL's interpretation of mass transit. Goldschmidt wrote a month later to Attorney General Benjamin R. Civiletti, challenging DOL's interpretation on both legal and policy grounds. In a memo prepared for Assistant Attorney General John B. Shenefield, dated June 16, 1980, the Office of Legal Counsel (OLC) agreed with DOL that mass transit is not a traditional governmental function.

In 1983, a district court concluded that municipal ownership and operation of a mass transit system was a traditional governmental function and thus exempt from the Fair Labor Standards Act. Three federal appellate courts and one state appellate court reached the opposite conclusion. Their research indicated that transit systems in the past had been owned and operated by private businesses. States became involved in mass transit only because of funding received from the federal government. Dove v. Chattanooga Area Reg. Transp. Auth., 701 F.2d 50 (6th Cir. 1983); Alewine v. City Council of Augusta, Ga., 699 F.2d 1060 (11th Cir. 1983); Kramer v. New Castle Area Transit Auth., 677 F.2d 308

(3d Cir. 1982); Francis v. City of Tallahassee, 424 So.2d 61 (Fla. App. 1982).

To resolve these conflicts in the lower courts, the Supreme Court held oral argument twice in 1984: on March 14 and on October 1. It asked the parties to address the question whether *National League* should be reconsidered and possibly overturned. Legal advisers in the Reagan administration found themselves in a difficult bind. The administration was committed strongly to federalism but did not disagree with DOL's conclusion from the Carter years. During the second oral argument, the Court signaled that it was prepared to overturn its 1976 ruling and shift to Congress the basic responsibility for monitoring and defending federalism. 159 Landmark Briefs 912-13.

Writing for a 5-4 Court, Justice Blackmun argued that the effort to distinguish between traditional and nontraditional state functions "is not only unworkable but is also inconsistent with established principles of federalism." Garcia v. San Antonio Metro. Transit Auth., 469 U.S. 528, 531 (1985). He said that the essential safeguard for federalism was not the judiciary but the political dynamics operating within Congress. Id. at 556.

An official in the Reagan administration, Attorney General Edwin Meese III, issued a spirited critique of *Garcia*. According to his reading, the Court disregarded "the framers' intention that state and local governments be a buffer against the centralizing tendencies of the national Leviathan." Edwin Meese, III, The Attorney General's View of the Supreme Court: Toward a Jurisprudence of Original Intention, 45 Pub. Adm. Rev. 701, 702 (Special Issue November 1985). During congressional hearings, the Justice Department sharply criticized *Garcia* for "reading out of the bill of rights" the Tenth Amendment and reducing states to the same status as other citizens and corporations who have to lobby Congress for assistance and protection. Fair Labor Standards Amendments of 1985: Hearings Before the Senate Comm. On Labor and Human Resources, 99th Cong., 1st Sess. 484 (1985).

Garcia threatened the states with massive costs. Most state employees were already receiving at least the minimum wage, but the financial burden of meeting the overtime provisions of the Fair Labor Standards Act could have reached several billion dollars, especially to cover firefighters and police in local governments. To prevent that cost from being transferred to the states, Congress passed legislation to postpone the effective date of *Garcia* (decided February 19, 1985) to April 15, 1986. It also permitted the use of compensatory time as a substitute for paying overtime. 99 Stat. 787 (1985). The bill did not affect *Garcia*'s principal holding that states must comply with the federal minimum wage law. The legislative debate on the bill emphasizes the role of Congress in making constitutional interpretations about federalism and the Commerce Clause (document 3).

D. Conclusion

The nine-year journey from *National League* to *Garcia* illustrates the powerful forces that determine the meaning of federalism. Presidential elections played a part, especially in the selection of Justices to the Supreme Court. The Court's effort in *National League* to establish a new legal doctrine that would strengthen states' rights proved to be unworkable in the lower courts, leading to another round of political activity within the executive branch and the eventual overrule of *National League* in 1985. The *Garcia* decision returned to Congress the principal responsibility for defining federalism. In the 1990s, the Court repeatedly challenged and invalidated congressional judgments about federalism and the commerce clause. With decisions limiting state workers access to either federal or state courts to enforce federal wages and hours laws, little life remains in the *Garcia* doctrine. Seminole Tribe v. Florida, 517 U.S. 44 (1996); Alden v. Maine, 527 U.S. 706 (1999).

DOCUMENTS

1. Oral Argument in *National League* Reveals Court's Concern for Congressional Power

Source: Oral argument in National League of Cities v. Usery, March 2, 1976; 86 Landmark Briefs 899-900

THE COURT [JUSTICE POWELL]: . . . I am concerned with whether or not, if we decide this case in favor of the Government, there will indeed be any limitation as to how far the Federal Government can go in regulating the affairs of the state and localities themselves. Give me the power of purse, give me the power to decide what you are paying—I control you. I think that is inevitable. I would like to stick to principle. . . . I am thinking about the long-time doctrine of Federalism that seems to me to be on the verge of being destroyed by vesting in the Federal Government, the power to put floors under and ceiling over the wages of Federal and State employees.

. . . .

MR. [Robert] BORK [Solicitor General]: . . . It would be appropriate for this Court, I think, to hold in the right case, that the Federal Government may not impose costs and burdens upon the states and local governments significantly greater than it bears itself. Here the costs and burdens, in terms of minimum wage, imposed upon the state and local governments, are less than the Federal Government imposes upon itself. . . .

---

2. Labor Department Identifies Traditional and Nontraditional Governmental Functions

Source: 44 Fed. Reg. 75628-30 (1979)

SUMMARY: The Supreme Court ruled in *National League of Cities v. Usery*, 426 U.S. 833 [1976], that the minimum wage and overtime compensation provisions of the Fair Labor Standards Act could not constitutionally be applied to State and local government employees who are engaged in traditional governmental activities. Pursuant to an enforcement policy and notification procedure approved by the district court on remand, the Department of Labor periodically publishes in the Federal Register a list of those governmental functions which it has determined to be nontraditional. . . . This final interpretation sets forth those governmental functions which have been determined to be nontraditional. . . .

Because the Supreme Court did not establish a test for distinguishing between traditional and nontraditional governmental functions . . ., the three-judge district court . . . requested the Secretary to propose a means of providing interpretative guidance to public employers in identifying the nontraditional functions. . . .

In response to this request, the Secretary submitted a proposal for the amendment of the Secretary's enforcement policy stated in 29 CFR 775. This proposal was approved by the court and published in the Federal Register on June 24, 1977 (see 42 FR 32253), by adding §§775.2 and 775.3 to Part 775.

§775.3 Nontraditional functions of States and their political subdivisions.

(a) In the *National League* decision, it was made clear that the operation of a railroad by a State or its political subdivision is not an integral operation in the area of traditional governmental functions. 426 U.S. 833, 854 n.18.

(b) For the purpose of the notice referred to in §775.2(b), the Administrator has determined that the following functions of a State or its political subdivisions are not traditional. From time to time, this section will be amended to list other such functions determined not to be traditional. The date listed after each function is the date of original publication in the Federal Register. . . .

(1) Alcoholic beverage stores. December 21, 1979.

(2) Off-track betting corporations. December 21, 1979.

(3) Local mass transit systems. December 21, 1979.

(4) Generation and distribution of electric power. December 21, 1979.

(5) Provision of residential and commercial telephone and telegraphic communication. December 21, 1979.

(6) Production and sale of organic fertilizer as a by-product of sewage processing. December 21, 1979.

(7) Production, cultivation, growing or harvesting of agricultural commodities for sale to consumers. December 21, 1979.

(8) Repair and maintenance of boats and marine engines for the general public. December 21, 1979.

4. There is added to Part 775 a new §775.4, which reads as follows:

§775.4 Traditional functions of States and their political subdivisions.

(a) In the *National League* decision, it was made clear that schools and hospitals, fire prevention, police protection, sanitation, public health, and parks and recreation are traditional functions or activities of States and their political subdivisions.

(b) In addition, the Administrator has determined that the following functions of a State or its political subdivisions are traditional (From time to time, this section will be amended to list other such functions determined to be traditional.)

(1) Libraries.

(2) Museums.

---

3. Legislative Response to the *Garcia* Ruling

Source: 131 Cong. Rec.
28984 (1985)

Mr. [Howard] METZENBAUM [D-Ohio]. Mr. President I am pleased to be a principal cosponsor of the Fair Labor Standards Public Employee Overtime Compensation Act of 1985. State and local governments across the country have expressed serious budgetary concerns in having to comply with the overtime provisions of the FLSA ever since the Supreme Court—in its Garcia decision issued in February of this year—reinstated the FLSA amendments of 1974. The budgetary problems faced by public employers could affect millions of taxpayers, forcing them to endure a loss in vital public services, or a burdensome increase in taxes, or both. . . .

At the same time, it is equally clear to me that 7 million State and local government employees deserve the protection of the FLSA. That protection has been afforded to workers in the private sector since the new deal, and to employees of the Federal Government since 1974. State and local employees should not be treated as second class citizens.

This bill, which reflects the considerable efforts of many individuals, represents a fair and equitable compromise. . . . The bill is in many respects a textbook example of how the legislative process should work.

It is significant that this compromise has been enthusiastically endorsed by the National League of Cities, the U.S. Conference of Mayors, the National Associations of Counties, and the National Conference of State Legislators. These public employer groups have praised the bill as "provid[ing] a solution to the problems created by Garcia which is ba-lanced and equitable for all parties. It maintains the principles of the Fair Labor Standards Act and at the same time recognizes the special circumstances faced by public employers and public employees." The AFL-CIO has praised the bill in similar terms, stating that it "Preserves the integrity of the Fair Labor Standards Act which is so vital to the interests of employees while addressing the concerns of public employers."

I also consider it significant that the bill vindicates the Supreme Court's faith in the role of Congress as a cornerstone of our Federal system of government. As expressed by the Garcia court, our Constitution contemplates that the proper protection for the sovereign interests of States and their political subdivisions lies not in directives issued by the Federal Judiciary but rather in the give-and-take of our federal system—especially the role of the States and cities in the political process. In responding to the concerns expressed so strongly by public employers, we have confirmed that the political process works, and works in the responsible fashion envisioned by our Founding Fathers.

V. FEDERALISM IN THE 1990s

The 1990s witnessed a dramatic revival of federalism. For the first time since the New Deal, the Supreme Court placed limitations on Congress's commerce power. The Justices also breathed new life into the state sovereignty protections in the Tenth and Eleventh Amendments. For the *New York Times'* Linda Greenhouse, the message of these decisions was clear: "The Supreme Court rules." Supreme Court; The Justices Decide Who's in Charge, N.Y. Times, June 27, 1999, at 4-1.

Upon further examination, however, a different message emerges. 1990s' federalism decisions are a testament to the power of elected government to shape the Court. Through judicial appointments, executive orders, the Contract with America, and the potent lobbying of state officials, the Supreme Court's revival of federalism is very much a product of its times.

A. Ronald Reagan's Crusade for Federalism

The genesis of the modern day revival of federalism is Ronald Reagan's 1980 run for the White House. A former governor of California, Reagan embraced the "traditional American principle that the best government is the one closest to the people" and, with it, the need to appoint judges whose "philosophy" is "consistent with the belief in the decentralization of the federal government and efforts to return decisionmaking power to state and local elected officials." 1980 Republican Party Platform, reprinted in 36 Cong. Q. Almanac 71-B, 74-B (1980). In his inaugural address, Reagan reaffirmed this campaign pledge, promising "to curb the size and influence of the federal establishment and to demand recognition of the distinction between the powers granted to the federal government and those reserved to the states or to the people." Pub. Papers, 1981, at 2.

Federalism figured into Reagan's efforts to reshape the federal judiciary. Sandra Day O'Connor, Reagan's first Supreme Court nominee, began her Senate Judiciary Committee testimony this way: "I want to make only one substantive statement to you at this time. My experience as a State court judge and as a State legislator has given me a greater appreciation of the important role the States play in our federal system. . . ." (document 1). By appointing Antonin Scalia, Anthony Kennedy, and elevating William Rehnquist to Chief Justice, moreover, Reagan ensured that his most enduring federalism legacy would come in the form of Supreme Court opinions. The Court became even more sympathetic to federalism when President George Bush nominated Clarence Thomas to be Associate Justice.

In a 1991 interpretation of the federal Age Discrimination in Employment Act, the Justices emphasized that a state's retirement provision "is a decision of the most fundamental sort for a sovereign entity." Gregory v. Ashcroft, 501 U.S. 452, 460 (1991). The Court was more assertive a year later when it rejected Congress's demand that states come up with a way to dispose of low-level radioactive waste by 1996 or be forced to become the owners of it. New York v. United States, 505 U.S. 144 (1992).

In many ways, the law on radioactive waste seemed a model of federal-state cooperation. The bill had been drafted by the National Governors' Association. According to bill sponsor Mo Udall (D-Colo.), the bill was "primarily a resolution of the conflicts between the States that do not have disposal capacity and the three States that have capacity." 131 Cong. Rec. 35203 (1985). In defending the statute's constitutionality, Solicitor General Kenneth Starr argued: "In light of the origin of the problem as a dispute among the States, the requests of the States for a state-oriented solution and the assiduous care Congress displayed in attending to the interests and concerns of the several States, the Act is a constitutionally permissible example of cooperative federalism designed to preserve, rather than preempt, state authority." 213 Landmark Briefs 314-15.

These points did not impress the Court. It invalidated the statute and returned the issue to Congress. The decision had little impact on public policy. Instead of trying to draft another statute to correct problems identified by the Court, Congress merely relied on the existing compacts that states had formed to dispose of radioactive waste.

B. The Contract with America

A more fundamental shift towards states' rights resulted from the 1994 national elections. The Republican "Contract with America," announced on September 24, 1994, pledged a smaller federal government and a larger role for the states. The Republican victory in the elections gave them control of both Houses of Congress, converting the Contract into a blueprint for legislative action.

Along with welfare and other reforms that returned major responsibilities and liabilities to the states, the Contract promised to do away with the practice of the federal government imposing expensive mandates on the states without providing federal funds. According to Contract architects Newt Gingrich (R-Ga.) and Dick Armey (R-Tx.), unfunded mandates "threaten to bankrupt local communities" "with one-size-fits-all policies on areas as diverse as New York City and rural Iowa." Newt Gingrich, Dick Armey et al., Contract with America, 133 (1994). Legislation was enacted into law on March 22, 1995, but it did not end unfunded mandates. Many of the mandates concerning civil rights, the disabled, and other categories are specifically exempted. For the mandates that are covered, the statute merely requires the Congressional Budget Office to flag any bill that creates an unfunded mandate of $50 million or higher on the states.

The Contract also guaranteed "the first ever vote on a constitutional amendment" to establish term limits for members of Congress. The purpose of this initiative was to punish the national legislature for being "out of touch" with middle America and to return political power to the states and localities. In 1995, however, Congress voted down several term limit proposals.

By the 1996 elections, much of the Contract with America had fizzled. While Republican presidential candidate Bob Dole spoke of the 1994 elections as a mandate "[t]o rein in government" by "getting it out of matters best left to the states, cities, and families across America," the people rejected Dole, Newt Gingrich, and much of the Contract. Bob Dole, Remarks to the National Newspapers Association, Washington,

D.C. (March 10, 1995). At the same time, Democrats and Republicans alike spoke in favor of downsizing the federal government.

For the Supreme Court, the 1994 elections proved transformative. Its burgeoning federalism revival became the centerpiece of Rehnquist era reforms. Through a series of "states' rights" rulings, the Justices effectively overturned *Garcia*. Moreover, for the first time since 1936, the Court rejected federal legislation as outside the scope of the commerce power.

C. The Rehnquist Court and the Commerce Clause

In a closely watched decision in 1995, *United States v. Lopez*, the Court ruled that a statute banning guns within 1,000 feet of a school exceeded Congress's authority under the Commerce Clause. 514 U.S. 549 (1995). The statute was controversial from the start. Congress made no findings to support its conclusion that gun possession affected interstate commerce, a fact that the National Conference of State Legislatures seized upon in a brief attacking the statute (document 2). George Bush also spoke out against the gun ban. When signing the bill into law, Bush argued that the ban "unnecessarily constrain[s] the discretion of State and local governments" and that "[t]he policies reflected in these provisions could legitimately be adopted by the States, but they should not be imposed on the States by the Congress." Pub. Papers, 1990 (II), at 1715.

During oral argument, the Justices called into question Clinton administration claims that Congress had "ample basis . . . to conclude that disruption of the educational process would have substantial deleterious effects on the national economy." In questioning Solicitor General Drew Days, the Justices wondered what limits, if any, the administration's theory would place on Congress's commerce power (document 3). Divided 5 to 4, the Court castigated Congress both for intruding into matters traditionally associated with state control and for failing to show a linkage between gun possession and interstate commerce.

Within two weeks of the Court's decision, a "terribly disappointed" President Clinton submitted legislation to Congress to amend the earlier statute by requiring the federal government to prove that the firearm has "moved in or the possession of such firearm otherwise affects interstate or foreign commerce." Pub. Papers, 1995 (I), at 678. Before the Senate Judiciary Committee, Clinton officials defended this proposal. Walter Dellinger, head of the Office of Legal Counsel, explained that *Lopez* did not call into question "congressional authority to regulate articles of commerce such as firearms that have moved across state lines"—even if the linkage to commerce was remote and even if Congress did not hold hearings or otherwise engage in formal factfinding (document 4). On the question of whether gun possession affects interstate commerce, the sponsor of the bill, Senator Herb Kohl (D-Wisc.), testified that "[a]lmost every gun is made from raw material from one State, assembled in a second State, and transported to the schoolyards in yet another State." Guns in Schools: A Federal Role?: Hearing before the Subcommittee on Youth Violence of the Senate Committee on the Judiciary, 104th Cong., 1st Sess. 4 (1995). On the basis of this hearing, Congress enacted the Clinton proposal in 1996, finding that crime at the local level "is exascerbated by the interstate movement of drugs, guns, and criminal gangs," that the occurrence of violent crime in school zones has resulted in a decline in the quality of education, and that it has the power under the commerce clause to enact the legislation.   110 Stat. 3009-369, §657 (1996).

Following *Lopez*, there was some reason to think that the principal problem with the gun ban was Congress's failure to present adequate findings to show an interstate commerce link. In May 2000, however, the same coalition of Reagan-Bush appointees that invalidated the gun ban (Rehnquist, O'Connor, Kennedy, Scalia, and Thomas) made clear that extensive congressional factfinding was not enough. In striking down part of the 1994 Violence Against Women Act (VAWA), these Justices rejected Clinton administration arguments that "the connection between gender-motivated violence and interstate commerce is both direct and expressly established in Congress's findings and the supporting legislative record" (document 5). By holding that "[t]he Constitution requires a distinction between what is truly national and what is truly local," United States v. Morrison, 120 S.Ct. 1740, 1754 (2000), these Justices also rejected the claims of 36 state attorneys general that the Act was "a particularly appropriate remedy for the harm caused by gender-motivated violence." Amicus Curiae Brief for the States of Arizona et al., United States v. Morrison, Nos. 99-5 & 99-29, at 2. However, at hearings held in 1993, the Conference of State Chief Justices submitted a resolution opposing VAWA as intruding upon the responsibilities of state courts "for administering a coherent and comprehensive system of civil, criminal, and domestic relations law" (document 6).

D. The States and Federalism

Throughout the 1990s, state and local officials have played a significant role in shaping the federal-state balance of powers. By challenging federal mandates, state and local actors have set the stage for most of the Rehnquist Court's federalism decisions. Even when they are not a party to the litigation, state and local actors have made extensive use of amicus briefs to communicate their perspectives to the Court.

Before Congress and the White House, state and local officials have played an equally prominent role. The most influential of these state and local lobbyists is the so-called "Big Seven," comprising the Council of

State Governments, International City Management Association, National Association of Counties, National Conference of State Legislatures, National Governors' Association, National League of Cities, and the U.S. Conference of Mayors. Whether the issue is unfunded mandates, welfare reform, or VAWA, Washington's willingness to embrace policy arguments grounded in the Tenth Amendment and other federalism protections is a by-product of the efforts of the "Big Seven" lobby.

An incident in President Clinton's second term underscores the capacity of state and local organizations to protect their interests. In May 1998, Clinton issued an executive order on federalism, setting forth a number of principles to define the boundaries between the national government and the states. Unlike earlier executive orders (including one Clinton issued in 1993), the 1998 order specified instances in which federal preemption is warranted without any reference to the traditional boundaries of state and local authority. Exec. Order No. 13,083, 63 Fed. Reg. 27,651 (1998). The "Big Seven" immediately issued a sharp protest, complaining that no state or local government official had been consulted in the drafting of the order. Congress passed legislation prohibiting the use of any appropriated funds to implement the order. 112 Stat. 2681-116, §623 (1998). The Clinton White House agreed to withdraw its order and start over, this time working in concert with state and local organizations. On August 4, 1999, Clinton issued a new order—this one satisfying state and local interests. Exec. Order No. 13,132, 64 Fed. Reg. 43,255 (1999).

E. Conclusion

The Rehnquist Court's revitalization of federalism, while significant, has mostly gone unnoticed by Congress. A survey of the Congressional Record, for example, reveals that these decisions have had "little serious impact on dialogue or decisions by Congress." Matthew D. Adler and Seth F. Kreimer, The New Etiquette of Federalism: New York, Printz, and Yeskey, 1998 Sup. Ct. Rev. 71, 138. With that said, the Rehnquist Court may be poised to enter into a battle royale with Congress. In a April 2000 speech, Justice Antonin Scalia served the following notice on Congress: "My Court is fond of saying that acts of Congress come to the Court with the presumption of constitutionality. But if Congress is going to take the attitude that it will do anything it can get away with and let the Supreme Court worry about the Constitution . . . then perhaps that presumption is unwarranted." Tony Mauro, Little Deference to Congress as the Court Curbs Federal Power, Legal Times, May 22, 2000, at 8.

Social and political forces will determine whether this battle takes place. With the Court sharply divided 5 to 4, the November 2000 elections will play a determinative role in defining federalism's future. In particular, the Rehnquist Court's federalism legacy may well be in the hands of the next two or three justices appointed to the Court.

DOCUMENTS

1. O'Connor Testifies on Federal-State Relations

Source: The Nomination of Judge Sandra Day O'Connor of Arizona to Serve As An Associate Justice of The Supreme Court of The United States: Hearings Before the Senate Comm. on the Judiciary, 97th Cong., 1st Sess. 59, 121-122 (1981)

[Senator Strom Thurmond (R-S.C.)] Judge O'Connor, you have been nominated to serve on the highest court in our country. What experience qualifies you to be a Justice of the U.S. Supreme Court?

Judge O'CONNOR. Mr. Chairman, I suppose . . . that my experience in all three branches of State government will provide some very useful background for assuming the awesome responsibility of an Associate Justice of the U.S. Supreme Court.

. . .

My experience in State government has also given me a greater appreciation, as I have indicated, for the strengths and the needs of our federal system of government, which envisions, of course, an important role for the States in that process.

. . .

[Senator Howell Heflin (D-Ala.)]:
. . . I would like to know your general philosophy of the role of the Judiciary in preserving Federalism.

Judge O'CONNOR. Mr. Chairman, Senator Heflin, the judiciary in my view has an important obligation in that regard. The Federal Government was the outgrowth or product of the States' willingness to band together and form a Federal Government, and it of course assumed that it had created a Federal Government of limited powers and, indeed, had delegated expressly to the Federal Government those powers that the States then thought were appropriate, and reserved in the 10th amendment to the people and to the State those powers that were not delegated.

. . .

I am sure that we have not seen the last of the inquiries that the Court will make, by any

stretch, into the application of the 10th amendment, but it sets forth a very vital pronouncement of the role of the States in the Federal system and indeed—as a product if you will of State government, which I am—I have some concerns about seeing that State governments and local government are maintained in their abilities to deal with the problems affecting the people. . . .

2. State Lawmakers Challenge Gun Ban at Schools

Source: Brief Amicus Curiae of The National Conference of State Legislatures, at 13-15, United States v. Lopez, 514 U.S. 595 (1995) (No. 93-1260)

. . . Although this Court has sanctioned a broad use of the commerce power, its decisions nonetheless make clear that the commerce clause has real and substantial limits. Were it otherwise, it would be meaningless to speak of a "Federal Government of limited powers."

. . .

. . . [I]n order to criminalize conduct under the commerce clause, Congress must be regulating interstate commerce. Congress cannot, under the guise of regulating interstate commerce, legislate beyond its delegated authority. And Congress's regulation of intrastate activity must reach activity that has a real and "substantial economic effect on interstate commerce."

The Gun-Free School Zones Act plainly does not meet these standards. The nature of the conduct it criminalizes (simple possession of a gun in or near a school) has no obvious connection to interstate commerce. The Act itself, which was enacted as Section 1702 of the Crime Control Act of 1990, contains no findings concerning the effect of firearm possession in the schools on interstate commerce. Nor did the report which accompanied the Crime Control Act discuss the impact on interstate commerce caused by firearms in the schools. Indeed, as the court of appeals noted, the report did not "even

mention the Gun-Free School Zones Act."
Moreover, while the Act was the subject of a
hearing by a House subcommittee, this
hearing does not remotely establish that
firearms possession in the schools has a
substantial effect on interstate commerce.
Indeed, the legislative record indicates that
Congress did not view itself as doing
anything other than regulating violent
criminals.

---

3. Solicitor General Days
Defends Gun Ban at Schools

Source: Oral Argument of Drew Days
for the United States at 4-5, 13-15,
United States v. Lopez, 514 U.S. 549
(1995) (No. 93-1260)

QUESTION: If this is covered, what's left
of enumerated powers? What is there that
Congress could not do, under this rubric, if
you are correct?

GENERAL DAYS: Justice O'Connor, that
certainly is a Question that one might ask, but
this Court has asked that Question in a
number of other circumstances, and rather
than starting from the assumption that
something was inherently local, it's looked at
the degree to which Congress had a
reasonable basis for extending its authority
under the commerce power to regulate that
particular activity.

QUESTION: But in some of those very
cases, General Days, the statement is found
that the power is not limitless.

GENERAL DAYS: Well, that is certainly
the case, Chief Justice Rehnquist. That's an
understanding from the Constitution, but one
has to look at where the limitations are that
are imposed by the Constitution itself.

QUESTION: Well, what would be—if this
case is—Congress can reach under the
interstate commerce power, what would be an
example of a case which you couldn't reach?

GENERAL DAYS: Well, Your Honor, I'm
not prepared to speculate generally, but this
Court has found that Congress, for example,
in New York v. United States could not
regulate—could not require New York State
to carry out certain responsibilities, because it
was commandeering the instrumentalities of
the State.

QUESTION: Well, the objection there was
that it was objecting the State governmental
machinery to operate in a certain way. The
Question here, it seems to me, is quite
different. The Question here is the universe
of transactions that the Congress may reach.

GENERAL DAYS: Yes.

QUESTION: Can you tell me, Mr. Days,
has there been anything in our recent history
in the last 20 years where it appears that
Congress made a considered judgment that it
could not reach a particular subject?
(Laughter.)

GENERAL DAYS: I don't know whether
there's been a conscious effort to do that, but
I think as this Court has said in its Tenth
Amendment jurisprudence that Congress
reflects the will of the people, and it has built
into it, and into its operations, a concern
about the extent to which its regulations and
its legislation would encroach on matters that
have been traditionally left to the State.

. . .

QUESTION: General Days, I think it's
well-established that a factor in both the
education of children and in the law-abiding
nature of children, a major factor is the
stability of families. I suppose, under your
reasoning, Congress could enact a Federal
domestic relations law providing a Federal
marriage, Federal divorce procedures, and
what-not. I mean, there's nothing that affects
levels of crime and levels of education as
much as that. Why not?

GENERAL DAYS: Justice Scalia, Congress
has legislated, for example, with respect to
problems of—

QUESTION: Domestic violence, I'm
aware.

GENERAL DAYS: —domestic violence, or
the disappearance of children—

QUESTION: That doesn't—

GENERAL DAYS: —or interstate divorce
problems, so it's not that Congress hasn't
dealt with those issues, but I think we would
look to the—

QUESTION: The Question is whether it has
dealt with them constitutionally.
(Laughter.)

GENERAL DAYS: —Justice Scalia, that is
really your department. . . .

. . .

QUESTION: The only limitation, then, that you're recognizing, is the narrow reading—well, strike narrow, is a reading of U.S. v. New York that Congress could not impose certain affirmative obligations upon the State, but so far as concurrent regulation, and, indeed, even displacement of State regulation, presumably there is no limit, if, in fact, it can reach the case before us?

GENERAL DAYS: Well, I think there are limits, Justice Souter. The Question is whether there's anything left of the State once the Federal Government gets done. . . .

---

4. Clinton Official Encourages Congress to Respond to *Lopez*

Source: Guns in Schools: A Federal Role?: Hearing Before the Subcomm. on Youth Violence of the Senate Comm. on the Judiciary, 104th Cong., 1st Sess. 9-13 (1995)

[Mr. Walter Dellinger, Assistant Attorney General, Office of Legal Counsel.] The *Lopez* opinion was devoted to a single Question, and that was whether the possession of a firearm in a school zone, where that firearm had no connection whatsoever with interstate commerce, could be regulated by Congress on the grounds that possession of a firearm in a school zone substantially affected the national economy.

The revised statute, however, will rest on a different source of commerce clause power, the power of Congress to regulate articles of commerce themselves, articles that have moved in interstate commerce, in order to prevent the use of interstate commerce as the means of spreading and perpetuating activity which Congress has deemed harmful or injurious. . . .

Senator [Fred] THOMPSON [(R-Tn.)]. Thank you, Mr. Dellinger, I take it that you feel that the changes that have been made in the current proposed bill fulfill all of the constitutional deficiencies of the prior legislation that was addressed in *Lopez*.

Mr. DELLINGER. Yes, I do, Senator.

Senator THOMPSON. And I take it that your conclusion has to do with the findings that are in the bill, and also from the fact that the illegality is based on possession of a weapon that was previously transported in interstate commerce.

Mr. DELLINGER. That is correct, Senator. . . .

Senator THOMPSON. I am wondering about what you would perceive to [be] the limits of that. What if the handgun, if we are dealing with a handgun, traveled in interstate commerce 10 years prior? Would that make any difference?

Mr. DELLINGER. It would not under the statute.

Senator THOMPSON. Twenty years, 30 years?

Mr. DELLINGER. I don't think that the time—

Senator THOMPSON. Well, I don't mean under the statute. We are talking about constitutional tests now.

Mr. DELLINGER. I believe that constitutionally it is the fact that this is moved in interstate commerce that is essential to the constitutionality of Congress' authority to regulate. . . .

Senator THOMPSON. Do you think that these findings in the proposed legislation are essential to its constitutionality, or do you think the prior interstate aspect standing alone would pass constitutional muster?

Mr. DELLINGER. I think in this setting that in the absence of the findings, it would still be constitutional because of the prior interstate effect. . .

Senator THOMPSON. My time is running out. Can Congress just put down any findings in a piece of legislation and vote on them, do you think, or must there more than that? In other words, we come back here after having had a problem with a bill and say to the court OK, we will give you some findings now, and we list a bunch of findings and we vote that we make those findings, but they are based on no hearings, they are based on no particular scientific documentation or anything like that. Do you think just the nature of findings and Congress' use of them, in general, is sufficient?

Mr. DELLINGER. Mr. Chairman, I think that the court acts on the assumption that when Congress votes on a set of findings that

Members have given their reflective judgment to that. It takes them seriously, and by that same token Congress itself should take seriously the fact that it is voting on matters and you ought to really believe yourself that you have some basis for those conclusions before you vote on an act. I think both the Congress and the court ought to take those seriously.

---

5. Clinton Administration Defends Violence Against Women Act

Source: Brief for The United States, United States v. Morrison, 17, 28-29, 35 (Nos. 99-5 & 99-29)

. . . Congress had far more than the rational basis that this Court has required to conclude that gender-motivated violence substantially affects interstate commerce. Congress found that gender-motivated violence burdens the national economy and interstate commerce in several distinct ways: by deterring women from seeking jobs, including jobs in interstate businesses, that would require them to work at certain hours or in certain places; by inhibiting women from traveling, interstate as well as intrastate, and from engaging in other economic activity; by impeding victims' ability to work at all, or to work productively, thereby forcing many into dependence, poverty, and even homelessness; and by imposing increased medical and other costs on victims, their employers and insurers, and state and local governments. All of those burdens were documented in the extensive legislative record. . . .

This Court's conclusion in *Lopez* that the Gun-Free School Zones Act of 1990 (GFSZA) did not possess the requisite nexus to interstate commerce does not suggest the same conclusion with respect to Section 13981. Whereas the connection between gun possession near schools and interstate commerce in *Lopez* was both attenuated in fact and unarticulated by Congress, the connection between gender-motivated violence and interstate commerce is both direct and expressly established in Congress's findings and the supporting legislative record.

As the Court explained in *Lopez*, such congressional findings are particularly significant where, as here, the connection between the regulated activity and interstate commerce may not be "visible to the naked eye." . . .

[Furthermore,] [t]he vindication of civil rights has long been a paradigmatic federal responsibility. . . . It is a responsibility that, to be sure, is shared with the States. But in contrast to general criminal law as involved in *Lopez*, civil rights historically has not been an area in which "the States possess primary authority."

---

6. State Chief Justices Oppose Violence Against Women Act

Source: Crimes of Violence Motivated By Gender: Hearing Before the Subcomm. on Civil and Constitutional Rights of the House Comm. on the Judiciary, 103rd Cong., 1st Sess. 83-84 (1993)

WHEREAS, The Constitution of the United States reserves to the states, or to the people, all powers not expressly delegated to the United States, nor prohibited by it to the states; and

WHEREAS, spousal and sexual violence and all legal issues involved in domestic relations historically have been governed by state criminal and civil law; and

WHEREAS, state courts have the primary responsibility for administering a coherent and comprehensive system of civil, criminal, and domestic relations law and have the structure, experience and procedures for the proper disposition of all cases within their systems; and

WHEREAS, the United States Senate is considering S.15, the Violence Against Women Act of 1991, which proposes federal programs intended to assist in solving problems of sexual and domestic violence; and

WHEREAS, states also have recognized, and are giving serious attention to, these problems and are developing effective programs for dealing with them; and

WHEREAS, Section 301(c) of S.15 may be construed to create a federal cause of action against any person who commits a "crime of violence motivated by gender". . . ; and

WHEREAS, the federal cause of action created by Section 301(c) would impair the ability of state courts to manage criminal and family law matters traditionally entrusted to the states;

NOW, THEREFORE, BE IT RESOLVED that the Conference of Chief Justices commends Congress for addressing the critical problems of sexual and spousal violence and supports the intended objectives of S.15; and

BE IT FURTHER RESOLVED that Section 301(c) be eliminated.

VI. BOERNE v. FLORES

Rehnquist Court efforts to limit Congress's power over the states were again on display in *Boerne v. Flores.* 521 U.S. 507 (1997). Through its power to enforce the Fourteenth Amendment, Congress, in 1993, sought to overturn a restrictive 1990 Supreme Court interpretation of the free exercise of religion clause. As another round in the public dialogue over the meaning of religious freedom, a unanimous Supreme Court invalidated this statute in 1997. Rather than settle the issue definitively, the Court's decision has returned the question of religious liberty protections back to both Congress (which is now considering new legislative language) and the states (many of whom have enacted their own versions of the federal statute).

A. The Supreme Court and Religious Liberty

In 1984, Oregon denied unemployment benefits to two members of the Native American Church (NAC), Alfred Smith and Galen Black, whose ingestion of peyote at a religious ceremony led to their dismissal. Unlike the federal government and several states, Oregon did not exempt from their criminal statutes "the nondrug use of peyote in bona fide religious ceremonies." 21 CFR § 1307.31 (1999). The Oregon Supreme Court agreed with Smith and Black that this denial of benefits violated their First Amendment religious liberty protections, pointing to constitutional judgments by Congress on this issue as well as exemption legislation approved by other states. Smith v. Employment Division, 763 P. 2d 146 (Ore. 1988).

David Frohnmayer, Attorney General of Oregon, objected strongly to the reliance by the state supreme court on congressional interpretations of the Constitution. In asking the U.S. Supreme Court to hear the case, he contended that "[t]his process of canvassing congressional understanding to resolve an important first amendment question would be troubling under any circumstance." 196 Landmark Briefs 425. NAC leaders regarded the Court's decision to hear the case as an invitation to disaster and pressured Smith to withdraw his claim. In the end, however, Smith decided that he would rather fight in court than be known as "the guy that sold out." Garrett Epps, To an Unknown God: The Hidden History of Employment Division v. Smith, 30 Ariz. St. L.J., 953, 1009 (1998).

During oral argument, Frohnmayer insisted that there was no principled way of distinguishing the NAC claim from the claims of Rastafarians and others who sought a religion-based exemption from drug laws. For Frohnmayer: "I went in there with two sorts of slogans in my mind: Slippery Slope, Slippery Slope, and Drugs are Bad, Drugs are Bad." Epps at 1010. The Justices agreed. Unlike earlier rulings, which placed a heavy burden on the government to justify infringements on religious practices, the Court concluded that it should only ask whether the government's action is rationally related to a legitimate state interest. Employment Division v Smith, 494 U.S. 872 (1990).

Following the Court's decision, interest groups turned their attention to Congress and the legislative process. Relying on Congress's Section 5 power to enforce the Fourteenth Amendment, religious interests helped draft the 1993 Religious Freedom Restoration Act (RFRA). Under this legislation, the government could not burden a person's free exercise of religion unless the burden was "essential to further a compelling government interest and is the least restrictive means of furthering that interest." One year later, Congress approved of a measure making lawful "the use, possession, or transportation of peyote by an Indian for bona fide traditional ceremonial purposes." 108 Stat. 3125 (1994).

B. Congress, the Court, and RFRA

Legislative consideration of RFRA showcased representatives from an unprecedented coalition of religious and other interest groups. With few exceptions, congressional testimony heralded RFRA as a necessary response to the Court's decision in *Smith*. Illustrative of this testimony are comments from three members of the "Coalition for the Free Exercise of Religion." Robert Dugan, Jr., representing the National Association of Evangelicals, said that *Smith* "has deprived us of our birthright as Americans" and must be "overrule[d]." Religious Freedom Restoration Act of 1991: Hearings before the Subcomm. on Civil and Constitutional Rights of the House Comm. on the Judiciary, 102d Cong., 2d Sess. at 10, 14 (1992). Dallin H. Oaks, from the Church of Jesus Christ of the Latter-Day Saints (the Mormon Church), regarded the statutory restoration of the compelling interest standard as "both a legitimate and a necessary response by the legislative branch to the degradation of religious freedom resulting from the *Smith* case." Id. at 25. Oliver S. Thomas, general counsel of the Baptist Joint Committee on Public Affairs, referred to *Smith* as "the *Dred Scott* of first amendment law." The Religious Freedom Restoration Act: Hearings before the Senate Committee on the Judiciary, 102d Cong., 2d Sess. 42 (1992).

Lawmakers read from a nearly identical script. Unwilling to cede, as Congressman Henry Hyde (R-Ill.) urged, that "Congress is institutionally unable to restore a prior interpretation of the first amendment once the Supreme Court has rejected that interpretation," 1992 House Judiciary Committee Hearings at 7, most lawmakers condemned *Smith* as "disastrous," "dastardly and unprovoked," "devastating," and "degrad[ing]." 139 Cong. Rec. 9683 (1993) (statement of Rep. Nadler); 137 Cong. Rec. 17035-36 (1991) (statement of Rep. Solarz); 139 Cong. Rec. 9684 (1993) (statement of Rep. Schumer); id. at 9685 (statement of Rep. Orton). The Senate approved the bill by a vote of 97 to 3. 139 Cong. Rec. 26416 (1993). The House passed the bill without taking a roll call vote. 139 Cong. Rec. 9687 (1993).

For his part, Bill Clinton, invoking "the power of God," spoke of his conviction that RFRA "is far more consistent with the intent of the Founders of this Nation than the [*Smith*] decision" (document 1). When a constitutional challenge to RFRA made its way to the Supreme Court, moreover, the Justice Department argued that RFRA "deters violations of the Free Exercise Clause and promotes equal treatment for all faiths" by "ensur[ing] that minority, unpopular, and emerging faiths enjoy the same freedom as religious adherents who possess the political means to obtain legislative exemptions from burdensome laws." 257 Landmark Briefs 320-21.

During oral arguments, however, the Justices greeted this administration claim with skepticism. Pointing to numerous religious-based exemptions to generally applicable laws, the Justices suggested that state lawmakers were sensitive to the claims of religious minorities (document 2). In looking to state officials to defend religious liberty, the Justices signaled their concern that RFRA threatened federalism. According to an amicus brief filed by sixteen state attorneys general: "[T]he Fourteenth Amendment," in taking "power from the states and g[iving] it to the federal government[,]. . . did not repeal the Tenth Amendment or the principles of federalism for which it stands" (document 3).

The Supreme Court, in *Boerne v. Flores*, agreed with this federalism argument, holding that Congress does not have "the power to decree the substance of the Fourteenth Amendment's restrictions on the States." 521 U.S. at 519. The Court also ruled that RFRA violated the separation of powers. Invoking *Marbury v. Madison* for the proposition that the "powers of the legislature are defined and limited," the Court suggested that constitutional interpretation is a judicial monopoly. Id. at 519. For this very reason, there was some question about the constitutionality of

RFRA as applied not to the states but to the federal government. In 1998, however, a federal appeals court held that RFRA was constitutional as applied to federal law. In re Young, 141 F. 3d 854 (8th Cir. 1998), cert. denied, 525 U.S. 811.

Following the *Boerne* decision, Congress and the Clinton administration considered alternative means of protecting religious liberty. On August 14, 1997 the White House released comprehensive guidelines on religious exercise and religious expression in the federal workforce. The White House, Office of the Press Secretary, Guidelines on Religious Exercise and Religious Expression in the Federal Workplace, Aug. 14, 1997. Congress sought to impose RFRA-like obligations on the states through its powers to regulate interstate commerce and to control Federal spending.

In July 1999, the House enacted the Religious Liberty Protections Act, a measure supported by 92 religious and civil liberty groups, including Protestant, Catholic, Jewish, Muslim, and Native American organizations. 145 Cong. Rec. H5608 (daily ed. July 15, 1999). The bill states that a government shall not "substantially burden" a person's religious exercise (1) in a program or activity, operated by a government, that receives Federal financial assistance or (2) in any case in which the substantial burden on religious exercise affects commerce with foreign nations, among the states, or with Indian tribes. A report by the House Judiciary Committee defended the measure's constitutionality (document 4). The prospects of the 106th Congress enacting this measure are remote, however, for it is doubtful that the Senate will consider this proposal.

C. The States and Religious Liberty

Congress is hardly alone in seeking to expand religious liberty protections. Following the Supreme Court's 1990 decision, state lawmakers began to fill the void left open by the Court's ruling. The Oregon legislature, for example, responded to the Court's decision by enacting a bill that protects the sacramental use of peyote by Native Americans. Enacted in 1991, the bill exempts from criminal prosecution the ingestion of peyote in connection with the good faith practice of a religious belief. Oregon Laws, Chapt. 329, § 1 (June 24, 1991).

Several other states have enacted RFRA styled statutes. Two states, Connecticut and Rhode Island, passed legislation in 1993—the same year that Congress enacted RFRA. Following the Supreme Court's invalidation of the federal RFRA, several more states passed legislation in an attempt to guarantee religous freedom. From 1998 to 2000, Arizona, Florida, Idaho, Illinois, New Mexico, South Carolina, and Texas have also passed statutes modeled on RFRA. In explaining why he signed Texas' RFRA, Governor George W. Bush remarked: "Recent court decisions have chipped away at the rock of religious freedom, one small action at a time: one bureaucratic rule, one regulatory decision, one threatened lawsuit. . . . The Religious Freedom Restoration Act says loud and clear: Texas will not stand for government interference with the free exercise of religion." Press Release, Governor Signs Bills to Restore Religious Freedoms Protections, Expand Faith-Based Initiatives, June 10, 1999.

In several states, there was no reason to enact RFRA styled statutes. State supreme courts, interpreting their state constitutional provisions, concluded that their states "afford the same protection for religious exercise as the Federal Constitution [did] before [the U.S. Supreme Court's 1990 decision in] *Employment Division v. Smith.*" Smith v. Fair Employment and Housing Commission, 12 Cal. 4th 1143, 1177 (1996). These states include Alaska, California, Maine, Michigan, Minnesota, Ohio, New York, and Washington. For this very reason, California governor Pete Wilson vetoed a RFRA bill approved by the California Assembly in 1998.

D. Conclusion

The future of religious liberty protections remains uncertain. The ongoing constitutional dialogue about the appropriate balance between state prerogatives and the free exercise of religion is likely to continue for many years to come. Ironically, as more and more states respond to the Supreme Court's restrictive definition of religious liberty, the principal antagonists in this controversy—Congress and the Supreme Court—will play an increasingly small role in defining the ultimate meaning of religious liberty protections.

DOCUMENTS

1. Clinton Condemns *Smith*, Applauds RFRA

Source: Pub. Papers 1993 (II) at 2000-01

We all have a shared desire here to protect perhaps the most precious of all American liberties, religious freedom. Usually the signing of legislation by a President is a ministerial act, often a quiet ending to a turbulent legislative process. Today this event assumes a more majestic quality because of our ability together to affirm the historic role that people of faith have played in the history of this country and the constitutional protections those who profess and express their faith have always demanded and cherished.

The power to reverse legislation by legislation, a decision of the United States Supreme Court, is a power that is rightly hesitantly and infrequently exercised by the United States Congress. But this is an issue in which that extraordinary measure was clearly called for. As the Vice President said, this act reverses the Supreme Court's decision Employment Division against Smith and reestablishes a standard that better protects all Americans of all faiths in the exercise of their religion in a way that I am convinced is far more consistent with the intent of the Founders of this Nation than the Supreme Court decision.

More than 50 cases have been decided against individuals making religious claims against Government action since that decision was handed down. This act will help to reverse that trend by honoring the principle that our laws and institutions should not impede or hinder but rather should protect and preserve fundamental religious liberties.

The free exercise of religion has been called the first freedom, that which originally sparked the development of the full range of the Bill of Rights. Our Founders cared a lot about religion. And one of the reasons they worked so hard to get the first amendment into the Bill of Rights at the head of the class is that they well understood what could happen to this country, how both religion and Government could be perverted if there were not some space created and some protection provided. They knew that religion helps to give our people the character without which a democracy cannot survive. They knew that there needed to be a space of freedom between Government and people of faith that otherwise Government might usurp.

---

2. Solicitor General Dellinger Defends RFRA

Source: 258 Landmark Briefs 575-76

[Solicitor General Walter Dellinger] . . . State and local legislative bodies cannot be relied upon to craft exemptions from laws of general application that will protect the ability of religious minorities to the same extent as the majority.

QUESTION: The irony to that argument is, they did it in the peyote case.

GENERAL DELLINGER: In the—well—

QUESTION: After our decision.

GENERAL DELLINGER: And Congress—yes, but Justice Stevens, Congress was concerned—and they are the specialists on the perils of special interest exemption processes. They were concerned that if you have a case-by-case process, religions that, for whatever reasons, have more political

influence are able to get their specific exemptions.

QUESTION: General—

QUESTION: Well, certainly the peyote smokers don't have a great deal of influence, and yet they succeeded in Oregon.

GENERAL DELLINGER: It is not clear to me how well one can parse what—sometimes some minorities are particularly well-situated. Others, like the Amish, have a very difficult time in the legislative process—

QUESTION: Perhaps the peyote smokers had help from those outside of religion. [General laughter.]

QUESTION: General Dellinger, we've just been told by the representative of the Ohio attorney general that the states want to do even more than Congress has done, but they don't want Congress to tell them.

That's where they say they see the princip[al] constitutional problem, and you've just said that the states—you know, we can't trust them, and I'm asking you what basis is there for making that judgment when we're being told by the states, leave us alone. We'll do even better.

GENERAL DELLINGER: Justice Ginsburg, there was an eight-hundred-page record of testimony, groups—one religious group after another testified as to the difficulties that particularly marginal religious groups have getting accommodations. . . .

---

3. State Attorneys General Attack RFRA on Federalism Grounds

Source: 258 Landmark Briefs 308-09

Amicus State of Ohio and 15 other Amici States and Territories write to urge the Court to reverse the decision below and in the process to declare The Religious Freedom Restoration Act ("RFRA" or the "Act") unconstitutional as applied to the States. In doing so, they join at least four other States— California, New York, Illinois, Wisconsin—that have already challenged the validity of RFRA in separate actions.

The Amici States do not make this request lightly. RFRA tries to advance a commendable goal—religious liberties— and does so at the end of a legislative process that is as deserving of respect as each of the State legislative processes that it seeks to replace. But in the last analysis the pathmarking means used to further this legislative scheme exceed Congress's enumerated powers and disregard vital principles of federalism.

In the three short years since RFRA was enacted, it has disrupted several core functions of State governance. Whether it be running prisons, educating children, defining criminal laws, or exercising other police powers, RFRA has undermined the traditional discretion given to the States in these areas. Because the plain language of the Act enshrines the "least restrictive means" test as the across-the-board minimum for free exercise claims, it is difficult to be hopeful about regaining State authority over these areas any time soon or about ultimately confining the damage to these areas alone.

No less promising is the impact that this theory of congressional authority could have on future federal-state relations. If blessed by the Court, this expansive theory of congressional authority—applicable any time Congress chooses to protect constitutional "values" covered by the due process or equal protection clauses—would have no fathomable stopping point. It would open most, if not all, areas of State governance to federal regulation, threatening to destroy the Constitution's most important liberty safeguard—a distribution of power among the States and a balance of power between the national and State governments.

---

4. The House Considers the Federalism Implications of a "Son of RFRA" Proposal

Source: H.R. Rep. No. 106-219, 106th Cong., 1st Sess. 15-16, 25 (1999)

H.R. 1691 relies on Congress' power to regulate commerce among the States and includes a jurisdictional element to be proven in claims resting on this power. . . .

The commerce provision of H.R. 1691 provides as an element of the claim that the burden on religious exercise or the removal of that burden must affect commerce. Thus, H.R. 1691 protects only as much religious exercise as Congress is constitutionally empowered to protect. . . .

. . .

H.R. 1691 lifts burdens on religious exercise without dictating the means by which governments might accomplish this. H.R. 1691 does not impose any specific affirmative duty, implement a federal regulatory program, or conscript state officers. Its core policy is not to regulate the states, but to deregulate the exercise of religion. H.R. 1691 pre-empts state laws that fall within the scope of Congressional power and substantially burden religious exercise without a compelling reason, and it provides a cause of action to enforce that policy. . . .

H.R. 1691 does not violate the Tenth Amendment as interpreted by the Supreme Court in *New York v. United States* and *Printz v. United States*. Both cases explicitly recognize Congressional power to make "compliance with federal standards a precondition to continued state regulation in an otherwise pre-empted field." What is prohibited by *New York* and *Printz* is any attempt by Congress to require a state, in its sovereign capacity, to regulate its own citizens according to federal dictate, or to impress state officials to implement or enforce federal policy. Put another way, the federal government may not "commandeer" state legislatures or state officials to affirmatively enact or enforce federal policy. But it may prohibit them from violating federal policy regulating or deregulating private activity in fields subject to Congressional power.

4

SEPARATION OF POWERS: DOMESTIC CONFLICTS

The constitutional doctrine of separation of powers is ambiguous because it appears to contradict another basic principle of government: checks and balances. The record shows that the framers were more interested in an *overlapping* of powers as a means of securing this system of checks and balances, and never seriously entertained a strict separation of powers. Nevertheless, the picture is confused by a series of contradictory rulings from the Supreme Court. At times the Court adopts a strict, doctrinaire view of separated powers, and on other occasions promotes a pragmatic, functional theory that tolerates a substantial overlapping of power.

This chapter begins with the Watergate tapes case, *United States* v. *Nixon* (1974), which not only helped define the President's power to withhold documents from other branches (executive privilege) but was pivotal in forcing the resignation of President Richard Nixon. The Court's decision is comprehensible only by understanding the political context of the case and the limited reach of the decision in resolving disputes over executive privilege. Most of these controversies are settled through executive-legislative accommodations, not court decisions.

In *INS* v. *Chadha* (1983), discussed in Section II, the Court used a strict approach to strike down Congress' use of a "legislative veto" to control agency actions. The decision forced Congress to rewrite a number of statutes containing the forbidden legislative veto, but this form of congressional control survives as a practical accommodation between executive agencies and congressional committees. More than four hundred new legislative vetoes have been enacted since *Chadha*. Clearly in this area the "last word" in constitutional law has not been a court decision but rather the agreements worked out between Congress and the executive branch.

Section III focuses on *Bowsher* v. *Synar* (1986), which struck down a provision of the Gramm-Rudman Act that gave the Comptroller General (a legislative officer) crucial executive duties in implementing this deficit-reduction statute. Another effort by Congress to control deficits led to the Line Item Veto Act of 1996, struck down in *Clinton* v. *City of New York* (1998), an issue covered in Section IV. *Bowsher* stands in sharp contrast to *Morrison* v. *Olson* (1988), discussed in Section V, where the Court upheld a congressional statute that created the office of independent counsel. Why did two statutes fall so readily while the other was sustained with only one dissenting Justice? The legislative history reveals that Congress was careless in considering the constitutional issues raised by Gramm-Rudman and the Item Veto Act, while it acted thoughtfully and responsibly on the independent counsel statute. Section VI covers the power of impeachment, a constitutional power governed almost entirely by the political branches.

I. THE WATERGATE TAPES CASE

A 1972 burglary of the Democratic National Committee in the Watergate Office Building, Washington, D.C., raised questions about the involvement of the Nixon White House. Congressional and judicial requests for documents from the administration were rebuffed by assertions of "executive privilege"—the claim that the President has a constitutional right to withhold sensitive documents from other branches. The matter gradually unfolded to produce an impeachment effort in Congress, judicial demands for tapes recorded in the White House office, a decision in *United States* v. *Nixon* (1974) that the tapes be turned over to the courts, and President Nixon's subsequent resignation. These experiences, as will be discussed in Section V, prompted Congress in 1978 to create a permanent mechanism for the appointment of independent counsels.

A. The Break-in

During the early morning hours of June 17, 1972, James McCord and four other men illegally entered the sixth floor headquarters of the Democratic National Committee in the Watergate Office Building. Assisting in the burglary operation were Howard Hunt and G. Gordon Liddy. They remained nearby in a room in the Watergate Hotel and communicated by walkie-talkie with Alfred Baldwin, who served as a lookout in the Howard Johnson Motor Lodge across the street. All eight men were connected with the Nixon reelection committee. Several had worked for the CIA and the FBI.

A guard at the Watergate Office Building had noticed masking tape on the edge of a door in the garage leading to the office building. The tape allowed the door to be opened without a key. The guard contacted the police and a plainclothes squad was sent to the building in an unmarked car. The police arrested the five burglars. Indictments were brought against them and against Hunt and Liddy. Baldwin, given a grant of immunity, became the government's chief witness.

At a news conference on June 22, President Nixon said that the White House "has had no involvement whatever in this particular incident." Pub. Papers, 1972, at 691. At a news conference on August 29, he reported on an investigation conducted by White House Counsel John Dean: "I can say categorically that his investigation indicates that no one in the White House Staff, no one in this Administration, presently employed, was involved in this very bizarre incident." Nixon added that such incidents are not unusual—overzealous people in campaigns act in ways that are wrong—but that what "really hurts is if you try to cover it up." Pub. Papers, 1972, at 828. In the fall 1972 elections, Nixon won reelection by an overwhelming margin.

B. Snowballing Effect in 1973

At the January 1973 trial, Hunt and the four men who accompanied McCord pleaded guilty. McCord and Liddy were found guilty. The trial begged the question: who had helped organize the burglary? Was it a "third-rate burglary," as some in the Nixon administration maintained? Was it, instead, sponsored and funded by the Republican campaign staff and administration officials? Federal district judge John J. Sirica conceded at the end of the trial that he had been unable to reveal a motive behind the burglary.

Sirica selected March 23 as the date for sentencing the seven men. The trial had been frustrating for him because he felt that none of the defendants had told the truth. John J. Sirica, To Set the Record Straight 46-67 (1980). His suspicion was confirmed three days before sentencing when McCord walked into his office with a letter. McCord charged that political pressure had been applied to the defendants—to have them plead guilty and remain silent—and that perjury had been committed throughout the trial. The letter also revealed McCord's lack of confidence in the Justice Department. The thrust of these charges would be substantiated over the coming months. Perjury had been committed and higher-ups in the administration had participated in a cover-up. Sirica, noting that McCord's letter was dated March 19 (Sirica's birthday), remarked: "This is the best damned birthday present I've ever gotten. I always told you I felt someone would talk. This is going to break this case wide open." Sirica, To Set the Record Straight, at 74.

During the trial, Congress conducted its own investigation. At a news conference on March 2, President Nixon said that he would object if a congressional committee asked White House Counsel John Dean to testify on the Watergate affair. The objection, Nixon said, was based on executive privilege. Pub. Papers, 1973, at 160-61. Nixon developed his position in greater detail on March 12, arguing that executive privilege "is rooted in the Constitution." Although he said that executive privilege would not be used "as a shield to prevent embarrassing information from being made available but will be exercised only in those particular instances in which disclosure would harm the public interest," he signaled a likely constitutional confrontation:

Under the doctrine of separation of powers, the manner in which the President personally exercises his executive powers is not subject to questioning by another branch of government. If the President is not subject to such questioning, it is equally appropriate that members of his staff not be so questioned, for their roles are an extension of the Presidency. Pub. Papers 185 (1973).

During a news conference on March 15, President Nixon continued to oppose John Dean's appearance before a congressional committee (document 1). However, within a few days he began to shift ground. On March 21 (the day after McCord walked into Judge Sirica's office) Nixon said that "serious charges" had come to his attention and "major developments" had occurred. Pub. Papers, 1973, at 299. Nixon was now prepared, under special procedures, to permit White House aides to appear before the Senate Select Committee on Presidential Campaign Activities, chaired by Senator Sam J. Ervin, Jr. (D-N.C.). Witnesses could appear in executive session, if appropriate; executive privilege could be asserted during the course of the questioning; the hearings could be televised; and all members of the White House Staff would appear voluntarily, testifying under oath and "they will answer fully all proper questions." Pub. Papers, 1973, at 298-99.

By this time, enormous public pressures were building. On April 30, Nixon announced the resignation of Dean and two other key White House aides, H.R. Haldeman and John D. Ehrlichman. On the same day, Nixon announced the resignation of Attorney General Richard G. Kleindeinst and his replacement by Elliot L. Richardson. In an address to the nation that evening, Nixon said that he had given Richardson "absolute authority to make all decisions bearing upon the prosecution of the Watergate case and related matters. I have instructed him that if he should consider it appropriate, he has the authority to name a special supervising prosecutor for matters arising out of the case." Pub. Papers, 1973, at 330. As a condition for sending Richardson's name to the floor for confirmation, the Senate Judiciary Committee insisted that he appoint a special prosecutor to handle the Watergate investigation; that his choice for special prosecutor would appear before the Committee and if the Committee did not support this candidate Richardson would search for someone else; and the special prosecutor would be granted a large measure of independence. Richardson agreed to all of these conditions. "Nomination of Elliot L. Richardson to be Attorney General," hearings before the Senate Committee on the Judiciary, 93d Cong., 1st Sess. 4-6 (1973). The confirmation hearings also explored the scope of executive privilege, with Richardson conceding that in a criminal prosecution it would be necessary for courts to adjudicate the extent to which the President could withhold documents. Id. at 158-59.

Richardson returned to the Committee with his choice for special prosecutor—former Solicitor General Archibald Cox—and supplied the Committee with a statement (which the Committee had helped draft) that detailed the duties and responsibilities of the Watergate special prosecutor. Id. at 143-46. The Committee questioned Cox extensively on his independence, including the ability to hire his own staff and conduct the investigation without interference from Richardson. After the Senate confirmed Richardson, he issued a regulation that contained the specific powers for a special prosecutor, providing unusual authority and independence. The special prosecutor could not be removed from his duties "except for extraordinary improprieties on his part" (document 2). Cox began to assemble an investigative team.

C. Discovery of the Tapes

Senate hearings disclosed to the public a remarkable fact about White House operations. Alexander P. Butterfield testified about his duties at the White House from January 21, 1969 to March 14, 1973. He had told committee staff, a few days before the hearings, about the existence of listening and recording devices in the Oval Office of the President. He explained this system at the hearings (document 3).

President Nixon, citing executive privilege, rejected the Ervin Committee's request for access to presidential papers and tape recordings. Pub. Papers, 1973, at 636, 657, 668. The Committee then went to court to get the White House tapes but that effort was rebuffed. Judge Sirica held that his court lacked jurisdiction. After Congress passed a special statute conferring jurisdiction, another district court (Judge Gesell) ruled that release of the material to the Committee would create undue risk of pretrial publicity in the pending Watergate prosecutions. The latter decision was upheld on appeal. Senate Select Com. on Pres. Campaign Activities v. Nixon, 498 F.2d 725 (D.C. Cir. 1974).

Acting by grand jury subpoena, Cox sought access to the tapes. Nixon insisted that the President "is not subject to compulsory process from the courts" and that it was "inadmissible for the courts to seek to compel some particular action from the President." Pub. Papers, 1973, at 669-670. On August 29, Judge Sirica ruled that he had jurisdiction to decide the issue of executive privilege, that he had authority to order a President to obey the command of a grand jury subpoena, and that inspection of the tape recordings in the judge's chambers was required to balance the rights of the grand jury against the need for protection of presidential deliberations. In re Subpoena to Nixon, 360 F.Supp. 1 (D.D.C. 1973). Sirica's decision was upheld by the D.C. Circuit on October 12. Nixon v. Sirica, 487 F.2d 700 (D.C. Cir. 1973).

D. The Saturday Night Massacre

In response to the appellate court's decision, President Nixon on October 19 offered a compromise that he felt would avoid the necessity of Supreme Court review. First, he instructed White House Counsel not to seek Supreme Court review from the decision of the appellate court. Second, he directed Cox "to make no further attempts by judicial process to obtain tapes, notes, or memoranda of Presidential conversations." Third, he offered to submit to Judge Sirica a statement making a "full disclosure" of everything contained in the subpoenaed tapes that had any bearing on Watergate. The authenticity of this summary, prepared by President Nixon, would be assured by giving "unlimited access" to Senator John Stennis, allowing him to listen to every requested tape to verify that Nixon's statement was full and accurate. Pub. Papers, 1973, at 887-89.

Cox rejected this procedure, in part because he believed that a trial judge might reject the use of summaries as evidence on the ground they were not original documents. On October 20, President Nixon ordered Attorney General Richardson to fire Cox. Richardson, citing his promises to the Senate Judiciary Committee and his regulation giving Cox full authority to contest the assertion of executive privilege, refused and resigned. Nixon then ordered Deputy Attorney General William Ruckelshaus to fire Cox. Ruckelshaus also refused and resigned. Nixon next ordered Solicitor General Robert Bork (now Acting Attorney General) to fire Cox, and Bork complied by abolishing the Special Prosecutor's Office.

The resignations of Richardson and Ruckelshaus and the firing of Cox provoked a public uproar and the call by 84 members of Congress for Nixon's impeachment. Responding to these events, Nixon announced on October 23 that he would hand over nine tapes to Judge Sirica and that a new special prosecutor would be appointed to investigate Watergate. Pub. Papers, 1973, at 897-99. Sirica's review of the tapes revealed evidence of a coverup, such as Nixon's remark at a March 22, 1973 meeting: "And, uh, for that reason, I am perfectly willing to—I don't give a shit what happens. I want you to stonewall it, let them plead the Fifth Amendment, cover-up or anything else, if it'll save the plan." Sirica, To Set the Record Straight, at 162.

On November 1, Leon Jaworski succeeded Cox as Special Prosecutor for Watergate. Nixon announced on November 17 that Jaworski would not be removed unless there was a consensus of the top leadership of both Houses of Congress: the Speaker and the majority and minority leaders of the House, the President pro tem and the majority and minority leaders of the Senate, and the ranking two members of the House and Senate Judiciary Committees. Pub. Papers, 1973, at 951.

The fallout continued when the White House disclosed that two of the tapes to be turned over to Sirica did not exist. President Nixon said that the tape had run out on one of the conversations and the other conversation was not recorded because it took place in his family quarters which did not have a recording system. Pub. Papers, 1973, at 929-31. Moreover, on November 26 it was revealed that a tape of a June 20, 1972 conversation contained an 18 minute gap. A panel of electronics specialists determined that the gap was caused by at least five separate, manual erasures.

E. Gearing up for Impeachment

On November 15, 1973, the House by a 367 to 51 vote adopted a resolution appropriating $1 million for an investigation by the House Judiciary Committee as to whether President Nixon should be impeached. On February 6, 1974, the House formally granted the Judiciary Committee the power to conduct an impeachment inquiry. This time the vote was 410 to 4. After two months of closed hearings and televised debates, the Committee recommended late in July three articles of impeachment: obstruction of justice (supported in the Committee by a vote of 27 to 11), abuse of presidential powers (28 to 10), and contempt of Congress for refusing to comply with subpoenas (21 to 17).

The House impeachment action occurred at the same time that Jaworski was seeking further documentation from the administration. On February 14, 1974, Jaworski reported to the Senate Judiciary Committee that President Nixon had refused to release any more presidential tapes or documents related to Watergate. James D. St. Clair, special counsel to President Nixon, developed the legal position for withholding presidential documents. Jaworski went to court seeking 64 post-Watergate conversations, most of them involving Nixon. The legal dispute made its way to the Supreme Court. During oral argument, St. Clair equivocated on Nixon's willingness to accept the Court's judgment on executive privilege as binding on the President (document 4).

On July 24, the Supreme Court held that the President's generalized assertion of executive privilege had to yield to the demonstrated, specific need for evidence in a pending criminal trial. United States v. Nixon, 418 U.S. 683 (1974). As if to anticipate Nixon's warning that he would comply with a court ruling only if it were "definitive," the Court's decision was unanimous. On August 5, Nixon released three previously undisclosed transcripts from among the 64 the Supreme Court required him to give to Sirica. The conversations with chief of staff H. R. Haldeman on June 23, 1972, provided further evidence of Nixon's participation in a coverup, Nixon agreeing that the CIA should put a halt to the FBI investigation (document 5). With the release of these tapes, Nixon said that a House vote of impeachment "is, as a practical matter, virtually a foregone conclusion." Pub. Papers, 1974, at 622. He announced his resignation on August 8, to be effective noon the following day.

F. Consequences of *Nixon*

The Court's ruling in this case was extraordinary, not only because of its political impact but the mere fact that it had been issued. Most of the collisions involving executive privilege are resolved by the political branches. If the President invokes executive privilege, Congress and its committees must decide whether to do battle to gain access to disputed documents. *United States* v. *Nixon* does not provide much guidance here, as this case involved a collision between the judiciary and the President, not between the executive and legislative branches. In most cases the crucial ingredients are congressional determination and the likely political costs to the executive branch of not complying with a congressional request for information. The powers of Congress are formidable, beginning with political pressure and eventually leading to the issuance of subpoenas and holding executive officials in contempt.

Throughout this process the two political branches decide for themselves what is essential in defending their constitutional prerogatives and the particular accommodation that can be fashioned to settle the dispute. For the most part, Congress and the executive have strong incentives to work with each other. In particular, Congress' willingness to leave the details of administration with the executive is often hinged on the executive's willingness to share with Congress information necessary to monitor the administration of federal programs. On those rare occasions when courts are involved, they typically guide the other branches toward a solution rather than impose one. As Judge Harold Leventhal said on one such occasion: "A compromise worked out between the branches is most likely to meet their essential needs and the country's constitutional balance." United States v. AT&T, 551 F.2d 384, 394 (D.C. Cir. 1976). See also United States v. AT&T, 567 F.2d 121 (D.C. Cir. 1977). For this reason, as Louis Henkin observed, *United States* v. *Nixon*, "like other great-hard cases, will not have made bad law, but hardly any law at all." Executive Privilege: Mr. Nixon Loses but the Presidency Largely Prevails, 22 UCLA L. Rev. 40, 46 (1974).

DOCUMENTS

1. Nixon Explains Executive Privilege

Source: Pub. Papers,
1973, at 203-04

Q. Mr. President, do you plan to stick by your decision not to allow Mr. Dean to testify before the Congress, even if it means the defeat of Mr. Gray's nomination? [L. Patrick Gray III was nominated to be FBI Director.]

THE PRESIDENT. I have noted some speculation to the effect that the Senate might hold Mr. Gray as hostage to a decision on Mr. Dean. I cannot believe that such responsible Members of the United States Senate would do that, because as far as I am concerned, my decision has been made.

. . .

Mr. Dean is Counsel to the White House. He is also one who was counsel to a number of people on the White House Staff. He has, in effect, what I would call a double privilege, the lawyer-client relationship, as well as the Presidential privilege.

And in terms of privilege, I think we could put it another way. I consider it my constitutional responsibility to defend the principle of separation of powers. I recognize that many Members of the Congress disagree with my interpretation of that responsibility.

But while we are talking on that subject—and I will go on at some length here because it may anticipate some of your other questions—I am very proud of the fact that in this Administration we have been more forthcoming in terms of the relationship between the executive, the White House, and the Congress, than any administration in my memory. We have not drawn a curtain down and said that there could be no information furnished by members of the White House Staff because of their special relationship to the President.

All we have said is that it must be under certain circumstances, certain guidelines, that do not infringe upon or impair the separation of powers that are so essential to the survival of our system.

. . .

In this case, . . . [Dean] will furnish all pertinent information. He will be completely forthcoming—something that other administrations have totally refused to do until we got here. . .

2. Richardson Establishes a Special Prosecutor for Watergate

Source: 38 Fed. Reg.
14688 (1973)

There is appointed by the Attorney General, within the Department of Justice, a Special Prosecutor to whom the Attorney General shall delegate the authorities and provide the staff and other resources described below.

The Special Prosecutor shall have full authority for investigating and prosecuting offenses against the United States arising out of the unauthorized entry in Democratic National Committee headquarters at the Watergate, all offenses arising out of the 1972 Presidential election for which the Special Prosecutor deems it necessary and appropriate to assume responsibility, allegations involving the President, members of the White House staff, or Presidential appointees, and any other matters which he consents to have assigned to him by the Attorney General.

In particular, the Special Prosecutor shall have full authority with respect to the above matters for:

Conducting proceedings before grand juries and any other investigations he deems necessary;

Reviewing all documentary evidence available from any source, as to which he shall have full access;

Determining whether or not to contest the assertion of "Executive privilege" or any other testimonial privilege;

Determining whether or not application should be made to any Federal court for a grant of immunity to any witness, consistently with applicable statutory requirements, or for warrants, subpoenas, or other court orders;

Deciding whether or not to prosecute any individual, firm, corporation, or group of individuals;

Initiating and conducting prosecutions, framing indictments, filing informations, and handling all aspects of any cases within his jurisdiction . . . .

In exercising this authority, the Special Prosecutor will have the greatest degree of independence that is consistent with the Attorney General's statutory accountability for all matters falling within the jurisdiction of the Department of Justice. The Attorney General will not countermand or interfere with the Special Prosecutor's decisions or actions. The Special Prosecutor will determine whether and to what extent he will inform or consult with the Attorney General about the conduct of his duties and responsibilities. The Special Prosecutor will not be removed from his duties except for extraordinary improprieties on his part.

3. Senate Hearings Reveal a White House Taping System

Source: Presidential Campaign Activities of 1972 (Book 5), hearings before the Senate Select Committee on Presidential Campaign Activities, 93d Cong., 1st Sess. 2074-76, 2079, 2080 (1973)

Mr. [Fred] THOMPSON [Minority Counsel]. Mr. Butterfield, are you aware of the installation of any listening devices in the Oval Office of the President?

Mr. [Alexander P.] BUTTERFIELD. I was aware of listening devices; yes, sir.

Mr. THOMPSON. When were those devices placed in the Oval Office?

Mr. BUTTERFIELD. Approximately the summer of 1970 [later corrected as the spring of 1971.] . . .

Mr. THOMPSON. Are you aware of any devices that were installed in the Executive Office Building office of the President? [The Old Executive Office Building is on White House grounds.]

. . .

Mr. BUTTERFIELD. . . . They were installed, of course, for historical purposes, to record the President's business and they were installed in his two offices, the Oval Office and the EOB office. Within the west wing of the White House, there are several, at least three, perhaps four—the three that I know of—boxes called Presidential locator boxes.

. . .

Mr. [Samuel] DASH [Chief Counsel and Staff Director]. . . . I think what you are saying was that at all times certainly in the White House itself, either in the Oval Office or in the Executive Office of the President where there was a locator light that whenever the President moved the locator light moved where the President was, it triggered the microphones and then whenever anybody started to speak in that office where the microphones were as the voice activated the device, the recording devices began to operate, is that not true?

Mr. BUTTERFIELD. That is true, yes, sir.

. . .

Mr. DASH. To your knowledge, did the President ever ask while he was in the Oval Office to have the system not operate, the locator light not show in that office so as to trigger the device?

Mr. BUTTERFIELD. No, sir. As a matter of fact, the President seemed to be totally, really oblivious, or certainly uninhibited by this fact.

4. St. Clair during Oral Argument before the Supreme Court

Source: 79 Landmark Briefs 871-72, 879 (1975)

Mr. JUSTICE MARSHALL: The tapes that they ask for in this subpoena *duces tecum*, which is the only thing before us—has any effort been made to say what if any part of that can be released?

Mr. ST. CLAIR: Other than the 20 that are already published, no effort has been made as yet, sir.

Mr. JUSTICE MARSHALL: Why not?

Mr. ST. CLAIR: Because, if Your Honor please, we have not felt that it has been necessary to do·so, because we firmly feel that the President has every right to refuse to produce them.

Mr. JUSTICE MARSHALL: You don't think that a subpoena *duces tecum* is sufficient reason for you to try? You just ignored it, didn't you?

Mr. ST. CLAIR: [No], sir, we did not. We filed a motion to quash it.

Mr. JUSTICE MARSHALL: The difference between ignoring and filing a motion to quash is what?

Mr. ST. CLAIR: Well, if Your Honor please, we are submitting the matter—

Mr. JUSTICE MARSHALL: You are submitting the matter to this Court—

Mr. ST. CLAIR: To this Court under a special showing on behalf of the President—

Mr. JUSTICE MARSHALL: And you are still leaving it up to this Court to decide it.

Mr. ST. CLAIR: Yes, in a sense.

Mr. JUSTICE MARSHALL: In what sense?

Mr. ST. CLAIR: In the sense that this Court has the obligation to determine the law. The President also has an obligation to carry out his constitutional duties.

Mr. JUSTICE MARSHALL: You are submitting it for us to decide whether or not executive privilege is available in this case.

Mr. ST. CLAIR: The problem is the question is even more limited than that. Is the executive privilege, which my brother [Jaworski] concedes, absolute or it is only conditional?

Mr. JUSTICE MARSHALL: I said "in this case." Can you make it any narrower than that?

Mr. ST. CLAIR: No, sir.

Mr. JUSTICE MARSHALL: Well, do you agree that that is what is before this Court, and you are submitting it to this Court for decision?

Mr. ST. CLAIR: This is being submitted to this Court for its guidance and judgment with respect to the law. The President, on the other hand, has his obligations under the Constitution.

Mr. JUSTICE MARSHALL: Are you submitting it to this Court for this Court's decision?

Mr. ST. CLAIR: As to what the law is, yes.

.   .   .   .

Mr. JUSTICE MARSHALL: You are still saying the absolute privilege to decide what shall be released and what shall not be released is vested in one person and nobody can question it.

Mr. ST. CLAIR: Insofar as it relates to the Presidential conversations, this is correct, sir—

---

5. White House Conversation, June 23, 1972

Source: H.R. Rept. No. 93-1305, 93d Cong., 2d Sess. 53 (1974)

HALDEMAN: Now, on the investigation, you know the Democratic break-in thing, we're back in the problem area because the FBI is not under control, because [Acting FBI Director Patrick] Gray doesn't exactly know how to control it and they have—their investigation is now leading into some productive areas—because they've been able to trace the money—not through the money itself—but through the bank sources—the banker. And, and it goes in some directions we don't want it to go. Ah, also there have been some things—like an informant came in off the street to the FBI in Miami who was a photographer or has a friend who is photographer who developed some films through this guy Barker and the films had pictures of Democratic National Committee letterhead documents and things. So it's things like that are filtering in. . . .

NIXON: That's right.

HALDEMAN: That the way to handle this now is for us to have [CIA Deputy Director Vernon L.] Walters call Pat Gray and just say, "Stay to hell out of this—this is ah. business here and we don't want you to go any further on it." That's not an unusual development, and ah. that would take care of it.

NIXON: What about Pat Gray—you mean Pat Gray doesn't want to?

HALDEMAN: Pat does want to. He doesn't know how to, and he doesn't have . . . any basis for doing it. Given this, he will then have the basis. He'll call [FBI Deputy Associate Director] Mark Felt in. . .

NIXON: Yeah.

HALDEMAN: He'll call him and say, "We've got the signal from across the river [the CIA] to put the hold on this." And that will fit rather well because the FBI agents who are working the case, at this point, feel that's what it is . . . .

HALDEMAN: And you seem to think the thing to do is get them to stop?

NIXON: Right, fine.

NIXON: . . . I'm not going to get that involved. I'm [unintelligible].

HALDEMAN: No, sir, we don't want you to.

NIXON: You call them in.

II. LEGISLATIVE VETO

The Supreme Court in *INS v. Chadha* declared that "legislative vetoes" were an invalid form of congressional control. 462 U.S. 919 (1983). For more than fifty years, Congress had relied on this device to control its delegation of legislative power in such areas as the President's authority to reorganize the executive branch, immigration, rulemaking, impoundment, foreign trade, and national emergencies. The legislative veto allowed Congress to control executive activities without having to pass another public law. Congress exercised control merely by passing "simple resolutions" (adopted by either House), "concurrent resolutions" (passed by both Houses but not sent to the President), and even committee actions.

Under the Court's ruling, all of the statutory provisions authorizing legislative vetoes were unconstitutional. As Justice White noted in his dissent, the Court in "one fell swoop" struck down more laws enacted by Congress than the Court had cumulatively invalidated in the entire history of the Court. 462 U.S. at 1002. Yet Congress continues to rely on the legislative veto to control agency actions. Instead of acting through the full legislative process (action by both Houses and presentment of a bill to the President) as required by *Chadha,* statutes enacted since 1983 enable Congress to rely on controls short of a public law, usually some form of committee-approval mechanism.

What accounts for this gap between what the Court said and what the two political branches continue to do? Why has there been so little compliance with what all observers regard as an "epic" separation of powers decision? Did the Court attempt too broad a remedy and fail to recognize the practical needs that led Congress and the executive branch to adopt the legislative veto in the first place? Evidently those needs were present before *Chadha* and continue to exist after the Court's decision.

A. The Lawmaking Process

No one disputes that the making of a public law requires action by both Houses of Congress and presentment of a bill to the President for his signature or veto. Article I, Section 7, of the Constitution provides that "Every Order, Resolution, or Vote to which the Concurrence of the Senate and House of Representatives may be necessary (except on a question of Adjournment)" shall be presented to the President. Bills and "joint resolutions" must comply with bicameralism and presentment before becoming public laws. "Joint resolutions" and "bills" are legally identical. They must pass both Houses and be presented to the President.

Congress can adopt simple resolutions or concurrent resolutions for internal matters, such as procedural rules and punishing or expelling members, without sending either measure to the President. These resolutions are not considered "legislative in effect." Instead, they are passed pursuant to congressional powers under Article I. A Senate report in 1897 concluded that the meaning of "legislative in effect" depended on substance, not form. If a simple resolution or concurrent resolution contained matter that was "legislative in its character and effect," it had to be presented to the President. S. Rep. No. 1335, 54th Cong., 2d Sess. 8 (1897).

On these questions there was little dispute. But what if a public law, enacted by both Houses and signed by the President, authorized use of a simple or concurrent resolution to control the executive branch? Would those resolutions then be legally binding? In 1854, Attorney General Cushing concluded that a President, by signing the enabling statute, would in effect consent to the coerciveness of such resolutions (document 1). Specific examples were forthcoming. In 1905 Congress passed legislation giving it the power by concurrent resolution to direct the Secretary of War to make investigations in rivers and harbors matters. 33 Stat. 1147, §2 (1905). Two years earlier Congress also resorted to simple resolutions to direct the Secretary of Commerce to make investigations and to issue reports. 32 Stat. 829, §8 (1903).

B. Legislative Vetoes Initiated by the President

In an effort to cut federal spending and increase "economy and efficiency," President Herbert Hoover wanted Congress to delegate to him broad authority to reorganize the executive branch. Hoover could have made reorganization proposals through the regular legislative process, but he feared that his proposals would either be amended beyond recognition or else never enacted. In his 1929 Annual Message to Congress, he suggested that Congress delegate reorganization powers to him, subject to some form of congressional approval or disapproval. As one possibility, Hoover suggested that the President could act "upon approval of a joint committee of Congress" (document 2). In essence, the constitutional tables would be turned. Instead of Congress presenting a bill to the President for his approval or rejection, the President would submit proposals subject to a congressional veto.

During the election year of 1932, Hoover asked Congress for authority to consolidate various executive and administrative activities. He proposed that the President incorporate the reorganization changes in an Executive Order, which would lie before Congress for 60 days during which time Congress could "request suspension of action." Pub. Papers, 1932-33, at 58. The precise form of congressional control was left indefinite.

As an amendment to the Legislative Branch Appropriations Act for fiscal year 1933, Hoover finally received his reorganization authority, subject to a one-House legislative veto. The procedure required the President to submit reorganization proposals in an Executive Order, which would become effective within 60 days unless either House disapproved by simple resolution. Congress could shorten the time period by passing a concurrent resolution of approval. 47 Stat. 414-15, Sec. 407 (1932).

When Congress reconvened on December 5, 1932, Hoover issued eleven Executive Orders consolidating some 58 governmental activities. By that time, Hoover had been overwhelmingly defeated for reelection, and Congress decided to leave reorganization changes to his successor, Franklin D. Roosevelt. · On January 19, 1933, the House of Representatives passed a resolution disapproving all of Hoover's reorganization proposals.

On January 24, 1933, shortly before leaving office, Hoover vetoed a bill that required the Joint Committee on Internal Revenue Taxation to approve any refunds or credits in excess of $20,000. Hoover argued that Congress should not be involved in executive and administrative functions. To his veto message he attached an opinion by Attorney General William Mitchell, who challenged not only the committee control over tax refunds but also the one-House veto over executive reorganization proposals. 37 Op. Att'y Gen. 56 (1933). One day before Roosevelt's inauguration, Congress extended the President's reorganization authority for two years, but eliminated the one-House veto. 47 Stat. 1517-19 (1933). Roosevelt could exercise the authority without the check of a legislative veto.

C. Presidential Accommodations, With Misgivings

In 1937, Roosevelt asked Congress to renew the authority to reorganize the executive branch, subject to a joint resolution of disapproval. He advised Congress the next year that any action short of a bill or joint resolution would merely represent "an expression of congressional sentiment," without binding effect on the President. The Senate passed legislation acceding to his request, but the House of Representatives balked. Members of the House did not want to oppose a reorganization plan by joint resolution, have it vetoed by the President, and then scramble for the necessary two-thirds in each House for an override. Within a matter of days, after realizing that his bill was dead, Roosevelt reversed course and supported an amendment to allow Congress to reject reorganization plans by a concurrent resolution (a two-House legislative veto). A number of ingenious arguments were advanced to justify the administration's switch. 83 Cong. Rec. 4487, 5004-05 (1938). The reorganization bill passed in 1939, including the two-House veto. Roosevelt signed the bill, expressing no constitutional objections.

Whatever constitutional objections Presidents harbored about the legislative veto, they acquiesced because Congress insisted that it would not delegate certain authorities without attaching some sort of legislative veto. Presidents who wanted additional statutory authority had to take the strings attached to it. For example, President Roosevelt signed the Lend Lease Act of 1941, which permitted Congress to terminate the President's emergency authority by concurrent resolution. Roosevelt had strong misgivings about the constitutionality of this procedure, but swallowed his doubts for two reasons. He wanted the authority and feared that publicizing his constitutional position would delight his opponents and alienate his friends. Roosevelt expressed his constitutional objections in a memorandum to his Attorney General, Robert H. Jackson, directing him at some future date to publish the memorandum as an official document. Jackson chose to publish the memorandum as part of an article for the Harvard Law Review in 1953, eight years after Roosevelt's death (document 3).

Presidents Truman and Eisenhower also signed reorganization bills that contained the legislative veto. When the authority was extended in 1949, Congress tightened its control by substituting a one-House veto for the concurrent resolution of disapproval. In the meantime, the legislative veto had proliferated. Legislation in 1940 authorized the Attorney General to suspend deportation of an alien, subject to a two-House veto (later changed to a one-House veto). During the emergency conditions of World War II, it was impracticable to expect Congress to authorize each defense installation or public works project. Beginning with an informal system in 1942, all proposals for acquisitions of land and leases were submitted in advance to the Naval Affairs Committees for their approval. That understanding was formalized in a public law in 1944. Congress enacted other "coming into agreement" provisions in 1949 and 1951, requiring the Armed Services Committees to approve the acquisition of land and real estate transactions.

In an effort to stop this spread of legislative vetoes, Attorney General Brownell issued an opinion in 1955 that characterized the committee veto as an unconstitutional infringement on executive power by engrafting executive duties on legislative members. 41 Op. Att'y Gen. 230 (1955). However, the Eisenhower administration soon learned that if it shut the door to one form of congressional involvement in administrative decisions, Congress could easily create substitutes that gave committees the same level of control without raising constitutional issues. Legislation was drafted to prohibit appropriations for certain real estate transactions unless the Public Works Committees first approved the contracts. The "committee veto" thus operated within the halls of Congress rather than against executive agencies. Eisenhower signed the bill after Brownell assured him that this new procedure was constitutional because it was based on the power of Congress to control its authorization and appropriation procedures. While the form changed, the substance of the committee veto remained in force. Joseph P. Harris, Congressional Control of Administration 230-31 (1964).

D. The Accommodation Begins to Unravel

Executive-legislative relations experienced new strains in the 1970s when Congress included the legislative veto in statutes involving the war power, national emergencies, impoundment, presidential papers, federal salaries, and selected agency regulations. By the late 1970s, Congress threatened to extend the legislative veto to control regulations issued by every agency of government.

In an effort to combat this growth, Attorney General Griffin Bell issued an opinion in 1977 that attempted to justify the one-House veto in the reorganization statute, while casting doubt on other forms of the legislative veto. 43 Op. Att'y Gen. No. 10 (1977). The following year, President Carter released a major critique of the legislative veto. He warned that the legislative vetoes already enacted into law would be treated merely as "report-and-wait" provisions. Any congressional disapproval by committee action, simple resolution, or concurrent resolution would be given "serious consideration by executive officials but would not be regarded as legally binding" (document 4).

Nevertheless, on the same day that Carter issued his statement, two officials from his administration backpedaled from Carter's broad threat. During a press conference on June 21, 1978, Attorney General Bell and White House aide Stuart Eizenstat announced that they could live with certain types of legislative vetoes, especially those in the War Powers Resolution and legislation governing arms sales to foreign countries.

By the time the *Chadha* case reached the Supreme Court, briefs in opposition to the legislative veto were filed by the Reagan administration, the American Bar Association, and the attorneys for Chadha. The Senate and the House of Representatives filed briefs that defended the constitutionality of the legislative veto.

Writing for the Court, Chief Justice Burger insisted that any action of Congress that has the effect of "altering the legal rights, duties, and relations" of persons outside the legislative branch must conform to two procedural requirements: action by both Houses (to satisfy bicameralism) and presentment of a bill or joint resolution to the President for his signature or veto. INS v. Chadha, 462 U.S. 919, 952 (1983). According to the Court, Congress could affect agency activities only by passing a public law. Newspapers and the media featured bold headlines: "Court Decision Axes Congressional Power," "Congressional Veto Killed," and "Justices Strip Congress of Veto Power." The actual results proved to be less sweeping.

E. Declared Unconstitutional, Legislative Vetoes Persist

Following the Court's ruling, Congress amended a number of statutes by deleting legislative vetoes and replacing them with joint resolutions. Legislation changed to comply with *Chadha* include statutes dealing with the D.C. Home Rule Act, executive reorganization, national emergencies, export administration, and federal pay. Yet Congress also put legislative vetoes in bills and Presidents continued to sign them into law. From the date of the Court's decision in *Chadha* to the end of 1999, Congress enacted more than four hundred new legislative vetoes. Most of these require the executive branch to obtain the approval of specific committees. Here are examples from some statutes in 1998: None of the funds available to the Forest Service may be reprogrammed without the advance approval of the Appropriations Committees. 112 Stat. 2681-272. Not to exceed five percent of any appropriation to the IRS may be transferred to any other IRS appropriation upon the advance approval of the Appropriations Committees. 112 Stat. 2681-488, Sec. 101. Money in the Federal Buildings Fund may be expended for emergency repairs only when advance approval is obtained from the Appropriations Committees. 112 Stat. 2681-502.

In addition to the new legislative vetoes that appear in public laws, a number of committee vetoes were driven underground, relying on informal, nonstatutory understandings. A good example is a conflict that arose in 1984, when President Reagan signed an appropriations bill and objected to several provisions that required executive agencies to seek the prior approval of the Appropriations Committee. His signing statement implied that committee-veto provisions would be regarded by the administration as having no legal effect. After notifying the committees, agencies could do as they liked without obtaining the committee's approval (document 5).

The House Appropriations Committee responded quickly to this challenge. It reviewed a procedure that had worked well with the

National Aeronautics and Space Administration for about four years. Statutory ceilings ("caps") were placed on various NASA programs, usually at the level requested in the President's budget. NASA could exceed those caps only if it received permission from the Appropriations Committees. Because the administration now threatened to ignore the committee controls, House Appropriations said that it would repeal both the committee veto *and* NASA's authority to exceed the caps. If NASA wanted to spend beyond the caps, it would have to do what the Court mandated in *Chadha*: pass a bill through both Houses and present it to the President. H.R. Rep. No. 916, 98th Cong., 2d Sess. 48 (1984).

NASA groaned at the thought of having to get a new public law every time it needed to exceed spending caps. To avoid that kind of administrative rigidity, NASA Administrator James M. Beggs wrote to the Appropriations Committees and suggested a compromise. Instead of putting the caps in a public law, he recommended that they be placed in the conference report that explains how Congress expects a public law to be carried out. He then pledged that NASA would not exceed any ceiling identified in the conference report without first obtaining the prior approval of the Appropriations Committees (document 6). NASA would abide by informal and nonstatutory agreements, which are permissible under *Chadha*. NASA is not legally bound by these agreements, but violations of trust would provoke the Appropriations Committees to return the caps to the public law and force NASA to seek a separate law each time it needed to exceed the caps.

Informal, nonstatutory committee controls are used frequently to monitor agency spending. For decades, congressional committees have insisted on approving agency "reprogramming" (when agencies want to shift funds from one program to another within the same appropriations account). In return for the discretion to reprogram funds, agencies are expected to notify congressional committees and in some cases obtain committee approval. These understandings were first spelled out in committee reports, as part of the legislative history of a bill, and later incorporated in agency budget manuals. Louis Fisher, *Presidential Spending Power* 75-98 (1975). Despite *Chadha*, these committee vetoes continue to be accepted by executive agencies. Even if Congress entirely removed legislative vetoes from statutes, their equivalent would be embedded in agency manuals.

A dramatic example of informal agreements that permit committee control involves the "Baker Accord." In the early months of the Bush administration, Secretary of State James A. Baker, III, decided to give four committees of Congress a veto power over the fractious issue of funding the Nicaraguan Contras. In return for receiving $50 million in humanitarian aid for the Contras, Baker agreed that a portion of the funds could be released only with the approval of certain committees and party leaders. White House counsel C. Boyden Gray objected to this level of involvement by Congress in foreign policy, especially through what seemed to him an unconstitutional legislative veto. Wash. Post, March 26, 1989, at A5. Robert H. Bork regarded the Baker Accord as "even more objectionable" than the legislative veto struck down in *Chadha*, because it permitted control by committees instead of a one-House veto. 135 Cong. Rec. 6528 (1989). However, the informal nature of the Baker Accord is not prohibited by *Chadha*, and Baker agreed to the compromise (document 7).

F. Conclusion

To minimize the risk of self-inflicted wounds, the Supreme Court usually follows the sensible guideline that it will not "formulate a rule of constitutional law broader than is required by the precise facts to which it is to be applied." Ashwander v. TVA, 297 U.S. 288 (1936). The Court violated that principle in *Chadha* by issuing a decision that not only reached beyond the immigration statute but exceeded the Court's understanding of executive-legislative relations. Through an endless variety of formal and informal agreements, congressional committees will continue to exercise control over administration decisions.

The predictable and inevitable result of *Chddha* is a system of lawmaking that is now more convoluted, cumbersome, and covert than before. In many cases the Court's decision simply drives underground a set of legislative and committee vetoes that used to operate in plain sight. Effective government requires comity and cooperation among the branches. In one form or another, legislative vetoes will remain an important mechanism for reconciling legislative and executive interests.

DOCUMENTS

1. Opinion by Attorney General Cushing

Source: 6 Op. Att'y Gen. 680, 682, 683 (1854)

[Attorney General Cushing wrote this letter analyzing the legal effect of certain votes taken in the Senate and the House of Representatives regarding a refund to a private citizen who claimed that the federal government owed him money. The claim had been rejected by the Commissioner of Pensions; the Secretary of the Interior affirmed that ruling. Each House of Congress passed separate resolutions, directing that the claim be returned to the Secretary for "liquidation." Cushing concluded that the resolutions had no legal effect unless their force had been recognized in a previous public law.]

SIR:

. . . It is for Congress to pass laws; but it cannot pass any law, which, in effect, coerces the discretion, of the President, except with his approbation, unless by concurrent vote of two-thirds of both Houses, upon his previous refusal to sign a bill. . . .

If, then, the President approves a law, which imperatively commands a thing to be done, ministerially, by a Head of Department, his approbation of the law, or its repassage after a veto, gives constitutionality to what would otherwise be the usurpation of executive power on the part of Congress.

Of course, no separate resolution of either House can coerce a Head of Department, unless in some particular in which a law, duly enacted, has subjected him to the direct action of each; and in such case it is to be intended, that, by approving the law, the President has consented to the exercise of such coerciveness on the part of either House.

2. President Hoover Proposes Legislative Veto

Source: Pub. Papers,
1929, at 431-32

[The subject of department reorganization] has been under consideration for over 20 years. It was promised by both political parties in the recent campaign. It has been repeatedly examined by committees and commissions—congressional, executive, and voluntary. The conclusions of these investigations have been unanimous that reorganization is a necessity of sound administration; of economy; of more effective governmental policies and of relief to the citizen from unnecessary harassment in his relations with a multitude of scattered governmental agencies. But the presentation of any specific plan at once enlivens opposition from every official whose authority may be curtailed or who fears his position is imperiled by such a result; of bureaus and departments which wish to maintain their authority and activities; of citizens and their organizations who are selfishly interested, or who are inspired by fear that their favorite bureau may, in a new setting, be less subject to their influence or more subject to some other influence.

. . .

With this background of all previous experience I can see no hope for the development of a sound reorganization of the Government unless Congress be willing to delegate its authority over the problem (subject to defined principles) to the Executive, who should act upon approval of a joint committee of Congress or with the reservation of power of revision by Congress within some limited period adequate for its consideration.

3. Roosevelt's Confidential Memo Attacking Legislative Veto

Source: Robert Jackson, A Presidential Legal Opinion, 66 Hare. L. Rev. 1353, 1357-58 (1953)

[The Lend-Lease Act of 1941 permitted Congress, by concurrent resolution, to terminate the emergency authorities delegated to the President. Roosevelt signed the bill, without expressing any constitutional reservations, but several days later wrote to Robert Jackson (at that time Attorney General) and asked that an official memorandum be prepared stating why the legislative veto was constitutionally deficient. The Justice Department drafted the memo and Roosevelt signed it, although it was not made public until Jackson's article in 1953.]

THE WHITE HOUSE
WASHINGTON
April 7, 1941

MEMORANDUM FOR THE
ATTORNEY GENERAL

On March 11, 1941, I attached my approval to the bill (H.R. 1776) entitled "An Act to Promote the Defense of the United States." The bill was an outstanding measure which sought to meet a momentous emergency of great magnitude in world affairs. In view of this impelling consideration, I felt constrained to sign the measure, in spite of the fact that it contained a provision which, in my opinion, is clearly unconstitutional. I have reference to the clause of Section 3(c) of the Act, providing that after the passage of a concurrent resolution by the two Houses before June 30, 1943, which declares that the powers conferred by or pursuant to subsection (a) are no longer necessary to promote the defense of the United States, neither the President nor the head of any Department or agency shall exercise any of the powers conferred by or pursuant to subsection (a), with certain specified exceptions. In effect, this provision is an attempt by Congress to authorize a repeal by means of a concurrent resolution of the two Houses, of certain provisions of an Act of Congress.

The Constitution of the United States, Article I, Section 7, prescribes the mode in which laws shall be enacted. . . . The Constitution contains no provision whereby the Congress may legislate by concurrent resolution without the approval of the President. . . .

It is too clear for argument that action repealing an existing Act itself constitutes an Act of Congress and, therefore, is subject to the foregoing requirements. A repeal of existing provisions of law, in whole or in part, therefore, may not be accomplished by a concurrent resolution of the two Houses.

In order that I may be on record as indicating my opinion that the foregoing provision of the so-called Lend-Lease Act is unconstitutional, and in order that my approval of the bill, due to the existing exigencies of the world situation, may not be construed as a tacit acquiescence in any contrary view, I am requesting you to place this memorandum in the official files of the Department of Justice. . . .

/s/ Franklin D. Roosevelt

---

4. President Carter Attacks the Legislative Veto

Source: Pub. Papers,
1978 (1), at 1146-49

To the Congress of the United States:
. . . [T]he legislative veto injects the Congress into the details of administering substantive programs and laws. These new provisions require the President or an administrator of a government agency to submit to Congress each decision or regulation adopted under a program. Instead of the decision going into effect, action is blocked for a set time—typically 60 congressional working days—while Congress studies it. A majority of both Houses, or either House, or even a single committee, is authorized to veto the action during that period.

Such intrusive devices infringe on the Executive's constitutional duty to faithfully execute the laws. They also authorize Congressional action that has the effect of legislation while denying the President the opportunity to exercise his veto. Legislative vetoes thereby circumvent the President's role in the legislative process established by Article I, Section 7 of the Constitution.

These are fundamental constitutional issues. The Attorney General is seeking a definitive judgment on them from the courts, but no immediate resolution is in prospect. Pending a decision by the Supreme Court, it is my view, and that of the Attorney General, that these legislative veto provisions are unconstitutional.

. . .

I urge Congress to. avoid including legislative veto provisions in legislation so that confrontations can be avoided. For areas where Congress feels special oversight of regulations or other actions is needed, I urge the adoption of "report-and-wait" provisions instead of legislative vetoes. Under such a provision, the Executive "reports" a proposed action to Congress and "waits" for a specified period before putting it into effect. This waiting period permits a dialogue with Congress to work out disagreements and gives Congress the opportunity to pass legislation, subject to my veto, to block or change the Executive action. . . .

As for legislative vetoes over the execution of programs already prescribed in legislation and in bills I must sign for other reasons, the Executive Branch will generally treat them as "report-and-wait" provisions. In such a case, if Congress subsequently adopts a resolution to veto an Executive action, we will give it serious consideration, but we will not, under our reading of the Constitution, consider it legally binding.

5. President Reagan Protests Legislative Vetoes After *Chadha*

Source: Pub. Papers, 1984 (II), at 1056-57

In signing H.R. 5713 into law, I note that seven of its provisions purport to limit my authority, and the authority of the affected department or agency heads, to use funds otherwise appropriated by this bill, unless the Committees on Appropriations of both the House of Representative and the Senate approve of those expenditures. . . .

I fully recognize the interest of Congress and its committees in preserving oversight and accountability over the discretion Congress grants to the executive in such important areas as the obligation of appropriations. I do believe, however, that the time has come, with more than a year having passed since the Supreme Court's decision in *Chadha*, to make clear that legislation containing legislative veto devices that comes to me for my approval or disapproval will be implemented in a manner consistent with the *Chadha* decision. I strongly urge Congress to discontinue the inclusion of such devices in legislation, because doing so serves no constructive purpose after *Chadha* beyond introducing confusion and ambiguity into the process by which the executive's obligations are discharged.

6. NASA Agrees to Informal Legislative Vetoes

Source: Letter of Aug. 9, 1984, from NASA Administrator James M. Beggs to the House and Senate Appropriations Committees

Dear Mr. Chairman:

As you are aware, the Supreme Court in 1983 held legislative vetoes to be unconstitutional, and the Department of Justice, in applying that decision to the FY 1985 HUD-Independent Agencies appropriation act (P.L. 98-371), has indicated that provisions for Committee approval to exceed ceilings on certain programs specified in the legislation are unconstitutional.

We have now operated under the present operating plan and reprogramming procedures for several years and have found them to be workable. In light of the constitutional questions raised concerning the legislative veto provisions included in P.L. 98371, however, the House Committee on Appropriations has proposed in H.R. 6040, the FY 1984 general supplemental, deletion of all Committee approval provisions, leaving inflexible, binding funding limitations on several programs. Without some procedure for adjustment, other than a subsequent separate legislative enactment, these ceilings could seriously impact the ability of NASA to meet unforeseen technical changes or problems that are inherent in challenging R&D programs. We believe that the present legislative procedure could be converted by this letter into an informal agreement by NASA not to exceed amounts for Committee designated programs without the approval of the Committees of Appropriations. This agreement would assume that both the statutory funding ceilings and the Committee approval mechanisms would be deleted from the FY 1985 legislation, and that it would not be the normal practice to include either mechanism in future appropriations bills. Further, the agreement would assume that future program ceiling amounts would be identified by the Committees in the Conference Report accompanying NASA's annual appropriations act and confirmed by NASA in its submission of the annual operating plan. NASA would not expend any funds over the ceilings identified in the Conference Report for these programs without the prior approval of the Committees.

We appreciate the support NASA has received from the Committees of both the House and the Senate, and wish to assure the Committees that NASA will comply with any ceilings imposed by the Committees without the need for legislative ceilings which could cause serious damage to NASA's ongoing programs.

/s/ James M. Beggs
Administrator

---

7. Secretary of State Baker Accepts Committee Vetoes

Source: Letter of April 28, 1989,
from Secretary of State Baker
to Speaker Jim Wright

Dear Mr. Speaker:

Pursuant to the bipartisan agreement on Central America between the Executive and the Congress, the Congress has now voted to extend humanitarian assistance to the Nicaraguan Resistance at current levels through February 28, 1990. This assistance has been authorized and appropriated but will not be obligated beyond November 30, 1989, except in the context of consultation among the Executive, the Senate Majority and Minority leaders, the Speaker of the House of Representatives and the Majority and Minority leaders, and the relevant authorization and appropriation committees, and only if affirmed via letters from the Bipartisan Leadership of Congress and the relevant House and Senate authorization and appropriations committees.

This bipartisan accord on Central America represents a unique agreement between the Executive and the Legislative Branches. Thus, it is the intention of the parties that this agreement in no way establishes any precedent for the Executive or the Legislative Branch regarding the authorization and appropriation process.

Sincerely yours,

/s/ James A. Baker, III

III. GRAMM-RUDMAN

The Reagan administration's victory in *Chadha* whetted the appetite of political appointees within the Justice Department, the White House, and the Office of Management and Budget (OMB). They began to press for a "unitary executive" model in which the President would have total control over all executive agencies. Headed for extinction under that model were the independent commissions (Interstate Commerce Commission, Federal Trade Commission, Securities and Exchange Commission, etc.) that Congress had created to be somewhat autonomous from presidential influence. A measure of independence was granted by restricting the President's power to remove the commissioners, giving the commissioners lengthy terms (longer than the President's four-year term), and other statutory protections. The administration would lose the battle for subordinating independent commissions to the President, but its strategy and objectives colored the lawsuits contesting the constitutionality of the Gramm-Rudman Act.

A. The Gramm-Rudman Act

The economic experiment launched by the Reagan administration and approved by Congress in 1981 helped trigger a massive increase in budget deficits. "Supply-side economics" promised the use of tax cuts to stimulate majority economic growth and increase revenues. Instead, budget deficits exploded of the to $150 billion to $200 billion a year. The political situation was near deadlock because Reagan threatened to veto any tax increase passed by Congress. Tax increases were in fact enacted in 1982 and 1984, but the deficits remained huge. An effort by Congress in 1985 to deal with the deficit problem through the regular legislative process collapsed, setting the stage for the complicated mechanics of the Gramm-Rudman Act.

The goal of Gramm-Rudman was to eliminate the deficits gradually over a five-year period. The question remained, however: Who would enforce these deficit targets? Congress was unwilling to delegate enforcement powers to the administration, given its ongoing battles with OMB. One of the early proposals would have authorized the Congressional Budget Office (CBO) to play a coequal role with OMB in reporting economic forecasts. The two agencies would estimate revenues and outlays, determine excess deficits, and estimate economic growth rates. They would also determine whether excess deficits were "statistically significant" and therefore subject to being withheld to stay on target. This process of withholding funds is called "sequestration."

Without holding hearings, the Senate agreed to this complex procedure by adding an amendment to a statute on the public debt. The only hearings were held by the House Committee on Government Operations. Of the four persons invited to testify, only Louis Fisher of the Congressional Research Service examined the constitutionality of Gramm-Rudman. He found that it violated presidential powers and vested unconstitutional powers in the CBO (document 1). After the hearings, Laurence H. Tribe of the Harvard Law School also raised constitutional questions about infringing presidential power and giving executive functions to CBO.

In subsequent drafts of the bill, Congress decided to shift the enforcement powers to the Comptroller General, who is the head of the General Accounting Office. After CBO and OMB made their estimates, the Comptroller General would give due regard to their work but could make whatever changes he thought necessary to draft a sequestration order. The President would have to sign that order with no opportunity for making changes or vetoing it. Although the Comptroller General has some executive duties dating back to 1921, he is generally regarded as an agent of Congress. The Comptroller General is appointed by the President, subject to the advice and consent of the Senate, and can be removed by joint resolution. A joint resolution has to be submitted to the President and can be vetoed, but the removal process at least gives Congress the opportunity to initiate a removal. The Gramm-Rudman statute raised this question: Could Congress delegate executive functions to an officer removable by Congress?

Congress, sufficiently in doubt about the constitutionality of this process, included within the Gramm-Rudman statute a procedure that would guarantee expedited review by the Supreme Court. A case challenging the statute would go first to a three-judge court and from there directly to the Supreme Court. The provision for expedited review seemed to advertise Congress' admission that the statute was highly suspect on constitutional grounds. There was a further danger. If the Court found the role of CBO or GAO to be unconstitutional, that would place the sole power in OMB. Instead of a joint legislative-executive effort, the power would be concentrated in a presidential agency.

To avoid that possibility, Congress added a fallback procedure that would be constitutional while at the same time protecting legislative prerogatives. If the Court declared the sequestration process unconstitutional, the CBO and OMB estimates would be sent to a special committee of Congress responsible for placing the budget cuts in a bill that would have to pass both Houses and be presented to the President. 99 Stat. 1100 (1985). This fallback procedure simplified the task of the Supreme Court. It could declare the delegation of power to the Comptroller General unconstitutional with the confidence that Congress could achieve the same result through constitutional means. President Reagan signed the Gramm-Rudman Act, indicating in his signing statement that he regarded the powers given to the Comptroller General to be unconstitutional (document 2). Both branches decided to sidestep their duties to act constitutionally.

B. Litigation

In the government's brief to the Supreme Court, Solicitor General Charles Fried argued that the constitutional doctrine of separation of powers bars the Comptroller General from participating in the execution of the Gramm-Rudman Act. Fried gave two basic reasons: (1) the Comptroller General "is subject to removal by Congress and indeed is an officer of the Legislative Branch," and (2) the performance of those functions "in a manner that binds the President and the heads of the executive departments and agencies under his control can be undertaken only by the President or by an Officer of the United States who serves at the pleasure of the President." 160 Landmark Briefs 334. Fried pushed a view that would be rejected later by the Court in the independent counsel case: "[T]here must be a unitary, vigorous, and independent Executive who is responsible directly to the people, not to Congress (except by impeachment)." Id. at 336. Finally, Fried took a swipe at the independent commissions in a footnote: "There is no occasion here to consider the current soundness of the premises underlying *Humphrey's Executor* [which placed some restraints on the President's removal power over commissioners in independent commissions]. As the district court concluded . . . , developments since *Humphrey's Executor* do, however, appear to have cast a shadow over those premises." Id. at 367, n. 32. During oral argument, Fried told the Court that the administration's position did not challenge the constitutionality of the independent agencies, but that point was sharply questioned by Justice O'Connor.

In declaring Gramm-Rudman unconstitutional, the Court focused on the powers given to the Comptroller General. Under the sequestration process, he would receive budget estimates from OMB and CBO and proceed to draft the sequestration order, making whatever adjustments to the OMB/CBO figures he thought necessary. The Court held that the sequestration duties of the Comptroller General were executive in nature and that Congress could not vest those functions in an officer over which it had removal power. Bowsher v. Synar, 478 U.S. 714 (1986).

DOCUMENTS

1. Fisher Testifies on Constitutional Problems With Gramm-Rudman

Source: The Balanced Budget and Emergency Deficit Control Act of 1985: Hearing Before the House Comm. on Government Operations, 99th Cong., lst Sess. 202-208, 212-13 (1985)

Mr. [Louis] Fisher [Congressional Research Service]. . . .

Mr. Chairman, . . . the debt-limit bill raises profound questions about executive-legislative relations and budget control. . . .

The Budget and Accounting Act of 1921 placed upon the President the responsibility to prepare and submit a national budget. Congress did not attempt to tell the President what should be in his budget. The very point of an executive budget was to present precisely what the President considered necessary and appropriate for the country.

1. *Dictating the President's Budget.* H.J. Res. 372 [Gramm-Rudman] allows the President to set budget outlays and federal revenues "at such levels as (he) may consider most desirable and necessary." However, the bill also requires that the President's budget be prepared "in such a manner as to ensure that the deficit for such fiscal year shall not exceed the maximum deficit amount specified" in the bill.

I doubt that Congress can compel the President to submit a budget with a particular deficit. While it is true that the U.S. Code contains numerous directives regarding the President's budget with regard to format, deadlines, and other matter, I do not believe that Congress can tell the President what deficit to include. An executive budget expresses what the President wants, not what Congress wants.

5. *Role of CBO.* H.J. Res. 372 calls upon the Director of the Congressional Budget Office to produce jointly with the Director of the Office and Management and Budget a report on economic forecasts. They are to estimate revenues and outlays, determine excess deficits, and estimate economic growth rate. They also determine whether excess deficits are "statistically significant" (greater than 5 percent of the maximum deficit allowed, except for 7 percent for fiscal 1986). These reports therefore constitute a key trigger on presidential action to cut indexed amounts for entitlements or to sequester funds.

Under *Buckley v. Valeo*, 424 U.S. 1 (1976), it appears to be unconstitutional for Congress to impose substantive and enforcement responsibilities on legislative officers, which the CBO Director clearly is. The inclusion of CBO is apparently an effort to counter the criticism of too much power in the hands of OMB, but this provision adds further doubts about the constitutionality of H.J. Res. 372.

2. Reagan Challenges Constitutionality of Gramm-Rudman

Source: Pub. Papers, 1985
(II), at 1471-72

Today I have signed H.J. Res. 372, which increases the statutory limit on the public debt and includes the Balanced Budget and Emergency Deficit Control Act of 1985, also known as the Gramm-Rudman-Hollings amendment. . . .

In signing this bill, I am mindful of the serious constitutional questions raised by some of its provisions. The bill assigns a significant role to the Director of the Congressional Budget Office and the Comptroller General in calculating the budget estimates that trigger the operative provisions of the bill. Under the system of separated powers established by the Constitution, however, executive functions may only be performed by officers in the executive branch. The Director of the Congressional Budget Office and the Comptroller General are agents of Congress, not officers in the executive branch. The bill itself recognizes this problem and provides procedures for testing the constitutionality of the dubious provisions. The bill also provides a constitutionally valid alternative mechanism should the role of the Director of the Congressional Budget Office and the Comptroller General be struck down. It is my hope that these outstanding constitutional questions can be promptly resolved.

IV. THE ITEM VETO

The explosion of deficits in the 1980s prompted members of Congress to consider some form of item-veto power. There were many options, but legislators generally wanted a statutory solution rather than having to mount an uphill and uncertain battle for a constitutional amendment. Although legislators continued to talk about giving the President an "item veto" by statute, this was always a misnomer. A true item veto would allow the President to strike sections and language *before* the bill became law. That is the procedure available to 43 governors. Such a change, most lawmakers and executive officials agreed, would require an amendment to the Constitution. The complicated task was to give the President a comparable power by statute by allowing him to cancel items *after* they became law.

President Ronald Reagan, by persistently and dramatically advocating the item veto, supplied the major force for change. Year in and year out, he urged Congress to act. Members recognized that they were being asked to shift some of the power of the purse to the President. The methods for expanding presidential power ranged the gamut from an "inherent item veto" to altering the President's existing authority to rescind (cancel) appropriations. These ideas, discussed below, culminated in the Line Item Veto Act of 1996.

A. The Inherent Item Veto

One of the early proposals, popularized by the *Wall Street Journal* in 1987, was to recognize that the President already had an "inherent item veto." Advocates of this power argued that the growth of "omnibus" appropriations bills and the practice of adding unrelated "riders" to bills had so eroded the President's original veto power that he could act in self-defense by vetoing individual items.

In 1988, the Office of Legal Counsel in the Justice Department released a lengthy analysis of the inherent item veto, concluding that the Constitution does not allow the President to veto portions of a bill while signing the remainder into law (document 1). The idea that the Justice Department, typically a defender of presidential power, would throw cold water on a proposal designed to augment executive authority was quite extraordinary.

Senator Robert Dole (R-Kans.), running for President in 1988, said that although no President had used the power, "it might be worth a try." If it meant provoking a constitutional test when he received a bill "larded with fat, I will do it. Then we'll let the courts decide." Cong. Q. Weekly Rept., May 14, 1988, at 1284. Dole's presidential bid failed, but other legislators urged President Reagan in his last two years and President Bush during his term to use the inherent item veto and provoke a court test. However, Bush announced in 1992 that his constitutional advisers had convinced him that there was no legal support for an inherent item veto. Pub. Papers, 1992 (II), at 479.

B. Expedited and Enhanced Rescission

The Impoundment Control Act of 1974 authorized the President to submit proposals to Congress to rescind (cancel) appropriations. If Congress failed to support his recommendations during a 45-day review period, agencies would have to release the funds for obligation and expenditure. Over the years, many legislators criticized this process as erecting too high a hurdle for the President.

In 1992, 1993, and 1994, the House of Representatives passed legislation to make it easier for the President to rescind funds. Instead of allowing Congress to ignore the President's rescission proposals, "expedited rescission" required at least one House to vote on the President's recommendations. The Senate took no action on these bills, focusing on a rival procedure called "enhanced rescission." The Senate wanted to allow presidential proposals for rescissions to become law unless Congress passed a bill disapproving them. Of course the President could then veto the disapproval bill, forcing Congress to muster a two-thirds majority in each House to override the President. Of the two proposals, enhanced rescission shifted much more power to the President than expedited rescission.

With the Republican victories in the 1994 elections and the drafting of the "Contract with America" by House Republicans, Congress had the votes and the legislative platform to pass strong item-veto powers for the President. On January 12, 1995, the House Committee on Government Reform and Oversight and the Senate Committee on Governmental Affairs held joint hearings to consider enhanced rescission. This legislation passed the House in February.

On January 24, 1995, the Senate Judiciary Committee held hearings on proposals to give the President an item veto. Walter Dellinger, head of the Office of Legal Counsel in the Justice Department, testified on a range of issues, including the House bill on enhanced rescission. He expressed concern that some of the words used in the House bill—particularly "veto" and "repeal"—could make it difficult for the two branches to defend the statute in court (document 2). Congress made numerous changes in the bill to address this problem, but by the time the issue was decided by the Supreme Court in 1998, the statute had never shaken its reputation for allowing the President to "repeal" law in violation of the Constitution.

C. Separate Enrollment

In 1995, the Senate wrestled with two competing rescission proposals. Senator John McCain advocated enhanced rescission, while Senator Pete Dominici supported expedited rescission. The committees of jurisdiction—Senate Budget and Senate Governmental Affairs—couldn't decide which version to recommend. They reported both versions, inviting a floor fight to see which one would prevail.

The McCain and Domenici bills were yanked in favor of a substitute that had been considered and rejected a decade back: "separate enrollment." This procedure would convert the present 13 appropriations bills into about ten thousand bills. A clerk would take an appropriations bill after it had passed both Houses and break it into separate paragraphs, sections, and numbers, with each part made into a bill and presented to the President. The Senate, anxious to pass something, embraced separate enrollment on March 23.

Senator Spencer Abraham flagged a serious constitutional problem. Would the individual bills fashioned by the clerk be "bills" as contemplated by the Constitution? Although each House had passed the larger bill, could it be argued that they had also passed the mini-bills? To remove this constitutional shadow, Senator Abraham successfully offered an amendment to have the individual bills returned to each chamber to be voted on en bloc. 141 Cong. Rec. 8883, 8905 (1995).

When a bill passes both Houses in different forms, conferees are appointed to work out a compromise. Republicans were slow to go to conference because they did not want to give President Clinton authority that he could exploit in 1995 and 1996 for political, partisan reasons (which is what he, or any other President, would do). By not acting, however, Republicans were vulnerable to the charge of hypocricy. If they thought the President should have an item veto to cut waste, why not produce a bill for his signature?

D. The Line Item Veto Act

The logjam broke in 1996. Dole, now a declared candidate for President, wanted to display his leadership abilities by getting a bill through Congress. Under these pressures, the bill popped out of conference. The conferees agreed basically with the House version: enhanced rescission. The new law put the burden on Congress to disapprove presidential rescission proposals within a 30-day period. Along with rescission of discretionary appropriations, the President could cancel any new item of direct spending (entitlements) and certain limited tax benefits.

Opponents of the measure warned that it will "take the appropriation process out of . . . [Congress and] transport it down to 1600 Pennsylvania Avenue." 141 Cong. Rec. 3455 (1995) (Cong. Kanjorski). Supporters of the Act described the shift of power as salutary. For John McCain: "Given Congress' predilection for unfunded and/or pork barrel spending, omnibus spending bills, and continuing resolutions, it would seem only prudent and constitutional to provide the President with functional veto power." 141 Cong. Rec. 102 (1995).

Clinton received the bill and signed it into law on April 9, 1996. He said that the "modern congressional practice of presenting the President with omnibus legislation reduces the President's ability to play the role in enacting laws that the Constitution intended. This new authority brings us closer to the Founders' view of an effective executive role in the legislative process." Pub. Papers, 1996 (I), at 559. To ease passage of the bill, the conferees decided to deny Clinton access to the authority during the remainder of 1996, making it available to whoever won the election. Many Republicans assumed that their candidate, Bob Dole, would be the first beneficiary of item-veto authority. Instead, Clinton won reelection. His use of the item veto had a very modest effect on the federal budget. Cancellations for fiscal year 1998 came to $355 million out of a total budget of $1.7 billion. Total savings, over a five-year period, fell short of $600 million.

E. Punting to the Courts

As though doubting their own legislation, members of Congress included in the Line Item Veto Act a procedure giving legislators and private individuals an opportunity—through expedited review—to challenge the constitutionality of the statute. Challenges would go directly from a district court to the Supreme Court. Senator Byrd, a strong opponent of the bill, objected also to expedited review. Congress, he said, should resolve constitutional issues within its own chambers rather than toss them to the courts (document 3). Some members in the House hoped the courts would protect legislative prerogatives and "save this Congress from itself," while others regarded constitutional issues as solely for the courts, not for Congress (document 4).

In 1997, a district court held that the Line Item Veto Act was unconstitutional because it violated the legislative procedures set forth in Article I. The court argued that presidential cancellations were equivalent to repeal, and that repeal could be accomplished only through the regular legislative process: passage by both Houses and presentment of a bill to the President. Byrd v. Raines, 956 F.Supp. 25 (D.D.C. 1997). On appeal, the Supreme Court ruled that the plaintiffs (members of Congress) lacked standing to bring the case. Raines v. Byrd, 521 U.S. 811 (1997).

The following year, a district court found standing for private plaintiffs and held the statute unconstitutional. City of New York v. Clinton, 985 F. Supp. 168 (D.D.C. 1998). When the Supreme Court heard oral arguments in this case, Solicitor General Seth Waxman contended that, unlike a "true line item veto, which everybody understands is unconstitutional," enhanced rescission legislation does not run afoul of Article I procedures. Nevertheless, the Supreme Court affirmed the district court's ruling, holding that the cancellation authority represented the "repeal" of law that could be accomplished only through the regular legislative process, including bicameralism and presentment. In his dissent, Justice Scalia noted that Congress "succeeded in faking out the Supreme Court" by dubbing its handiwork "The Line Item Veto Act." Clinton v. City of New York, 524 U.S. 417, 469 (1998).

Through this lengthy procedure, legislative and spending prerogatives were returned to Congress, but not because legislators were willing to defend their own institution. It took another branch to do the constitutional analysis that Congress should have performed by itself.

The matter is now back in Congress. Constitutional amendments have again been introduced to grant the President item-veto authority. For a statutory fix, bills rely on expedited rescission and separate enrollment. Meanwhile, the economic condition that popularized the item veto—massive deficits—has been replaced not only by budget surpluses but surpluses "as far as the eye can see."

DOCUMENTS

1. OLC Rejects the Inherent Item Veto

Source: 12 Ops. O.L.C. 128 (1988)

. . . Our review . . . of the relevant constitutional materials persuades us that there is no constitutional requirement that a "Bill" must be limited to one subject. The text and structure of Article I weigh heavily against any such conclusion. Moreover, historically "Bills" have been made by Congress to include more than one item or subject, and no President has viewed such instruments as constituting more than one bill for purposes of the veto. Indeed, the Framers foresaw the possibility that Congress might employ "the practice of tacking foreign matter to money bills," but gave no indication that this practice was inconsistent with their understanding of the term "Bill." Nor, we are constrained to conclude, does the recent commentary on this question provide persuasive support for an inherent item veto power in the President. . . .

We can discern nothing in the text or structure of the Constitution suggesting that the President possesses such enhanced authority. With respect to enrolled bills or any other completed legislative instrument, the Constitution authorizes the President only to "approve . . . *it*" or "not." (emphasis added). The Constitution does not suggest that the President may approve "parts of it" or indicate any presidential prerogative to delete or alter or revise the bill presented. . . .

Is it possible that the Founders, while debating the nature of the Presidential veto, would refrain from giving him an absolute veto, and yet simply assume that he would be able to veto portions of a measure and sign the remainder into law [thus exercising an absolute veto over items]? It seems inconceivable that such a feature of the President's veto power would have gone unremarked at the Constitutional Convention.

. . . On balance, the evidence indicates that the Framers did not intend to limit the contents of a bill. The early historical practice of Congress was to pass bills containing numerous items of appropriation. . . . [And] although Presidents have exercised the veto power differently, they have been unanimous in the view that they were without authority to approve or disapprove parts of a bill.

2. Dellinger Warns About Words

Source: The Line-Item Veto: A Constitutional Approach: Hearing before the Senate Committee on the Judiciary, 104th Cong., 1st Sess. 49 (1995)

[H.R. 2 would grant the President enhanced rescission over appropriations and limited tax benefits.] It does so by purporting to authorize the President to "veto" targeted tax benefits after they become law, thus resulting in their "repeal." . . . The use of the terms "veto" and "repeal" is constitutionally problematic. Article I, § 7 of the Constitution provides that the President only can exercise his "veto" power before a provision becomes law. As for the word "repeal," it suggests that the President is being given authorization to change existing law on his own. This arguably would violate the plain textual provisions of Article I, § 7 of the Constitution, governing the manner in which federal laws are to made and altered. To avoid these constitutional shoals, we believe that H.R. 2 should be recast so that it eliminates the word "veto" from the targeted tax benefit provision, and confers on the President the power to *suspend* (rather than "repeal") such benefits. . . .

3. Byrd Objects to Expedited Review

Source: 142 Cong. Rec. S2942-43 (daily ed. March 27, 1996)

Constitutional problems in the bill? Proponents say not to worry. Section 3 authorizes expedited review of constitutional challenges. Any member of Congress or any individual adversely affected by the item veto bill may bring an action, in the U.S. District Court for the District of Columbia, for declaratory judgment and injunctive relief on the ground that a provision violates the Constitution. . . .

Evidently the authors of this legislation had substantial concern about the constitutionality of their handiwork. A provision for expedited review to resolve constitutional issues is not boilerplate in most bills. You may remember that when we included a provision for expedited review in the Gramm-Rudman-Hollings Act of 1985, the result was a Supreme Court opinion that held that the procedure giving the Comptroller General the power to determine sequestration of funds violated the Constitution.

Why are we trying to pass a bill that raises such serious and substantial constitutional questions? We should be resolving these questions on our own. All of us take an oath of office to support and defend the Constitution. During the process of considering a bill, it is our our duty to identify—and correct—constitutional problems. . . . It is irresponsible to simply punt to the courts, hoping that the judiciary will somehow catch our mistakes.

4. Members Look to Courts for Constitutional Analysis

Source: 142 Cong. Rec. H3010 (daily ed. March 28, 1996)

[Congresswoman Marge Roukema (R-N.J.)]: We all recognize the genius of the framers of our U.S. Constitution. They did not want a king or a dictator or an oligarchy—a small group ruling the Nation. So they wrote the Constitution based on a delicate system of checks and balances and the separation of powers doctrine. . . .

I am convinced, however, that the Supreme Court of the United States will save this Congress from itself. This propos[al] violates the foundation of our Constitution and will be overturned at its first judicial challenge. . . .

[Congressman William Clinger (R-Pa.)]: It has been suggested that there are a number of reasons why we should not enact this legislation. It has been suggested that it is unconstitutional. It is not really our job to determine what is constitutional or what is not unconstitutional, but the fact is that we do provide severability in this measure. If a provision, any provision of the matter is considered to be unconstitutional, it can be stricken and the rest of the matter can stand.

V. INDEPENDENT COUNSELS

The Court's decision in *Bowsher* encouraged the Reagan administration to push its theory of a "unitary executive" even farther. That theory would be exploded two years later when the Court, with only one dissent, upheld the office of independent counsel (called special prosecutor in earlier years). The Reagan administration argued strongly that the independent counsel undermined the President's constitutional authority to supervise enforcement actions within the executive branch, but in both 1983 and 1987 President Reagan signed reauthorization bills.

In 1992, Congress refused to extend the authority, in large part because of Republican objections to independent counsel Lawrence Walsh's investigation of the Iran-Contra affair. Nevertheless, the office was reauthorized in 1994 to permit investigation of the Clinton White

House.   This cycle led to fresh complaints about the conduct of independent counsel Kenneth Starr, and Congress once again refused to reauthorize the office.

A. Origin of Statute

The special prosecutor statute, as discussed in Section I of this chapter, emerged from the politics of Watergate.   What began as a bungled attempt to burglarize the Democratic national party headquarters on June 17, 1972, quickly blossomed into a crisis that would engulf the Nixon administration.   When the magnitude of the scandal became apparent, Attorney General Elliot Richardson (with Nixon's support) appointed Archibald Cox to investigate the affair.   Nixon later fired Cox but—under heavy public pressure—agreed to a replacement, Leon Jaworski.

During the Ford administration, Congress considered a bill to establish a permanent office of special prosecutor.   Attorney General Edward H. Levi testified in 1976 that the office was of "questionable constitutionality."   He particularly disliked the proposal to place the power of appointment in a body of federal judges.   Provision for Special Prosecutor: Hearings Before the House Comm. on the Judiciary, 94th Cong., 2d Sess. 33-34 (1976).   Michael M. Uhlmann, an Assistant Attorney General, also testified that the proposal was unconstitutional, especially because the duty to enforce a criminal law was "the very core of 'executive functions.'" Watergate Reorganization and Reform Act of 1975: Hearings Before the Senate Comm. on Government Operations, 94th Cong., 1st Sess. 3 (1975).

Nevertheless, President Carter supported a court-appointed, temporary special prosecutor (document 1).   Assistant Attorney General John Harmon subsequently accepted the constitutionality of a special prosecutor.   However, one of the pending bills would have allowed the special court of federal judges to also remove the special prosecutor, a provision that Harmon said would present a serious constitutional question.   Special Prosecutor Legislation: Hearings Before the House Comm. on the Judiciary, 95th Cong., 1st Sess. 2 (1977).   Congress fixed that problem by placing the removal power with the Attorney General, subject to specific causes established by statute.   When President Carter signed the legislation establishing an office of special prosecutor, he considered the office a necessary response to the lessons learned from the Watergate affair.   Pub. Papers, 1978 (II), at 1854-55.

B. Reauthorizations

The office of special prosecutor had an initial statutory life of five years. When it was reauthorized in January 1983 for another five years, President Reagan signed the legislation and indicated no constitutional misgivings about the office. At that time, the statute had been used infrequently and there was little reason for the Justice Department or the White House to mount an all-out attack. The 1983 extension changed the office from "special prosecutor" to "independent counsel" and altered the ground for removal from "extraordinary impropriety" to "good cause." 96 Stat. 2039, 2042 (1983).

On June 23, 1983, the Supreme Court handed down *Chadha*. Three years later it decided *Bowsher*. Those two decisions gave the Justice Department grounds to believe that a successful legal challenge could be mounted against the independent counsel. After years of support from two administrations, the Reagan administration began to actively oppose the office of independent counsel in 1987. By that time the office of independent counsel had become a thorn in the side of the Reagan administration. It had been used to investigate the Iran-Contra affair and to investigate major figures within the White House, including Michael Deaver and Edwin Meese III.

During hearings in 1987, Assistant Attorney General John Bolton objected that independent counsels were executive officers carrying out prosecutorial functions and therefore had to be under the direction and control of the President. Independent Counsel Amendments Acts of 1987: Hearings Before the House Comm. on the Judiciary, 100th Cong., 1st Sess. 429-33 (1987). Bolton repeated his constitutional critique to the Senate Committee on Governmental Affairs (document 2).

Nevertheless, when the bill to reauthorize the independent counsel reached President Reagan later that year, he did not exercise his veto power. The President's acquiescence is hardly surprising, for the bill reached his desk in the midst of the Iran-Contra scandal. A veto in the context of Iran-Contra would have been too easily interpreted as an effort to conceal administration misdeeds (document 3). Reagan signed the bill, but expressed "strong doubts" about its constitutionality (document 4). When the constitutionality of the independent counsel was litigated, the Reagan administration filed an amicus brief pointing to constitutional defects in the statute.

C. The Statute Is Upheld

In 1988, an extraordinary 7-1 decision upheld the constitutionality of the independent counsel. Morrison v. Olson, 487 U.S. 654 (1988). The decision was remarkable both for the lopsided majority and because Chief

Justice Rehnquist wrote it. In previous decisions Rehnquist frequently seemed to be a defender of executive power. The Court upheld the appointment of the independent counsel by a special panel of federal judges, and also supported statutory limits that required the Attorney General to remove the independent counsel only "for cause." Moreover, unlike *Bowsher*, the independent counsel statute "does not involve an attempt by Congress to increase its own powers at the expense of the Executive Branch." Id. at 694.

Whereas Congress signalled in advance the constitutional infirmity of Gramm-Rudman, by authorizing expedited review by the courts and including a fallback provision, comparable language did not appear in the original special prosecutor law or its later extensions. Instead, Congress held repeated hearings to give careful consideration to constitutional requirements (document 5).

D. Post-*Morrison* Developments

The statute was again up for reauthorization in 1992. Republicans, angry with the investigation by independent counsel Lawrence E. Walsh into the Iran-Contra affair, blocked the reauthorization. Critics argued "that some people given an unlimited budget and subpoena power, become so convinced of the virtue of their cause that means and ends can become confused." Jacob A. Stein, Four Probes Endanger the Executive Branch, Natl. L. J., June 19, 1995, at A-21. Along these lines, Republicans complained that Walsh had spent tens of millions of the taxpayers dollars over more than six years, and had relatively little to show for it in the way of prosecutions of the principal defendants. In fact, the Walsh investigation produced a number of significant convictions and indictments, but many of those were nullified by President Bush's pardon orders and the decision of Congress to grant immunity to certain individuals.

With the election of Bill Clinton, Republicans reversed course and began to support reauthorization for the purpose of investigating Clinton's investment in an Arkansas land development venture (Whitewater Development Co.). Because the law had already lapsed, Attorney General Janet Reno had to rely on her own authority, on January 20, 1994, to name a special prosecutor, Robert B. Fiske, Jr., to investigate Whitewater. But, on June 30, 1994, the independent counsel law was extended for five years. The new law also gave the federal court panel the option of reappointing Fiske or selecting someone else. The panel selected a replacement, former Republican Solicitor General Kenneth W. Starr.

Just as Republicans castigated Walsh for his investigation of Reagan and Bush, so was Starr pummeled by Democrats for his probe of Clinton. Matters reached a crescendo when Starr reported to Congress that Clinton may have committed impeachable offenses (a subject considered in the next case study). So poisoned was the political atmosphere that Congress decided not to reauthorize the independent counsel statute. It expired on June 30, 1999.

Interestingly, when the Senate Judiciary Committee held hearings in 1999 on the independent counsel, not only did the Clinton administration recommend against reauthorizing the statute (document 6), but so did Starr (document 7). Although the political climate turned against reauthorization, the institutional problem persists: How can the Justice Department, given its conflict of interest, credibly investigate the President and other high-ranking executive branch officials?

DOCUMENTS

1. Carter Supports Special Prosecutor

Source: Pub. Papers, 1977
(I), at 786, 788

To complement the Ethics in Government Act, I am also announcing my support for legislation which would require appointment of a Special Prosecutor to investigate and prosecute alleged offenses by high government officials. . . . the Special Prosecutor would be appointed by a specially empaneled court. He or she could be removed from office only upon a finding of extraordinary impropriety or incapacity. . . .

This approach will eliminate all appearance of high-level interference in sensitive investigations and prosecutions. The American people must be assured that no one, regardless of position, is above the law.

2. Reagan Official Testifies Against Independent Counsel

Source: Oversight of the Independent Counsel Statute: Hearings Before the Senate Comm. on Governmental Affairs, 100th Cong., 1st Sess. 8-9 (1987)

Mr. [John R.] BOLTON [Assistant Attorney General, Legislative Affairs]. . . .

I would like to stress at the outset that we are not here today to oppose reauthorization [of the independent counsel]. We are here today to support reauthorization of a constitutional statute and we look forward to the opportunity to work with the subcommittee to fashion such a statute.

. . .

For the past 14 years, this Department has had an opportunity to testify on various occasions about independent counsel statutes and different kinds of proposals [and] with a single exception, on every such occasion our testimony has included questions concerning the constitutionality of legislation that would remove the function of prosecuting crimes from Executive Branch control. . . .

Mr. Chairman, our testimony summarizes the extensive constitutional learning that we believe applies in this case, beginning with *Buckley v. Valeo*, a case where the Supreme Court in 1976 held that the appointment mechanism of the Federal Election Campaign Act as then written, which vested appointment of four of the six members of the Federal Election Commission in officers of Congress was unconstitutional.

The court reasoned in that case that granting civil law enforcement authority to the Federal Election Commission when its members were not appointed by the President and confirmed by the Senate as required by the Constitution, was invalid.

Surely here where criminal law-enforcement authority is vested in the independent counsel, the appointment mechanism should conform to the

Constitution, which we believe requires both Executive appointment and Executive control over the work of the independent counsel.

3. Solicitor General Fried Explains Administration's Reluctance to Challenge the Independent Counsel Statute

Source: Charles Fried, Order and Law 137-40 (1991)

Many conservatives thought the Independent Counsel law was an outrage, but the politics were such that we were scared to challenge it. The challenges would have come most naturally in Iran-Contra and in respect to Attorney General Meese's own involvement with the Wedtech scandal. But these were terrible cases in which to challenge a law that the public was told guaranteed impartial justice. Accordingly, one of the most imaginative of the administration's legal officials, Richard Willard, proposed a solution that would both satisfy the public and save some shadow of the President's rights: to offer the Independent Counsels chosen by the court in accordance with the Act parallel appointments in the Department of Justice under departmental regulations guaranteeing them appropriate independence and discretion. Thus a challenge would not reach the courts, since every action such a prosecutor took—the indictments he signed, the subpoenas he issued—would be doubly valid, based in the Independent Counsel law and the President's inherent powers, and so no one could raise the separation-of-powers claim to question the prosecutor's authority. Lawrence Walsh and James McKay, the best and most conscientious of the court-appointed Independent Counsels, were most interested in getting about their work, and so accepted the arrangement. As a result, the Iran-Contra and Meese investigations were immunized from constitutional challenge. Alexia Morrison, the Independent Counsel in the EPA-Olson matter, would not accept the parallel appointment, and the stage was set for an inevitable challenge. Though the context of this case was far better, there was

still the political implication that we were just looking for a way to protect the President and his cronies. I dreaded the response of the courts in this atmosphere. But Ted Olson was the defendant, and there was no way for me to keep the case out of the courts.

4. Reagan Questions Constitutionality of the Independent Counsel

Source: Pub. Papers, 1987 (II), at 1524

Like its predecessors, H.R. 2939, the Independent Counsel Reauthorization Act of 1987, raises constitutional issues of the most fundamental and enduring importance to the Government of the United States. . . .

I fully endorse the goal manifested in the Independent Counsel Act of ensuring public confidence in the impartiality and integrity of criminal law investigations of high-level executive branch officials. Indeed, despite constitutional misgivings, my administration has faithfully and consistently complied with all of the requirements of the act. Even as the constitutional issues grew more clear, aided by the pronouncements of the Supreme Court in *INS* v. *Chadha* in 1983 and *Bowsher* v. *Synar* in 1986, we took extraordinary measures to protect against constitutional challenge the work of the more recently appointed independent counsel by offering each of them appointments in the Department of Justice.

Continuance of these independent counsel investigations was deemed important to public confidence in our government. Nevertheless, this goal, however sound, may not justify disregard for the carefully crafted restraints spelled out in the Constitution. An officer of the United States exercising executive authority in the core area of law enforcement necessarily, under our constitutional scheme, must be subject to executive branch appointment, review, and removal. There is no other constitutionally permissible alternative. . . .

Action on this bill, however, cannot await the resolution of [a case pending in the D.C. Circuit]. In order to ensure that public confidence in government not be eroded while the courts are in the process of deciding these questions, I am taking the extraordinary step of signing this bill despite my very strong doubts about its constitutionality.

---

5. Congress Interprets the Constitution

Source: Paul Gewirtz, Congress, As Well As Courts, Must Make Constitutional Law, Hartford Courant, July 24, 1988, at C3

Many have praised the U.S. Supreme Court's decision last month upholding the special prosecutor law, but the real credit belongs more to Congress than to the court itself.

The law was upheld because Congress did something that legislatures often fail to do. Rather than pass the buck to the courts, Congress carefully considered possible constitutional objections at the time it adopted the legislation. It wrote a balanced statute that took account of reasonable constitutional concerns and tried to minimize them.

In the end, the Supreme Court deferred to that effort. Its action illustrates the role legislatures can play in constitutional decision-making.

. . . Congress held hearings that assessed the views of a broad range of constitutional law experts. The drafters of the legislation sought to address many of the constitutional concerns raised—when the law was passed and through subsequent refinements.

The statute does not create special prosecutors who are altogether independent. It preserves a role for the president and attorney general in both the appointment and possible removal of special prosecutors. In addition, it avoids an excessive role for the other branches of government.

6. Attorney General Janet Reno Testifies Against Renewing the Independent Counsel Statute

Source: The Future of the Independent Counsel Statute: Hearings before the Senate Comm. on the Judiciary, 106th Cong., 1st Sess. 243-45 (1999)

Attorney General RENO.

. . . .

In 1993, I testified in support of the statute. I said that the law had been a good one, helping to restore public confidence in our system's ability to investigate wrongdoing by high-level Executive Branch officials. I believed then—and, Senator Lieberman, I believe now—that there are times when an Attorney General will have a conflict of interest. I also believed then as I do now that to keep the public's faith in impartial justice that in such a case someone other than the Attorney General must sometimes be put in charge of the investigation, and I think that is an important consideration.

. . . I have come to believe, after much reflection and with great reluctance, that the Independent Counsel Act is structurally flawed and that those flaws cannot be corrected within our constitutional framework.

In my view, the Act has failed to accomplish its primary goal—the enhancement of public confidence in the fair and impartial administration of the criminal law. This is so in large part because the Act requires the Attorney General to make key decisions at several critical stages of the process. . . .

. . . [A]n Attorney General, after all, is a member of the President's Cabinet, and as such his or her decisions will inevitably be second-guessed and criticized, no matter what decision is made.

On the other side of the equation, the decisions of an Independent Counsel are no less subject to criticism and second-guessing. Once again, I am not saying that this is fair or unfair, justified or unjustified, right or wrong. I am just saying that it is natural and that this climate of criticism and controversy weakens rather than strengthens the public's confidence in the impartial exercise of prosecutorial power, and that at the end of the day undercuts the purpose of the Act. . . .

    . . . In trying to ensure independence, the statute creates a new category of prosecutors who have no practical limits on their time or budgets. They have no competing public duties and no need to make difficult decisions about how to allocate scarce resources. . . .

An Independent Counsel typically is charged with investigating one person, and so all of his or her energy, ingenuity and resources are pointed in one direction. Add to this the fact that an Independent Counsel may labor in the public spotlight and under the watchful eye of history. An Independent Counsel will be judged not on the basis of a broad track record, but on one case alone. If the counsel uncovers nothing or fails to secure an indictment and conviction, some may conclude that he or she has wasted both time and money.

All of these factors combine, I believe, to create a strong incentive for the Independent Counsel to do what prosecutors should not be artificially pushed to do, that is to prosecute. . . .

---

7. Starr Testifies Against Independent Counsel Reauthorization

Source: The Future of the
Independent Counsel Statute:
Hearings before the Senate Comm.
on the Judiciary, 106th Cong. 1st Sess.
421-24 (1999)

[Independent Counsel Kenneth W. Starr]: . . . The statutory goal . . . is to bypass the administration's conflict of interest, to empower an outsider to investigate and, if appropriate, to prosecute; in other words, to do exactly what the Justice Department would do, but for the disabling conflict. That is the theory.

The reality is more complicated. For one thing, an Independent Counsel must start from scratch. Judge Walsh made this point well in his final report on Iran-Contra. In his words in the report: "[An] Independent Counsel is not an individual put in charge of an ongoing agency. He is a person taken from private practice and told to create a new agency . . . ." Doing so not only takes time; the costs can be substantial.

An Independent Counsel differs from a Justice Department prosecutor in another important respect, . . . the duty to report.

Independent Counsels originally were required to produce final reports discussing, among other things, their reasons for not prosecuting any matters within their jurisdiction. Federal prosecutors do not ordinarily allege improprieties without charging them in court. . . .

The witnesses before this Committee have been virtually unanimous in their opposition to final reports, and I concur in that . . . .

In addition, Independent Counsels are subject to a second reporting requirement that does not apply to ordinary prosecutors. . . . the requirement that an Independent Counsel inform the House of Representatives of particular information that, in the words of the statute, "may constitute grounds for an impeachment."

In our report to the House last fall, we summarized the evidence and its relevance [regarding Clinton's impeachment] . . .

While we did our best to heed this provision, I question its wisdom. For one thing, it is curious to impose the statutory duty on one, and only one, Federal prosecutor. In addition, this responsibility further politicizes Independent Counsel investigations.

To a much greater degree than people realize, the Department of Justice can help or hinder an Independent Counsel. The statute specifically provides that an Independent Counsel, in the words of the statute, may request assistance from the Department of Justice, and the Department of Justice shall provide that assistance, but the Department has the raw power to refuse to provide assistance or to drag its feet. . . .

. . . [T]he Department of Justice, which has incentives to come to the aid of a U.S. Attorney or a regulatory Independent Counsel, has no incentive to help a statutory Independent Counsel. With no institutional defender, Independent Counsels are especially vulnerable to partisan attack. In this fashion, the legislative effort to take politics out of law enforcement sometimes has the ironic effect of further politicizing it.

. . . .

After carefully considering the statute and its consequences, both intended and unintended, I concur with the Attorney General, who has aligned herself with her predecessors. The statute should not be preauthorized.

VI. IMPEACHMENT

The Constitution provides that the President, Vice President, and all civil officers of the United States shall be removed from office upon "Impeachment for, and Conviction of, Treason, Bribery, or other high Crimes and Misdemeanors." The House impeaches by a majority vote; a two-thirds vote of the Senate is needed for conviction.

Other than making the Chief Justice the presiding officer in the Senate after a President has been impeached, the framers excluded the judiciary and the courts have not tried to carve out a role. In 1993, the Supreme Court turned aside a challenge to the impeachment of federal judge Walter Nixon, who objected to the Senate's initial use of a 12-member committee to take testimony and gather evidence. He argued that the Constitution required the full Senate to "try all impeachments" and that "try" includes the taking of evidence and the hearing of testimony. Kenneth Starr, as Solicitor General, wrote a brief supporting the Senate procedure (document 1). Siding with Starr, the Court dismissed the case as a nonjusticiable political question. Nixon v. United States, 506 U.S. 224 (1993).

Legislators decide many key issues, such as the burden of proof. Is it clear and convincing evidence? Preponderance of the evidence? Beyond a reasonable doubt? Lawmakers are at liberty to select whatever test they are comfortable with. The two chambers determine crucial procedural issues, including the right of the accused to confront and cross-examine witnesses and the opportunity of House managers to call live witnesses. Legislators make judgments to accept or exclude evidence, determine issues of relevance and materiality, and Senators decide whether deliberations at the end of the trial should be open or closed.

What are the grounds for impeachment? Treason is defined in Article III, Section 3, of the Constitution, while bribery is generally understood to mean the giving, offering, or taking of rewards as payment for favors. However, there is continuing disagreement about the meaning of "other high Crimes and Misdemeanors." "Other" suggests that high crimes and misdemeanors are of the same order as treason and bribery, but precisely what this clause means is left to the individual interpretations of lawmakers, not courts.

In 1970, Minority Leader Gerald Ford claimed that an impeachable offense "is whatever a majority of the House of Representatives considers it to be at a given moment in history." 116 Cong. Rec. 11913 (1970). That kind of open-ended definition resembles the vague grounds of "maladministration" that James Madison successfully challenged at the Philadelphia convention. Such loose terms meant that the President would effectively serve at the pleasure of Congress. 2 Farrand 65-66, 550. The still undefined contours of the impeachment process were evident in late 1998 and early 1999 when the House impeached and the Senate considered the removal of President Bill Clinton.

A. Only Indictable Crimes?

In the phrase high crimes and misdemeanors, does the word "crimes" apply only to actions indictable in the courts (statutory offenses), or did the framers have in mind something broader, covering abuse of office and "political crimes" against government and society? The more comprehensive definition is widely accepted. At the constitutional convention, Madison said it was indispensable to defend the community against the "incapacity, negligence or perfidy of the chief Magistrate." 2 Farrand 65. In Federalist 65, Alexander Hamilton called the object of impeachment "those offenses which proceed from the misconduct of public men, or, in other words, from the abuse or violation of some public trust. They are of a nature which may with peculiar propriety be denominated POLITICAL, as they relate chiefly to injuries done immediately to the society itself."

Articles of impeachment often refer to behavior that falls short of criminal conduct. Impeachment is widely regarded as a political, not a judicial, act. The purpose is to remove an unfit person from office, not to punish someone for a crime. Impeachment and removal is for the political branches; punishment is done in the courts.

During the impeachment of President Richard Nixon, the impeachment inquiry staff of the House Judiciary Committee prepared a report on "Constitutional Grounds for Presidential Impeachment." The staff, including the future first lady Hillary D. Rodham, concluded that criminality was not essential to impeach and remove a federal official (document 2).

B. Can Congress Censure a President?

Supporters of President Clinton advocated a congressional resolution of censure as a substitute for impeachment and removal. Although Congress is authorized by the Constitution to censure its members for "disorderly Behavior," the act of censuring officials outside the legislative branch raises serious questions of separation of powers.

Some guidance on this issue comes from the Senate's adoption of a resolution in 1834 censuring President Andrew Jackson for assuming "authority and power not conferred by the Constitution, but in derogation of both." This resolution responded to Jackson's decision to remove a Secretary of the Treasury for refusing to transfer the government's deposits from the central U.S. Bank to state banks. The brainchild of the censure resolution was Senator Henry Clay of Kentucky, defeated by Jackson in the presidential election of 1832. Clay was a major sponsor of legislation to recharter the U.S. Bank., a bill that Jackson vetoed. Animosity between two politicians couldn't have run deeper. Jackson, outraged by the censure resolution, retaliated with a lengthy "Protest" (document 3). Three years later, the Senate ordered the censure resolution expunged from the record.

In December 1998, during the impeachment debate on Clinton, the House prevented a vote on a censure resolution offered by Democrats. Speaker-elect Bob Livingston (R-La.) said that censure "is out of the realm of responsibility of the House of Representatives. We have a constitutional responsibility to charge or not charge, impeach or not impeach." Eric Pianin, "Speaker-Elect's Vow Imperils His Hope to Pacify House," Washington Post, December 14, 1998, at A14. The House voted down a procedure that would have allowed a vote on a censure resolution. 144 Cong. Rec. H12031-39 (daily ed. December 19, 1998). Senate Democrats also drafted a censure resolution, but the Senate refused to take it up. The New York Times, February 13, 1999, at A8.

C. From Two Votes to One

From 1789 to 1936, the Senate followed a two-step process: first a two-thirds vote to determine guilt, and then a vote of two-thirds on removal. A Senator could vote for guilt and then decide, for other reasons, not to remove. The judgment on guilt was unaffected by the decision on removal.

Matters changed in 1936 when the Senate considered seven articles of impeachment against Judge Halsted Ritter. The vote on the first six articles was "not guilty." On the seventh article, however, the Senate reached the two-thirds margin for guilty and was about to vote on removal. At that point a Senator argued that there was no need for a separate vote because the Constitution expressly provides that any civil officer found guilty of an impeachable offense "shall be removed." Removal was automatic. The chair agreed with that reasoning and no one challenged his ruling. 80 Cong. Rec. 5607 (1936). Thereafter, whenever the Senate reached a verdict of guilty in an impeachment trial, the person was at the same time removed.

During the Senate's vote on Clinton, several Senators announced that he was guilty as charged (of perjury and obstruction of justice) but that the nature of the offenses did not justify removal. Faced with a single vote, they decided to vote "not guilty" even though they were convinced he was indeed guilty (document 4).

D. Alerting the House

How does the House learn of possible impeachment offenses? During the Watergate investigation, special counsel Leon Jaworski prepared a document indicating that President Nixon had conspired to obstruct justice, committed perjury, and obstructed a criminal investigation. He submitted grand jury evidence—called the "road map"—to the House Judiciary Committee to assist in its impeachment inquiry. The report referred to particular tapes and testimony of witnesses, but did not make conclusions about impeachable conduct.

In 1980, Congress authorized a judicial council to determine that a federal judge has engaged in conduct constituting one or more grounds for impeachment. The Judicial Conference then presents a report to the House of Representatives for possible impeachment proceedings. That statute, 94 Stat. 2035 (1980), was upheld by the D.C. Circuit in 1987. Hastings v. Judicial Conference of U.S., 829 F.2d 91 (D.C. Cir. 1987). The Judicial Conference used this procedure to recommend the impeachment of Judge Alcee L. Hastings, who was impeached by the House and removed by the Senate.

Independent Counsel Kenneth Starr relied on statutory language that directed him to submit to the House of Representatives "any substantial and credible information" about impeachable conduct. 28 U.S.C. § 595(c). His report to the House concluded that acts by President Clinton "may constitute grounds for an impeachment" (document 5).

E. Factors Beyond the Charges

Throughout Clinton's impeachment there were comments by legislators that had nothing to do with the specific articles being drafted and voted on. One issue was Starr's decision to bring impeachment charges to the House. Congressman John Conyers, ranking Democrat on the House Judiciary Committee, said "we are confronted with an overzealous and non-independent counsel report." 144 Cong. Rec. H11782-83 (daily ed. December 18, 1998). To Congressman Edward Markey (D-Mass.), Starr had "twisted and warped his task from one in which he was out to find the truth to one where he went out to get the President and First Lady of this country." Id. at H11822. For many Democrats, the dispute was not over the message but rather the messenger.

Second, legislators wondered whether it was proper for Congress, through the impeachment process, to "overturn" the wishes of the electorate. Senator Kent Conrad, Democrat of North Dakota, said that the process required members of Congress "to make a profound judgment on whether we should overturn the results of a national election. 67 members in this chamber can nullify the votes of the 47 million Americans who voted for President Clinton. That is an awesome power. It must be used with great restraint." 145 Cong. Rec. S1470 (daily ed. February 12, 1999). As Senator Conrad implied, this consideration is not wholly binding, for otherwise no President who had been elected could ever be impeached or removed, regardless of the gravity of the charges brought against him.

Third, many lawmakers thought they should take their cues not from constitutional requirements and the interpretation to be given to "other high crimes and misdemeanors," but rather to what constituents wanted. Under this approach, deference had to be given to public opinion (document 6).

Fourth, by the time the House began debate on the impeachment articles, President Clinton had initiated another bombing attack against Iraq. Democrats objected that the impeachment proceeding should be delayed to avoid undermining Clinton in his capacity as Commander in Chief. Congressman Martin Frost (D-Tex.) referred to "a great bipartisan tradition of supporting the Commander in Chief and supporting our soldiers, sailors, and airmen in the time of war. That tradition is being shattered today by a partisan majority." 144 Cong. Rec. H11779 (daily ed. December 18, 1998). The House actually suspended debate on the impeachment for a day to consider a resolution supporting the American soldiers conducting air operations against Iraq.

F. Conclusions

There is broad agreement that impeachment need not be limited to criminal misconduct, and that the nature of an impeachable offense must be serious abuse of office, including severe "political crimes" and injuries done to government and society. A heavy shadow falls over any effort by Congress to censure a President, particularly as a substitute for impeachment. On all these issues, however, precisely what constitutes a "high crime and misdemeanor" and to what degree partisan and political factors should affect the outcome is a matter left to legislators.

DOCUMENTS

1. Starr Defends Senate Trial Procedures

Source: Brief for the Respondents and Amicus Curiae United States Senate in Opposition, Nixon v. United States, October Term, 1991, at 8-9; 225 Landmark Briefs 374-75

[Solicitor General Kenneth W. Starr:] The court of appeals correctly determined that petitioner's challenge to his conviction on articles of impeachment is nonjusticiable. . . .

1. Petitioner's claim that the Senate violated the Constitution by utilizing a committee to compile an evidentiary record is not justiciable because it asks the courts to review a determination that the Constitution plainly commits to the Senate alone. The Impeachment Trial Clause expressly instructs:

The Senate shall have the sole Power to try all Impeachments. Art. I, § 3, Cl. 6. As the court of appeals explained, that Clause gives the Senate exclusive—and hence unreviewable—power to conduct impeachment trials. . . . The Constitution's grant of that authority necessarily gives the Senate sole authority to determine how evidence shall be taken for that body's use—a detail on which the Constitution is silent.

That conclusion finds additional textual support in the Rulemaking Clause, which states that "[e]ach House may determine the Rules of its Proceedings." Art. I, § 5, Cl. 2. . . .

2. Grounds for Impeachment

Source: "Constitutional Grounds for Presidential Impeachment," report by the Staff of the Impeachment Inquiry, House Committee on the Judiciary, 93d Cong., 2d Sess. 26-27 (Feb. 1974)

Impeachment is a constitutional remedy addressed to serious offenses against the system of government. . . .

While it may be argued that some articles of impeachment have charged conduct that constituted crime and thus that criminality is an essential ingredient, or that some have charged conduct that was not criminal and thus criminality is not essential, the fact remains that in the English practice and in several of the American impeachments the criminality issue was not raised at all. The emphasis has been on the significant effects of the conduct— undermining the integrity of office, disregard of constitutional duties and oath of office, arrogation of power, abuse of the governmental process, adverse impact on the system of government. Clearly, these effects can be brought about in ways not anticipated by the criminal law. Criminal standards and criminal courts were established to control individual conduct. Impeachment was evolved by Parliament to cope with both the inadequacy of criminal standards and the impotence of courts to deal with the conduct of great public officials. . .

. . . Because impeachment of a President is a grave step for the nation, it is to be predicated only upon conduct seriously incompatible with either the constitutional form and principles of our government or the proper performance of constitutional duties of the presidential office.

3. Jackson Condemns Censure Resolution

Source: 3 A Compilation of the Messages and Papers of the Presidents 1289, 1291-93 (J. Richardson ed. 1897)

. . . [W]ithout notice, unheard and untried, I thus find myself charged on the records of the Senate, and in a form hitherto unknown in our history, with the high crime of violating the laws and Constitution of my country.

. . . [T]he resolution of the Senate is wholly unauthorized by the Constitution, and in derogation of its entire spirit. It assumes that a single branch of the legislative department may for the purposes of a public censure, and without any view to legislation or impeachment, take up, consider, and decide upon the official acts of the Executive. . . .

The resolution above quoted charges, in substance, that in certain proceedings relating to the public revenue the President has usurped authority and power not conferred upon him by the Constitution and laws, and that in doing so he violated both. Any such act constitutes a high crime—one of the highest, indeed, which the President can commit—a crime which justly exposes him to impeachment by the House of Representatives, and, upon due conviction, to removal from office and to the complete and immutable disfranchisement prescribed by the Constitution. . . .

The impeachment, instead of being preferred and prosecuted by the House of Representatives, originated in the Senate, and was prosecuted without the aid or concurrence of the other House. The oath or affirmation prescribed by the Constitution was not taken by the Senators, the Chief Justice did not preside, no notice of the charge was given to the accused, and no opportunity afforded him to respond to the accusation, to meet his accusers face to face, to cross-examine the witnesses, to procure counteracting testimony, or to be heard in his defense. . . .

4. Voting "Not Guilty" After Concluding Guilt

Source: 145 Cong. Rec. S1636 (daily ed. February 12, 1999)

Mr. [Robert C.] BYRD [D-W.Va.]. . . . Does not this misconduct constitute an injury to the society and its political character? Does not such injury to the institutions of Government constitute an impeachable offense, a political high crime or high misdemeanor against the state? How would Washington vote? How would Hamilton vote? How would Madison or Mason or Gerry vote? My head and my heart tell me that their answer to these questions would be, "Yes."

. . . A vote to convict carries with it an automatic removal of the President from office. It is not a two-step process. Senators can't vote maybe. The only vote that the Senator can cast, under the rules, as written, is a vote either to convict and remove or a vote to acquit. [Concluding that Clinton's removal "could create an unstable condition," Byrd voted "Not Guilty" on both articles after being convinced that Clinton was guilty as charged.]

[Senator Susan Collins (R-Me.) voted not guilty on both articles, yet explained that the House managers had proved to her satisfaction that Clinton "did, in fact, obstruct justice." 145 Cong. Rec. S1568. Another Republican Senator, Olympia Snowe of Maine, voted not guilty on the articles after concluding that Clinton had "unlawfully" influenced a potential witness, Betty Currie. Id. at S1546-47, S1669-71. Senator James Jeffords (R-Vt.) voted not guilty on both articles despite agreeing that the House managers had proven that Clinton had obstructed justice. Id. at S1595.]

[Similarly, on the perjury issue, Senator Fred Thompson (R-Tenn.) voted against that article after concluding that Clinton had perjured himself a number of times. Thompson voted not guilty because he believed that the perjurious statements did not justify removal. Id. at S1554-55. Senator Ted Stevens (R-Alas.) voted against the perjury article, although he said that if he were sitting as a juror in a criminal case he would find Clinton "guilty of perjury as charged." Id. at S1599. Senator Slade Gorton (R-Wash.) had "no reasonable doubt" that Clinton committed perjury but voted "not guilty" because he thought removal was unwarranted. Id. at S1462-64.]

5. Starr Reports to the House

Source: Referral to the United States House of Representatives Pursuant to Title 28, United States Code, § 595(c), September 11, 1998

[Independent Counsel Kenneth W. Starr:] The information reveals that President Clinton:

• lied under oath at a court deposition while he was a defendant in a sexual harassment lawsuit;

• lied under oath to a grand jury;

• attempted to influence the testimony of a potential witness who had direct knowledge of facts that would reveal the falsity of his deposition testimony;

• attempted to obstruct justice by facilitating a witness's plan to refuse to comply with a subpoena;

• attempted to obstruct justice by encouraging a witness to file an affidavit that the President knew would be false, and then by making use of that false affidavit at his own deposition;

• lied to potential grand jury witnesses, knowing that they would repeat those lies before the grand jury; and

• engaged in a pattern of conduct that was inconsistent with his constitutional duty to faithfully executive the laws.

6. Seeking Guidance from Public Opinion

Source: 144 Cong. Rec. H11792 (daily ed. December 18, 1999)

Mr. [John] DINGELL [D-Mich.]. Listen to the people. This is a political process. It was expected by the Framers of the Constitution that this same political process would function as such. Politics and political process requires involvement of the people and that we who hold this responsibility listen carefully and respectfully to their wishes.

Listen to the people of America. They do not believe impeachment is a proper remedy for President Clinton's misbehavior. The people do not approve of Mr. Clinton's behavior, but they do not believe that the President's action rises to the level of impeachable offenses. They find no basis for us to take such action. . . .

We are now deciding whether to precipitate a Constitutional crisis. We are deciding whether to create a great public controversy where the people will be divided by a process they do not want to go forward. We must now decide whether to put at risk the powers of the Presidency, not the well being [of] a Bill Clinton.

All this is set against the wishes of the people who have spoken to us with clarity.

5

THE WAR POWER

Executive-legislative conflicts over foreign affairs and war have sparked a series of constitutional disputes in our nation's history. Few of those controversies, however, ever find their way to the judiciary. For the most part, they are resolved through political settlements agreed to by Congress and the President. Thus, the momentous decision to commit the nation's blood and deplete its treasury is left almost solely to nonjudicial officials.

Section I of this chapter covers the constitutional principles of the war power, its implementation over the early decades, and the unique circumstances of the Civil War. The latter part of Section I traces the developments leading to the Vietnam War, the national debate that produced the War Powers Resolution of 1973, the constitutional implications created when President Bush decided to introduce troops into the Persian Gulf in 1990, and military initiatives by President Clinton.

Section II concentrates on the decision by President Truman in 1952 to seize the nation's steel mills as part of the effort to prosecute the war in Korea. Political circumstances combined with a dubious legal position to hand Truman a stinging defeat in the courts.

Executive-legislative accommodations are debated within the framework of the text of the Constitution and the intent of the framers. However, text and intent are only a starting-point. They must be interpreted in light of historical developments, judicial rulings, institutional understandings, and public reactions.

I. THE POWER TO MAKE WAR

At the time that America declared its independence from England in 1776, the prevailing model of government in other nations placed the power of foreign affairs and war solely with the king. John Locke's *Second Treatise of Government* (1690) recognized three basic powers: legislative, executive, and federative. The latter consisted of "the power of war and peace, leagues and alliances, and all the transactions with all persons and communities without the commonwealth." To Locke it was "always almost united" with the executive. §§146-147. Placing the executive and federative powers in separate hands would invite "disorder and ruin." §148.

Sir William Blackstone, the distinguished eighteenth century English jurist, also gave a broad reading to the king's prerogative. The king had the absolute right to send and receive ambassadors, make treaties and alliances, make war or peace, coin money, issue letters of marque and reprisal (authorizing private citizens to engage in war), command the military, raise and regulate fleets and armies, and represent the nation in its intercourse with foreign nations. 2 William Blackstone, Commentaries on the Laws of England 237-80 (1803).

A. Framers' Intent

The framers broke decisively with those models of government. The draft Constitution transferred many of Locke's federative powers and Blackstone's royal prerogatives to Congress. For more than four of the five months at the Philadelphia Convention, the framers gave the Senate the exclusive power to make treaties and appoint ambassadors. After the Great Compromise established a House of Representatives based on population and gave each state two Senators to be elected by state legislatures, the framers feared that an aristocratic Senate might abuse its powers. To introduce a check, they added the President to the treaty-making and appointment processes. Alexander Hamilton explained in Federalist 69 that the President had "concurrent power with a branch of the legislature in the formation of treaties," whereas the British king "is the *sole possessor* of the power of making treaties." The Federalist 450 (Benjamin Wright ed. 1961).

The framers gave Congress other express powers over foreign affairs and war. The Constitution vests in Congress the power to regulate foreign commerce. Because commercial conflicts between nations were often a prelude to war, the most significant foreign policy in 1787 consisted of foreign commerce, a power the framers placed explicitly in Congress. The Constitution grants other foreign powers to Congress: the power to "lay and collect Taxes, Duties, Imposts, and Excises, to pay the Debts and provide for the common Defence and general Welfare of the United States"; the power to define and punish piracies and felonies committed on the high seas, and offenses against the law of nations; the power to declare war, grant letters of marque and reprisal, and makes rules concerning captures on land and water; the power to raise and support armies and provide and maintain a navy; the power to make regulations of the land and naval forces; the power to provide for calling forth the militia to execute the laws of the union, suppress insurrections, and repel invasions; and the power to provide for organizing, arming, and disciplining the militia.

The power of Congress to "declare" war resulted from a change of language at the convention. Initially Congress was empowered to "make" war. The debate on this language illuminates the scope of presidential power and the framers' determination to reserve all but defensive actions to Congress (document 1). Later, at the Pennsylvania ratification convention in 1787, James Wilson stated that the system of checks and balances "will not hurry us into war; it is calculated to guard against it. It will not be in the power of a single man, or a single body of men, to involve us in such distress; for the important power of declaring war is vested in the legislature at large." 2 Elliot 528.

The constitutional authority of Congress to control foreign affairs and war relies heavily on its power to appropriate funds. Article I, Section 9, states that no money shall be drawn from the Treasury "but in Consequence of Appropriations made by Law." In Federalist 58, James Madison said that the power of the purse represents the "most complete and effectual weapon with which any constitution can arm the immediate representatives of the people, for obtaining a redress of every grievance, and for carrying into effect every just and salutary measure." The Federalist 391 (Benjamin Fletcher Wright ed. 1961).

Hamilton had British history in mind when he explained in Federalist 69 why the American President was less threatening to individual rights than the king of England. Among other differences, Hamilton pointed out that the power of the king "extends to the declaring of war and to the *raising* and *regulating* of fleets and armies," whereas the Constitution placed those powers squarely in Congress. The Federalist 446 (B. Wright ed. 1961). James Madison warned against placing the power of commander in chief in the same hands as the power to go to war:

> Those who are to *conduct a war* cannot in the nature of things, be proper or safe judges, whether a *war ought to* be *commenced, continued,* or *concluded.* They are barred from the latter functions by a great principle in free government, analogous to that which separates the sword from the purse, or the power of executing from the power of enacting laws. 6 Writings of James Madison 148 (Gaillard Hunt ed. 1900-10) (emphasis in original).

The framers empowered the President to be "Commander in Chief of the Army and Navy of the United States, and of the Militia of the several States, when called into the actual Service of the United States." The President directs the armed forces after Congress decides to declare war. In addition, the debates at the Philadelphia convention suggest that the President also has an implied power to take certain actions to "repel sudden attacks" upon the United States (document 1). Designating the President Commander in Chief was an important method for preserving civilian supremacy over the military. 10 Op. Att'y Gen. 74, 79 (1861). What else the title implies is a subject of continuing dispute. In a concurrence, Justice Jackson once remarked that the commander-in-chief clause implies "something more than an empty title. But just what authority goes with the name has plagued presidential advisers who would not waive or narrow it by nonassertion yet cannot say where it begins or ends." Youngstown Co. v. Sawyer, 343 U.S. 579, 641 (1952).

B. Early Historical Precedents

Once the Constitution was ratified, Congress and the President slowly established the precedents that would shape the allocation of foreign affairs and the war power. Although Congress is empowered to declare war, it has done so only on five occasions: the War of 1812, the Mexican War, the Spanish-American War, World War I, and World War II. In addition, American forces have fought in "quasi wars" never formally declared by Congress but nevertheless authorized by statute. Two decisions in 1800 and 1801 interpreted congressional statutes that authorized hostilities on the high seas. The Supreme Court recognized the constitutional legitimacy of these undeclared wars. Military conflicts could be "limited," "partial," and "imperfect," without Congress having to issue a formal declaration. Bas v. Tingy, 4 U.S. 37 (1800); Talbot v. Seeman, 5 U.S. 1 (1801). In the latter case, Chief Justice Marshall wrote for the Court: "The whole powers of war being, by the constitution of the United States, vested in Congress, the acts of that body can alone be resorted to as our guides in this inquiry." Talbot, 5 U.S. at 28. Subsequent Presidents would use military force without Congress either authorizing or declaring war.

A speech by John Marshall, delivered in 1800 when he was a member of the U.S. House of Representatives, is often cited by the Supreme Court and advocates of executive power to support the proposition that the President is the sole authority in foreign affairs. However, this speech is wrenched from context to attribute to Marshall a position he never advanced. Marshall's statement that the President "is the sole organ of the nation in its external relations" suggests that he promoted an exclusive power for the President in foreign affairs. But Marshall merely argued that the President was responsible for carrying out national policy *after* it had been established by treaty or by statute. Marshall meant that the President, as sole organ, *announced* policy; he did not *make* it (document 2).

Four years later, as Chief Justice, Marshall decided a case in which Congress established one foreign policy by statute and the executive branch pursued another. Legislation in 1799 authorized the President to seize vessels sailing *to* French ports. President Adams issued an order directing American ships to capture vessels sailing *to or from* French ports. Captain George Little seized a Danish ship sailing from a French port and was sued for damages. Marshall decided that congressional policy, as expressed in the statute, necessarily prevailed over presidential orders or military actions pursuant to those orders. Captain Little was personally liable. Little v. Barreme, 6 U.S. 169 (1804).

C. The Civil War

Throughout the nineteenth century, various practices and judicial rulings established that the war power lay with Congress and that it shared significantly in foreign policy. The closest the nation came to a presidential war prior to the Civil War was in 1846, when President Polk ordered General Zachary Taylor to occupy disputed territory on the Texas-Mexico border. The action precipitated a clash between American and Mexican soldiers, leading Polk to tell Congress a few weeks later that "war exists." Although Congress declared war against Mexico, Polk's action was censured by the House in 1848 because the war had been "unnecessarily and unconstitutionally begun by the President of the United States." Cong. Globe, 30th Cong., 1st Sess. 95 (1848). One of Polk's critics at the time was Congressman Abraham Lincoln, who wrote to a friend:

> Allow the President to invade a neighboring nation, whenever *he* shall deem it necessary to repel an invasion, and you allow him to do so, *whenever he may choose to say* he deems it necessary for such purpose—and you allow him to make war at pleasure. . . . This, our Convention understood to be the most oppressive of all Kingly oppressions; and they resolved to so frame the Constitution that *no one man* should hold the power of bringing this oppression upon us. 1 The Collected Works of Abraham Lincoln 451-52 (Roy Basler ed. 1953) (emphasis in original).

During his own years as President, Lincoln exercised military force without first obtaining congressional authorization, but it would be inaccurate to call his actions "dictatorial." In April 1861, with Congress in recess, he issued proclamations calling forth the state militia, suspending the writ of habeas corpus, and placing a blockade on the rebellious states. When Congress returned he explained that his actions, "whether strictly legal or not, were ventured upon under what appeared to be a popular demand and a public necessity, trusting then, as now, that Congress would readily ratify them." 7 Richardson 3225. In short, he conceded that he had acted without proper authority and asked Congress to legalize what he had done. Congress passed legislation "approving, legalizing, and making valid all the acts, proclamations, and orders of the President, etc., as if they had been issued and done under the previous express authority and direction of the Congress of the United States." 12 Stat. 326 (1861).

Lincoln distinguished between his exercise of the war power to preserve the Union and the actions of Polk, who had acted against a foreign nation. Lincoln said he was compelled to use force to put down an internal rebellion. Vessels that violated his blockade in rebellious states were seized and their cargo taken as prize. Lincoln's action was upheld by the Supreme Court, divided 5 to 4. Writing for the majority, Justice Grier said that the President as Commander in Chief "has no power to initiate or declare a war either against a foreign nation or a domestic State." But if a foreign nation invaded, the President was not only authorized "but bound to resist force by force. He does not initiate the war, but is bound to accept the challenge without waiting for any special legislative authority." The Prize Cases, 67 U.S. 635, 668 (1863). Richard Henry Dana, Jr., representing the executive branch, acknowledged that Lincoln's actions had nothing to do with "the right *to initiate a war, as a voluntary act of sovereignty*. That is vested only in Congress." Id. at 660.

Lincoln invoked other extraordinary powers during the Civil War. Although the authority to suspend the writ of habeas corpus is found in Article I under congressional power, Lincoln told Congress when it returned that he had suspended the writ. His message to Congress explained that he found it necessary during the emergency to exercise both Article I and Article II powers (document 3).

A resulting lawsuit sheds light on who decides the meaning of the Constitution. John Merryman, suspected of secessionist activities, was arrested by federal troops on May 25, 1861, and held at Fort McHenry. On the following day, a writ of habeas corpus was issued by Chief Justice Taney, sitting as circuit judge, directing the military to deliver Merryman to the Chief Justice two days later. The military refused, stating that the arrest had been authorized by the President. Although ruling that Lincoln had no power under the Constitution to suspend the writ, Taney realized that he could not prevail in a confrontation with the President. The concluding words of his decision gave Lincoln the "final word" on this part of the Constitution:

> I have exercised all the power which the constitution and laws confer upon me, but that power has been resisted by a force too strong for me to overcome. . . . I shall . . . order all the proceedings in this case, with my opinion, to be [transmitted] . . . to the president of the United States. It will then remain for that high officer, in fulfillment of his constitutional obligation to "take care that the laws be faithfully executed," to determine what measures he will take to cause the civil process of the United States to be respected and enforced. Ex parte Merryman, 17 F. Cas. 144, 153 (C.C. Md. 1861) (No. 9,487).

D. Developments Leading to Vietnam

The Civil War was exceptional in many respects. Hostilities were turned inward rather than against a foreign nation. Because of the emergency, the President operated at first solely on his own prerogative, trusting that Congress when it convened would ratify his actions, which it did. Despite the magnitude of military operations, there was no declaration of war by Congress. A formal declaration was considered necessary only for conflicts with other nations, such as the War of 1812 and the Mexican War. Similarly, Congress issued a declaration for the Spanish-American War of 1898, World War I, and World War II.

Two developments during and immediately after World War II served to widen presidential power: the United Nations Charter and mutual security treaties (particularly NATO). During negotiations over the U.N. Charter of 1945, procedures were developed to permit the U.N. to employ military force to deal with threats to peace and acts of aggression. All U.N. members would make available to the Security Council, on its call, armed forces for the purpose of maintaining international peace and security. These agreements, concluded between the Security Council and member states, would be in accordance "with their respective constitutional processes."

While the Senate debated the U.N. Charter, President Truman wired a note from Potsdam, pledging that when any agreements "are negotiated it will be my purpose to ask the Congress for appropriate legislation to approve them." 91 Cong. Rec. 8185 (1945). That same understanding was incorporated into the U.N. Participation Act of 1945, section 6 of which states that the agreements "shall be subject to the approval of the Congress by appropriate Act or joint resolution." 59 Stat. 621, § 6 (1945). Yet the very procedural mechanism to safeguard congressional prerogatives has never been followed. No U.N. member has ever entered into an agreement with the Security Council.

Also muddying up the legal waters are the mutual security treaties entered into after World War II: the Rio Treaty of 1947, the NATO Treaty of 1949, the SEATO Treaty of 1949, and others. Executive officials assured Congress that its prerogatives were fully protected, and yet these treaties would become another source of "authority" for presidential action.

Truman took the initiative in June 1950 to involve the nation in war in Korea. He acted solely on his interpretation of presidential power, seeking no authority from Congress. Truman tried to justify his actions in Korea by calling it a U.N. "police action" rather than a war. Pub. Papers, 1950, at 504, 522. However, the U.N. exercised no real authority over the war, which remained an American operation—measured by troops, money, casualties, and deaths—from start to finish. The legality of Truman's action has been debated ever since. What is not debatable is the fact that the President, for the first time, had committed U.S. troops abroad into a major conflict on what he considered to be adequate executive authority. He acted without a declaration of war or specific authorization from Congress.

Truman later experienced an unusual judicial rebuff. In the midst of a nationwide strike in 1952, he ordered the seizure of steel mills to help prosecute the war in Korea. His theory of inherent presidential power, as explained in Section II of this chapter, was soundly rejected by the Supreme Court.

When Dwight D. Eisenhower became President in 1953, he regarded Truman's actions in Korea as a mistaken exercise of executive power. Eisenhower believed that the country was on more solid constitutional and political footing when the President acted in concert with Congress. Toward that end he requested, and received, "area resolutions" giving the President authority to use military force in specific areas of the world. He received area resolutions for Formosa in 1955 and for the Middle East in 1957. 69 Stat. 7 (1955); 71 Stat. 4 (1957). He regarded executive-legislative coordination as essential: "I deem it necessary to seek the cooperation of the Congress. Only with that cooperation can we give the reassurance needed to deter aggression . . . ." Pub. Papers, 1957, at 11.

Unlike Eisenhower, President John F. Kennedy was prepared to act solely on what he claimed to be his constitutional authority when he confronted the Soviet Union during the Cuban missile crisis in 1962. He said he had full authority as Commander in Chief to take whatever actions were necessary to prevent the Soviet Union from placing missiles in Cuba. Pub. Papers, 1962, at 674, 679. Congress passed the Cuba Resolution of 1962, but did not authorize presidential action. It merely expressed the sentiments of Congress. 76 Stat. 697 (1962).

The next area resolution was the ill-fated Southeast Asia Resolution of 1964 (also called the Gulf of Tonkin Resolution). In response to President Lyndon Johnson's report of attacks on U.S. vessels in the Gulf of Tonkin Congress hastily passed legislation to approve and support "the determination of the President, as Commander in Chief, to take all necessary measures to repel any armed attack against the forces of the United States and to prevent further aggression." The United States was "prepared, as the President determines, to take all necessary steps, including the use of armed force . . . ." 78 Stat. 384 (1964).

The resolution represented a careless abdication of congressional authority. The administration said that the attacks occurred on August 2 and 4, although subsequent studies indicate that the second "attack" probably never occurred. President Johnson requested the resolution on August 4. Without taking the time to independently investigate the facts, the Senate began debate on August 6 and passed the resolution the following day, 88-2. A unanimous House passed the resolution a day later, voting 414-0. In the midst of a presidential election year, only two members of Congress were willing to challenge the President. One of the dissenters in the Senate, Wayne Morse (R-Ore.), displayed an uncanny gift for prophecy: "Unpopular as it is, I am perfectly willing to make the statement for history that if we follow a course of action that bogs down thousands of American boys in Asia, the administration responsible for it will be rejected and repudiated by the American people. It should be." 110 Cong. Rec. 18427 (1964). Four years later, after heavy casualties in a war that seemed to have no end and no possible victory, Johnson was driven from office.

Beginning with hearings in 1967, the Senate Foreign Relations Committee reexamined the constitutional responsibilities of Congress in war and foreign affairs. It concluded that the President should obtain congressional approval before committing U.S. economic and military resources to another country. The concentration of power in the executive branch had progressed to the point that the President had acquired "virtual supremacy over the making as well as the conduct of the foreign relations of the United States." S. Rep. No. 129, 91st Cong., 1st Sess. 7 (1969).

In 1969, the Senate passed the National Commitments Resolution by the top-heavy majority of 70-16. Passed in the form of a Senate resolution, the measure has no legal effect. However, it marked a significant expression of constitutional principles by a bipartisan Senate. The Democrats supported it 43-3; the Republicans voted in favor 17-13. The resolution defined a national commitment as the use of U.S. armed forces on foreign territory, or a promise to assist a foreign country by using U.S. armed forces or financial resources "either immediately or upon the happening of certain events." The resolution provides that "it is the sense of the Senate that a national commitment by the United States results only from affirmative action taken by the executive and legislative branches of the United States Government by means of a treaty, statute, or concurrent resolution of both Houses of Congress specifically providing for such commitment." 115 Cong. Rec. 17245 (1969). During floor debate, Senator J. William Fulbright (D-Ark.) explained the history and purpose of the resolution (document 4).

E. From Vietnam to Clinton

From 1970 to 1973, the House and the Senate drafted legislation to curb the President's power to initiate war. A compromise product was finally presented to President Nixon in 1973, but he vetoed it for a number of policy and constitutional reasons (document 5). Both Houses were able to override him, the House narrowly (284 to 135) and the Senate by a more comfortable margin (75 to 18).

The War Powers Resolution of 1973 calls for the "collective judgment" of both Congress and the President before U.S. troops are sent into combat. It recognizes that the President may use military force without prior congressional authorization for 60 days (with the option of extending this period to 90 days), but longer military engagements would require congressional action. Presidents Ford, Carter, Reagan, Bush, and Clinton all used military force without seeking congressional authorization, but many of these operations were of a short-term nature: Ford's rescue of the U.S. merchant ship *Mayaguez*, which had been seized by Cambodians; Carter's attempted rescue of American hostages in Iran; Reagan's invasion of Grenada and air strikes against Libya; Bush's intervention in Panama in 1989; and Clinton's sending of cruise missiles into Baghad. More extensive operations, such as the commitment of troops to Lebanon in 1983 and to the Middle East in 1991, were authorized by Congress. Clinton's use of military force in Haiti, Iraq, Bosnia, and Yugoslavia were for longer periods, but lacked any authorization from Congress.

In August 1990, President Bush sent military forces to Saudi Arabia after Iraq invaded Kuwait. Although members of Congress expressed concern about the President's deployment of troops, there was little discussion about his constitutional authority until November when he more than doubled the size of American forces to create an offensive capability and obtained from the U.N. Security Council a resolution authorizing member states to use "all necessary means" to force Iraqi troops out of Kuwait. Administration officials claimed that President Bush could use U.S. forces for offensive operations without first obtaining authority from Congress.

Congressman Ronald Dellums (D-Cal.) and other legislators took the issue to a federal district court, which held on December 13 that the dispute was not ripe for judicial determination. Nevertheless, the court forcefully rejected many of the sweeping claims for presidential authority advanced by the Justice Department. Dellums v. Bush, 752 F.Supp. 1141 (D.D.C. 1990). The oral argument before the court reveals the conflicting positions on presidential power (document 6).

The decision in *Dellums* might have prompted the Bush administration to rethink its constitutional theories about presidential power. On January 8, 1991, about a week before a deadline established by the United Nations for Iraq to withdraw from Kuwait if it wanted to avoid war, President Bush sent a letter to congressional leaders recommending legislative action. Although his letter does not explicitly acknowledge the need for congressional authority, it recognizes that the United States would be on firmer ground if it proceeded with joint action between Congress and the President (document 7). Congress passed legislation on January 12, 1991, authorizing the use of military force. 105 Stat. 3 (1991).

In his eight years in office, President Bill Clinton invoked military force on a number of occasions without seeking congressional support or approval. He sent cruise missiles into Iraq, ordered air strikes in Bosnia, conducted military operations in Somalia, threatened to invade Haiti, sent

20,000 troops to Bosnia, conducted an air war against Serbia, bombed Iraq repeatedly, and sent cruise missiles into Afghanistan and Sudan. In each case he based his actions solely on what he considered to be the President's constitutional power. Congress used the power of the purse to put an end to military operations in Somalia, denying funds after March 31, 1994. 107 Stat. 1475-77, sec. 8151 (1993). On the other military initiatives, Congress was either inactive or uncertain of the proper legislative response.

When Clinton was prepared to send ground troops to Bosnia in 1995, Congress responded by adopting a variety of amendments to limit him, but often they were "sense of Congress" or "sense of Senate" formulations and therefore legally non-binding. The response in Congress depended greatly on what Bob Dole, the Senate Majority Leader, would do. In key speeches, he made it clear that legislative prerogatives were to be subordinated to presidential interests (document 8). There would be no checks and balances system, no tussling for power. Once the President had announced his policy, legislators would dutifully fall in line. Congress, as a separate and independent branch, did not exist. It was not remotely coequal.

Clinton engaged in other military initiatives. In August 1998, he ordered cruise missiles into Afghanistan to attack paramilitary camps and into Sudan to destroy a pharmaceutical factory, both actions as retaliation for bombings earlier in the month against U.S. embassies in Africa. In September 1996, he ordered the launching of cruise missiles against Iraq and conducted four days of bombing against Iraq in December 1998. Military strikes continued against Iraq in 1999 and 2000. Other than some consultation, Congress had no role in any of these decisions to use force.

The largest military commitment was Clinton's decision to initiate war against Yugoslavia in 1999. Here there was no claim of acting in a defensive manner or to protect American lives. The use of force marked an unambiguous, unvarnished example of a President taking the country from a state of peace to a state of war, without ever asking Congress for authority. Lawmakers took a number of votes, but none of them authorized what Clinton did and none of them prohibited him from doing what he did. Consequently, what the framers thought had been vested in Congress was now in the hands of the President. By failing to act, Congress effectively stood by on the sidelines unable—or unwilling—to protect its institutional interests. Congressman Tom Campbell (R-Cal.) attempted to litigate the constitutionality of the war in Yugoslavia (document 9). However, federal courts held that the matter was foreclosed from judicial scrutiny because of standing and the political question doctrine. Campbell v. Clinton, 203 F.3d 19 (D.C. Cir. 2000); Campbell v. Clinton, 52 F. Supp. 2d 34 (D.D.C. 1999).

F. Conclusion

The system of checks and balances was meant to apply both to domestic and military policy, and particularly to the conduct of war abroad. There are practical as well as constitutional reasons for making sure that foreign policy and national security are not in the hands of an unchecked Executive. In a speech to the Center for Strategic & International Studies on November 19, 1999, Congressman Lee Hamilton (D-Ind.) pointed to the value of joint action by Congress and the President: "I believe that a partnership, characterized by creative tension between the President and the Congress, produces a foreign policy that better serves the American national interest—and better reflects the values of the American people—than policy produced by the President alone." Those are sound values, both legally and politically, but unless Congress is willing to use the ample constitutional powers at its disposal, and unless the public puts pressure on legislators to assert their prerogatives and insist on a coequal role, the framework developed by the founding fathers and written into the text of the Constitution will be of only theoretical interest.

DOCUMENTS

1. Debate on War Power at Philadelphia Convention

Source: 2 Farrand 318-19

[On August 17, 1787, the delegates at the constitutional convention in Philadelphia considered language giving Congress the power to "make war."]

Mr PINKNEY opposed the vesting this power in the Legislature. Its proceedings were too slow. It wd. meet but once a year. The Hs. of Reps. would be too numerous for such deliberations. The Senate would be the best depositary, being more acquainted with foreign affairs, and most capable of proper resolutions. If the States are equally represented in Senate, so as to give no advantage to large States, the power will notwithstanding be safe, as the small have their all at stake in such cases as well as the large States. It would be singular for one—authority to make war, and another peace.

Mr. BUTLER. The Objections agst the Legislature lie in a great degree agst the Senate. He was for vesting the power in the President, who will have all the requisite qualities, and will not make war but when the Nation will support it.

Mr. MADISON and Mr. GERRY moved to insert "*declare*," striking out "*make*" war; leaving to the Executive the power to repel sudden attacks.

Mr. SHARMAN thought it stood very well. The Executive shd. be able to repel and not to commence war. "Make" better than "declare" the latter narrowing the power too much.

Mr. GERRY never expected to hear in a republic a motion to empower the Executive alone to declare war.

Mr. ELSEWORTH. [T]here is a material difference between the cases of making *war*, and making *peace*. It shd. be more easy to get out of war, than into it. War also is a simple and overt declaration. Peace attended with intricate & secret negociations.

Mr. MASON was agst giving the power of war to the Executive, because not <safely> to be trusted with it; or to the Senate, because not so constructed as to be entitled to it. He was for clogging rather than facilitating war; but for facilitating peace.   He preferred "*declare*" to "*make*".

On the Motion to insert *declare*—in place of *Make*, <it was agreed to.>

N.H. no. Mas. abst. Cont. no.* Pa. ay. Del. ay. Md. ay. Va. ay. N.C. ay. S.C. ay. Geo. ay. [Ayes—7; noes—2; absent—I.]

*On the remark by Mr. King that "*make*" war might be understood to "conduct" it which was an Executive function, Mr. Elseworth gave up his objection <and the vote of Cont. was changed to—ay.>

---

2. President as "Sole Organ" in Foreign Affairs

Source: Annals of Cong., 6th Cong. 613-14 (1800)

[The following remarks by Congressman John Marshall came in response to a proposal to impeach President John Adams for interfering with judicial proceedings in the trial of Jonathan Robbins. In carrying out an extradition treaty with England, Adams had decided to return Robbins to England.]

The [dispute] was in its nature a national demand made upon the nation. The parties were the two nations. They cannot come into court to litigate their claims, nor can a court decide on them. Of consequence, the demand is not a case for judicial cognizance.

The President is the sole organ of the nation in its external relations, and its sole representative with foreign nations.   Of consequence, the demand of a foreign nation can only be made on him.

He possesses the whole Executive power. He holds and directs the force of the nation. Of consequence, any act to be performed by the force of the nation is to be performed through him.

He is charged to execute the laws. A treaty is declared to be a law. He must then execute a treaty, where he, and he alone, possesses the means of executing it.

The treaty, which is a law, enjoins the performance of a particular object.   The person who is to perform this object is marked out by the Constitution, since the person is named who conducts the foreign intercourse, and is to take care that the laws be faithfully executed. The means by which it is to be performed, the force of the nation, are in the hands of this person. Ought not this person to perform the object, although the particular mode of using the means has not been prescribed? Congress, unquestionably, may prescribe the mode, and Congress may devolve on others the whole execution of the contract; but, till this be done, it seems the duty of the Executive department to execute the contract by any means it possesses.

---

3. Lincoln's Message to Congress on July 4, 1861

Source: 7 A Compilation of the Messages and Papers of the Presidents 3224, 3225-26 (James Richardson ed. 1897-1925)

. . . [T]his issue embraces more than the fate of these United States. It presents to the whole family of man the question whether a constitutional republic, or democracy—a government of the people by the same people—can or can not maintain its territorial integrity against its own domestic foes. . . . It forces us to ask, Is there in all republics this inherent and fatal weakness?   Must a government of necessity be too *strong* for the liberties of its own people, or too *weak* to maintain its own existence?

So viewing the issue, no choice was left but to call out the war power of the Government and so to resist force employed for its destruction by force for its preservation.

.   .   .

Recurring to the action of the Government, it may be stated that at first a call was made for 75,000 militia, and rapidly following this a proclamation was issued for closing the ports of the insurrectionary districts by proceedings in the nature of blockade. So far all was believed to be strictly legal. At this point the insurrectionists announced their purpose to enter upon the practice of privateering.

Other calls were made for volunteers to serve three years unless sooner discharged, and also for large additions to the Regular Army and Navy. These measures, whether strictly legal or not, were ventured upon under what appeared to be a popular demand and a public necessity, trusting then, as now, that Congress would readily ratify them. It is believed that nothing has been done beyond the constitutional competency of Congress.

Soon after the first call for militia it was considered a duty to authorize the Commanding General in proper cases, according to his discretion, to suspend the privilege of the writ of *habeas corpus*, or, in other words, to arrest and detain without resort to the ordinary processes and forms of law such individuals as he might deem dangerous to the public safety. This authority has purposely been exercised but very sparingly. Nevertheless, the legality and propriety of what has been done under it are questioned, and the attention of the country has been called to the proposition that one who is sworn to "take care that the laws be faithfully executed" should not himself violate them. Of course some consideration was given to the questions of power and propriety before this matter was acted upon.

The whole of the laws which were required to be faithfully executed were being resisted and failing of execution in nearly one-third of the States. Must they be allowed to finally fail of execution, even had it been perfectly clear that by the use of the means necessary to their execution some single law, made in such extreme tenderness of the citizen's liberty that practically it relieves more of the guilty than of the innocent, should to a very limited extent be violated? To state the question more directly, Are all the laws *but one* to go unexecuted, and the Government itself go to pieces lest that one be violated? Even in such a case, would not the official oath be broken if the Government should be overthrown when it was believed that disregarding the single law would tend to preserve it? . . .

---

4. The National Commitments Resolution of 1969

Source: 115 Cong. Rec.
16615-17, 16618 (1969)

Mr. [J. William] FULBRIGHT [D-Ark.]. . . .
[T]he Senate has allowed an imbalance to arise within our governmental structure and that by a process of erosion and by a process of acceptance of executive action some of the most significant powers of the Senate have been lost or at least they have been neglected.

They are not permanently lost. The purpose of this commitment resolution is to reestablish the proper role of the Senate.

.   .   .

What we have in mind are important commitments of the Nation, commitments which involve particularly the sending of armed forces, the sending abroad of armed men, in whatever branch of the forces they may be, to engage in hostilities in a foreign country. There is no question, as I shall point out later, about the use and participation of our Armed Forces in defense of the homeland, so to speak. That is not really involved in this resolution at all. The classic example, of course, is the one in which [we] are involved at present—the commitment of over 500,000 men in Vietnam.

. . .

Although Senate Resolution 85 will not carry the force of law, it does express the judgment or opinion of the Senate as to the appropriate constitutional procedures for initiating war and undertaking commitments to foreign nations. At best, the resolution will help to create a new attitude within the Congress, an attitude of diligence in defense of congressional prerogatives, of caution and precision in legislative authorizations, of care in the oversight of the foreign activities of our Government, and of healthy skepticism toward the urgings and opportunities of the executive—especially those involving speedy action and sweeping grants of power.

In the long run, however, neither Senate resolutions nor any organizational or procedural devices are likely to restore congressional authority in foreign affairs. The restoration of constitutional balance will depend on decisions of a more fundamental nature, decisions as to the kind of country we want America to be and the kind of role we want it to play in the world. . . .

---

5. Nixon's Veto of War Powers Resolution

Source: Pub. Papers, 1973, at 893-94

To the House of Representatives:

I hereby return without my approval House Joint Resolution 542—the War Powers Resolution. While I am in accord with the desire of the Congress to assert its proper role in the conduct of our foreign affairs, the restrictions which this resolution would impose upon the authority of the President are both unconstitutional and dangerous to the best interests of our Nation.

The proper roles of the Congress and the Executive in the conduct of foreign affairs have been debated since the founding of our country. Only recently, however, has there been a serious challenge to the wisdom of the Founding Fathers in choosing not to draw a precise and detailed line of demarcation between the foreign policy powers of the two branches.

The Founding Fathers understood the impossibility of foreseeing every contingency that might arise in this complex area. They acknowledged the need for flexibility in responding to changing circumstances. . . .

CLEARLY UNCONSTITUTIONAL

House Joint Resolution 542 would attempt to take away, by a mere legislative act, authorities which the President has properly exercised under the Constitution for almost 200 years. One of its provisions would automatically cut off certain authorities after sixty days unless the Congress extended them. Another would allow the Congress to eliminate certain authorities merely by the passage of a concurrent resolution—an action which does not normally have the force of law, since it denies the President his constitutional role in approving legislation.

I believe that both these provisions are unconstitutional. The only way in which the constitutional powers of a branch of the Government can be altered is by amending the Constitution—and any attempt to make such alterations by legislation alone is clearly without force.

. . .

FAILURE TO REQUIRE POSITIVE CONGRESSIONAL ACTION

I am particularly disturbed by the fact that certain of the President's constitutional powers as Commander in Chief of the Armed Forces would terminate automatically under this resolution 60 days after they were invoked. No overt Congressional action would be required to cut off these powers—they would disappear automatically unless the Congress extended them. In effect, the Congress is here attempting to increase its policymaking role through a provision which requires it to take absolutely no action at all.

---

6. Authority of President Bush to Take Offensive War Against Iraq

Source: Oral Argument in Dellums v. Bush, U.S. District Court for the District of Columbia, Dec. 4, 1990, Transcript of Hearing

---

Mr. [Jules] LOBEL [for the plaintiffs, challenging the President]: Your Honor, the question before this court is straightforward: Can the President initiate a war against Iraq for the purpose of driving it from Kuwait without first obtaining the prior authorization of Congress. The President says he can; the Constitution says he cannot.

Here the threat that an explicit constitutional provision will be violated is clear. The President has repeatedly threatened Iraq with attack unless it withdraws from Kuwait. Just yesterday, Secretary Cheney said, "We cannot wait for sanctions to work. We must have the option to use force."

. . .

Finally, the administration has stated that it does not need congressional authorization to go to war, and it has stated so unequivocally and repeatedly. Your Honor, there is great wisdom in the framers' judgment that the time for the representatives of the American people to debate whether we should make war in another country is before the war begins and not while it is going on.

. . .

. . . In 1973, Congress passed by overwhelming majorities the War Powers Resolution. Section 2(c) of the War Powers Resolution states that the President cannot introduce troops into hostilities unless (1), there is a congressional declaration of war; (2), there is other explicit congressional authorization, which does not include budgetary authorization; or (3), there is an attack on U.S. troops or U.S. territory. None of these three things have occurred here. It is therefore clear that Congress has spoken and has passed a law which is still the law of the land.

. . .

Mr. [Stuart M.] GERSON [defending the Administration]: Needless to say, I view constitutional language and constitutional history somewhat differently than my brother. Disputes of the sort that are embodied in this lawsuit are far from novel and were well within the compass of understanding and address of the Constitution's framers. . . .

The COURT: Are you suggesting that the War Power's Clause at Article I, Section 8, Clause 11, I think, it is, means nothing?

Mr. GERSON: No, I'm not suggesting that at all.

The COURT: When does it apply?

Mr. GERSON: . . . [T]he framers, and those in government since the framers, envisioned self-initiated military action—that is what these plaintiffs would call offensive military action—but short of war and its profound domestic and international consequences. Perhaps the best evidence, while it has some constitutional problems that are not relevant here, and I read the literal language significantly differently from Mr. Lobel, is the so-called War Powers Resolution itself, which clearly envisions, by its literal terms, the introduction of troops into hostility before a declaration of war.

The Congress, which spoke in 1973, had the same understanding that the framers had that has been since the early days of this country. A declared war means plenty. It's extremely consequential. One need only look to what has gone on during declared wars and how hard it is to get out of one once one starts. International law questions are raised. That's understood.

. . .

There are contexts in which a court legitimately can talk about whether or not there is a war—whether an insurance payment ought to be made, whether a policy kicks in, whether certain kinds of contractual arrangements are activated, as was the case with the Iranians' claims matter that counsel cited. But when the two political branches are involved, when the juridical definition of a war is at issue, the courts universally, uniformly have abjured answering that question.

The COURT: Isn't there some historical evidence, legislative history, so to speak, indicating that one reason for this clause was to make certain that one person does not get the country involved in war? They were not talking about insurance payments; they were talking about getting the country involved in a war.

---

7. President Bush Requests Congress to Support Military Action Against Iraq

Source: Pub. Papers, 1991, I, at 13-14

Dear _____:

The current situation in the Persian Gulf, brought about by Iraq's unprovoked invasion and subsequent brutal occupation of Kuwait, threatens vital U.S. interests. The situation also threatens the peace. It would, however,

greatly enhance the chances for peace if Congress were now to go on record supporting the position adopted by the UN Security Council on twelve separate occasions. Such an action would underline that the United States stands with the international community and on the side of law and decency; it also would help dispel any belief that may exist in the minds of Iraq's leaders that the United States lacks the necessary unity to act decisively in response to Iraq's continued aggression against Kuwait.

. . .

I therefore request that the House of Representatives and the Senate adopt a Resolution stating that Congress supports the use of all necessary means to implement UN Security Council Resolution 678. . . .

Sincerely,

George Bush

Note: Identical letters were sent to Thomas S. Foley, Speaker of the House of Representatives; George J. Mitchell, Senate majority leader; Robert Dole, Senate Republican leader; and Robert H. Michel, House Republican leader.

---

8. Dole Defers to the President

Source: 141 Cong. Rec. S17529, S17862 (daily ed. November 27 & 30, 1995)

Now, in my view the President has the authority and the power under the Constitution to do what he feels should be done regardless of what Congress does. But we also have a responsibility to our constituents and, I think, to the President of the United States to give him our best advice.

. . .

. . . . It is time for a reality check in the Congress. The fact is that President Clinton has decided to send United States Forces to

Bosnia. The fact is that these troops will be sent—and indeed some are already there. The fact is by next week, there will be a couple thousand American soldiers on the ground in Bosnia.

The President has the constitutional power as Commander in Chief to send these forces. The Congress cannot stop this troop deployment from happening. The President and senior advisers have repeatedly said they will proceed with the deployment, whatever the Congress does. If we would try to cut off funds we would harm the men and women in the military who have already begun to arrive in Bosnia.

. . . We have one President at a time. He is the Commander in Chief. He has made this decision. I do not agree with it. I think it is a mistake.

---

9. Congressman Campbell Challenges Unilateral Presidential Wars

Source: Brief for Plaintiffs-Appellants, Campbell v. Clinton, No. 99-5214, D.C. Circuit, at 8-10, 20-21

This case poses the extremely important question of whether it is legal under the Constitution and the War Powers Resolution . . . for the President, acting alone and without the approval of a Congress that specifically addressed the issue, to initiate and continue offensive military action against the Republic of Yugoslavia. Despite the requirements of the Constitution and the WPR mandating that the President obtain the affirmative consent of Congress to engage in hostilities, and despite congressional votes refusing to give him that authority, the District Court dismissed the Complaint on the basis that plaintiffs lacked standing. . . .

This Circuit and others have rejected defendant's claim that a court can never determine whether the President's deployment of military force against another country requires the authorization of Congress. Rather, it has decided that a decision to wage war requires congressional approval and that courts are competent to decide whether combat activities are of such magnitude and duration as to require that approval.

Likewise, plaintiffs' claim that the President is in violation of the WPR can be decided by the District Court. Defendant has not and cannot claim that the WPR was inapplicable to the military action against Yugoslavia. The Resolution sets judicially manageable standards for determining when the sixty-day termination requirement is triggered—48 hours from when a Presidential report is submitted or required to be submitted. The President has submitted the report required under the WPR, and the Congress has treated it as the required report. Moreover, Congress has considered congressional resolutions pursuant to the WPR's priority procedures. In addition, the undisputed facts regarding the level of hostilities and administration admissions demonstrate that even had the President not submitted a report, he was required to do so. Thus, the lower court is not being asked to make a policy choice; it is being asked to perform the traditional function of courts: the interpretation of statutes and the application of the law to the facts.

. . .

Defendant argued below that the Constitution is ambiguous and contains no clear standard as to the respective competencies of the political branches to initiate a war against another nation. Article I, § 8 of the Constitution does however clearly set forth the respective competencies of the political branches. Only Congress can decide to go to war except where the President acts in an emergency to repel an enemy attack. *Mitchell v. Laird,* 488 F.2d

611, 613-14; *Dellums v. Bush*, 752 F. Supp. 1141, 1144-46 (D.D.C. 1990).

Our Constitution provides that a decision to initiate war be made by Congress. The framers were opposed to giving one person the power to initiate war. . . .

II. THE STEEL SEIZURE CASE

A 1952 case presented the Supreme Court with the penultimate conflict of whether the President should be allowed to win a war or act in a manner that is pursuant to the Constitution and to statutes passed by Congress. In the midst of a threatened nationwide strike affecting the steel industry in 1952, President Truman decided to forego the statutory option available to him: a cooling-off period of 80 days. That procedure had been included in the Taft-Hartley Act of 1947, a measure vetoed by Truman. The veto message objected that the bill discriminated against employees, deprived workers of basic rights, and weakened the trade union movement. Pub. Papers, 1947, 288-97. After both Houses overrode the veto, Truman said "[w]e must all respect its provisions" and pledged to see "that this law is well and faithfully administered." Id. at 306.

A. The Making of a Crisis

In June 1950, North Korea invaded South Korea. President Truman reacted by sending U.S. forces to Korea, without ever seeking approval or authority from Congress. What was initially referred to as a "police action," operating under the United Nations Charter, dragged on and became a full-scale war with mounting U.S. casualties. As the military conflict moved into 1951, Truman feared an escalation of wages and prices in the steel industry, with inflationary pressures then spreading to the rest of the economy.

Instead of availing himself of the process provided in the Taft-Hartley Act, Truman turned to informal procedures for working out an acceptable contract between labor and industry to replace the steel contract scheduled to expire on December 31, 1952. Months passed by without agreements. With a strike looming on April 9, 1952, Truman had in effect, through these efforts, invoked his own cooling-off period, one that had lasted 99 days. Politically, he could not then tack on an additional 80 days, especially under a statute he so opposed.

On the evening of April 8 he issued an Executive Order directing the Secretary of Commerce to seize steel mills (document 1). On the same evening, Truman delivered a radio and television speech to the nation to build public support for his action. In a message larded with criticism of 'the business community, he blasted the steel companies for selfish behavior and explained why he did not invoke the Taft-Hartley Act (document 2). Throughout this period, Truman attempted to shore up his support among labor.

B. Congress Responds

The legality of Truman's action was immediately challenged by some members of Congress, who pointed out that in 1951 Congress had specifically considered granting a President seizure authority and chose to reject that course (document 3). Newspapers from around the country published editorials that condemned Truman's theory of inherent and emergency power. The editorials (document 4) ripped him for acting in a manner they regarded as arbitrary, dictatorial, dangerous, destructive, high-handed, and unauthorized by law. 98 Cong. Rec. 4029-30, 4033-34 (1952).

At a news conference on April 17, Truman was asked by reporters whether he could also seize newspapers and radio stations. His reply: "Under similar circumstances the President of the United States has to act for whatever is for the best of the country. That's the answer to your question." Pub. Papers, 1952, at 273. Truman's remark was picked up in the press with this flavor: "The President has the power to do what is right for the people, Truman replied grimly. His sharp tone cut off further discussion of the point." Senators Homer Ferguson (R-Mich) and Henry Styles Bridges (R-N.H.) offered these interpretations:

> Mr. FERGUSON. . . . I have read history to some extent, and I think I am correct in saying that no ruler, no matter how great a tyrant he may have been, has failed to contend that he was acting for the good of the people regardless of his acts. In other words, the implication is that the President knows best what is right for the people.
> Mr. BRIDGES. Mr. President, will the Senator yield?
> Mr. FERGUSON. I am glad to yield to the Senator from New Hampshire.
> Mr. BRIDGES. The inference is that the President, himself, is to determine what is good for the people, rather than to allow the people to make the determination for themselves.
> Mr. FERGUSON. That is correct. [98 Cong. Rec. 4090 (1952)]

Truman's definition of executive power so offended the public that he soon found himself backtracking, noting ways in which legal and constitutional limits operate on the President. On April 21 he pointed out that Congress could act legislatively to check his action. He argued that Congress could not meet its responsibilities through inaction or passivity.

'Congress should, he said, either reject his course of action or pass legislation providing an alternative solution to the labor dispute. Pub. Papers, 1952, at 284. Congress refused to bite. Truman had gotten himself out on a limb and Congress felt no obligation to either rescue him or saw him down. He continued to dangle.

At a news conference on April 24, Truman equivocated on his legal authority, dismissing talk of seizing the press and the radio as "a lot of hooey" while insisting on a broad power to act unilaterally in times of emergency (document 5). Three days later he tried to quiet fears in the country by declaring that the President, like any public official, is under the law. To a private citizen he wrote:

> . . . I believe that I was acting within the powers of the President under the Constitution—and indeed, that it was the duty of the President under the Constitution to act to preserve the safety of the Nation. The powers of the President are derived from the Constitution, and they are limited, of course, by the provisions of the Constitution, particularly those that protect the rights of individuals. The legal problems that arise from these facts are now being examined in the courts, as is proper, but I feel sure that the Constitution does not require me to endanger our national safety by letting all the steel mills shut down in this critical time. Pub. Papers, 1952, at 301.

C. The Dispute Goes to Court

The steel companies took the matter to court, where the Justice Department presented a remarkable argument that the judiciary had no power to constrain the President. According to the theory of presidential power developed by the administration, the President could be controlled only in two ways: by impeachment and through elections (document 6). On April 29, District Judge David A. Pine wrote a blistering opinion that repudiated this theory of inherent presidential power. In holding Truman's seizure of the steel mills to be unconstitutional, Pine acknowledged that a nationwide strike could do extensive damage to the country, but believed that a strike "would be less injurious to the public than the injury which would flow from a timorous judicial recognition that there is some basis for this claim to unlimited and unrestrained Executive power, which would be implicit in a failure to grant the injunction." Youngstown Sheet & Tube Co. v. Sawyer, 103 F.Supp. 569, 577 (D.D.C. 1952).

On May 22, with the case pending before the Supreme Court, Truman seemed once again adamant about the existence of inherent presidential powers. Such powers, he said, could not be taken away by the other branches, although after several confrontations with reporters he conceded that a Court decision would be binding on him (document 7).

One of the law clerks on the Supreme Court at that time was William Rehnquist, now Chief Justice. In terms of legal precedents, he thought that the administration would prevail. Nevertheless, on June 2, a 6 to 3 majority declared the seizure unconstitutional. Youngstown Co. v. Sawyer, 343 U.S. 579 (1952). Reflecting on that decision, Rehnquist came to realize the extent to which the political climate influenced the Court. Truman's definition of presidential power unsettled the country and a strong, negative public sentiment pressed upon the Court. As Rehnquist remarked many years later: "I think that this is one of those celebrated constitutional cases where what might be called the tide of public opinion suddenly began to run against the government, for a number of reasons, and that this tide of public opinion had a considerable influence on the Court" (document 8).

DOCUMENTS

---

1. Truman Seizes the Steel Mills (Exec. Order 10340)

Source: 17 Fed. Reg. 3139, 3141 (1952)

WHEREAS on December 16, 1950, I proclaimed the existence of a national emergency which requires that the military, naval, air, and civilian defenses of this country be strengthened as speedily as possible to the end that we may be able to repel any and all threats against our national security and to fulfill our responsibilities in the efforts being made throughout the United Nations and otherwise to bring about a lasting peace; and

WHEREAS American fighting men and fighting men of other nations of the United Nations are now engaged in deadly combat with the forces of aggression in Korea, and forces of the United States are stationed elsewhere overseas for the purpose of participating in the defense of the Atlantic Community against aggression; and

WHEREAS the weapons and other materials needed by our armed forces and by those joined with us in the defense of the free world are produced to a great extent in this country, and steel is an indispensable component of substantially all of such weapons and materials; and

[Truman cites other "whereas" provisions, including the failure to settle the labor dispute through collective bargaining procedures, with a strike called for April 9, 1952, and the threat that a work stoppage would cause on national defense.]

NOW, THEREFORE, by virtue of the authority vested in me by the Constitution and laws of the United States, and as President of the United States and Commander in Chief of the armed forces of the United States, it is hereby ordered as follows:

1. The Secretary of Commerce is hereby authorized and directed to take possession of all or such of the plants, facilities, and other property of the companies named in the list attached hereto, or any part thereof, as he may deem necessary in the interests of national defense . . .

HARRY S. TRUMAN

THE WHITE HOUSE,
April 8th, 1952; 9:50 p.m. e.s.t.

2. Truman Appeals for Public Support

Source: Pub. Papers,
1952, at 246-50

My fellow Americans:

Tonight, our country faces a grave danger. We are faced by the possibility that at midnight tonight the steel industry will be shut down. This must not happen.

Steel is our key industry. It is vital to the defense effort. It is vital to peace.

We do not have a stockpile of the kinds of steel we need for defense. Steel is flowing directly from the plants that make it into defense production.

If steel production stops, we will have to stop making the shells and bombs that are going directly to our soldiers at the front in Korea. . . .

. . . In normal times, unions are entitled to whatever wages they can get by bargaining, and companies are entitled to whatever prices they can get in a competitive market.

But today, this is different. There are limitations on what wage employees can get, and there are limitations on what prices employers can charge. [Truman explains some rules established by the federal government regarding wage and price increases.]

.   .   .

You may think this steel dispute doesn't affect you. You may think it's just a matter between the Government and a few greedy companies. But it is not. If we granted the outrageous prices the steel industry wants, we would scuttle our whole price control program. . . .

A lot of people have been saying I ought to rely on the procedures of the Taft-Hartley Act to deal with this emergency.

This has not been done because the so-called emergency provisions of the Taft-Hartley Act would be of no help in meeting the situation that confronts us tonight. [Truman explains that the procedures of the Act required the President to establish a board of inquiry, which would report findings after a week or two. Meanwhile, the steel plants would be shut down. After that, the 80 day cooling-off period would begin.] But the fact is that in the present case, the steelworkers' union has already postponed its strike since last December 31—99 days. [In other words, instead of following the Taft-Hartley procedure the previous December, Truman chose an informal negotiation period that preempted a statutorily authorized process.]

3. Senators Challenge Truman's Action

Source: 98 Cong. Rec.
3956 (1952)

Mr. [Arthur] WATKINS [R-Utah]. Will the Senator tell us what the law is which restricts [labor unions from collective bargaining]?

Mr. [Homer] FERGUSON [R-Mich.]. It is the order of the President of the United States, Executive Order 10340, directing the Secretary of Commerce to take possession of and operate the plants and facilities of certain steel companies. The names of 86 steel companies are listed in that order.

Mr. WATKINS. Does the Senator seriously state now that the mere declaration by the President, or the order of the President, is the law of the land? I should like to know if the Senator is being facetious, or if he really believes that this is a law.

Mr. FERGUSON. I am merely stating that the President in his order is laying down what he believes to be law, and that the Secretary of Commerce, so far as the employers are concerned, will carry out that order until some way is found—which I shall discuss later—of bringing this question before the court to determine whether or not the seizure is legal.

Mr. WATKINS. Would the Senator say that in effect this is an edict of the President?

Mr. FERGUSON. It is a decree.

Mr. WATKINS. A decree of the President; and he refers to it as a law.

Mr. FERGUSON. That is correct. It is a decree of the President.

Mr. WATKINS. The Senator from Michigan is a fine lawyer, and he has been a judge. I should like to ask him, if, after a day's reflection, he has been able to find anything in the law or the Constitution which would give the President the right to do what he has done in issuing that order.

Mr. FERGUSON. I have not. Nor does the order itself specify any law under which the President was operating. He merely says that he is operating under the law of the land, the Constitution of the United States, the inherent powers of the President of the United States, and the inherent powers of the President as Commander in Chief of the Army and Navy of the United States. His statement deals in generalities. . . .

Mr. [Karl] MUNDT [R-S.D.]. . . .

. . .[W]hen we were debating the Defense Production Act on June 28, 1951, an amendment was offered by the Senator from Connecticut [Mr. Benton], the Senator from New York [Mr. Lehman], the Senator from Michigan [Mr. Moody], and one or two other Senators, by which they proposed to give the President precisely the power he is now exercising. They offered that when, in the judgment of the President, it would aid in the national defense, the President should be authorized to take over and operate such industries as the steel industry.

That amendment was thoroughly debated. . . . By a yea-and-nay vote, with only 25 Senators voting in the affirmative and 57 Senators recorded as voting in the negative,

the United States Senate specifically denied the President the authority which he is now usurping.

---

4. Newspaper Editorials Condemn Truman's Action

Source: 98 Cong. Rec. 4030, 4033-34 (1952)

A real liberal doesn't oppose arbitrary executive action only when it is directed against his own political interests. He opposes it wherever it shows itself, because he knows that while his political foe may be the victim today, tomorrow his friend or he himself may be the victim. (The New York Times)

There is grave danger—danger of the most vital character—in confirmation of dictatorial powers by the Executive: What is used to seize control of reluctant capital today will be used to compel obedience of reluctant labor tomorrow, and on the same grounds of urgency and necessity. (New York Daily Compass)

We believe that all segments of our population should share in the bounties of our land within the framework of a free economy which is regulated by laws instead of executive decrees. As for the Presidential order seizing the steel mills, we see it as dangerous. (Atlanta Constitution)

Mr. Truman should not be allowed dictatorially to bypass legislation in force and make his own law. The precedent he is attempting to establish would allow the President to take over any property, institution, or concern as he desired. (Boston Herald)

The President is behaving like a dictator, ignoring the lawful procedures set up by the Congress for Government intervention in strikes. If he gets away with this, there's no telling what might be the next step in confiscation of private property and infringement of personal liberties. (Cleveland News)

Mark this day and date on our calendar. It is the day on which, without the formality of an election, the Government of the United States ceased to be a Government by and for the people and came into the open frankly and nakedly as a labor dictatorship. (Indianapolis News)

President Truman's seizure of the steel industry will probably go down in history as one of the most high-handed acts committed by an American President. (Washington Post)

---

5. Truman Discusses Emergency Power

Source: Pub. Papers, 1952, at 290-92, 294

There has been a lot of hooey about the seizure of the press and the radio. As I told you last week, the President of the United States has very great inherent powers to meet great national emergencies. Until those emergencies arise a President cannot say specifically what he would do or would not do. I can say this, that the thought of seizing press and radio has never occurred to me. I have difficulty imagining the Government taking over and running those industries.

.   .   .

Q. Mr. President, you say that during an emergency you have very great inherent powers to act. Are there any limitations at all over a President's actions during an emergency?

THE PRESIDENT. Well, you had better read your history and find out. There are a lot of Presidents who have had to make decisions in emergencies, and if you will read history

you will find out why they had to make them. But it did not hurt the Republic. In fact, it made the Republic better.

.   .   .

Q. Mrs. May Craig, Portland (Maine) Press Herald. Mr. President, if I might return to the steel [seizure], please. I listen up at the Capitol all the time, and the feeling up there is that one of the greatest protections for our liberty is that we live by written law, and they dread a departure into unwritten or inherent powers, fearing that precedent. Do you recognize the danger of that too?

THE PRESIDENT. Well, of course I do, May. But then when you meet an emergency in an emergency, you have to meet it.

---

6. Oral Argument in Steel Seizure Case (District Court)

Source: H.R. Doc. No. 534, 82d Cong., 2d Sess. 255-58, 371-72 (1952)

Mr. [Homer] BALDRIDGE [Assistant Attorney General]: I call your Honor's attention to Article 2 of the Constitution which provides that the executive power shall be vested in the President of the United States; . . .

The COURT [U.S. District Judge David A. Pine]: What is meant by "executive powers," Mr. Baldridge? Isn't it the power to execute statutes?

Mr. BALDRIDGE: Well, among other things it is the power to protect the country in times of national emergency by whatever means seem appropriate to achieve that end.

The COURT: Well, how far would you carry that?

Mr. BALDRIDGE: Well, we don't think we have carried it too far in this particular instance, Your Honor. I don't know as I can discuss it—

Mr. BALDRIDGE: . . .

. . . as to the President's power to seize: I think in the last analysis it is fair to say that magnitude of the emergency itself is sufficient to create the power to seize under these circumstances.

The COURT: I think Chief Justice Hughes said in one of his opinions that emergencies do not create power. They may give an occasion for the exercise of power that has been dormant, but they do not create power.

Mr. BALDRIDGE: Well, under our Constitutional system, Your Honor, it seems to me that there is enough residual power in the executive to meet an emergency situation of this type when it comes up.

The COURT: I think that whatever decision I reach, Mr. Baldridge, I shall not adopt the view that there is anyone in this Government whose power is unlimited, as you seem to indicate.

. . .

The COURT: So you contend the Executive has unlimited power in time of an emergency?

Mr. BALDRIDGE: He has the power to take such action as is necessary to meet the emergency.

The COURT: If the emergency is great, it is unlimited, is it?

Mr. BALDRIDGE: I suppose if you carry it to its logical conclusion, that is true. But I do want to point out that there are two limitations on the Executive power. One is the ballot box and the other is impeachment.

The COURT: Then, as I understand it, you claim that in time of emergency the Executive has this great power.

Mr. BALDRIDGE: That is correct.

The COURT: And that the Executive determines the emergencies and the Courts cannot even review whether it is an emergency.

Mr. BALDRIDGE: That is correct.

7. Truman Again Defends Inherent Executive Powers

Source: Pub. Papers,
1952, at 361-64

THE PRESIDENT. There must be some provision to meet the situation. Whether seizure is the answer or not, I don't know. That is what we have had to use, because that is the only we had.

Q. Who would have that authority? The President would have that as statutory power in reserve, or would you have him go to Congress at each emergency?

THE PRESIDENT. The President *has* the power, and they can't take it away from him.

. . .

Q. Mr. President, as I understood you to say that the President *has* the power, that is, of seizure—

THE PRESIDENT. That's correct.

Q. —and "they" can't take it away—

THE PRESIDENT. That's correct.

Q. —who did you mean, sir, Congress—

THE PRESIDENT. Yes—

Q. —the courts, who?

THE PRESIDENT. —nobody can take it away from the President, because he is the Chief Executive of the Nation, and he has to be in a position to see that the welfare of the people is met.

. . .

Q. Isn't that what is up before the Supreme Court now?

THE PRESIDENT. No, I don't think so. No. As you will find out when the decision comes down.

Q. It might lead to some confusion. Would you explain—

THE PRESIDENT. I have—

Q. —what you feel is before the Court—

THE PRESIDENT. —I have no explanation to make, because I am not going to comment on what the Court is going to do.

Q. No. No, I am not asking you to do that, but you see, as it stands now, it appears that you have said the Court can't take the power away.

THE PRESIDENT. Nobody can take it away from the President, because it is inherent in the Constitution of the United States. I have cited you some precedents, now go and read them.

. . .

Q. Mr. President, you said on a previous occasion on the same subject, that you would abide by whatever—

THE PRESIDENT. That's correct.

Q. —decision the Supreme Court handed down.

THE PRESIDENT. That is exactly what I expect to do.

Q. Well, getting back to Joe's question, if the Court hands down a decision that you do not have the power, would you—

THE PRESIDENT. I will turn the steel companies—turn the steel industry back to the companies, and see what happens.

---

8. Rehnquist Reflects on Steel Seizure Case

Source: William H. Rehnquist, The Supreme Court 95-98 (1987)

The manner in which the case proceeded in the district court before Judge Pine had a considerable influence on public opinion. The government's original arguments in the district court, to the effect that the president's power was plenary unless some provision of the Constitution expressly denied authority to him, was rightly regarded as an extraordinary argument. The newspapers and commentators denounced it, and it obviously played a part in Judge Pine's decision in favor of the steel companies. The government quickly sensed that it had made a mistake in making these arguments, and recanted them almost immediately; by the time the case was argued in the Supreme Court, the arguments made by Holmes Baldridge in the district court had been entirely abandoned, but speaking as one who was on the scene at the time, I don't think they could be erased from anyone's mind. The government's litigation strategy in the district court, reported blow by blow in the Washington newspapers, undoubtedly had an effect on how the case was finally decided by the Supreme Court.

But I also think another, more deep-seated factor played a part in the tides of public opinion that were running at this time.

There was a profound ambivalence on the part of much of the public about the Korean War . . . . When North Korea invaded South Korea, President Truman and his top advisers deliberately refrained from asking Congress for a declaration of war, and the United States continued to refer to the Korean conflict as a "police action" under the aegis of the United Nations rather than as a war. But in fact it seemed indistinguishable to most people from a war . . .

. . . In the spring of 1952, the Korean conflict appeared to be pretty much of a stalemate; the result was an erosion of public willingness to sacrifice. We had a draft, we had price controls, we had rent controls, we had production controls, but these measures, which had been borne resolutely during the Second World War, were borne less resolutely and with considerably more grumbling during the Korean conflict. After President Truman forbade General MacArthur to authorize air strikes beyond the Yalu River, which separated North Korea from China, it seemed very difficult to figure out how the United States could "win" in Korea, and sacrifices that will be cheerfully borne when related to a clearly defined objective will not be so cheerfully borne when the objective seems confused and uncertain. . . .

Finally, although President Truman has today been accorded at least his just deserts by historians who have written since he left office, his standing in public opinion at the time of the Steel Seizure Case was at its nadir. . . .

These are the factors that I think played a considerable part in the way the Steel Seizure Case was decided. I was recently asked at a meeting with some people in Washington, who were spending a year studying various aspects of the government, whether the justices were able to isolate themselves from the tides of public opinion. My answer was that we are not able to do so, and it would probably be unwise to try. We read newspapers and magazines, we watch news on television, we talk to our friends about current events. No judge worthy of his salt would ever cast his vote in a particular case simply because he thought the majority of the public wanted him to vote that way, but that is quite a different thing from saying that no judge is ever influenced by the great tides of public opinion that run in a country such as ours. Judges are influenced by them, and I think that such influence played an appreciable part in causing the Steel Seizure Case to be decided the way it was.

6

PRIVACY

The Constitution explicitly protects a range of individual rights from governmental intrusion. What happens, however, when governmental action is not prohibited by express constitutional protections? Do implied fundamental rights limit governmental power? This question has bedeviled jurists, theorists, and politicians since Justices Chase and Iredell squared off in *Calder* v. *Bull*, 3 U.S. (3 Dall.) 386 (1798). For Chase: "There are certain vital principles in our free Republican governments, which will determine and overrule an apparent and flagrant abuse of legislative power," Id. at 388; for Iredell: "the Court cannot pronounce [legislation] to be void, merely because it is, in their judgment, contrary to the principles of natural justice. The ideas of natural justice are regulated by no fixed standard." Id. at 399.

The availability of implied rights raises questions about the judiciary's role in a democratic society. "Judicial review expresses," as Alexander Bickel observed, "a form of distrust of the legislature." Alexander M. Bickel, The Least Dangerous Branch 21 (1962). The greater the protection accorded unenumerated rights, the greater the judiciary's countermajoritarian role, and the greater the distrust. Likewise, limiting protections to explicit textual guarantees restricts the judicial role.

The current battlefield for this perennial debate over the judicial role is the so-called right to personal privacy. Abortion, homosexual sodomy, parental authority, and the termination of life-sustaining medical treatment are all part of this battle. On the one side, proponents of privacy speak of the Court's role as a countermajoritarian check and the Constitution as a "living charter." For these proponents, the Court may infuse natural law theories into Fourteenth Amendment due process protections of "life, liberty, and property." Michael H. v. Gerald D., 491 U.S. 110, 141 (1989) (Brennan, J., dissenting). On the other side, opponents argue that the Court "comes nearest to illegitimacy when it deals with judge-made constitutional law having little or no cognizable roots in the language or design of the Constitution." Bowers v. Hardwick, 478 U.S. 186, 194 (1986). For these opponents, the infusion of natural law theories into due process protections—better known as substantive due process decisionmaking—is nearly always (if not always) illegitimate.

This chapter examines three facets of this debate. Section I, by examining the Bork confirmation hearings and Supreme Court arguments in *Webster* v. *Reproductive Health Services*, 492 U.S. 490 (1989), considers elected branch efforts to shape Supreme Court privacy doctrine. Section II examines elected branch efforts to limit a woman's abortion right through its power of the purse (prohibiting federally funded abortions).   Section III describes state and federal responses to the Supreme Court's recent recognition of broad state authority to regulate abortions. Insights into what might happen if *Roe* v. *Wade* is overturned will be gleaned through this discussion.

I. THE REAGAN ADMINISTRATION v. PRIVACY

In 1980 and again in 1984, presidential candidate Ronald Reagan pledged to appoint judges "who respect traditional family values and the sanctity of innocent human life . . . [and] who share our commitment to *judicial restraint*." 1984 Republican Party Platform, reprinted in 40 Cong. Q. Almanac 55-B, 56-B (1984) (emphasis added).   The most visible mechanism for putting this philosophy of "judicial restraint" into action was administration attacks on Supreme Court privacy decisionmaking.

Attorney   General   William   French   Smith   summarized   the administration's position on privacy, arguing that the judiciary is wrong to "discern such an abstraction in the Constitution, arbitrarily elevate it over   other   constitutional   rights   and   powers   by   attaching   the   label 'fundamental,' and then resort to it as, in the words of one of Justice Black's dissents, a 'loose, flexible, uncontrolled standard for holding laws unconstitutional.'" William French Smith, Urging Judicial Restraint, 68 A.B.A.J. 59, 61 (1982) (quoting Griswold v. Connecticut, 381 U.S. 479, 521 (1965)). Privacy therefore was depicted as an unprincipled judicial powergrab which lessened the power of the people to govern themselves through the election of their representatives.

The fulcrum of the privacy wars is the Supreme Court's 1973 establishment of a woman's right to terminate her pregnancy. Roe v. Wade, 410 U.S. 113 (1973). Reagan often spoke of the need to "[a]ffirm [ ] the humanity of the unborn child in our society" and criticized the *Roe* decision as an unjustified "usurpation of the role of legislatures and State courts." Pub. Papers, 1982 (II), at 1104, 1105. The administration's challenge to judge-made law, however, necessarily extended beyond *Roe*. It encompassed the Supreme Court's approval of a parent's right to direct the upbringing of her child as well as the sanctity of the marital bedroom. These widely accepted manifestations of privacy doctrine proved the chief stumbling block in the administration's attack on unenumerated rights.

A. From *Lochner* to *Griswold*

The judicial tradition that serves as backdrop to family and marriage cases is the *Lochner* era, a period from 1905 to 1937 in which the Court infused *laissez-faire* economics into the due process clause to strike down roughly   two   hundred   social   and   economic   laws.   Overwhelmingly condemned as a symbol of unprincipled judicial overreaching, the *Lochner* era helped prompt FDR's court-packing plan.

In 1905, the Court invalidated a New York law limiting bakery workers to sixty hours a week or ten hours a day. Lochner v. New York, 198 U.S. 45 (1905). The Court concluded that, rather than serve public health objectives, the law created "meddlesome" and "unreasonable" interferences with an individual's right to enter into contracts. Labor unions, the press, and a host of social and economic groups openly challenged the Court. By 1937, with the popularity of the New Deal reinforced by Roosevelt's landslide victory in the 1936 election and the factual premise of Lochner's free market philosophy savaged by the enduring Depression, the Court seemed to put to rest its judicial veto of economic legislation and, with it, substantive due process decisionmaking.

The death of substantive due process ultimately proved short lived. The judicial lawmaking debate again took center stage with *Griswold* v. *Connecticut*, a 1965 Supreme Court decision invalidating a Connecticut statute that criminalized the use by married persons of any drug or medicinal article to prevent conception. 381 U.S. 479 (1965). Writing for the Court, Justice Douglas emphasized that a "zone of privacy [was] created by several fundamental constitutional guarantees," id. at 485, including the "penumbras, formed by emanations" of the First, Third, Fourth, Fifth, and Ninth Amendments. Id. at 484. Douglas explicitly rejected substantive due process' recognition of unenumerated rights as a basis for his decision. For Douglas: "We do not sit as a super-legislature to determine the wisdom, need, and propriety of laws that touch economic problems, business affairs, or social conditions." Id. at 482. This rejection is rooted in the prior discrediting of the *Lochner* era. By 1973, however, all nine Justices in *Roe v. Wade* agreed that due process protections extended beyond explicit Bill of Rights guarantees.

B. Bork's Challenge to *Griswold*

With the 1980 election of Ronald Reagan, substantive due process decisionmaking was again under attack. The defining moment was the July 1987 nomination of Robert Bork to the U.S. Supreme Court. Bork was nominated to replace judicial moderate Lewis Powell, the swing vote on a sharply divided Court and the justice who often stymied much of the Reagan revolution through decisive votes on abortion, affirmative action, and church-state matters. The Bork nomination, then, threatened to alter fundamental doctrines of the Court. Indeed, Senate Judiciary Committee Chairman Joseph Biden (D-Del.) suggested that the Bork controversy was more about the loss of Justice Powell than about Bork himself, remarking that if "Bork were about to replace Rehnquist or . . . Scalia, this would be a whole different ball game." Edward Walsh, Court Change Elevates Biden's Profile, Wash. Post, July 12, 1987, at A7.

In addition to these high stakes, the Bork nomination was controversial because the Reagan administration said that Bork embodied all that the courts should be. In Reagan's words, Bork shared his "belief in judicial restraint: that a judge is bound by the Constitution to interpret laws, not make them." Pub. Papers, 1987 (II), at 1230. For example, in a controversial 1971 law review article, Bork used *Griswold* v. *Connecticut* to illustrate the problems of judge-made law. Bork thought *Griswold* embodied the Warren Court's tendency to make its own value choices supreme and thereby displace elected government. For Bork, *Griswold* is "an unprincipled decision" which "fails every test of neutrality" (document 1).

Bork's attack on *Griswold* was not lost on his opponents. Although their principal concern was abortion, the Block Bork Coalition feared that turning the confirmation hearings into a divisive public referendum on abortion would play into White House charges that the Bork opposition was merely a thinly-veiled pro-choice special interest group. The solution was to "pluck the heartstrings of [the] middle class" by having abortion subsumed into the larger issue of privacy. Ann Lewis, an anti-Bork political consultant, describes how the campaign seized upon "privacy" as the salient issue:

> It was the right to privacy that he had challenged, so it wasn't that we sat around and thought "we can't talk about abortion, what's another word." He had handed us that because his attack was on the right to privacy. In addition, it was the strongest way to make the case, because when you talk about privacy, everyone has their own private ideas for private behavior. Michael Pertschuk & Wendy Schaetzel, The People Rising 257-58 (1989).

This strategy was implemented in a full page ad that appeared in *The Washington Post* and other newspapers on September 14, 1987. Planned Parenthood warned that the stakes of the Bork nomination were "[d]ecades of Supreme Court decisions uphold[ing] your freedom to make your own decisions about marriage and family, childbearing and parenting" and that "[i]f the Senate confirms Robert Bork, it will be too late. Your personal privacy, one of the most cherished and unique features of American life, has never been in greater danger."

Competing reports prepared by the White House and Senate Judiciary Committee Chairman Joseph Biden served as an opening volley in this debate. The White House Report defended Bork's position on privacy. The White House Report: Information on Judge Bork's Qualifications, Judicial Record & Related Subjects, reprinted in 9 Cardozo L. Rev. 187, 205-209 (1987). Characterizing the contemporary debate over privacy as "remarkably similar to the debate of the *Lochner* era," Bork's "judicial philosophy" was depicted as the simple demand that, "without a clear constitutional warrant, judges may not displace the considered judgments of elected officials." Id. at 209. In contrast, the Biden Report argued that Bork's "rejection of constitutional protection[s] against unwarranted intrusions into the intimacies of one's personal life" revealed an unprincipled disregard for "the text, history and tradition of the Constitution." The Biden Report, reprinted in 9 Cardozo L. Rev. 219, 244 (1987).

The real battle began on September 15, 1987, when Bork and members of the Senate Judiciary Committee went head-to-head on the privacy issue. Biden pressed Bork on his assertion that "the economic gratification of a utility company is as worthy of as much protection as the sexual gratification of a married couple, because neither is mentioned in the Constitution." Senator Edward Kennedy (D-Mass.) told Bork that he had "serious questions . . . about placing someone on the Supreme Court that . . . find[s] some rationale not to respect [privacy rights]." Bork responded that the founders "banked a good deal upon the good sense of the people [and their elected representatives]" and asked rhetorically: "Privacy to do to what[?] . . . to take cocaine in private? Privacy for businessmen to fix prices in a hotel room?" (document 2).

The Senate Judiciary Committee voted 9-5 against Bork's nomination. A cornerstone of the majority report was Bork's refusal to recognize a constitutional right to privacy (document 3). Although Senators such as Robert Dole (R-Kan.) labelled this privacy attack as "unfair" and "absurd," the Senate defeated the Bork nomination 58-42, in large measure because of the privacy issue (document 4).

After Bork, it seems unlikely that a judicial nominee will challenge privacy in such a direct manner. Indeed, Anthony Kennedy was quick to embrace privacy at his confirmation hearing. Kennedy noted that "the concept of liberty in the due process clause is quite expansive, quite sufficient, to protect the values of privacy that Americans *legitimately* think are part of their constitutional heritage." Nomination of Anthony M. Kennedy to be Associate Justice of the Supreme Court of the United States: Hearings Before the Senate Comm. on the Judiciary, 100th Cong., 1st Sess. 164 (1987) (emphasis supplied). Kennedy was confirmed by a unanimous Senate.

George Bush and Bill Clinton's Supreme Court nominees have also bowed to the altar of unenumerated privacy rights. The first question asked of David Souter at his confirmation hearings concerned his views on *Griswold,* to which he replied: "I believe that the Due Process Clause of the 14th Amendment does recognize and does protect an unenumerated right of privacy." Nomination of David H. Souter to be Associate Justice of the Supreme Court of the United States: Hearings Before the Senate Comm. on the Judiciary, 101st Cong., 2d Sess. 54 (1990). Even Clarence Thomas told Senator Biden on the first day of his hearings that "[my] view

is that there is a right to privacy in the Fourteenth Amendment."
Nomination of Judge Clarence Thomas to be Associate Justice of the
Supreme Court of the United States: Hearings before the Senate
Committee on the Judiciary, 102d Cong., 1st Sess. at 127 (1991).
Needless to say, Clinton nominees Ruth Bader Ginsburg and Stephen
Breyer embraced privacy rights at their confirmation hearings. For
Ginsburg, the decision whether or not to bear a child "is central to a
woman's life, to her well-being and dignity. It is a decision she must
make for herself." Nomination of Ruth Bader Ginsburg to be Associate
Justice of the Supreme Court of the United States: Hearings before the
Senate Comm. on the Judiciary, 103d Cong., 1st Sess. 207 (1993).

C. The Abortion Issue

Before the Supreme Court, the Reagan administration simultaneously
defended *Griswold* and attacked *Roe*. In *Webster* v. *Reproductive Health
Services*, 492 U.S. 490 (1989), the administration's brief "assum[ed]" that
Griswold "establish[ed] a general right to privacy or personal autonomy"
and then argued that *Roe* should be overturned because "abortion is
'inherently different' from decisions concerning marital privacy and the
use of contraceptives" (document 5). In oral arguments, moreover,
Special Assistant to the Attorney General and former Solicitor General
Charles Fried argued that "we are not asking the Court to unravel the
fabric of unenumerated and privacy rights which the court has woven in
cases like . . . *Griswold*" (document 6).

The narrowness of the Reagan administration attack against privacy
is also revealed in the administration's failure to participate in nonabortion
privacy cases. Court opinions limiting the scope of privacy doctrine in
Bowers v. Hardwick, 478 U.S. 186 (1986) (homosexual sodomy), and
Michael H. v. Gerald D., 491 U.S. 110 (1989) (unwed fathers), were
decided without the benefit of administration filings. When asked about
the Reagan administration's failure to participate in these cases, Charles
Fried said that administration actions were "*not* an attack against privacy."
He further stated that the Reagan administration and the Department of
Justice felt "no particular concern about privacy in general." Their
concern about privacy, he said, came only from a desire to narrow its
scope in regards to *Roe* v. *Wade*. Telephone interview of Charles Fried by
Carolyn Kimbler, Nov. 16, 1990.

D. Conclusion

The politics of *Griswold* is ultimately the politics of abortion. Bork
opponents championed privacy to avoid a divisive fight over abortion; the
Reagan administration spoke generally about judicial restraint but
defended *Griswold* in court and declined to involve itself in nonabortion

privacy cases. That both sides concealed the abortion question in the interest of *realpolitik* is hardly surprising. As long as abortion remains controversial, the debate over *Griswold* and judge-made law is likely to continue.

DOCUMENTS

1. Bork Attacks *Griswold*

Source: Robert H. Bork, Neutral Principles and Some First Amendment Problems, 47 Ind. L.J. 1, 2-3, 6-7, 9 (1971)

The requirement that the Court be principled arises from the resolution of the seeming anomaly of judicial supremacy in a democratic society. If the judiciary really is supreme, able to rule when and as it sees fit, the society is not democratic. The anomaly is dissipated, however, by the model of government embodied in the structure of the Constitution, a model upon which popular consent to limited government by the Supreme Court also rests. This model we may for convenience, though perhaps not with total accuracy, call "Madisonian."

A Madisonian system is not completely democratic, if by "democratic" we mean completely majoritarian. It assumes that in wide areas of life majorities are entitled to rule for no better reason that they are majorities. . . . The model has also a counter-majoritarian premise, however, for it assumes there are some areas of life a majority should not control. There are some things a majority should not do to us no matter how democratically it decides to do them. These are areas properly left to individual freedom, and coercion by the majority in these aspects of life is tyranny.

Some see the model as containing an inherent, perhaps an insoluble, dilemma. Majority tyranny occurs if legislation invades the areas properly left to individual freedom. Minority tyranny occurs if the majority is prevented from ruling where its power is legitimate. Yet, quite obviously, neither the majority nor the minority can be trusted to define the freedom of the other. This dilemma is resolved in constitutional theory, and in popular understanding, by the Supreme Court's power to define both majority and minority freedom through the interpretation of the Constitution. Society consents to be ruled undemocratically within defined areas by certain enduring principles believed to be stated in, and placed beyond the reach of majorities by, the Constitution.

If I am correct so far, no argument that is both coherent and respectable can be made supporting a Supreme Court that "chooses fundamental values" because a Court that makes rather than implements value choices cannot be squared with the presuppositions of a democratic society. The man who understands the issues and nevertheless insists upon the rightness of the Warren Court's performance ought also, if he is candid, to admit that he is prepared to sacrifice democratic process to his own moral views. He claims for the Supreme Court an institutionalized role as perpetrator of limited coups d'etat.

. . . The problem may be illustrated by *Griswold* v. *Connecticut*, in many ways a typical decision of the Warren Court. . . .

The *Griswold* opinion fails every test of neutrality. The derivation of the principle was utterly specious, and so was its definition. In fact, we are left with no idea of what the principle really forbids. . . .

Griswold, then, is an unprincipled decision, both in the way in which it derives a new constitutional right and in the way it defines that right, or rather fails to define it. We are left with no idea of the sweep of the right of privacy and hence no notion of the cases to which it may or may not be applied in the future. The truth is that the Court could not reach its result in *Griswold* through principle. The reason is obvious. Every clash between a minority claiming freedom and a majority claiming power to regulate involves a choice between the gratifications of the two groups. When the Constitution has not spoken, the Court will be able to find no scale, other than its own value preferences, upon which to weigh the respective claims to pleasure. . . .

---

2. Senators Question Bork About Privacy

Source: Nomination of Robert H. Bork to Be Associate Justice of the Supreme Court of the United States: Hearings Before the Senate Comm. on the Judiciary, 100th Cong., 1st Sess. (Part I) 114-17 (1987)

The CHAIRMAN [Senator Joseph Biden (D-Del.)]

. . . In your 1971 article, "Neutral Principles and Some First Amendment Problems," you said that the right of married couples to have sexual relations without fear of unwanted children is no more worthy of constitutional protection by the courts than the right of public utilities to be free of pollution control laws.

You argued that the utility company's right or gratification, I think you referred to it, to make money and the married couple's right or gratification to have sexual relations without fear of unwanted children . . . "are identical." Now, I am trying to understand this. It appears to me that you are saying that the government has as much right to control a married couple's decision about choosing to have a child or not, as that government has a right to control the public utility's right to pollute the air. Am I misstating your rationale here?

Judge [Robert] BORK. With due respect, Mr. Chairman, I think you are. I was making the point that where the Constitution does not speak—there is no provision in the Constitution that applies to the case—then a judge may not say, I place a higher value upon a marital relationship than I do upon an economic freedom. Only if the Constitution gives him some reasoning. Once the judge begins to say economic rights are more important than marital rights or vice versa, and if there is nothing in the Constitution, the judge is enforcing his own moral values, which I have objected to. Now, on the *Griswold* case itself—

The CHAIRMAN. So that you suggest that unless the Constitution, I believe in the past you used the phrase, textually identifies, a value that is worthy of being protected, then competing values in society, the competing value of a public utility, in the example you used, to go out and make money—that economic right has no more or less constitutional protection than the right of a married couple to use or not use birth control in their bedroom. Is that what you are saying?

Judge BORK. . . . [A]ll I am saying is that the judge has no way to prefer one to the other and the matter should be left to the legislatures who will then decide which competing gratification, or freedom, should be placed higher.

The CHAIRMAN. Then I think I do understand it, that is, that the economic gratification of a utility company is as worthy of as much protection as the sexual gratification of a married couple, because neither is mentioned in the Constitution.

Judge BORK. All that means is that the judge may not choose.

The CHAIRMAN. Who does?

Judge BORK. The legislature.

---

3. The Senate Judiciary Committee Disapproves the Bork Nomination

Source: S. Exec. Rep. No. 7, 100th Cong., 1st Sess. 8, 20-21 (1987)

The Bork hearings opened on the eve of the celebration of the 200th anniversary of our Constitution. The hearings proved to be about that Constitution, not just about a Supreme Court nominee.

The hearings reaffirmed what many understand to be a core principle upon which this nation was founded: Our Constitution recognizes inalienable rights and is not simply a grant of rights by the majority.

. . .

The image of human dignity has been associated throughout our history with the idea that the Constitution recognizes "unenumerated rights." These are rights beyond those specifically mentioned in the Constitution itself, rights that are affirmed by the grand open-ended phrases of the document: "liberty," "due process," "equal protection of the laws" and others. The sober responsibility of preserving the meaning and content of these rights has fallen to the judiciary, and especially to the Supreme Court.

Judge Bork's narrow definition of liberty sets him apart from the tradition and history from which this nation was conceived. . . .

4. The Senate Debates the Bork Nomination

Source: 133 Cong. Rec. 29107, 29109, 29110 (1987)

Mr. [Robert] DOLE [R-Kan.]. . . .
We have heard a lot about the right of privacy. One of the most unfair criticisms leveled at Judge Bork suggests that he is an "extremist who believes —Americans—have no constitutional right to personal privacy." This charge is absur[d] on its face, since, as Judge Bork has noted, the Constitution explicitly protects certain rights of personal privacy, including, for example, the "right of people to be secure in their persons, houses, papers, and effects against unreasonable search and seizures."
What Judge Bork has found unsettling is the judicial creation of a vague, generalized right to privacy based on the "penumbras"—the vague, indefinite borderline areas—of these specific constitutional guarantees.

Whether or not one agrees with Judge Bork's positions on Griswold versus Connecticut or Roe versus Wade, it is simply irresponsible to label those positions as extreme or unsupported. In taking those positions, he is in good and numerous company with some of the best legal thinkers in our Nation. The brickbats that [have] been

hurled at him on this subject, therefore, are simply one more example of slogans passing for legal reasoning.

Mr. [Robert] BYRD [D-W.Va.]. . . .
Mr. President, among the many concerns I have about Judge Bork's jurisprudential views none ranks higher than the unease with which I observe his constricted view of the rights all of us have. In stark briefness, Judge Bork thinks that those rights are very limited in number and subject to majority limitation. Even as to the rights which are spelled out in the Constitution and the Bill of Rights, his respect is tentative and hesitant. . . .
What radical interests these [substantive due process] decisions protected, Mr. President. The right to have your child taught a foreign language or educated in a religious school. The right not to have your powers to conceive children taken away. The right to have your grandchildren in your home. The right to marry. Are these privacy rights, these liberties, so [foreign] to our values that Judge Bork finds it impossible to discern any protection for them in the Constitution? . . .

5. The Reagan Administration Seeks to Overturn *Roe*

Source: Brief for the United States as Amicus Curiae Supporting Appellants at 5-6, 11-15, Webster v. Reproductive Health Services, 492 U.S. 490 (1989) (No. 88-605)

Roe v. Wade, as the Court is well aware, has been intensely controversial from the day it was decided. That controversy is more than simply a reflection of the deep divisions in American society over the underlying question of abortion. Rather, the controversy has, in substantial measure, been a product of the decision itself. *Roe* rests on assumptions that are not firmly grounded in the Constitution; it adopts an unworkable framework tying permissible state regulation of abortion to particular periods in pregnancy; and it has allowed courts to usurp the function of legislative bodies in weighing competing social, ethical, and scientific factors in reaching a judgment as to how much state regulation is appropriate in this highly sensitive area. In similar circumstances, the Court has "not hesitated" to overrule a prior interpretation of the Constitution. It should do so here as well.

. . .

The primary source for fundamental rights lies in the provisions of the Constitution other than the Fourteenth Amendment itself. . . . In contrast, the right to abortion identified in *Roe* was grounded only in the liberty clause of the Fourteenth Amendment. As this Court recently reaffirmed, "[t]he Court is most vulnerable and comes nearest to illegitimacy when it deals with judge-made constitutional law having little or no cognizable roots in the language or design of the Constitution."

---

6. *Roe* Challenged in *Webster* Oral Arguments

Source: 183 Landmark Briefs
934-935, 939-940

[The Department of Justice]:

Mr. [Charles] FRIED: . . . Today the United States asks this court to reconsider and overrule its decision in Roe v. Wade. At the outset, I would like to make quite clear how limited that submission is. First, we are not asking the Court to unravel the fabric of unenumerated and privacy rights which this court has woven in cases like *Meyer* and *Pierce* and *Moore* and *Griswold.* Rather, we are asking the Court to pull this one thread.
. . .

QUESTION: Your position, Mr. Fried, then is that *Griswold v. Connecticut* is correct and should be retained?

Mr. FRIED: Exactly, Your Honor.

QUESTION: Is that because there is a fundamental right involved in that case?

Mr. FRIED: In *Griswold v. Connecticut*, there was a right which was well established in a whole fabric of quite concrete matters, quite concrete. It involved not an abstraction such as the right to control one's body, an abstraction such as the right to be let alone, it involved quite concrete intrusions into the details of marital intimacy. And that was

emphasized by the Court and is a very important aspect of the Court's decision.

QUESTION: Does the case stand for the proposition that there is a right to determine whether to procreate?

Mr. FRIED: *Griswold* surely does not stand for that proposition.

QUESTION: What is the right involved in Griswold?

Mr. FRIED: The right involved in *Griswold* as the court clearly stated was the right not to have the state intrude into, in a very violent way, into the details—inquire into the details of marital intimacy. There was a great deal of talk about inquiry into the marital bedroom and I think that is a very different story from what we have here.

[Reproductive Health Services]:

Mr. [Frank] SUSMAN: . . . I think the Solicitor General's submission is somewhat disingenuous when he suggests to this court that he does not seek to unravel the whole cloth of procreational rights, but merely to pull a thread. It has always been my personal experience that when I pull a thread, my sleeve falls off. There is no stopping.

It is not a thread he is after. It is the full range of procreational rights and choices that constitute the fundamental right that has been recognized by this court. For better or for worse, there no longer exists any bright line between the fundamental right that was established in *Griswold* and the fundamental right of abortion that was established in *Roe*. These two rights, because of advances in medicine and science, now overlap. They coalesce and merge and they are not distinct.

QUESTION: Excuse me, you find it hard to draw a line between those two, but easy to draw a line between first, second and third trimester.

Mr. SUSMAN: I do not find it difficult—

QUESTION: I don't see why a court that can draw that line can't separate abortion from birth control quite readily?

Mr. SUSMAN: If I may suggest the reasons in response to your question, Justice Scalia. The most common forms of what we generically in common parlance call contraception today—IUDs, low-dose birth control pills, which are the safest type of birth control pills available—act as abortifacients. They are correctly labeled as both.

Under this statute, which defines fertilization as the point of beginning, those forms of contraception are also abortifacients. Science and medicine refers to them as both. We are not still dealing with the common barrier methods of *Griswold*. We are no longer just talking about condoms and dia- phragms. Things have changed. The bright line, if there ever was one, has now been extinguished. That's why I suggest to this court that we need to deal with one right, the right to procreate. We are no longer talking about two rights.

II. EXECUTIVE AND LEGISLATIVE RESPONSES TO *ROE*

Roe v. *Wade* spurred elected government into action. It functioned as a political catalyst rather than the last word on abortion. In the decade before the decision, only ten abortion-related bills were introduced in Congress. During the decade after *Roe*, 500 abortion bills were introduced. Congress' record here is mixed. It has accepted numerous restrictions on federal abortion funding, prohibited the performance of abortions at military hospitals and federal penitentiaries, and funded pro- life counselling programs. However, efforts to statutorily repeal *Roe* by either defining life at conception or curtailing federal court jurisdiction in this area have been rejected.

Congress, moreover, has refused to act on two proposed constitutional amendments: one a "human life" amendment that would outlaw abortion by extending constitutional protection to fetuses at the "moment of fertilization," S.J. Res. 8, 98th Cong., 1st Sess., reprinted in 129 Cong. Rec. 685-90 (1983); the other a Human Life Federalism Amendment which provided that "[t]he Congress and the several states have the concurrent power to restrict and prohibit abortions; *provided*, That a law of a State [which is] more restrictive than a law of Congress shall govern." S.J. Res. 110, 97th Cong., 1st Sess., reprinted in 127 Cong. Rec. 21383 (1981).

The executive branch, especially during the Reagan and Bush presidencies, has been extremely active in its efforts to restrict abortion. It has participated in numerous lawsuits, prohibited research on fetal tissue, and adopted restrictive regulations on family planning counselling. In addition, the executive has launched varied and numerous rhetorical attacks against abortion, including speeches, legislative proposals, and Surgeon General reports. Through the threatened and actual use of the veto power, the executive has pressured Congress to maintain strict anti- abortion funding prohibitions. With the election of Bill Clinton, however, Reagan and Bush-era initiatives were rescinded. Clinton, moreover, appointed pro-choice judges and vetoed a Congress-approved ban of partial birth abortion.

A. From *Roe* to Hyde

On January 22, 1973, the Supreme Court issued its decision in *Roe* v. *Wade*. 410 U.S. 113 (1973). Holding that the state's interest in potential human life is not compelling until the third trimester of pregnancy (once the fetus becomes viable) and that the state's interest in promulgating *reasonable* maternal health regulations is not compelling until after the first trimester of pregnancy, the decision to have a first trimester abortion was left to the woman (in consultation with her physician). By valuing a woman's right to privacy over potential human life and by imposing a trimester standard that reads like a legislative abortion code, *Roe* became a lightening rod for anti-abortion forces.

Within months of the decision, numerous anti-abortion measures had been introduced in Congress. One statute would have defined a "person" for Fourteenth Amendment purposes to include "any animate combination of viable human cells;" another statute would have limited abortion protections to instances where the life of a pregnant woman was at stake; a constitutional amendment would return abortion policy to the states; and another amendment proposal would extend Fourteenth Amendment protections to "unborn offspring." See 119 Cong. Rec. 37113 (1973). However, these proposals were not passed, in part because the congressional committees with jurisdiction to consider these proposals refused to act. After the House Judiciary Committee rejected a motion to hold hearings on abortion, a proposal was offered to "relieve the Judiciary Committee from jurisdiction" over abortion. See id. Frustrated by these tactics, anti-abortion forces turned their attention to the subterranean world of appropriations-based policymaking. Riders were attached to appropriations bill to prohibit the use of appropriated funds to finance abortions.

In 1974, Congress considered and *rejected* limitations on federal funding of abortions. At that time, the prevailing view in Congress was that "an annual appropriation bill is an improper vehicle for such a controversial and far-reaching legislative provision whose implications and ramifications are not clear, whose constitutionality has been challenged, and on which no hearings have been held." H.R. Rep. No. 1489, 93rd Cong., 2d Sess., reprinted in 120 Cong. Rec. 36928, 36933 (1974). After this action, chief bill opponent Bella Abzug (D-N.Y.)—who had characterized the bill as a "blunderbuss restriction" and "mindless legislation"—happily declared that Congress had "at last conceded the wisdom of *Roe*." 30 Cong. Q. Almanac 101 (1974). This "concession" was short-lived, however. Starting in 1976, Congress has prohibited most forms of federal abortion assistance.

B. The Hyde Amendments

After defeats in 1974 and 1975, anti-abortion forces scored a stunning victory in 1976.   During debates on the appropriations bill for the Department of Health, Education, and Welfare (now the Department of Health and Human Services), Representative Henry Hyde (R-Ill.) decided that it would be "a nice idea if we could just sneak an amendment in there that would halt this nefarious practice [of government supported abortion]" and "scribbled . . . out" a funding prohibition "in longhand right on the spot." Peg O'Hara, Congress and the Hyde Amendment . . . How the House Moved to Stop Abortions, 38 Cong. Q. Weekly Rep. 1038 (Apr. 19, 1980). At that time, the Health, Education, and Welfare appropriation was paying for 250,000 to 300,000 of an estimated one million abortions a year at an estimated cost of $45 million. Id. The Hyde Amendment specified that "[n]one of the funds appropriated under this Act shall be used to pay for abortions or to promote or encourage abortions." 122 Cong. Rec. 20410 (1976).

Debate over this proposal was dramatic and emotional (document 1). Hyde spoke of the "unborn child" as deserving "better than to be flushed down a toilet or burned in an incinerator." Hyde opponent Daniel Flood (D-Pa.) characterized the measure as "blatantly discriminatory" because the denial of Medicaid funds effectively "prohibits abortion for poor people."   After eleven weeks and dozens of compromise proposals, Congress agreed to a prohibition on abortion-related Medicaid funds "except where the life of the mother would be endangered if the fetus were carried to term." 90 Stat. 1418, 1434 (1976).

The 1977 battle over abortion funding proved more divisive than its predecessor. Representative Hyde reintroduced the 1976 compromise language with rhetorical flourish:

> Theology does not animate me; biology does. That is a human life; that is not a potential human life; it is a human life with potential.
>
> When a pregnant woman, who should be the natural protector of her unborn child, becomes its deadly adversary, then it is the duty of this legislature to intervene on behalf of defenseless human life. 123 Cong. Rec. 19701 (1977).

Opponents returned to their arguments of class-based legislation and the misuse of the appropriations process. Over the next five months (from June 17 to December 7), the mother of all appropriations battles took place. Before the matter was decided, 28 roll call votes were taken (seventeen in the Senate and eleven in the House), two continuing resolutions expired, and thousands of federal employees were threatened with delays in their paychecks. When the dust had finally settled, the 1977 Hyde Amendment provided:

[N]one of the funds provided for in this paragraph shall be used to perform abortions except where the life of the mother would be endangered if the fetus were carried to term; or except for such medical procedures necessary for the victims of rape or incest, when such rape or incest has been reported promptly to a law enforcement agency or public health service; or except in those instances where severe and long-lasting physical health damage to the mother would result if the pregnancy were carried to term when so determined by two physicians. 91 Stat. 1460 (1977).

This compromise language did not survive. In 1979, the exemption for medically necessary abortions was dropped. 93 Stat. 923, 926 (1979). In 1980, a caveat, added to the rape exemption, demanded that rape victims report the crime within 72 hours. 94 Stat. 3166, 3170 (1980). Finally, in 1981, Congress dropped the rape and incest exemption. The 1981 language remained unaltered until 1993. With the election of Bill Clinton, anti-Hyde forces found an ally in the White House. As a result, the funding ban was moderated. Congress restored the rape and incest exception and eliminated restrictions on District of Columbia abortion funding. 107 Stat. 1350, §142 (1993).

The Hyde Amendment typifies Congress' use of appropriations as the principal weapon in its anti-*Roe* arsenal. Other funding restrictions apply to appropriations for the Department of Defense, 97 Stat. 1421, 1447 (1983) (which prohibits use of funds to perform abortions unless the life of the woman would be endangered); Peace Corps, 101 Stat. 1329-145 (1987) (no funds may be used to pay for abortions); Legal Services Corporation, 88 Stat. 378, 385 (1974) (prohibiting legal assistance for the procurement of abortions in federally funded legal assistance programs); Bureau of Prisons, 101 Stat. 1329-17, 18 (1987) (prohibiting use of funds to perform abortions); and family planning, 84 Stat. 1504, 1508 (1970) (prohibiting the use of funds for programs in which abortion is a method of family planning).

Congress' continuing reliance on appropriations-based policymaking in this area seems surprising. Although the single-year nature of appropriations affords Congress the luxury of fine tuning, the annual ritual of reenacting Hyde has cost all three branches. Congress is forced to address this acrimonious issue each year; annual changes in appropriations-based policy create a moving target for courts to interpret; and agencies struggle to develop a long-term enforcement structure.

Appropriation measures are preferred over constitutional amendment and direct statutory repeals because they are easier to enact. A funding ban leaves the right intact and hence appears to be a moderate response. Congress' decision not to finance an activity which many find morally reprehensible does not necessarily call into question the correctness of

Roe. Women continued to have access to abortions, but had to rely increasingly on private rather than federal funds.

C. From *Harris* to Reagan

The controversy over the Hyde Amendment was not limited to the halls of Congress. In the courts, the amendment came under sharp constitutional attack. A brief filed by the Center for Constitutional Rights emphasized privacy concerns, arguing that the Hyde Amendment was premised on the belief that "abortion is . . . murder" and therefore served an unconstitutional purpose. Brief for Appellees, 115 Landmark Briefs at 238. Equality concerns were highlighted by the National Organization for Women (NOW), which argued that "[t]he purpose and effect of this exclusionary funding scheme is to induce indigent women to carry unwanted pregnancies to term." Brief for National Organization for Women as Amici Curiae, 115 Landmark Briefs at 657-58. Finally, the American Civil Liberties Union (ACLU) characterized the Hyde Amendment as "'religious gerrymandering' which cannot survive the neutrality demanded by the Establishment Clause." Brief of Appellees, 115 Landmark Briefs, at 247.

Briefs filed by the Carter Department of Justice and a coalition of over 200 members of Congress answered these charges. The Justice Department argued that Congress' decision to treat abortion differently from other health programs was not malicious, for "abortion is the only medically necessary service that involves the purposeful termination of potential human life." Brief for the Secretary of Health, Education, and Welfare, 115 Landmark Briefs at 29. This brief also answered the establishment clause charge, noting that the "belief that life begins at conception is not exclusively religious in character and is not solely attributable to the Roman Catholic Church." Id. at 35. The congressional brief spoke almost exclusively to separation of powers concerns, namely, the Constitution's Article I, Section 9 demand that "[n]o money shall be drawn from the Treasury but in Consequence of Appropriations made by Law" (document 2).

In *Harris* v. *McRae*, 448 U.S. 297 (1980), the Supreme Court upheld the Hyde Amendment. The Court ruled that "[w]hether freedom of choice that is constitutionally protected warrants federal subsidization is a question for Congress to answer, not a matter of constitutional entitlement." Id. at 318. *Harris* was a victory both for Congress and the Carter administration. Although President Carter opposed a constitutional amendment to prohibit abortion because "my solemn oath and my duties as President" required him "to carry out the ruling of the Supreme Court," he also spoke against federal funding of abortions. Pub. Papers, 1980 (III), at 2354. Indeed, when questioned about the disproportionate burden that poor women suffer under the Hyde Amendment, Carter answered: "[A]s you know, there are many things in life that are not fair, that wealthy people can afford and poor people can't. But I don't believe that the Federal Government should take action to try to make these opportunities exactly equal, particularly when there is a moral factor involved." Pub. Papers, 1977 (II), at 1237.

Despite this ostensible support for abortion funding prohibitions, the Carter administration came under sharp attack from anti-abortion forces for its implementation of the Hyde Amendment. Representative Hyde angrily labelled Carter administration regulations "the weakest . . . possible, inviting massive fraud and providing no protection whatever to prenatal life." 124 Cong. Rec. 1476 (1978).

President Carter's skirmishes with anti-abortion interests over his implementation of the Hyde funding ban highlight the extraordinarily important role that the executive plays in putting legislative programs into effect. Nowhere is this more clear than in comparing both the rhetoric and the initatives of the Carter and Reagan administrations. In the 1980 presidential campaign, for example, Carter ran on a platform which "oppose[d] government interference in the reproductive decisions of Americans" and "recognize[d] reproductive freedom as a fundamental human right." 1980 Democratic Party Platform, reprinted in 36 Cong. Q. Almanac 91-B, 106-B (1980). In sharp contrast, Reagan's 1980 Republican Party Platform "support[ed] a constitutional amendment to restore protection of the right to life for unborn children." 1980 Republican Party Platform, reprinted in 36 Cong. Q. Almanac 58-B, 62-B (1980). The election of Ronald Reagan then changed the face of White House abortion policy.

Once in office, Reagan's criticisms of *Roe* became more pitched. In the words of Reagan's Solicitor General Charles Fried, "[t]he Reagan administration made *Roe* v. *Wade* the symbol of everything that had gone wrong in law, particularly constitutional law." Charles Fried, Order and Law 72 (1991). In Reagan's view, *Roe* v. *Wade* was as divisive and as wrong as *Dred Scott*. Indeed, in one of his writings, Reagan proclaimed:

> Abraham Lincoln recognized that we could not survive as a free land when some men could decide that others were not fit to be free . . . [W]e cannot survive as a free nation when some men decide that others are not fit to live. . . . My Administration is dedicated to the preservation of America as a free land . . . [by preserving] the transcendent right to life of all human beings, the right without which no other rights have any meaning (document 3).

These sentiments are reflected in countless speeches and addresses given by Reagan on abortion.

Reagan did much more than use the bully pulpit to reverse *Roe*. He used the full arsenal of weapons available to a President: judicial and administrative appointments, court briefs, legislative proposals, constitutional amendment proposals, and regulatory initiatives. The principal weapon in this attack against *Roe* was regulation. The most significant regulatory initiatives were prohibitions on fetal tissue research and the so-called "gag order" limiting Title X family planning counseling.

D. Reagan's Regulatory Initiatives

The Reagan administration's reliance on agency regulations is to be expected. Direct attacks on *Roe* by way of repeal legislation and constitutional amendment, of course, require congressional support. Despite strong White House backing of human life legislation, a permanent Hyde Amendment, and several other proposals, Reagan's legislative campaign failed. Congress refused to enact any of these anti-abortion proposals. Regulatory action does not require formal congressional support. Executive regulations generally have the force of law unless Congress enacts overriding legislation (which is then subject to a presidential veto). In other words, just as Congress can make law by enacting a statute, the President exercises comparable authority by promulgating regulations.

In March 1988, the Reagan administration's placed a moratorium on funding research that uses aborted fetal tissue. Prompted by National Institute of Health (NIH) plans to seek a cure for Parkinson's disease through fetal tissue implants, Department of Health and Human Services official Robert Windom imposed the ban because of unresolved "ethical and legal" questions. Michael Specter, NIH Told to Stop Use of Aborted Fetuses, Wash. Post, Apr. 15, 1988, at A1. In spite of January 1989 recommendations to end the ban by both the NIH and a federally appointed Human Fetal Tissue Transplantation Research Panel, the moratorium was extended indefinitely—this time by Bush's Secretary of Health and Human Services Louis Sullivan. While recognizing that the use of aborted fetal issue "could potentially produce health benefits," Sullivan thought the "moral and ethical" costs too high. HHS Press Release, Nov. 2, 1989.

A more dramatic example of executive regulatory power is the controversy over family planning counselling. The story begins in 1970, when Congress added to Title X, a comprehensive family planning statute, an explicit prohibition against appropriating funds "where abortion is a method of family planning." 84 Stat. 1504, 1508 (1970).

The Nixon administration interpreted the funding ban "literally," prohibiting "financial support of programs in which abortions are provided." Ruth Marcus, Court's Conservatives Take Aggressive Path,

Wash. Post, June 3, 1991, at A7. These regulations, promulgated before *Roe* when the federal abortion controversy was dormant, prompted little reaction. When the Carter administration revised these regulations in 1981, the abortion question had clearly moved to the center stage of American political debate. The Carter administration fueled this debate by mandating that "non-directive counseling" on "pregnancy termination" and other alternative courses of action be given to women "requesting information options for the management of an unintended pregnancy." Program Guidelines for Project Grants for Family Planning Services, Part II, 8.6 at 13 (1981).

The Reagan administration vehemently opposed the Carter regulations. Noting that the requirement of nondirective counseling on pregnancy termination "has effectively barred family planning organizations that will not engage in abortion activity from participating in the title 10 program," the administration sought to repeal the Carter regulations. Pub. Papers, 1987 (II), at 895, 897. At first, the administration worked with Representative Jack Kemp (R-N.Y.), Senator Orrin Hatch (R-Utah), and others to legislatively prohibit family planning recipients from referring pregnant women for abortions. That measure failed and the administration elected to override the Carter scheme through its own regulatory initiatives. On July 30, 1987, Reagan briefed right-to-life leaders about "steps that I believe represent powerful examples of what can be done now to protect the lives of unborn children," including "a restriction on the use of Federal funds for activities that advocate abortion." Id. at 896, 898.

On September 1, 1987, proposed regulations were published. The Reagan proposal placed three controversial demands on funded clinics, namely: (1) that they maintain complete physical and financial separation of federally funded activities and abortion-related activities; (2) that they neither encourage, promote, nor advocate abortion as a method of family planning; and (3) that they refuse to provide abortion counselling or referrals. 52 Fed. Reg. 33214-15 (1987). The impact of this proposal was tremendous, affecting over one-third of the total public family planning funds (approximately $150 million per year). Specifically, 3,900 clinics serving 4.3 million people participate in the Title X program.

The proposal drew heavy criticism and a few compliments. Some members referred to the proposal as "long-awaited" and congratulated the administration on "restor[ing] a Congressionally-mandated wall of separation between family planning and abortion." Letter from Senator Gordon Humphrey to Secretary of Health and Human Services Otis Bowen, Nov. 2, 1987. Many members of Congress, however, were outraged by the President's decision to promulgate these regulations. Senator Edward Kennedy, joined by 34 other senators, described the proposal as "not in the best interest of the 5,000,000 low income [persons] that depend upon the program each year for family planning services."

Letter from Senator Edward Kennedy to Secretary of Health and Human Services Otis Bowen, Oct. 30, 1987. Efforts to block the Reagan proposal failed. On February 2, 1988, the Reagan proposal became final (document 4).

E. Judicial Challenges, Legislative and Executive Responses

The Reagan proposal was immediately challenged and quickly worked its way to the Supreme Court. In its Supreme Court brief and oral arguments, the Bush Administration picked up where the Reagan administration left off. Relying principally on *Harris* v. *McRae*, the government contended that the right to an abortion need not be subsidized by the state, and that the regulations did not amount to an unconstitutional obstacle to the exercise of that right. Against claims that the regulation violated the free speech rights of physicians, the government argued that the First Amendment does not require the state to subsidize all expression, but rather permits the state to pick and choose which values it seeks to promote. Brief for the United States, Rust v. Sullivan, 206 Landmark Briefs at 309.

The Supreme Court upheld the regulations in 1991. Rust v. Sullivan, 500 U.S. 173 (1991). The five-member majority agreed with the Bush administration claim that "the government may 'make a value judgment favoring childbirth over abortion, and . . . implement that judgment by the allocation of public funds.'" At the same time, Congress was considering a proposal to require Title X clinics to provide a pregnant woman with nondirective counseling on all her options, including abortion. The bill viewed the Reagan regulations as a denial of "quality health care" to low-income pregnant women and as "bizarre and cruel" (document 5). When this legislative repeal effort stalled, Congress turned to the appropriations process by approving a rider that prohibited federal funding of the Reagan regulations. President Bush vetoed that bill and Congress failed in its override effort.

Bill Clinton's victory in 1992 set the stage for another challenge to *Rust*. On January 22, 1993, two days after his inauguration, Clinton dismantled the pro-life regulatory initiatives of the Reagan and Bush administrations. Speaking of our national "[goal] to protect individual freedom" and his vision "of an America where abortion is safe and legal, but rare" (document 6), Clinton directed his Secretaries of Health and Human Services and Defense as well as the Administrators of the Food and Drug Administration and U.S. Agency for International Development (AID) to rescind existing anti-abortion regulations, including limits on the ability of family planning programs to mention abortion. 58 Fed. Reg. 7455 (1993). In addition to removing Title X restrictions, the ban on fetal tissue research was lifted, privately funded abortions at military hospitals were permitted, the moratorium on the importation of the abortifacient

RU-486 was suspended, and limitations on the use of private funds by pro-choice organizations that also receive AID funds were suspended.

Clinton also advanced his pro-choice agenda through legislative initiatives, court filings, and judicial appointments. He stood behind legislative efforts to guarantee access to abortion clinics and to fetal tissue for research; he proposed a budget that included neither the Hyde Amendment nor other abortion funding prohibitions. On the judicial front, Clinton told reporters that he had settled on Ruth Bader Ginsburg as his Supreme Court nominee "after he became convinced that she was clearly 'pro-choice.'" Michael Kranish & Joel P. Engardio, Clinton Defends Methods, Boston Globe, June 16, 1993, § 3, at 1. Finally, before the Supreme Court, Clinton's Solicitor General Drew Days successfully argued that federal racketeering laws apply to the activities of Operation Rescue and that federal judges may restrict abortion protests by placing a "buffer zone" around abortion clinics. National Organization for Women, Inc. v. Scheidler, 510 U.S. 249 (1994); Madsen v. Women's Health Center, Inc., 512 U.S. 753 (1994).

Clinton, finally, made effective use of his veto power to stymie pro-life initiatives. In 1998, a veto threat helped stall legislation that would have made it a federal crime to end-run state parental notification laws by transporting a minor across state lines for an abortion. More significant, in 1996 and 1997, Clinton successfully fended off congressional efforts to outlaw partial birth abortions. Arguing that such abortions should be lawful when health-related, Clinton condemned Congress for fashioning a bill "that is consistent neither with the Constitution nor with sound public policy" (document 7). While supporters of the ban depict partial birth abortions as "infanticide" and therefore "outside the concerns of *Roe v. Wade*" (document 8), opponents had just enough votes to sustain the veto. After the House voted 296 to 132 to override the veto, the Senate—by a vote to 64 to 36—fell three votes short of the necessary two-thirds majority. 144 Cong. Rec. S10564 (daily ed. Sept 18, 1998).

F. Conclusion

Executive and legislative responses to *Roe* reveal the extraordinary range of options available to elected government in the face of a Supreme Court decision with which it disagrees. Congress may utilize its appropriations power by prohibiting abortion-related expenditures, its exceptions power by forbidding Supreme Court review of abortion cases, its Fourteenth Amendment, Section 5 power by declaring that constitutional personhood protections begin at conception, its power to send anti-abortion constitutional amendments to the states for ratification, and its power to confirm or reject judicial and other nominees based on their attitudes towards *Roe*. The White House may exercise its power and recommend anti-abortion legislation (and constitutional amendments) to

Congress, its power to appoint judges and federal officials who oppose *Roe*, its power to file briefs and argue cases, its veto power to make anti-abortion language a condition to the President's approval of legislation, and its Article II, Section 1 power to promulgate implementing regulations.

Elected branch activity, however, has not shaken a woman's fundamental right under *Roe*. Direct repeal efforts have been rejected in favor of funding bans and regulations, permitting the elected branches to express their disapproval of *Roe* without engaging in direct battle with the judiciary. That *Harris* v. *McRae* and *Rust* v. *Sullivan* both upheld elected branch responses reaffirms the vitality of constitutional dialogues between the courts and elected government. By upholding elected branch actions, the Court helps forestall more drastic remedies of constitutional amendment or court stripping.

The Court's willingness to bend but not break has figured prominently in the forging of an emerging equilibrium on abortion rights. For example, rather than launch a frontal assault on *Roe*, Republican candidates increasingly sound a moderate tone on abortion rights. Bob Dole (in 1996) and George W. Bush (in 2000) both professed that there would be no abortion "litmus test" for their judicial appointments. Likewise, pointing to public opinion polls, Bush said that there was no sense in pursuing an anti-abortion constitutional amendment. In the end, while pro-choice and pro-life interests are too polarized and too powerful for there to be a common ground on abortion, abortion rights now seem a secure feature of our constitutional landscape.

DOCUMENTS

1. Congress Debates Abortion

Source: 122 Cong. Rec. 20410-11, (1976)

Mr. [Henry] HYDE [R-Ill.]. . . .

The unborn child facing an abortion can best be classified as a member of the innocently inconvenient and since the pernicious doctrine that some lives are more important than others seems to be persuasive with the pro-abortion forces, we who seek to protect that most defenseless and innocent of human lives, the unborn—seek to inhibit the use of Federal funds to pay for and thus encourage abortion as an answer to the human and compelling problem of an unwanted child.

We are all exercised at the wanton killing of the porpoise, the baby seal. We urge big game hunters to save the tiger, but we somehow turn away at the specter of a million human beings being violently destroyed because this great society does not want them.

And make no mistake, an abortion is violent.

I think in the final analysis, you must determine whether or not the unborn person is human. If you think it is animal or vegetable then, of course, it is disposable like an empty beer can to be crushed and thrown out with the rest of the trash.

We hear the claim that the poor are denied a right available to other women if we do not use tax money to fund abortions.

Well, make a list of all the things society denies poor women and let them make the choice of what we will give them.

Don't say "poor woman, go destroy your young, and we will pay for it."

An innocent, defenseless human life, in a caring and humane society deserves better than to be flushed down a toilet or burned in an incinerator.

The promise of America is that life is not just for the privileged, the planned, or the perfect.

. . .

Mr. [Daniel] FLOOD [D-Pa.]. . . .

. . . I have supported for many, many years constitutional amendments which would address this very serious matter, and the Members know it. So, what am I doing down here now? Well, I will tell you. I oppose this amendment, and I will tell you why. Listen. This is blatantly discriminatory; that is why.

The Members do not like that? Of course they do not. It does not prohibit abortion. No, it does not prohibit abortion. It prohibits abortion for poor people. That is what it does. . . . It does not require any change in the practice of the middle-income and the upper-income people. Oh, no. They are able to go to their private practitioners and get the service done for a fee. But, it does take away the option from those of our citizens who must rely on medicaid—and other public programs for medical care.

---

2. Congressional Amici Defend Hyde Amendment

Source: 115 Landmark Briefs 733, 741-42, 756

Independently of any other issue involved in this appeal is the primary concern of the members of Congress who are *amici* here, with respect to the separation of powers, the law-making power of the Congress, and . . . appropriations power of the Congress as given in Article I, Section 9, Clause 7 of the Constitution. . . .

This issue is not limited to the abortion question; the inviolable and exclusive power of the purse is one that touches on all of what Congress does. To tamper with that exclusive power is to tamper with the very essence of constitutional, representative government. Once done, Congress could become a mere bookkeeper for a judiciary, or even executive, that has arrogated unto itself a power denied it by the framers of our system.

So clearly has this been understood that some of the harshest language ever used to describe a violation of the separation of powers has been used with respect to this problem. . . .

Madison [discussed] the appropriations power in his Federalist Paper No. 58: "The House of Representatives cannot only refuse, but they alone can propose the supplies requisite for the support of government. . . . This power over the purse may, in fact, be regarded as the most complete and effectual weapon with which any constitution can arm the immediate representatives of the people, for obtaining a redress of every grievance, and for carrying into effect every just and salutary measure."

. . .

Hamilton was equally adamant in his Federalist Paper No. 78: "The legislature not only commands the purse but prescribes the rules by which the duties and rights of every citizen are to be regulated. The judiciary, on the contrary, has no influence over the sword or the purse."

. . .

Nothing can be clearer than the fundamentally legislative nature of appropriations decisions. . . . Any judicial order to expend money for abortion puts the federal judiciary squarely in the legislative area. . . .

---

enough for all of us to insist on protecting the unborn.

---

3. Reagan Attacks *Roe*

Sources: R. Reagan, Abortion
and the Conscience of the
Nation 15, 19-21 (1984)

The tenth anniversary of the Supreme Court decision in *Roe* v. *Wade* is a good time for us to pause and reflect. Our nationwide policy of abortion-on-demand through all nine months of pregnancy was neither voted for by our people nor enacted by our legislators—not a single state had such unrestricted abortion before the Supreme Court decreed it to be national policy in 1973. But the consequences of this judicial decision are now obvious: [from 1973 to 1983], more than 15 million unborn children have had their lives snuffed out by legalized abortions. That is over ten times the number of Americans lost in all our nation's wars.

. . .

Despite the formidable obstacles before us, we must not lose heart. This is not the first time our country has been divided by a Supreme Court decision that denied the value of certain human lives. The *Dred Scott* decision of 1857 was not overturned in a day, or a year, or even a decade. . . .

What, then, is the real issue? I have often said that when we talk about abortion, we are talking about two lives—the life of the mother and the life of the unborn child. Why else do we call a pregnant woman a mother? I have also said that anyone who doesn't feel sure whether we are talking about a second human life should clearly give life the benefit of the doubt. If you don't know whether a body is alive or dead, you would never bury it. I think this consideration itself should be

---

4. Reagan Title X Regulations

Source: 53 Fed. Reg.
2922-23, 2935, 2945
(Feb. 2, 1988)

Title X of the Public Health Service Act . . . contains the following prohibition [§ 1008], which has not been altered since enacted in 1970:

"None of the funds appropriated under this title shall be used in programs where abortion is a method of family planning."

This language clearly creates a wall of separation between Title X programs and abortion as a method of family planning. It embodies a view that abortion is inappropriate as a method of family planning.
. . .

. . .

There is no question, of course, that Congress has now become acutely aware of Title X. . . . Unless and until Congress enacts new legislation, however, Title X remains in effect as law, and the Department's obligation is to interpret existing law and—based on its experience in administering the program—to exercise its delegated administrative authority by adopting the policies that best effectuate the statute.

. . .

§ 59.8 Prohibition on counseling and referral for abortion services; limitation of program services to family planning.

(a)(1) [A] Title X project may not provide counseling concerning the use of abortion as a method of family planning. . . .

(2) Because Title X funds are intended only for family planning, once a client served by a Title X project is diagnosed as pregnant, she must be referred for appropriate prenatal

and/or social services by furnishing a list of available providers that promote the welfare of mother and unborn child. . . .

§ 59.10   Prohibition on activities that encourage, promote or advocate abortion.

(a) A Title X project may not encourage, promote or advocate abortion as a method of family planning. . . .   Prohibited actions include the use of Title X project funds for the following:

(1) Lobbying for the passage of legislation to increase in any way the availability of abortion as a method of family planning;

(2) Providing speakers to promote the use of abortion as a method of family planning;

(3) Paying dues to any group that as a significant part of its activities advocates abortion as a method of family planning;

(4) Using legal action to make abortion available in any way as a method of family planning; and

(5) Developing or disseminating in any way materials (including printed matter and audiovisual materials) advocating abortion as a method of family planning.

---

5. Chafee Urges Legislative Repeal of *Rust*

Source: John Chafee, Congress Should Remedy the Court's Decision, Wash. Post, June 7, 1991, at A-23

Imagine that a patient with severe chest pains is found to have heart disease. A doctor, acting responsibly, legally and ethically, would tell the patient of *all* potential treatments and medical options available.   The doctor would not even consider withholding information when counseling that patient, even if the doctor would not choose certain treatments for himself were he in the same circumstances.

A system in which the doctor is forbidden to tell the patient each of the options available seems inconceivable.   Yet on May 23, the Supreme Court, by a 5-to-4 decision, said such a withholding of information is perfectly all right if the patient is a low-income pregnant woman at a health care facility receiving any portion of its funds pursuant to Title X of the Public Health Service Act.

What a bizarre and cruel turn of events. A poor woman, frequently in a desperate situation, asks the doctor for her options, and the doctor is forbidden to tell her.

. . . The Court has spoken, and now it is time for Congress to take action.   We need to speak clearly and decisively, without ambiguity.

The regulations to be imposed are bad policy for a number of reasons.   First, they create a two-tiered health care system where low-income women receive more limited care and information. . . .

Second, the regulations conflict with the professional ethics of major medical organizations, including the American Medical Association and the American College of Obstetricians and Gynecologists, which insist on the patient's right to full information. . . .

Third, the regulations place health care professionals at risk for medical malpractice. Physicians are routinely held liable for failing to provide complete information to a patient about his or her medical condition and medical options.

Finally, the regulations would compel family planning providers to choose between offering only government-approved information to poor pregnant women and forgoing their federal funds.   As more clinics forgo federal funds in order to avoid these restrictive regulations and the possible result of increased exposure to medical malpractice, fewer low-income women will receive critical family planning services. . . .

6. Clinton Rescinds Abortion Restrictions

Source: Pub. Papers 1993 (I), at 7-8

. . . Today I am acting to separate our national health and medical policy from the divisive conflict over abortion. This conflict, which stems from the *Roe v. Wade* decision of 20 years ago, has brought to a halt promising research on treatment for serious conditions and diseases [Parkinson's disease, Alzheimer's disease, diabetes, and leukemia] that affect millions of Americans, millions of American men, women, and children who include the members of the family and friends of mine and I'm sure virtually every other set of family and friends in the United States. We must free science and medicine from the grasp of politics and give all Americans access to the very latest and best medical treatments.

. . . As a nation, our goal should be to protect individual freedom while fostering responsible decisionmaking, an approach that seeks to protect the right to choose while reducing the number of abortions. Our vision should be of an America where abortion is safe and legal, but rare.

So today I am also directing Secretary Shalala to act immediately to implement her intended suspension of the Title X family planning regulations that are also known as the "gag rule." . . . As a result of today's action, every woman will be able to receive medical advice and referrals that will not be censored or distorted by ideological arguments that should not be a part of medicine.

7. Clinton Vetoes Partial Birth Legislation

Source: Pub. Papers, 1996 (I), at 567-68

I am returning herewith without my approval H.R. 1833, which would prohibit doctors from performing a certain kind of abortion. I do so because the bill does not allow women to protect themselves from serious threats to their health. By refusing to permit women, in reliance on their doctors' best medical judgment, to use this procedure when their lives are threatened *or* when their health is put in serious jeopardy, the Congress has fashioned a bill that is consistent neither with the Constitution nor with sound public policy.

I have always believed that the decision to have an abortion generally should be between a woman, her doctor, her conscience, and her God. I support the decision in *Roe v. Wade* protecting a woman's right to choose, and I believe that the abortions protected by that decision should be safe and rare. Consistent with that decision, I have long opposed late-term abortions except where necessary to protect the life or health of the mother. In fact, as Governor of Arkansas, I signed into law a bill that barred third trimester abortions, with an appropriate exception for life or health.

The procedure described in H.R. 1833 has troubled me deeply, as it has many people. I cannot support use of that procedure on an elective basis, where the abortion is being performed for non-health related reasons and there are equally safe medical procedures available.

There are, however, rare and tragic situations that can occur in a woman's pregnancy in which, in a doctor's medical judgment, the use of this procedure may be necessary to save a woman's life or to protect her against serious injury to her health. In these situations, in which a woman and her family must make an awful choice, the Constitution requires, as it should, that the ability to choose this procedure be protected.

. . .

I understand the desire to eliminate the use of a procedure that appears inhumane. But to eliminate it without taking into consideration the rare and tragic circumstances in which its use may be necessary would be even more inhumane.

The Congress chose not to adopt the sensible and constitutionally appropriate proposal I made, instead leaving women unprotected against serious health risks. As a result of this Congressional indifference to women's health, I cannot, in good conscience and consistent with my responsibility to uphold the law, sign this legislation.

---

8. Congress Debates Partial Birth Legislation

Source: 145 Cong. Rec. S12863-64, 12869-70, 12873, 12881, 12883 (daily ed. October 20, 1999)

[Mr. Rick Santorum (R-Pa.)]: . . . Some have tried to turn this into a broader debate about abortions and view this as just the first shot at *Roe v. Wade*, an attempt to put a chink in the armor, intimating there is a grand agenda to try to chip away abortion rights that were given by the Supreme Court in *Roe v. Wade*.

Let me assure my colleagues that is not my intention. . . . In fact, one of the reasons we are offering this amendment is because we believe this comports with *Roe v. Wade*; that this is a constitutional restriction and, in fact, it falls outside the concerns of *Roe v. Wade* because the baby is outside of the mother. The baby is no longer in the mother's womb.

. . .

What I want to show today, looking at this procedure, is this is not like abortion. This is like infanticide. This is a baby who is all but born and then killed. So I think we need to look at it and have this debate focus on not the issue of abortion because there are plenty, as is evidenced by the numbers, of other procedures available to perform abortions. This is a rogue procedure that is infanticide. . . .

. . .

[Mrs. Barbara Boxer (D-Calif.)]: This is the third time the Republican leadership has brought this bill before the Senate. Again, it is playing doctor without one obstetrician or one gynecologist among us. . . .

. . . [W]e were elected to be Senators. We have a lot of work to do. We weren't elected to be the American College of Obstetricians and Gynecologists. They have their own organization. We should vote down this unconstitutional bill. If we do not—because I know this is political—why else would it be before the Senate? This is politics at its worst. This is the third time the President will veto this bill. We all know we will have the votes to sustain that veto. Why go through this if not for politics?

. . .

[Mr. Richard Durbin (D-Ill.)]: Nineteen Federal courts in 19 States have enjoined, have stopped, the enforcement of the so-called partial-birth abortion bans Senator Santorum brings to the floor. The States include: Alaska, Arkansas, Arizona, Florida, Georgia, Idaho, Illinois, Iowa, Kentucky, Louisiana, Michigan, Missouri, Montana, Nebraska, New Jersey, Ohio, Rhode Island, Wisconsin, and West Virginia.

. . .

[Mr. Tim Hutchison (R-Ark.)]: It is always ironic to me that those who say Government should not be involved in this issue are the first to say Government should pay for this procedure, or at least abortions in general.

Then there was the argument that the courts may rule this unconstitutional; therefore we should not even be voting on this because the courts, and the Supreme Court eventually, might rule this legislation unconstitutional.

. . .

I think it is an absolute red herring to say: Well, ultimately when the Supreme Court makes a definitive ruling on this subject, they may or may not rule that it is constitutional. That, in no way, abrogates our responsibility to debate it and to pass legislation that we believe is not only constitutional but in the best interests of this country.

. . .

[Mr. Joseph Lieberman (D-Conn.)]: Partial birth legislation has been challenged 22 times in the courts resulting in 19 injunctions. The court-imposed constraints must be reflected in legislative efforts if we are going to achieve our goal of reducing late-term abortions. Enacting legislation that courts have struck down time and again is unlikely to reduce abortions.

III. RETURNING ABORTION TO THE STATES: THE CONSEQUENCES OF *WEBSTER* AND *CASEY*

On July 3, 1989, the Supreme Court dealt a severe blow to the stringent trimester approach of *Roe* v. *Wade*. In *Webster* v. *Reproductive Health Services*, a plurality applied a less exacting "reasonableness" standard in approving a Missouri abortion-regulation statute. 492 U.S. 490 (1989). Three years later, the Court again signalled its willingness to uphold state antiabortion restrictions. Planned Parenthood v. Casey, 505 U.S. 833 (1992). Concluding that *Roe's* trimester standard inappropriately limited the states' compelling interests in maternal health and future life, a plurality of the Court ruled that state regulations which do not "unduly burden" a woman's right to terminate her pregnancy are constitutional.

The consequences of this returning of abortion to elected government are mixed. On the one hand, from 1989 to 1999, abortion rights hardly changed at all. Although several hundred abortion-related bills were introduced at the state level in the wake of these decisions, only a few became law (with nearly as many post-1989 measures protecting reproductive rights as regulating abortion). On the other hand, *Webster* did change the landscape of abortion politics. As Barbara Boxer (D. Calif.) put it, "[prior to *Webster*] [w]hen the court was protecting our right to choose, people in this country took it for granted, and so they didn't really pay attention to the politicians." Julie Rovner, Congress Puts Bush on Spot Over Funding of Abortion, 47 Cong. Q. Weekly Rep. 2708, 2710-11 (1989). With *Webster*, abortion became a dominant electoral issue and these high stakes are reflected in state and federal debates over abortion regulation.

This section examines state abortion politics after 1989. What types of laws, if any, were the states likely to enact? Might state courts provide broader "privacy" protections than federal courts through their interpretations of state constitutional provisions? In answering these questions, the starting point for discussion is state abortion politics that predate *Webster*.

A. State Abortion Politics: 1962-1989

Abortion politics did not begin with the Supreme Court's 1973 decision in *Roe* v. *Wade*. Prior to 1820, most states—following the common law—placed no restrictions on abortion. Between 1820 and 1840, however, a movement led by physicians known as "regulars" prompted ten of the nation's 26 states to pass restrictive abortion legislation. This campaign against "irregular" medical practitioners such as pharmacists and midwives has been attributed to these physicians' desire "to upgrade themselves professionally and become the exclusive providers of health care services in the United States." Marian Faux, Roe v. Wade 53 (1988). From that time until 1960, the perceived immorality of abortion supported further restrictions.

In the decade preceding *Roe* the abortion pendulum began to swing. Seventeen states liberalized criminal statutes governing abortion. The triggering event for these reforms was the 1962 Model Penal Code, which authorized abortions when the health of the mother was endangered, when the infant might be born with incapacitating physical or mental deformities, and when the pregnancy was a result of rape or incest. Actions in the late 1960s by the American Medical Association (AMA) and religious organizations furthered these efforts. In 1967, the AMA endorsed the Model Penal Code's limited approval of abortion. In 1968, the American Baptist Convention, the Unitarian Universalist Association and various Jewish groups favored liberalizing existing laws. By 1971, more far-reaching reform seemed likely. The National Conference of Commissioners on Uniform State Laws drafted a Uniform Abortion Act which would have placed no limitations on abortion during the first twenty weeks of pregnancy.

However, many states rejected the Model Penal Code reform, and some states that did enact reform legislation imposed so many restrictions that the number of legal abortions actually decreased. When *Roe* was decided, strict antiabortion laws remained on the books in nearly every state. Furthermore, the legislative battles leading up to *Roe* had led to the birth of the modern pro-life movement, which, in 1972, helped defeat Michigan and North Dakota referenda that would have repealed the laws that criminalized abortion in those states. In the months before the *Roe* decision, moreover, pro-life interests scored key legislative victories in Pennsylvania, where legislation allowing abortions only when the mother's life was threatened was approved by a 157 to 34 vote; and in Massachusetts, which approved by a 178 to 46 margin a bill that specified conception as the beginning of a human life.

The *Roe* litigation is a testament to state resistance to abortion rights. Arizona, Connecticut, Georgia, Kentucky, Nebraska, and Utah joined Texas in arguing against abortion rights (with no state arguing in support of abortion rights). At the same time, state advocacy before the Court got off to a rather inauspicious start. Texas Assistant Attorney General Jay Floyd began his argument awkwardly. Referring to Jane Roe's counsel, Sarah Weddington and Linda Coffee, Floyd commented, "It's an old joke, but when a man argues against two beautiful ladies like this, they are going to have the last word" (document 1).

The winds of political change in this area changed dramatically with *Roe*. By providing women an unqualified abortion right in the first trimester of pregnancy, *Roe* turned abortion rights advocates' principal objective into a constitutional mandate. Pro-life interests, in contrast, viewed *Roe* as a battle call. Determined to chip away at, if not destroy, *Roe*, these groups launched a massive political campaign.

Anti-abortion interests had huge success. From 1973 to 1989, 306 abortion measures were passed by 48 states. The principal weapons of *Roe* opponents were attempts to make abortion less attractive through so-called "burden creation" strategies. These strategies included increasing the risks of undergoing an abortion (statutes forbidding a safe abortion method—saline amniocentesis—while permitting more dangerous abortion techniques); reducing accessibility to medical facilities that perform abortions (statutes demanding that all abortions be performed in a hospital and zoning laws restricting the number of abortion clinics); increasing the cost of abortions (statutes requiring physician or pathologist involvement in abortion procedures); and establishing detailed pre-abortion procedures (statutes requiring women to be informed of the "medical risks" of abortion and to wait at least twenty-four hours after consenting to the abortion procedure). During this period, however, the Supreme Court stymied most of these reform efforts. With few exceptions, these regulations were invalidated prior to *Webster*.

B. *Webster* and the New Politics of Abortion

Webster's approval of abortion regulations signalled a new era in abortion politics. The Missouri statute at issue in *Webster* prohibited public employees from performing abortions in public hospitals and, more significantly, required physicians, prior to performing an abortion, to determine the viability of a fetus twenty or more weeks of gestational age. In upholding the law, Chief Justice Rehnquist, writing for a plurality of the Court, argued that *Roe's* rigid trimester approach is unworkable. For

Rehnquist: "Since the bounds of the [*Roe*] inquiry are essentially indeterminate, the result has been a web of legal rules that have become increasingly intricate, resembling a code of regulations rather than a body of constitutional doctrine." Webster, 492 U.S. at 518. This challenge to *Roe* sent a clear signal to elected government that previously suspect abortion regulations might now pass constitutional muster.

Leaders of groups on both sides of the issue proclaimed that the ruling would "set off a political firestorm throughout America." Joan Biskupic, New Limits on Abortion Rights Are Upheld by 5-4 Majority, 47 Cong. Q. Weekly Rep. 1698, 1700 (July 8, 1989) (quoting Kate Michelman, Executive Director of NARAL). Polls showed a dramatic increase in support for abortion rights: 57 percent of Americans said they opposed *Webster*, 61 percent said they agreed with *Roe* and 70 percent said they opposed a constitutional amendment banning abortions.   William Schneider, Wrong Way for Women's Movement, 21 Nat'l J. 2018 (1989). Yet instead of accentuating the sharp ideological divisions which had characterized the abortion debate before *Webster*, the public's increased interest in abortion created a less polarized, more ambiguous political situation. Many restrictions on abortion continued to command broad public support. For example, 83 percent of Americans said that a girl younger than 18 should be required to notify at least one parent before having an abortion, 65 percent favored mandatory viability tests for fetuses more than 20 weeks old, and a majority opposed public financing of abortions. R.W. Apple, Limits on Abortion Seem Less Likely, N.Y. Times, Sept. 29, 1989, at A1.

But the pro-choice "sleeping giant" was stirring. Acknowledging that it had been "lazy, complacent, and, because of that, caught off guard," the movement picked up steam. In the weeks just prior to the *Webster* decision, pro-choice groups experienced unprecedented growth in contributions and membership. NARAL increased its paid membership by 50 percent during the first six months of 1989 and saw its income surge from $3.3 million a year to $1 million a month. Federal Election Commission (FEC) records show that pro-choice political action committees (PACs) raised nearly $2.5 million during the 1989-90 election cycle, more than twice the amount that they raised in 1987-88. Likewise, the number of pro-choice PACs registered at the FEC jumped from five in 1988 to fifteen in 1990. NARAL's budget grew from $3.4 million in 1986 to more than $9 million in 1989, while membership in the organization grew from about 150,000 in 1986 to more than 500,000 in 1992. Pro-choice groups declared that public concern was the reason for the sudden swell in membership and funding. Pro-life groups, such as the NRLC, the American Life League, and Americans United for Life, experienced substantial yet less dramatic increases in contributions, a difference their leaders attributed to the widespread support their groups had enjoyed before the Supreme Court decided to hear *Webster*.

Irrespective of whether the pro-choice or pro-life side is stronger in absolute terms, one conclusion is inescapable: Improvements in pro-choice funding, membership figures, and organization after *Webster* created a new political force. In particular, *Webster* forced pro-choice groups out of the courtrooms and into state capitals. "I don't think you can get a clearer message about the fate of privacy rights [in the Supreme Court]. They don't fare very well," said Kathryn Kolbert, an attorney with the ACLU's Reproductive Freedom Project. "In the short term at least, some of our greater victories will have to come on the legislative level." Marcia Coyle, Is the Court Avoiding the Big Question?, Nat'l L.J., July 9, 1990, at 1. Pro-choice leaders nevertheless were reluctant to try to pass laws which would guarantee abortion rights at the state level, and instead sought to prevent the enactment of anti-abortion legislation.

Webster also played a critical role in the 1989 gubernatorial races in Virginia and New Jersey where pro-choice candidates Douglas Wilder and James Florio defeated anti-abortion candidates Marshall Coleman and James Courter. In 1990, abortion was "the most critical non-money issue" in gubernatorial races. Holly Idelson, Budgets, Jobs and Abortion Are Big Issues in States, 48 Cong. Q. Weekly Rep. 2840 (Sept. 8, 1990).

C. From *Webster* to *Casey*: The States and Abortion

Florida was the first battleground in the new abortion wars. Just two days after *Webster*, Republican Governor Bob Martinez announced that he would call a special session of his state's legislature to enact new abortion restrictions. He put forward a menu of proposals, including a seven-day wait before clinics could perform abortions, a ban on public funding of abortions, and fetal viability tests. However, the legislature killed all his bills in committee and adjourned without passing a single abortion restriction. "Once a right is established, it's not easily removed," said Democrat Tom Gustafson, Speaker of the Florida House of Representatives. "There has been a very clear response from people that they felt a right was being taken away." Jeffrey Schmalz, Abortion Access Stands in Florida, N.Y. Times, Oct. 12, 1989, at A23.

Because the abortion question reentered the political arena with such force, politicians who attacked the constitutional deficiencies of anti-abortion bills often concealed their real reasons. This may have been the case in Idaho, where the legislature passed a restrictive abortion bill on March 23, 1990. Based upon National Right to Life's model legislation, the bill sought to ban abortions except in cases involving rape, incest, or danger to the mother's life and probably would have outlawed between 93 to 98 percent of all abortions in the state. While the bill awaited the signature of Idaho's anti-abortion Governor, Democrat Cecil Andrus, the Idaho pro-choice movement suddenly came alive.

The pro-choice groups' most well-publicized tactic was their announcement of a national boycott of Idaho's chief cash crop, potatoes. The boycott attracted national media attention, and in a final dramatic gesture staged the day before Andrus announced his decision, pro-choice college students dumped 10,000 Idaho potatoes on the steps of the capitol. Some of their signs read, "Veto House Bill 625: No dic-tater-ship." When Andrus finally announced that he had decided to veto the bill, he cited its inadequate rape and incest provisions as his primary justification. But he also objected to the bill's constitutional deficiencies: "I am advised by legal scholars of both political parties that, in their opinion, there is not the remotest chance of this legislation's being found constitutional by the Supreme Court." Andrus pointed out that the bill "was conceived outside our state for the sole purpose of getting this issue back before the Supreme Court," and that "the financial burden to Idaho will be excessive if we litigate this issue." He denied that boycotts and political pressure influenced his decision. Pro-lifers disagreed. The National Right to Life Committee targeted Andrus for defeat in November of 1990, but he easily won reelection, and abortion rights supporters gained a commanding majority in the Idaho Senate.

Andrus's resolve reveals that governors, armed with their veto power, wield enormous influence on the lawmaking process. In Louisiana, however, Governor Buddy Roemer was unable to fend off state legislature opposition to abortion through his veto power. On June 14, 1991, Roemer—for the third time in less than a year—vetoed restrictive antiabortion legislation. In each instance, he proclaimed that he was willing to sign an abortion bill but that the state legislature had approved measures without "meaningful exceptions . . . [and] I cannot close my eyes to that." Ed Anderson, Roemer Vetoes Bill on Abortion, New Orleans Times-Picayune, June 15, 1991, A1. Roemer's actions did not sit well with the Louisiana legislature. Ridiculing Roemer for statements such as "I still consider myself pro-life, but I'm more pro-choice now," Allen Bares, a co-sponsor of the bill, declared it was time to "send a loud and clear message to the people of this state and this nation that this [legislature] is pro-life." Ed Anderson, Legislature Bans Abortion, New Orleans Times-Picayune, June 19, 1991, A1. On June 18, 1991, the Louisiana legislature reinstated its antiabortion measure, overriding a gubernatorial veto for the first time in its history.

The Louisiana legislature's willingness to stare down Roemer's third veto is attributable to the political potency of the religious interests opposed to abortion, most notably fundamentalist religious groups from northern Louisiana, and Roman Catholics from southern Louisiana. Religious convictions and a desire to overturn *Roe* v. *Wade* also played an important role in Pennsylvania. On November 17, 1989, Pennsylvania passed a law banning most abortions at public hospitals, prohibiting them after the 24th week of pregnancy, requiring spousal notification and a waiting period, and outlawing abortion for sex selection. The

Pennsylvania House passed the measure by a vote of 143 to 58, and the Senate approved it 33 to 17. Michael deCourey Hinds, Pennsylvania Passes Anti-Abortion Measure, N.Y. Times, Nov. 15, 1989, at A19. Political analysts, however, said Pennsylvania was unrepresentative of national opinion on abortion, and pointed out that the state had a history of social conservatism due to its relatively large rural population and its many Roman Catholics and fundamentalist Christians.

Pro-choice groups held a vigil outside the Harrisburg mansion of Governor Robert P. Casey. Casey, however, signed the bill into law two days later, proudly proclaiming: "We are the first state in the country after the *Webster* case to move and speak forcefully on the subject of protection of unborn life. I have seen politicians cutting and running, and states waffling on that issue. Pennsylvania did not." Tom Troy, Casey "Satisfied" with 1989, Confronted Tough Issues Like Abortion, UPI, Dec. 20, 1989, BC Cycle.

Abortion foes expressed their hopes that the law would serve as a vehicle to challenge *Roe* became a reality when on January 21, 1992, the Supreme Court agreed to hear the case. Before the Supreme Court, however, Pennsylvania's Attorney General Ernest Preate argued that "*Roe v. Wade* need not be revisited by this Court except to reaffirm that *Roe* did not establish an absolute right to abortion on demand" (document 2). In contrast, pro-choice interests, including a coalition of sixteen states, argued that the Pennsylvania statute could not be upheld without reexamining *Roe* (document 3).

D. *Casey* and Beyond

Planned Parenthood v. *Casey* offered victories (and setbacks) for both the pro-life and pro-choice forces. By reaffirming the "central holding of *Roe*," 505 U.S. at 879, *Casey* made clear that five Reagan-Bush Supreme Court appointments were not enough to undo abortion rights. On the other hand, *Casey* utilized a deferential "undue burden" standard to uphold all but the spousal notification provision of the state's law.

Casey's middle-ground approach to both abortion rights and broad state regulatory authority matched public opinion, prompting some conservative commentators to claim that "the current Court is driven more by public opinion than by constitutional principle." Bruce Fein, Jurisprudence of Popular Opinion?, Washington Times, July 7, 1992, at F1. Nonetheless, the Court's decision seems to have stabilized state abortion politics. State attorneys general, for example, have resisted enforcing existing state laws with Pennsylvania-type restrictions. Most strikingly, according to Alan Guttmacher Institute studies, "antiabortion legislators [have] heeded [*Casey*] . . . and curtailed their attempts to make abortion illegal." Alan Guttmacher Institute, State Reproductive Health

Monitor 5, no. 2 (May 1994): ii. Nearly all of the abortion regulation measures adopted since *Casey* involve restrictions approved by the Court: waiting periods, informed consent, and parental notification.

In recent years, moreover, abortion has played a less prominent role in gubernatorial elections. For example, by arguing that they can do nothing to repeal the federally guaranteed right to abortion, some conservative Republicans have avoided the issue altogether. "I'm not going to waste political capital on things that aren't going to happen," explained Ellen Sauerbrey (the Republican candidate for the 1998 Maryland governorship). Robert Shogan, GOP Conservatives Tilt Toward Center, L.A. Times, Oct. 22, 1998, at 5A. In sharp contrast, Gray Davis, in his successful 1998 campaign for the California governorship, trumpeted his support for abortion rights through television advertisements.

The one exception to this relative placidity is partial-birth abortion. With President Clinton's vetoing of a nation-wide ban on this procedure, right to life activists turned to the states. And with only 7 percent of Americans supporting third trimester abortions, state lawmakers have gladly answered this call. In 1997 alone, 15 states outlawed partial-birth abortions. In 18 other states, lawmakers considered enacting a ban on this procedure. By 1999, 30 states had enacted bans on this procedure.

On April 25, 2000, Don Stenberg, Attorney General of Nebraska, appeared before the Supreme Court to defend his state's law criminalizing the performance of partial-birth abortions (document 4). In its first major ruling on abortion since *Casey*, the Court held that the statute violated the Constitution as interpreted in *Casey* and *Roe*. Stenberg v. Carhart, 120 S.Ct. 2597 (2000).

E. State Courts Step In

The federal Constitution is not the only source of fundamental rights. Each state has the "sovereign right to adopt in its own constitution individual liberties more expansive than those conferred by the Federal constitution." PruneYard Shopping Center v. Robins, 447 U.S. 74, 75 (1980). *Webster* and *Casey* have called attention back to state courts. That state courts are stepping in and filling a gap left open by the Supreme Court is hardly surprising. As Justice Brennan recognized: "State constitutions, too, are a font of individual liberties. . . . The legal revolution which has brought federal law to the fore must not be allowed to inhibit the independent protective force of state law—for without it, the full realization of our liberties cannot be guaranteed." William J. Brennan, Jr., State Constitutions and the Protection of Individual Rights, 90 Harv. L. Rev. 489, 491 (1977).

Before *Roe*, several state courts struck down anti-abortion laws. *See* Jean Gray Platt ed., Special Project, Survey of Abortion Law, 1980 Ariz. St. L.J. 67, 106-11 (1980). After the Supreme Court concluded in *Harris v. McRae*, 448 U.S. 297 (1980), that a congressional prohibition on the use of Medicaid funds for abortions did not violate the equal protection clause, courts in California, Connecticut, Massachusetts, Michigan, New Jersey, and Oregon interpreted their own constitutions to protect the right of indigent women to a state-funded abortion. The New Jersey Supreme Court pointed out that "state Constitutions are separate sources of individual freedoms and restrictions on the exercise of power by the Legislature. . . . Although the state Constitution may encompass a smaller universe than the federal Constitution, our constellation of rights may be more complete." Right to Choose v. Byrne, 450 A.2d 925, 931 (N.J. 1982).

Ten state constitutions contain explicit privacy provisions and several others contain clauses which have been interpreted to protect the right to privacy. Following *Webster*, some state courts have applied these provisions to protect abortion rights. In 1997, for example, the California Supreme Court struck down a law requiring pregnant minors to secure parental consent or judicial authorization before obtaining an abortion. For the court, the fact that the U.S. Supreme Court had approved an identical law was simply beside the point. Citing language from one of its earlier decisions, the court noted: "[O]ur state Constitution has been construed to provide California citizens with privacy protections encompassing procreative decisionmaking—*broader, indeed, than those recognized by the federal Constitution*." American Academy of Pediatrics v. Lundgren, 940 P.2d 797, 809 (Cal. 1997; emphasis in original). The court also cited the California Constitution's explicit right to privacy, which declares that "[a]ll people are by nature free and independent and have inalienable rights" and that "[a]mong these are . . . pursuing and obtaining safety, happiness, *and privacy*." *Id*. at 808 n.13 (emphasis in original).

In 1998, a Florida appeals court relied on an express privacy right in the state constitution ("Every natural person has the right to be let alone and free from governmental intrusion") to hold that the state is without authority to regulate first trimester abortions. The court enjoined enforcement of a law requiring physicians to provide detailed information about the gestational age of the fetus and alternatives to abortion (a law, coincidentally, that the U.S. Supreme Court upheld in *Casey*). State v. Presidential Women's Center, 707 So.2d 1145 (Fla. App. 4 Dist. 1998). Nine years earlier, the Florida Supreme Court voted 6-1 to strike down a statute that required a minor to obtain parental consent before undergoing an abortion, reasoning that the people of Florida would not have included an explicit privacy provision in the state constitution if they had been satisfied with the federal right to privacy. In re T.W., 551 So. 2d 1186, 1191-92 (Fla. 1989).

Victories in court do not end the political struggle. Although in 1981 the California Supreme Court declared that the legislature cannot restrict state funding for abortions for indigent women, over the next decade the legislature passed laws restricting the funding. Each year the courts struck the laws down and reinstated the funding. Philip Hager, Court Again Rejects Curbs on Abortions, L.A. Times, Nov. 17, 1989, at A3. Anti-abortion activists in Florida devoted energy to unseating justices who supported abortion rights. Florida's justices must undergo a "merit retention" vote every six years, and Justice Leander Shaw, author of the court's opinion in *In re T.W.*, faced his vote in November 1990. Shaw, the right-to-life groups' primary target, won sixty percent of the vote in his re-election bid.

F. Conclusion

Webster and *Casey*, while promising a revolution, have had a modest impact on abortion rights. State legislative initiatives have been few. State courts continue to serve as an independent voice on constitutional rights. In the years ahead, moreover, neither pro-choice nor pro-life advocates can reasonably expect a definitive Supreme Court decision to resolve the abortion question. Stung by *Roe*, the Court is unlikely to offer a detailed prescription on abortion rights. The issue has been returned to the political process, with periodic and limited review by the courts. As Gary Bauer, one of President Reagan's domestic policy advisors, put it: "It's going to be . . . a long, grind-out struggle by both sides." Robin Toner, Abortion Fight Goes On, State by State by State, N.Y. Times, Jan. 21, 1991, at A18.

DOCUMENTS

1. Oral Arguments in *Roe*

Source: 75 Landmark Briefs
798, 803-04

THE COURT: How do you suggest, if you're right, how do you — what procedure would you suggest for any pregnant female in the State of Texas ever to get any judicial consideration of this constitutional claim?

MR. FLOYD: Your Honor, let me answer your question with a statement, if I may. I do not believe it can be done. There are situations in which, of course as the Court knows, no remedy is provided. Now, I think she makes her choice prior to the time she becomes pregnant. That is the time of the choice. . . .

THE COURT: Maybe she makes her choice when she decides to live in Texas.

[Laughter]

MR. FLOYD: May I proceed?

There is no restriction on moving.

.   .   .

MR. FLOYD: We say there is life from the moment of impregnation.

THE COURT: And do you have any scientific data to support that?

MR. FLOYD: Well we begin, Mr. Justice, in our brief, with the development of the human embryo, carrying it through the development of the fetus from about seven to nine days after conception.

THE COURT: Well, what about six days?

MR. FLOYD: We don't know.

THE COURT: But the statute goes all the way back to one hour?

MR. FLOYD: I don't — Mr. Justice, there are unanswerable questions in this field. I —

[Laughter]

THE COURT: I appreciate it.

MR. FLOYD: This is an artless statement on my part.

THE COURT: I withdraw the question.

MR. FLOYD: Thank you.

When does the soul come into the unborn — if a person believes in a soul — I don't know. . . .

---

2. Pennsylvania Defends Its Restrictions on Abortion

Source: 216 Landmark Briefs 232, 237

Roe does not establish an absolute or unlimited right to abortion on demand, but instead attempts to establish a limited right which also respects the important state interests which exist in protecting fetal life and maternal health, and in other areas. As Justice O'Connor has demonstrated, the Court early formulated the undue burden test to accommodate these important state interests, and that test remains the most appropriate standard for fulfilling *Roe*'s promise that those interests will be respected.

.   .   .

Having said all this, it is nevertheless true that *Roe v. Wade* was incorrectly decided, and the Court may wish to take this occasion to review and overrule it. *Roe*'s identification of the abortion right as fundamental finds no support in the Constitution, in history, in a societal consensus, or in the Court's own precedents, and its use of trimesters and viability to define the contours of that right is at bottom arbitrary. Because of these flaws, *Roe* stands as a source of instability in the law and as a barrier to public understanding of the proper function of the Court in our system of government. *Roe* should share the fate of *Lochner v. New York*, its equally ill-conceived forerunner in substantive due process.

---

3. State Attorneys General Defend Abortion Rights

Source: 216 Landmark Briefs 1009, 1011-12

. . . Those who now urge this Court to abandon protection of the right to choose abortion and to thrust the issue back upon the states invite disaster. As chief legal officers, chief executives, and elected representatives of the people of our respective states, *amici* therefore urge the Court to be steadfast in its application of *Roe v. Wade*.

.   .   .

The need for stability and legitimacy in the law weighs heavily in favor of abiding by the precedent of *Roe v. Wade* regardless of individual views on how the case should be decided if it arose *res nova* today. Like *Brown v. Board of Education*, *Roe* has become part of the political and moral fabric of this country. Millions of women who have come of age in the last twenty years have structured their identities, their families, and their pursuits around the possession of a fundamental privacy right to decide whether or not or when to bear a child. *Roe* has also rooted itself in the practices and expectations of the States as sovereign entities, which have relied on *Roe* over the last two decades in developing a uniform statutory and regulatory framework within which health planning decisions are made.

This Court has consistently held that when individuals and governments have relied on a precedent, as they have on *Roe*, there should be extreme reluctance to overrule it. . . .

Because *Roe v. Wade* is so deeply embedded in both individual and governmental decisionmaking, reversal or modification of its holding would also substantially undermine the rule of law. Never before has this Court overruled a case that recognized a fundamental personal freedom. A departure from the guarantee of a fundamental liberty that coincides with a shift in the membership of the Court would run athwart the principal objective the doctrine of *stare decisis* is intended to serve: to enable citizens "to presume that bedrock principles are founded in the law rather than the proclivities of individuals. . . ."

---

4. Nebraska Defends its Ban on Partial Birth Abortions

Source: Oral Arguments 8, 14-16
Stenberg v. Carhart, No. 99-830
(argued April 25, 2000)

GENERAL STENBERG: For purposes of this case, the State's position would be that the State could not prohibit the D[ilation] & E[vacuation] procedure, but also the State has not attempted to prohibit the D & E procedure.

QUESTION: I know that's the position you take, but it is difficult to read the statute and be certain that that is so. . . .

.   .   .

GENERAL STENBERG: I think it's fair to say the statute might be amenable to more than one construction, but we believe that the State's construction is a reasonable one. It's

one that would uphold, hopefully uphold the cons–

QUESTION: Well, and we have held, have we not, that a Federal court in construing a State statute is obligated to, if there's constitutional doubt to construe in a reasonable way that will avoid the constitutional doubt?

GENERAL STENBERG: Yes, that is exactly right, Your Honor, and that's of course the rule that is followed by the Nebraska supreme court as well.

.   .   .

QUESTION: General, may I ask you this question: let's assume your construction of the statute is correct, and then the question is whether, could the State ban just D[ilation] & X[traction], and I understood you to say earlier that the American College of Obstetricians and Gynecologists said you don't need this procedure in substance.

But I notice in their brief they have a sentence, depending on the physician's skill and experience, the D & X procedure can be the most appropriate abortion procedure for some women in some circumstances, and then they have a footnote to the—a finding of the district court that there are at least 10 to 20 Nebraska women each year for whom the D & X is the most appropriate procedure.

Now, do we have to disagree with that finding to hold this statute valid?

GENERAL STENBERG: No, I don't believe so, Your Honor. I think you need to accept that the legislature could consider all of the competing—

QUESTION: And it can ban the most appropriate procedure for a small number of women?

GENERAL STENBERG: Well, I don't—I believe that the district court was simply erroneous—

QUESTION: Well, that's what I'm asking you. Do we have to find that finding erroneous in order to sustain your position?

7

GAY RIGHTS

Homosexuals do not possess the same privacy rights as heterosexuals. Through prohibitions in several states regarding same-sex marriage, homosexual sodomy, and homosexual adoption as well as limitations on the rights of a homosexual parent to obtain custody of or visit with their children, homosexuals face significant roadblocks when seeking to form families or to define their own sexuality. Moreover, through federal restrictions on military and other governmental service, homosexuals face some employment restrictions that heterosexuals do not. For the most part, federal courts have been unwilling to overturn federal and state restrictions on gay rights. Most notably, in *Bowers v. Hardwick*, the U.S. Supreme Court upheld Georgia's ban on consensual sodomy. Consequently, gay rights interests have turned their attention to state lawmakers and courts to overturn sodomy bans and other limitations on their personal privacy. Section I of this chapter examines *Bowers*.

Even when federal courts are willing to intercede on behalf of gay rights, state and federal officials have been able to short circuit these decisions. In *Romer v. Evans*, discussed in Section II, the Supreme Court's invalidation of a Colorado initiative prohibiting gays from seeking state antidiscrimination protections accomplished relatively little. The federal government distinguished *Romer* in defending its gays in the military policy. States too have continued to enact anti-gay initiatives.

I. BOWERS v. HARDWICK

The Supreme Court, in its 1986 *Bowers v. Hardwick* decision, placed its imprimatur on the authority of government to penalize homosexual conduct. Concluding that the right to privacy is tied to "family, marriage, [and] procreation," the Court refused to extend decisions recognizing the rights of married and unmarried heterosexuals to engage in sexual relations. 478 U.S. 186, 191 (1986). As a result, the Court upheld Georgia's authority to criminally sanction consensual homosexual sodomy.

Bowers, although shutting down most substantive due process challenges to the regulation of homosexual behavior, has hardly quieted efforts to eliminate the barriers of government restrictions against homosexuals and homosexual behavior. Most notably, by shifting their focus to state law claims, gay rights interests have scored several important victories. A number of state courts, including the Georgia Supreme Court, have invalidated state statutes that criminalize consensual sodomy. Other restrictions have also been rejected by state courts, including Vermont's ban on statutory benefits to same-sex couples. With that said, privacy-based restrictions on gay rights continue to be enacted, including the federal Defense of Marriage Act and state intiatives outlawing same sex marriage. Consequently, the story of *Bowers* and its aftermath suggests that the pendulum on gay rights may not fully turn unless and until there is a reversal of those social and political forces that deplore homosexual conduct as immoral.

A. Laws on Homosexuality

Government condemnation of homosexual conduct dates back to Plato, who, after "pointing out that male does not touch male in this way because the action is unnatural," asked "what precautions should we take against it?" Laws VIII at 836. English common law was equally strident. For Blackstone, sodomy—the "infamous crime against nature"—was described as being of a "deeper malignity" than rape, a "subject the very mention of which is a disgrace to human nature." 4 William Blackstone, Commentaries *215. Although Blackstone did not distinguish between homosexual and heterosexual sodomy, there is no doubt that English common law viewed homosexual conduct as so vile that it should be made a felony punishable by death.   For example, the original English enactments specifically targeted anal intercourse between males.

Common law prohibitions against sodomy in general and homosexual sodomy in particular were adopted by the American states. Thomas Jefferson made homosexual behavior a felony in the same class as rape in a criminal code which he drafted during the American Revolution. Thomas Jefferson, The Revisal of the Laws, 1776-1786, reprinted in 2 The Papers of Thomas Jefferson at 497, 664 (Julian P. Boyd, ed., 1950). In 1791, when the Bill of Rights was adopted, eleven of the thirteen states explicitly outlawed sodomy, with three states singling out sexual acts between men for special condemnation.

Government opposition to same-sex sexual conduct extended beyond sodomy laws to restrictions on government employment. In 1950, a subcommittee of the Senate Committee on Expenditures in the Executive Department concluded that homosexuals were not "proper persons to be employed in Government." S. Doc. 241, 81st Cong., 2d Sess. 3 (1950). "[I]t is generally believed," wrote the subcommittee, "that those who engage in overt acts of perversion lack the emotional stability of normal persons. . . . [Furthermore,] indulgence in acts of sex perversion weakens the moral fiber of an individual to a degree that he is not suitable for a position of responsibility." Id. at 4. Along the same lines, in 1953 President Dwight Eisenhower issued an executive order calling for the investigation and possible dismissal of government employees engaged in "sexual perversion." Exec. Order No. 10,450, 18 Fed. Reg. 2491 (1953). By linking same-sex sexual conduct to employability, sodomy laws were depicted by gay rights organizations as "the bedrock of legal discrimination against gay men and lesbians." Patricia A. Cain, Litigating for Lesbian and Gay Rights: A Legal History, 79 Va. L. Rev. 1551, 1587 (1993).

B. Reform Efforts

Efforts to reform sodomy laws began in 1955, when the American Law Institute considered proposals to decriminalize private homosexual conduct. In 1961, Illinois became the first state to repeal its sodomy law. With the emergence of gay rights groups in the mid-1960s, calls for the repeal of sodomy laws escalated. Inspired by the impressive advancements made by Martin Luther King and other civil rights leaders, leaders in the gay community began suggesting that homosexuals take a "vigorous civil-liberties, social-action approach" to end the criminalization of their behavior. Peter Irons, The Courage of their Convictions 384 (1988).

Reform efforts increased in the wake of a violent police raid of the Stonewall Inn in New York City. Beginning on June 27, 1969 and lasting for three days, the "Stonewall Riots" are widely credited for launching the Gay Liberation Movement. After Stonewall, the lobbying and litigation efforts of newly formed homosexual interest groups paid off. In 1973, the American Psychiatric Association removed homosexuality from its list of mental disorders. More significant, from 1969 to 1975, sodomy laws were either legislatively repealed or judicially invalidated in almost half the states. None of these states, however, was below the Mason-Dixon line. Irons at 385. Furthermore, opponents of sodomy statutes acknowledge that states have certain legitimate interests if the activity involves minors, unwilling participants, or actions that occur in public.

C. *Bowers v. Hardwick*

On August 3, 1982, Michael Hardwick was arrested for violating Georgia's sodomy statute. Unlike nearly all sodomy arrests (which are made in parks or other public places), Hardwick was arrested for committing sodomy with a consenting adult male in the privacy of his bedroom. Officer K.R. Torick had come to Hardwick's house with a warrant regarding a ticket Hardwick received for carrying an open container of alcohol. After being let into the house by Hardwick's roommate, Torick observed Hardwick and his friend engage in mutual oral sex through a partially open bedroom door.

Within days of his arrest, Hardwick was contacted by the American Civil Liberties Union. Because Hardwick was arrested in his home, the ACLU thought his "was a perfect test case" to challenge the Georgia law (document 1). In fact, ACLU lawyers "actually hoped for a guilty finding against Michael. Without an adverse judgment, they could not begin the appellate route that led through the state courts to the U.S. Supreme Court." Irons at 382. For this reason, after the county prosecutor effectively pulled the case by refusing to seek a grand jury indictment, Hardwick's lawyers took the initiative and filed a lawsuit in federal court. At first, this ACLU strategy carried the day. A federal appeals court struck down the Georgia statute, pointing out that, for some, homosexual sodomy "serves the same purpose as the intimacy of marriage." Hardwick v. Bowers, 760 F.2d 1202, 1212 (11th Cir. 1985).

Georgia appealed this ruling to a reluctant Supreme Court. At first, only Justices Byron White and William Rehnquist voted to hear the case (two votes short of the four required to grant a petition for certiorari). William Brennan "who had long wanted the Court to confront the [sodomy] issue and saw *Bowers* as an all-but-perfect case" next voted to grant certiorari. David J. Garrow, Liberty and Sexuality 656 (1994). Thurgood Marshall followed Brennan's lead, providing the critical fourth vote. However, after Justice Harry Blackmun explained to Brennan his fear that the case posed a serious threat to the doctrinal underpinnings of *Roe*, Brennan wrote his colleagues that "[I have] decided to change my vote. I vote to deny." Id. at 657. This prompted Chief Justice Warren Burger, after having "taken a second look," to change his vote to grant the petition. Id.

When argued before the Supreme Court, Georgia Attorney General Michael Bowers claimed that "neither the legal nor moral traditions of this nation can provide the necessary support for the recognition of consensual sodomy" as protected "under the guise of a right to privacy" (document 2). In sharp contrast, Laurence Tribe—representing Hardwick—pointed to the Court's prior invalidation of longstanding state prohibitions of interracial marriage to argue against "freez[ing]" into place a "historical vision" of individual rights (document 3).

When the Justices met in conference to discuss the case, a bare five-member majority was prepared to strike down the Georgia law. The critical fifth vote was that of Justice Lewis Powell. Within a week of the conference, however, Powell changed his position, concluding that his "bottom line" should be to uphold the sodomy law. John C. Jeffries, Jr., Justice Lewis F. Powell, Jr. 524 (1994). In the end, as revealed in his discussions with a law clerk who—unbeknownst to Powell—was gay, Powell sided with Georgia because he could not find in the Constitution a right to engage in sexual practices that he could not comprehend (document 4).

The Court boldly pronounced that it "is most vulnerable and comes closest to illegitimacy when it deals with judge-made constitutional law. . . ." 478 U.S. at 194. Pointing to longstanding prohibitions against sodomy, the Court rejected as "at best, facetious" the claim that the constitutional right to privacy extends to homosexual sodomy. Id. In a concurrence, Powell suggested that had Hardwick been "tried, much less convicted and sentenced" and had raised the Eighth Amendment, he might have decided differently.

The Court did not pretend to have the last word on consensual sodomy. It emphasized that its decision "raises no question about the right or propriety of state legislative decisions to repeal their laws that criminalize homosexual sodomy, or of state-court decisions invalidating those laws on state constitutional grounds," 478 U.S. at 190.

Immediately after its decision, the Court became the focal point of a fierce national debate which included academics, executive branch officials, members of Congress, and Supreme Court Justices. Academic commentary was "voluminous" and "almost universally negative." Earl M. Maltz, The Court, The Academy, and the Constitution, 1989 BYU L. Rev. 59, 60. For example, Reagan Solicitor General and Harvard law professor Charles Fried wrote that "[u]nless one takes the implausible line that people generally choose their sexual orientation, then to criminalize any enjoyment of their sexual powers by a whole category of persons is either an imposition of very great cruelty or an exercise in hypocrisy inviting arbitrary and abusive applications of the criminal law." Charles Fried, Order and Law 82-83 (1991). In Congress, *Bowers* was alternatively vilified as a "distressing setback" for individual liberties and applauded for "boldly reaffirm[ing] society's right to enact morals statutes" (document 5). Without doubt, the most surprising and revealing reaction came from Lewis Powell. Three years after his retirement, Powell described his vote in *Bowers* as "a mistake, . . . [w]hen I had the opportunity to reread the opinions. . . , I thought the dissent had the better of the arguments." Jeffries at 530.

D. Initiatives at the State Level

For gay rights litigants, *Bowers* was "the nail in the coffin" of federal judicial reform under substantive due process. David Lauter, Complex Issues Still Unresolved on Gay Rights, Natl. L.J., Apr. 14, 1986 at 1. As a result, the Gay and Lesbian Task Force, the Lamda Legal Defense and Education Fund, and other gay rights interests initially turned their attention to the states. In Nevada, Rhode Island, and the District of Columbia, legislatures repealed existing sodomy statutes. 1993 Statutes of Nevada 236 at 518; R.I. Gen. Law § 11-10-1 (1998); D.C. Act. 10-23 (D.C. Code Supp. 1994).

More striking, numerous state courts have struck down sodomy laws. In Georgia, for example, the state supreme court overturned the sodomy statute that the U.S. Supreme Court upheld in *Bowers*. Concluding that "unforced, private, adult" sexual activity "is at the heart of the Georgia Constitution's protection of the right to privacy," Powell v. State, 510 S.E.2d 18, 24 (Ga. 1998), the court rejected the state's claim that only "the General Assembly of Georgia" could change the sodomy ban (document 6). The court explained the breadth of independent constitutional judgment available to state courts:

> It is a well-recognized principle that a state court is free to interpret its state constitution in any way that does not violate principles of federal law, and thereby grant individuals more rights than those provided by the U.S. Constitution. . . . Thus, a state court may interpret a state constitutional provision as affording more protection to citizens, than have the federal courts in interpreting a parallel provision of the federal constitution. 510 S.E.2d at 22-23 n.3.

Other states that have looked to state law or state constitutions to strike down sodomy statutes include Kentucky, Michigan, Missouri, Montana, and Tennessee. Kentucky v. Wasson, 842 S.W. 2d 487 (Ky. 1992); Michigan Organization for Human Rights v. Kelley, No. 88-815820 CZ (Mich. Cir. Ct. July 9, 1990); State v. Cogshell, 997 S.W. 2d 534 (Mo. App. W.D. July 6, 1999); Gryczan v. State, 942 P. 2d 112 (Mont. 1997); Campbell v. Sundquist, 926 S.W.2d 250 (Tenn. Ct. App. 1996). Some state courts, however, have upheld their criminal sodomy statutes. Miller v. State, 636 So. 2d 391 (Miss. 1994); State v. Mitchell Smith, No. 99-0606, 2000 WL 1036302 (La. July 6, 2000).

E. Federal Initiatives

After the 1992 election of Bill Clinton, gay rights interests pushed for reforms at the federal level. Although Clinton promised the gay and lesbian community that he would "stand with you in the struggle for equality for all Americans," that promise has only been partially fulfilled. Pub. Papers, 1993 (I), at 510. Congress legislated on the issue, establishing conditions for gays in the military that are more stringent than the policy envisioned in the Clinton administration regulations. 107 Stat. 1670, §571 (1993). Years after the Clinton administration had adopted its "don't ask, don't tell" policy, more gay service members were being discharged than before it took effect.

Also interesting is Clinton's position on a federal law aimed at discouraging same-sex marriage, the 1996 Defense of Marriage Act (DOMA). 110 Stat. 2419. Under DOMA, states are not obligated to give "full faith and credit" to same-sex marriages that might be legally sanctioned in other states. Moreover, by defining marriage as "a legal union between one man and one woman as husband and wife," DOMA precludes gay couples from filing joint tax returns or applying for spousal benefits under Social Security and other federal programs. In approving this measure, Congress claimed that federal legislation was necessary to stop "the orchestrated legal campaign by homosexual groups to redefine the institution of marriage through the judicial process" (document 7). Clinton, while condemning DOMA as divisive and unnecessary, signed the bill "hav[ing] long opposed governmental recognition of same-gender marriages." Pub. Papers, 1996 (II), 1635.

Following the enactment of DOMA, gay rights interests continued their campaign to convince state courts and lawmakers to legalize same-sex unions. In Vermont, a 1997 lawsuit challenging that state's prohibition of same-sex marriage culminated in legislation, enacted in April 2000, allowing gays to form a "civil union," which gives them the same benefits, protections, and responsibilities that are granted to spouses in a marriage. In particular, after the Vermont Supreme Court prohibited the state from denying same-sex couples the statutory benefits and protections of marriage, Baker v. State, 744 A. 2d 864 (Vt. 1999), state lawmakers preferred to extend "equal rights, equal responsibilities, and equal benefits" to gays than to resist the court's ruling. Erin Kelly, Vermont Decision on Gay Marriage Benefits Cheered, Denounced, as Expected, Gannett News Service, April 26, 2000.

Outside of Vermont, the campaign for same-sex marriage has been a failure. No other state has sought to repeal or tone down their prohibition of same-sex marriage. Instead, lawmakers and voters in several states have signalled their disapproval of same-sex marriage by either amending their constitutions or enacting legislation. In 2000, anti-gay marriage initiatives appeared on the ballots of sixteen states. More significant, by August 2000, thirty-three states had adopted explicit prohibitions of same-sex marriage. For example, after the Hawaii Supreme Court suggested that it would require recognition of gay marriages, Baehr v. Lewin, 74 Haw. 645, 646 (1993), state lawmakers drafted a constitutional amendment limiting marriage to opposite-sex couples. On November 3, 1998, state voters ratified the amendment.

F. Conclusion

Fifteen years after *Bowers*, government restrictions on homosexual status and conduct continue. Unless the Supreme Court reverses course and intercedes on behalf of gay and lesbian interests, social and political forces will continue to drive reform efforts. These forces, especially in the post-*Bowers* period, have become more potent. For example, Barry Goldwater and other prominent conservatives have called for job protections for gays, including the lifting of the military ban (document 8). At the same time, with the Christian Coalition and other interest groups opposing reform initiatives, the future of gay rights remains uncertain.

Whatever the outcome, the current battles over gay rights will be principally defined by political action and not judicial rulings.

DOCUMENTS

1. Hardwick Describes His Arrest

Source: Peter Irons, The Courage of Their Convictions, 395-97 (1988)

. . . I retired with my friend. He had left the front door open, and Officer Torick came into my house about 8:30 in the morning. . . .

Officer Torick then came to my bedroom. The door was cracked, and the door opened up and I looked up and there was nobody there. I just blew it off as the wind and went back to what I was involved in, which was mutual oral sex. About thirty-five seconds went by and I heard another noise and I looked up, and this officer is standing in my bedroom. He identified himself when he realized I had seen him. He said, My name is Officer Torick. Michael Hardwick, you are under arrest. I said, For what? What are you doing in my bedroom? He said, I have a warrant for your arrest. I told him the warrant isn't any good. He said, it doesn't matter, because I was acting under good faith.

.   .   .

I was contacted about three days later by a man named Clint Sumrall who was working in and out of the ACLU. For the last five years, he would go to the courts every day and find sodomy cases and try to get a test case. . . .

I realized that if there was anything I could do, even if it was just laying the foundation to change this horrendous law, that I would feel pretty bad about myself if I just walked away from it. One thing that influenced me was that they'd been trying for five years to get a perfect case. Most of the arrests that are made for sodomy in Atlanta are of people who are having sex outside in public; or an adult and a minor; or two consenting adults, but their families don't know they are gay; or they went through seven years of college to teach and they'd be jeopardizing their teaching position. There's a lot of different reasons why people would not want to go on with it. I was fortunate enough to have a supportive family who knew I was gay. I'm a bartender, so I can always work in a gay bar. And I was arrested in my own house. So I was a perfect test case.

2. Georgia Defends Its Sodomy Law

Source: Brief for Michael J. Bowers, Attorney General of Georgia, Bowers v. Hardwick, 164 Landmark Briefs 383-86

Obviously, there is no textual support in the Constitution or laws of the United States for the proposition that sodomy is a protected activity. . . . No universal principle of morality teaches that homosexual sodomy is acceptable conduct. To the contrary, traditional Judeo-Christian values proscribe such conduct. . . .

. . . Sodomy was a capital crime in ancient Rome under the Theodosian law of 390 A.D. and under Justinian. Sodomy was proscribed by the teachings of St. Thomas Aquinas. Sodomy was prosecuted as heretical in the ecclesiastical courts throughout the Middle Ages. During the English Reformation when powers of the ecclesiastical courts were transferred to the King's courts, the first

English statute criminalizing sodomy was passed.

In the first half of the 17th Century, Lord Coke expounded upon the crimes of buggery and sodomy, noting that the "ancient authors doe conclude, that it deserveth death, *ultimum supplicium*, though they differ in the manner of punishment." Blackstone considered "the infamous crime against nature" as an offense of "deeper malignity" than rape, and an act as heinous, "the very mention of which is a disgrace to human nature," "a crime not fit to be named."

. . .

In 1816, the crimes of sodomy and bestiality were made punishable in Georgia by life imprisonment at hard labor . . . and have continuously been statutory crimes ever since.

While Respondents correctly note that 22 states have legislatively decriminalized homosexual sodomy . . . 25 states and the District of Columbia continue to maintain criminal statutes against this conduct. . . . Thus, neither the legal nor moral traditions of this nation can provide the necessary support for the recognition of consensual sodomy as falling within that class of rights deemed fundamental or implicit in the concept of ordered liberty. . . .

---

3. Tribe Condemns Sodomy Ban

Source: Oral Argument Transcript, Bowers v. Hardwick, 164 Landmark Briefs 648-49

MR. [LAURENCE] TRIBE: If history alone were the guide—surely, I have to concede that the framers of the Fourteenth Amendment . . . would have been prepared to assume that the kinds of sexual intimacies involved in this case would be outlawed. . . .

But, as this Court recognized in *Loving* against *Virginia*, where also a majority of the people of Virginia believed that interracial liaisons were inherently immoral and where for a long time a lot of people had believed that, this Court did not think that the Constitution's mission was to freeze that historical vision into place.

. . .

QUESTION: Mr. Tribe, if this evolution is taking place, as you suggest, and you may well be right, why isn't it more proper for this Court to let it be reflected in the majority rule where, you know, states have repealed these statutes.

MR. TRIBE: Justice Rehnquist, we do think that that trend is at least relevant for the question of whether this is self-evident evil. But, this Court has never before held that when a personal right protected by the Constitution, just because those persons might be able to obtain political redress, the right no longer deserves judicial protection.

---

4. Powell Searches For an Understanding of Homosexual Conduct

Source: John C. Jeffries, Jr., Justice Lewis F. Powell, Jr. 521-22 (1994)

Powell's search for a legal theory paralleled a search for personal understanding. Sexual activity between men was something he did not comprehend. Unable to say exactly what he wished to learn, he nonetheless realized that he needed to know more.

Unknown to Powell, one of his clerks was gay. Powell merely identified the young man as the most liberal of the four clerks and so sought out his views. . . . Powell came into the clerk's office and casually asked him to

review the arguments in this difficult case.
When told that (as the clerk believed) 10
percent of the population was gay, Powell
was incredulous. "I don't believe I've ever
met a homosexual," he told his astonished
clerk. "Certainly you have," came back the
reply, "but you just don't know that they are."
. . .

The discussion edged toward Powell's
true mission when he tried to find out from
his startled clerk just what it meant to be gay:

> "Are gay men not attracted to women at
> all?"
> "They are attracted to women, but there is
> no sexual excitement."
> "None at all?"
> "Justice Powell, a gay man could not get
> an erection to have sex with a woman."

The answer left Powell even more confused.
"Don't you have to have an erection to
perform sodomy?" he asked.

"Yes," he was told, "but that's because of
the sexual excitement."

What Powell found so difficult to grasp
was that homosexuality was not an act of
desperation, not the last resort of men
deprived of women, but a logical expression
of the desire and affection that gay men felt
for other men.

A few days later he made another run at
the same topic. Again the clerk tried to
explain that gay men "love other men like
straight men love women." Powell still found
it hard to follow. In the words of the clerk:
"He had no concept of it at all. He couldn't
understand the idea of sexual attraction
between two men. It just had no content for
him."

A third conversation took place just
before oral argument. Uncharacteristically,
Powell had still not decided how he would
vote. In great distress, the clerk debated
whether to tell Powell of his sexual
orientation. Perhaps if Powell could put a
familiar face to these incomprehensible urges,
they would seem less bizarre and threatening.

He came to the edge of an outright
declaration but ultimately drew back, settling
for a "very emotional" speech urging Powell
to support sexual freedom as a fundamental
right. "The right to love the person of my
choice," he argued, "would be far more
important to me than the right to vote in
elections." "That may be," Powell answered,
"but that doesn't mean it's in the
Constitution."

---

5. *Bowers*: The Reaction
in Congress

Source: 132 Cong. Rec. 19943 (1986);
135 Cong. Rec. 13950-51 (1989)

Mr. [Ted] WEISS [D-N.Y.]: Mr. Speaker,
the June 30 decision of the Supreme Court in
the Bowers versus Hardwick case marks a
distressing setback for people everywhere
concerned about individual liberties. . . .

. . .

The Court seems to believe that liberty
and homosexuality cannot coexist. But the
truth is that the State cannot police our
bedrooms and outlaw our most private,
personal, intimate relations with others
without destroying the most basic
constitutional notions of liberty and justice.

. . .

Ours is a secular society, one where
pluralism must take precedence over
moralism. Yet according to this decision, our
Constitution protects only those who follow
the "moral teachings" of religious authorities.
Adherence to this sanctimonious logic would
place our Nation firmly in the 14th century.

The Bowers versus Hardwick decision
assaults not just the sexual conduct, but the
very identity of millions of men and women.
There is no more personal decision a human
being can make than how to express their
inherent sexuality. . . .

Mr. [William] DANNEMEYER [R-Calif.]: . . . All too often militant homosexuals will insist that one person's values should not be forced upon another person. And that just because a man and woman enjoy sexual intercourse does not mean that two men cannot equally enjoy sodomy, or that sexual intercourse and sodomy should not be equally valued. "Anyway," they will proclaim, "You can't legislate morality."

These are powerful arguments on their surface. The rhetoric is appealing to our libertarian senses. After all, this is America, a land where anyone can do as they wish provided they do no harm to another. These thoughts comprise the homosexual liturgy.

Unfortunately for the homosexual movement, these arguments are specious and totally void of historical and legal claims of jurisprudence. . . . [T]he U.S. Supreme Court ruled that "There is no fundamental right to commit homosexual sodomy." In the case of Bowers versus Hardwick (1986), the Court boldly reaffirmed society's right to enact moral statutes of this nature.

---

6. Georgia Objects to State Supreme Court Reconsideration of its Sodomy Law

Source: Brief Amicus Curiae by the Attorney General in Support of the State's Motion for Rehearing at 1-2, 12, 14, Powell v. State, 510 S.E.2d 18 (Ga. 1998) (No. S98A0755)

On November 20, 1998, a majority of this Court ruled that the Constitution of Georgia protects as a fundamental right of privacy an act of sodomy . . . .

The majority opinion has forsaken established rules of constitutional interpretation and performed a purely legislative function, which rightly belongs to the General Assembly of Georgia.

Judge Learned Hand once said that liberty ". . . is not the ruthless, the unbridled will; it is not freedom to do as one likes. That is the denial of liberty and leads straight to its overthrow." . . . Eschewing this wisdom, this Court has established a rule of privacy that subsumes numerous well-worn laws designed for the protection of the health and decency of society as a whole.

It is certain that Georgia's laws against fornication and adultery will be challenged based on the new expansive right of privacy. These statutes, like many others, are commonly violated by two individuals acting privately and with mutual consent. . . .

[I]t might well be expected that the validity of laws prohibiting same-sex marriage, polygamy, consensual euthanasia, assisted suicide, necrophilia and bestiality, among others, will be questioned. These acts, it will be argued, are private and cause no harm to anyone other than those who are consenting to the acts. Thus the natural progression of this Court's declaration will raise questions about numerous public laws which embody values inherent in the traditions and experience of our state and nation.

---

7. House Judiciary Committee Defends DOMA

Source: H.R. Rep. No. 664, 104th Cong., 2d Sess. 12-15 (1996)

H.R. 3396, is appropriately entitled the "Defense of Marriage Act." The effort to redefine "marriage" to extend to homosexual couples is a truly radical proposal that would fundamentally alter the institution of marriage. To understand why marriage should be preserved in its current form, one need only ask why it is that society recognizes the institution of marriage and grants married persons preferred legal status. . . .

. . . [T]o discover the "ends of marriage," we need only reflect on this central, unimpeachable lesson of human nature [citing the testimony of Professor Hadley Arkes]:

"We are, each of us, born a man or a woman. The committee needs no testimony from an expert witness to decode this point: Our engendered existence, as men and women, offers the most unmistakable, natural signs of the meaning and purpose of sexuality. And that is the function and purpose of begetting. At its core, *it is hard to detach marriage from what may be called the "natural teleology of the body": namely, the inescapable fact that only two people, not three, only a man and a woman, can beget a child.*"

At bottom, civil society has an interest in maintaining and protecting the institution of heterosexual marriage because it has a deep and abiding interest in encouraging responsible procreation and child-rearing. Simply put, government has an interest in marriage because it has an interest in children.

. . .

There are two standard attacks on this rationale for opposing a redefinition of marriage to include homosexual unions. First, it is noted that society permits heterosexual couples to marry regardless of whether they intend or are even able to have children. But this is not a serious argument. Surely no one would propose requiring couples intending to marry to submit to a medical examination to determine whether they can reproduce, or to sign a pledge indicating that they intend to do so. Such steps would be both offensive and unworkable. Rather, society has made the eminently sensible judgment to permit heterosexuals to marry, notwithstanding the fact that some couples cannot or simply choose not to have children.

Second, it will be objected that there are greater threats to marriage and families than the one posed by same-sex "marriage," the most prominent of which is divorce. . . .

But the fact that marriage is embattled is surely no argument for opening a new front in the war. Indeed, it is precisely now, when marriage and the family are most in need of nurturing and care, that we should be the most wary of conducting new experiments with the institution. . . .

---

8. Goldwater Calls for an End to the Ban on Gays in the Military

Source: Barry Goldwater, The Gay Ban: Just Plain Un-American, Wash. Post., June 10, 1993, at A-23

After more than 50 years in the military and politics, I am still amazed to see how upset people can get over nothing. Lifting the ban on gays in the military isn't exactly nothing, but it's pretty damned close.

Everyone knows that gays have served honorably in the military since at least the time of Julius Caesar. They'll still be serving long after we're all dead and buried. That should not surprise anyone.

. . .

Some in Congress think I'm wrong. They say we absolutely must continue to discriminate, or all hell will break loose. Who knows, they say, perhaps our soldiers may even take up arms against each other.

Well, that's just stupid.

Years ago I was a lieutenant in charge of an all-black unit. Military leaders at the time believed that blacks lacked leadership potential—period. That seems ridiculous now, as it should. Now, each and every man and woman who serves his nation takes orders from a black man—our own Gen. Colin Powell.

.   .   .

We have wasted enough precious time, money and talent trying to persecute and pretend. It's time to stop burying our heads in the sand and denying reality for the sake of politics. It's time to deal with this straight on and be done with it. It's time to get on with more important business.

The conservative movement, to which I subscribe, has as one of its basic tenets the belief that government should stay out of people's private lives. Government governs best when it governs least—and stays out of the impossible task of legislating morality. But legislating someone's version of morality is exactly what we do by perpetuating discrimination against gays.

.   .   .

When the government sets policy, it has a responsibility to acknowledge facts, tell the truth and lead the country forward, not backward. Congress would best serve our national interest by finding the courage to rally the troops in support of ending this un-American discrimination.

II. ROMER v. EVANS

Starting in the early 1990s, gay rights opponents have made extensive use of state and local initiatives. By taking their case directly to the people, anti-gay interests have been able to overcome state and local lawmaker resistance to their agenda. Whether the issue is same-sex marriage, affirmative action, or the extension of antidiscrimination protections, gay rights opponents see these ballot initiatives as the best way to advance their cause.

In *Romer v. Evans*, 517 U.S. 620 (1996), the Supreme Court struck down a Colorado initiative prohibiting the granting of "protected status" to "homosexuals, bisexuals, and lesbians." *Romer*, however, did not put an end to the practice of government linedrawing on the basis of sexual orientation. Just as *Bowers* did little to deter gays from seeking the same privacy rights as heterosexuals, *Romer* has done little to quiet gay rights opponents in their efforts to limit employment, housing, and other opportunities to gay men and women. Following *Romer*, for example, voters in Hawaii and California registered their disapproval of same-sex marriage through ballot initiatives. *Romer*, moreover, has had no impact on the Clinton Justice Department's defense of restrictions on gay servicemen and women. In the end, the story of *Romer* and its aftermath makes clear that the battle over equal treatment for gays will largely be settled outside the courts.

A. Citizen Initiatives and Gay Rights

The most direct and most profound way state voters shape constitutional values is through initiatives and referenda. A majority of states, especially those in the West and South, allow voters to place legislative and constitutional reform proposals on the ballot. From 1898 to the early 1990s, voters in seventeen states considered 732 constitutional amendment initiatives, approving 223 of them. Of these 223 measures, 21 were ratified in the 1970s, rising to 33 in the 1980s, and rising even further to 42 in the period from 1991 to 1995.

Initiatives and referenda have been extraordinarily consequential. Examples include women's suffrage, voter election of U.S. senators, term limits, and much more. Moreover, since citizens typically use the initiative process to place issues on the ballot that elected officials are unwilling to deal with, direct democracy measures often touch on hot button constitutional issues. The emergence of the pro-life movement, for example, is tied to 1972 battles in North Dakota and Michigan over proposed referenda that would have repealed state laws that criminalized abortion. Also in 1972, overwhelming public support for a death penalty initiative prompted state lawmakers to support legislation authorizing capital punishment. In the 1990s, direct democracy proposals have focused on abortion, campaign finance reform, affirmative action, and gay rights.

During the 1990s, state-wide initiatives on gay rights issues occurred in Arizona, California, Florida, Hawaii, Idaho, Maine, Michigan, Missouri, Nevada, Oregon, and Washington. For the most part, these initiatives were championed by conservatives who oppose the extension of civil rights protections to homosexuals and lesbians. At one extreme, these measures, in addition to prohibiting homosexuality as a civil rights category, sought to group homosexuality with "pedophilia, sadism or masochism" and compel state education authorities to teach that homosexuality is "abnormal, wrong, unnatural, and perverse." State of Oregon, Measure Nine to Amend Constitution (1992), reprinted in William E. Adams, Jr., Pre-Election Anti-Gay Ballot Initiatives, 55 Ohio St. L.J. 583, 647 (1994). At another extreme, some of these measures do not even mention homosexuality. In Maine, for example, a 1995 referendum read: "Do you favor the changes in Maine law concerning the limitation of protected status to the existing classifications of race, color, sex, physical or mental disability, religion, age, ancestry, national origin, familial status, and marital status proposed by citizen petition?" State of Maine, An Act to Limit Protected Classes Under the Maine Human Rights Act (1995), reprinted in Adams at 632. Most of these initiatives, however, parallel the Colorado initiative struck down in *Romer*:

> . . . Neither the State of Colorado, through any of its branches or departments, nor any of its agencies, political subdivisions, municipalities or school districts, shall enact, adopt or enforce any statute, regulation, ordinance or policy whereby homosexual, lesbian or bisexual orientation, conduct, practices or relationships shall constitute or otherwise be the basis of, or entitle any person or class of persons to have any claim of

minority status, quota preferences, protected status or claim of discrimination. Colo. Const., Art. II, § 30b.

Colorado's Amendment 2 initiative, in large measure, was a response to the efforts of Aspen, Boulder, and Denver to prohibit discrimination in employment, housing, or public accommodations based on sexual orientation. In March 1991, Colorado Springs car dealer Will Perkins helped form Colorado for Family Values (CFV), the grassroots organization that initiated and campaigned for the passage of Amendment 2. According to CFV (in a pamphlet distributed to 750,000 registered voters across the state): "Militant homosexuals have flooded Colorado's media with claims that they're only after 'equal protection.' Truth is, they already share that with all Americans. What they really want will shock and alarm you." The pamphlet also spoke of "homosexual indoctrination in the schools" and linked homosexuality to pedophilia, disease, and promiscuity. Colorado for Family Values, Equal Rights-Not Special Rights! at 1-2 (1992).

Opponents of the measure compared the CFV's appeal to family values to "Hitler's appeals to traditional German family values." Opponents also distributed flyers calling for a boycott of Will Perkins's car dealership. "Don't pay him to hate" was written in the flyers. Timothy Egan, Anti-Gay Backlashes are on 3 States' Ballots, N.Y. Times, Oct. 4, 1992 at 4-4. Colorado governor Roy Romer joined in the opposition, saying that the intiative "is not a good thing to pass" and that Coloradans "are not intolerant . . . [but] on the question of gay and lesbian rights, it is foreign to them." Chuck Raash, Colorado Gay Rights Debate: Protection or Privilege?, Gannett News Service, June 22, 1992.

To help voters better understand the arguments for and against the amendment, the Colorado Legislative Council prepared a synthesis (without the incendiary rhetoric) of these arguments (document 1). On November 3, 1992, Amendment 2 was passed into law with 53.4% of the popular vote. Two weeks later, Richard Evans and other amendment opponents went into court to enjoin enforcement of the measure. Although he continued to oppose the measure (document 2), Governor Romer promised to exhaust all legal appeals in defending Amendment 2.

B. Amendment 2 and the Courts

On October 11, 1994 the Colorado Supreme Court ruled that Amendment 2, by prohibiting governmental entities in Colorado from enacting antidiscrimination protections for homosexuals and bisexuals, unconstitutionally infringed upon a "fundamental right . . . to participate equally in the political process." Evans v. Romer, 882 P.2d 1335, 1343 (Colo. 1994). In petitioning the Supreme Court to review this decision, lawyers for the state argued that the Colorado court's "creation of new constitutional 'rights' in response to socially worrisome issues" "places into constitutional doubt any attempt by state or federal governments to preempt countervailing social policies favored by lesser political units." 248 Landmark Briefs at 19. In its brief before the Supreme Court, Colorado likewise argued that the state court's decision cast doubt upon the "heart of state sovereignty" (document 3). Echoing this theme, an amicus brief filed by a coalition of seven states dubbed the Colorado Supreme Court decision a "serious[] threat[] [to] the right of all the people to participate collectively and directly in the political process." Id. at 385. A competing amicus brief, filed by a coalition of seven states and the District of Columbia, took issue with this states' rights claim. Contending that they "value their sovereignty equally with Colorado," this coalition depicted "Amendment 2 [as] the antithesis of the neutrality that the Equal Protection Clause requires." Id. at 1063, 1066.

At oral argument, the Justices picked up on this state sovereignty point, questioning Evans' lawyer about the propriety of municipalities trumping state preferences. The Justices also asked why Colorado could not deny protected group status to homosexuals if, under *Bowers*, it could criminalize homosexual conduct (document 4). In the end, however, the Justices ruled against the state. Concluding that Amendment 2 "deprives gays and lesbians even of the protection of general laws and policies that prohibit arbitrary discrimination in governmental and private settings," 517 U.S. at 630, the Court ruled that "the amendment seems inexplicable by anything but animus." Id. at. 632.

Immediately following the Court's ruling, Governor Romer urged Coloradans to accept the decision, expressing a hope that they would believe that "this is the highest court giving us good counsel" and that people would want to "live with this and make it work . . . find[ing] ways to include and understand the diversity in this culture." Keith White, Romer Urges Coloradans to Accept Supreme Court Ruling, Gannett News Service, May 21, 1996. Lawyers for the state were less compliant. In explaining their defeat, they pointed to "Colorado's political judgment confound[ing] . . . trends towards greater openness on matters of sexual conduct" and reasoned that "[t]he courts sensed something sinister about a statewide enactment that would quell the local and state debate raging across the state." Timothy M. Tymkovich, John Daniel Dailey, and Paul Farley, A Tale of Three Theories: Reason and Prejudice in the Battle Over Amendment 2, 68 U. Colo. L. Rev. 287, 332 (1997). For these lawyers, however, what Colorado did was not at all sinister but, instead, was part of an ongoing constitutional dialogue between municipalities and the state.

C. The Clinton Administration and *Romer*

One of the most striking features of the *Romer* litigation was the Clinton administration's decision to steer clear of the case. Although willing to speak out against Amendment 2 and, more generally, to embrace the extension of antidiscrimination protections to gays (document 5), Clinton concurred with Attorney General Janet Reno's conclusion that, since "[t]here was no federal program or federal statute involved," it was inappropriate for the Department of Justice to participate in the *Romer* litigation. At a news conference announcing the President's position, however, White House Press Secretary Mike McCurry was pressed by reporters who saw Clinton's decision as a political act, not a legal decision (document 6).

The reason reporters saw Clinton's decision as political is that, at the time of *Romer*, his administration was defending the so-called "Don't Ask, Don't Tell" policy governing gays in the military. According to Carter Phillips, one of Colorado's attorneys: "I don't think it's humanly possible to argue that Amendment 2 is unconstitutional but their gays-in-the-military policy is constitutional." David G. Savage, Government to Stay Out of the Battle Over Gay Rights, L.A. Times, June 9, 1995 at A36.

For the Clinton administration, its defense of "Don't Ask, Don't Tell" was critically important. When campaigning for the White House, Clinton argued that he would lift the ban against gays in the military. "One of my tenets," said candidate Clinton, is that "[w]e don't have a person to waste. We waste too many in America." Michael Frisby, Clinton Raps Perot on Gays, Boston Globe, May 31, 1992 at 14. But strong resistance from Congress and the military establishment prompted Clinton to compromise. Under this "Don't Ask, Don't Tell" policy, the military was forbidden from inquiring into sexual orientation. At the same time, openly gay individuals could not serve in the military (unless they could show that they do not engage in homosexual conduct). Since the policy was grounded in the belief that "open homosexuality" was at odds with "military effectiveness" (document 7), Clinton suffered much embarrassment for his apparent flip-flop.

While the administration may have been unwilling to jeopardize its gays-in-the-military policy by participating in *Romer*, Clinton nonetheless thought the decision "appropriate." One year later, lawyers for the Clinton administration distinguished *Romer* when opposing Supreme Court review of a "Don't Ask, Don't Tell" case. Arguing that, unlike Amendment 2, the military policy serves legitimate governmental purposes, Solicitor General Seth Waxman argued that *Romer* had no bearing on the constitutionality of "Don't Ask, Don't Tell" (document 8).

D. Conclusion

Romer v. Evans, while suggesting that the Supreme Court is willing to take a hard look at initiatives and referenda, has not slowed down the pace of direct democracy reforms. From 1996 to 2000, voters have spoken out on partial birth abortion, affirmative action, the right to die, same-sex marriage, and term limits. 1998, moreover, set a record for the most money ever spent on initiative campaigns.

For anti-gay interests, *Romer* has placed few limitations on their campaigns. Two years after the decision, the Supreme Court refused to review a federal court decision upholding a Cincinnati anti-gay initiative, the wording of which was almost identical to Colorado's Amendment 2. Equality Foundation of Greater Cincinnati v. City of Cincinnati, 128 F.3d 289 (6th Cir. 1997), cert. denied, 525 U.S. 943 (1998). In explaining that the Court may simply have concluded that the Cincinnati case did "not constitute an appropriate forum in which to decide a significant issue," Justices John Paul Stevens, David Souter, and Ruth Bader Ginsburg played down the Court's decision to deny cert. Nevertheless, for gay rights supporters and opponents, the decision makes clear that most of the battle over gay rights will be fought in the voting booth, not the courts.

DOCUMENTS

1. Colorado Legislative Council Analyzes Amendment 2

Source: Legislative Council of
the Colorado General Assembly,
An Analysis of 1992 Ballot
Proposals, Research Pub. No. 369
at 14-18 (1992)

Arguments For

1) There is no evidence that homosexual, lesbian, and bisexual individuals are sufficiently disadvantaged to warrant designation as a protected class. Protected class status is not a basic right guaranteed to all citizens by the United States Constitution. In general, protected class status has been afforded to groups which have historically been subjected to purposeful unequal treatment, or relegated to such a position of political powerlessness as to command extraordinary protection from the majoritarian political process, or been subjected to unique disabilities on the basis of stereotyped characteristics not truly indicative of their abilities. . . .

2) Homosexual, lesbian, and bisexual persons do not require protected status because they are entitled to recourse under the tort laws for libelous or slanderous abuse, wrongful discharge, emotional distress, or similar theories. . . .

3) Granting protected status to homosexual, lesbian, and bisexual persons may compel some individuals to violate their private consciences or to face legal sanctions for failure to comply. For some individuals, homosexuality, or bisexuality conflicts with their religious values and teachings or their private moral values. . . .

Arguments Against

1) All individuals should be accorded the same basic dignity, right to privacy, privileges, and protections guaranteed to every citizen. Discrimination against any class of individuals is wrong and, if tolerated, can easily spread to any and all groups in our society. In a pluralistic society, a threat to the rights of any one group should be viewed as a threat to the rights of all citizens. The amendment deprives homosexual, lesbian,

and bisexual persons of legal protection against discrimination based on sexual orientation by isolating them as a class which could not be protected by such civil rights laws. . . .

2) Because homosexual, lesbian, and bisexual persons face discrimination in employment, housing, and public accommodations and are victims of hate crimes, civil rights laws are needed that prohibit discrimination based on sexual orientation. Without the ordinances, existing laws inadequately protect these individuals and fail to address discrimination in employment, housing, and public accommodations. . . .

. . .

5) By singling out homosexual, lesbian, and bisexual persons in the state constitution and effectively denying them potential remedies for discrimination, the amendment denies them the same equal protections under the United States Constitution as other citizens. The proposed amendment may violate the equal protection clause of the United States Constitution, which prohibits any state from adopting a law which singles out a group for unfavorable or discriminatory treatment without a sufficient basis, or due to prejudice or irrational fears. . . .

---

2. Romer Speaks Out on Gay Rights

Source: Address by Gov. Roy Romer to the National Press Club, Federal News Service, at 11-12 (Jan. 29, 1993)

. . . I opposed Amendment Number 2 in Colorado, which said two things. Amendment 2 said you shall not create a special status or have quotas for someone who's homosexual, but it also said you shall not pass any law banning discrimination based upon sexual orientation.

I opposed that for the following reasons. I believe in the first part. I do not believe we ought to have special status, special class, or quotas based upon sexual orientation, but at the same time, I believe you ought not discriminate. In one sentence, I don't want special rights, I want equal rights. And that's my position.

Let me give it to you in just more human terms. You know, I'm from a small town, 800 people. I was a Methodist. Homosexuality is an awkward issue for me. I had to work to learn about it, but the best way I can communicate about it is to think of my brother. He's older than I. He's not gay.

But if he were gay, what would I want for my brother? I would want him to have as full a life as he could live. I wouldn't want somebody to discriminate against him on the job because he happened to be gay.

At the same time, I don't want my brother to have any special privilege or advantage, nor do I want to have his lifestyle forced upon others. Nor do I want others to have to associate together with him in a duplex if they choose not to do that. . . .

. . .

Basically I'm trying to get us in this nation to say there is diversity of sexual orientation. Let's try to learn to understand that diversity and try to enable all of us to live the fullest life that we can and not push our lifestyle off onto others.

I had a state of the state speech recently and I had to speak about this, and I used one sentence that I want to repeat here, and it's this. Whether we're within a church community or without, I would like to have us spend less time trying to legislate the morality of others and spend more time trying to create communities where we all can grow and learn what truth is for us. That, I think, would be a kind of a message that I would share with you about what I think we ought to do with the issue of homosexuality.

3. Colorado Defends Amendment 2

Source: 248 Landmark Briefs 183,
212-214

The intent and effect of Amendment 2 is to withdraw a deeply divisive social and political issue from elected representatives and place its resolution squarely in the hands of the people. Core principles of federalism have led this Court to grant States "extraordinarily wide latitude" in such internal allocations of authority among political institutions. Rare in any context, heightened scrutiny is almost never appropriate where, as here, the challenged state action goes to the heart of state sovereignty. Thus, on its face, Amendment 2 carries with it a strong presumption of constitutionality.

. . . .

The rational basis inquiry in this case does not depend upon mere theory, however, because the State argued, and presented convincing evidence, that in removing or preventing governmental regulation in this area, Amendment 2 promotes freedom of choice (relating to matters of personal and familial privacy, religion, and association), furthers several legitimate societal concerns (relating to the integrity of civil rights laws and the contours of social and moral norms), and achieves statewide uniformity.

Significantly, neither the trial court nor the Colorado Supreme Court found any of these purposes to be illegitimate or unreasonable. Indeed, between them, the two courts recognized that there are three "compelling" public purposes served—albeit inexactly—by Amendment 2. Those interests were the promotion of religious freedom, the promotion of familial privacy, and the preservation of associational privacy. . . .

. . . .

The supporters of Amendment 2 were acutely aware that laws and policies designed to benefit homosexuals and bisexuals could have an adverse effect on the ability of state and local governments to combat discrimination against suspect classes. . . .

When Amendment 2 was proposed, . . . the Colorado Civil Rights Division, had experienced steadily increasing demands upon a shrinking budget, and the existence of substantial evidence that homosexuals and bisexuals were not, as a class, in need of such protections.

4. Justices Call Into Question the Impact of Amendment 2

Source: 248 Landmark Briefs
1169-70, 1180-81

QUESTION: You mean no general laws can be applied to homosexuals now? They can be bashed, they can be murdered, they—all sorts of things. Is that what [Amendment 2] means?

. . . .

Ms. [Jean] DUBOFSKY [counsel for Richard G. Evans, who challenged the constitutionality of Amendment 2]: I think we're having trouble a little bit with semantics.

One of the difficulties is the use of the words special protection in this case. I don't think there is such a thing as special rights or special protections. I think there's a right which everyone has to be free from arbitrary discrimination.

QUESTION: No, but if I go and ask a homeowner to take me in on bed and breakfast and the homeowner says, I don't like Italians, that's my tough luck, unless there's a law against it. It's that person's house, and that person is entitled not to like Italians and not to rent rooms to Italians.

That's fine, unless there's a law against it, and you can have such a law prohibiting the rental of rooms, or refusal to rental on the basis of racial discrimination or on the basis of homosexuality, if you want to make that a category, and I think that this law says, no special protection on that basis. Why isn't that a special protection, one that is not given to everyone?

QUESTION: Ms. Dubofsky, do you contend that—are you asking us to overrule *Bowers v. Hardwick*?

Ms. DUBOFSKY: No, I am not.

QUESTION: Well, there we said that you could make homosexual conduct criminal. Why can a state not take a step short of that and say, we're not going to make it criminal, but on the other hand, we certainly don't want to encourage it, and therefore we will neither have a state law giving it special protection, nor will we allow any municipalities to give it special protection.

It seems to me the legitimacy of the one follows from the legitimacy of the other. If you can criminalize it, surely you can take that latter step, can't you?

Ms. DUBOFSKY: What you've done is deprived people, based on their homosexual orientation, of a whole opportunity to seek protection from discrimination, which is a very different thing.

QUESTION: So do you do it when you throw them in jail for a felony?

Ms. DUBOFSKY: No—

QUESTION: I'm not talking about orientation, now. I'm talking about conduct. If we have held it constitutional to make the conduct criminal, how could it be unconstitutional to go so much short of that?

We don't want to get into the hassle of intrusion into private life, and all of that, that that requires. We're not going to criminalize it. On the other hand, we do not think it is conduct that ought to be encouraged, and therefore we will not allow any special

protections for it, neither at the state level, nor locally.

Doesn't—if the one is constitutional, must not the other one be?

Ms. DUBOFSKY: If homosexuals were put into the language of Amendment 2 only in terms of, those people who engage in homosexual conduct shall not be entitled to ever seek protection under the civil rights laws, we would say that is unconstitutional. That's a very different thing from saying that you can criminalize homosexual sodomy.

QUESTION: But isn't it also true that this law applies to this class of people even if they abstain from the prohibited conduct?

Ms. DUBOFSKY: That's correct, and it also could apply to people who aren't gay, but who may be perceived to be gay and are discriminated against on that basis.

---

5. Clinton Seeks Equal Rights for Gays

Source: 35 Weekly Comp. Pres. Doc. 1089-90 (1999)

I am proud of the measures my Administration has taken to end discrimination against gays and lesbians and ensure that they have the same rights guaranteed to their fellow Americans. Last year, I signed an Executive order that amends Federal equal employment opportunity policy to prohibit discrimination in the Federal civilian work force based on sexual orientation. We have also banned discrimination based on sexual orientation in the granting of security clearances. As a result of these and other policies, gay and lesbian Americans serve openly and proudly throughout the Federal Government. My Administration is also working with congressional leaders to pass the Employment Non-Discrimination Act, which would prohibit most private employers from firing workers solely because of their sexual orientation.

America's diversity is our greatest strength. But, while we have come a long way on our journey toward tolerance, understanding, and mutual respect, we still have a long way to go in our efforts to end discrimination. During the past year, people across our country have been shaken by violent acts that struck at the heart of what it means to be an American and at the values that have always defined us as a Nation. In 1997, the most recent year for which we have statistics, there were more than 8,000 reported hate crimes in our country—almost one an hour. Now is the time for us to take strong and decisive action to end all hate crimes, and I reaffirm my pledge to work with the Congress to pass the Hate Crimes Prevention Act.

But we cannot achieve true tolerance merely through legislation; we must change hearts and minds as well. Our greatest hope for a just society is to teach our children to respect one another, to appreciate our differences, and to recognize the fundamental values that we hold in common. . . .

---

6. Reports Challenge White House Position on *Romer*

Source: Office of the White House Press Secretary [Mike McCurry], Press Briefing, June 8, 1995

Q: Well, Mike, the rationale that is being given here is that this was not a federal case, that this did not involve federal laws. However, this does deal with an issue that is coming up all across the nation in a number of states and a number of cities and it does have some national impact. Why then is it not appropriate for the federal government to step in and file a brief?

Mr. [Mike] McCURRY: Well, for all the reasons that the Attorney General indicated today.

. . .

Q: Mike, back on the Colorado case just for a second. Just to be clear, are you telling us that the administration took no position one way or the other—the White House took no position—the President—one way or the other on the case and that you agree with the decision that the Attorney General has made?

Mr. McCURRY: I'm saying that the President understands the reasoning of the Attorney General as she articulated it today and he fully supports her reasoning and her determination that the government not file on this case.

Q: Political question on that. Gay rights issues have dogged this administration from the beginning. You had problems with the gays in the military questions, with which the gay community was in an uproar over. You're have—the gay community is again, at least in terms of current comments, seems to be angered by this recent decision. How do you deal with this constituency group that helped the President is 1992 with money and with votes, looking ahead to the reelection?

Mr. McCURRY: Well, there was a long question there, and I don't—without accepting any of the premise of the question, I'll say, as we do with a variety of—any group of Americans that are organized and seek the administration's viewpoints and talk to them. We try to help them understand the direction and thrust of our policy. And if I'm not mistaken there's a group of leaders from various gay organizations that will be here as early as next week sometime. So we continue to keep a close dialogue underway.

. . .

Q: In the Colorado case, you indicated the President agrees with Reno's view that there's no underlying federal issue. But obviously the lawyers for the gay rights people feel this is a federal issue or else they wouldn't be going to the Supreme Court. The President is a legal and constitutional scholar in his right. If you go back to the early civil rights movement, they were exactly these same debates and discussions as to whether what was happening in the South was a state issue or a federal issue. Isn't he taking a rather cramped view of federal enforcement of civil rights by saying there's no federal issue?

Mr. McCurry: I haven't had an opportunity to review the constitutional issues with the President, so I'm not in a position to answer that.

---

7. Powell Testifies on Gays in the Military

Source: Policy Concerning Homosexuals in the Armed Forces: Hearings Before the Senate Comm. On Armed Services, 103d Cong., 1st Sess. 707-08 (1993)

General [Colin] Powell [Chair, Joint Chiefs of Staff]. . . I am pleased . . . to speak in full support of the President's new policy on homosexuals in the military. As the President described it yesterday, it is a policy that I think constitutes an honorable compromise, and it is also a policy that I and my colleagues on the Joint Chiefs of Staff feel that we will be able to implement successfully.

.   .   .

The challenge we faced was to try to reconcile or compromise two sets of conflicting views. On the one hand are those who believe that homosexuals should be allowed to openly serve. They note correctly that homosexuals have privately served well in the past and are continuing to serve well today.

There are some, however, who advanced a view much more aggressively than that and sought acceptance in the military of the entire gay rights agenda, to include not only open service within the military but the introduction of all of the associated benefits of partnership and other benefits that accrue to partnerships within the military. On the other hand are those of us who believe that the presence of open homosexuality would have an unacceptable detrimental and disruptive impact on the cohesion, morale, and esprit of the Armed Forces.

Our concern has not been about homosexuals seducing heterosexuals or heterosexuals attacking homosexuals. The first of these so-called problems is manageable and the second so-called problem is punishable. For us the issue is also not what is acceptable in civilian life, and it is also not our place as the uniformed leaders of the Armed Forces to use our official position to make moral or religious judgments on this issue.

Our perspective is a unique one, and it is the unique perspective of the military and what is best for military effectiveness. The military exists to fight the Nation's wars, to accomplish our war-fighting mission. . . .

And to win wars, we create cohesive teams of warriors who will bond so tightly that they are prepared to go into battle and give their lives if necessary for the accomplishment of the mission and for the cohesion of the group and for their individual buddies. We cannot allow anything to happen which would disrupt that feeling of cohesion within the force.

We are the best force in the world, and to be the best requires subjugating individual rights to the benefit of the group and the benefit of the team. Homosexuals over history who have been willing to keep their orientation private have been successful members of those teams.

Congress and the courts have consistently upheld the unique circumstances of military service, and I believe the American people understand these unique circumstances and support them as well. Because in the military we discriminate in many ways that would be absolutely unthinkable and unacceptable in civilian life. We have rules and regulations that are unique to our calling and could not pass any constitutional test if they were applied in civilian life.

We impose on our troops conditions of service unlike any other field of endeavor. We tell them who they will work with, where to live, and we tell them who they will be living with. . . .

. . . We have successfully mixed rich and poor, black and white, urban and rural. But open homosexuality in units is not just the acceptance of benign characteristics such as color or race or background. It involves matters of privacy and human sexuality that, in our judgment, if allowed to exist in the force would affect the cohesion and well-being of the force. . . .

---

8. Department of Justice Defends "Don't Ask, Don't Tell"

Source: Brief for the Respondents in Opposition, Thorne v. Department of Defense (No. 98-91), at 7-10

The court below also correctly rejected petitioner's argument that 10 U.S.C. 654 ["Don't Ask, Don't Tell"] and its implementing directive violate equal protection. The court of appeals relied upon its decision in *Thomasson*, which held that . . . this acts-based classification in a military context is not suspect and does not burden any fundamental right, so that it is therefore reviewable under the rational-basis test. . . .

. . .

Petitioner's reliance on *Romer v. Evans* is misplaced because there are at least four important distinctions between Amendment 2 to the Colorado Constitution at issue in *Romer* and the statute challenged here. First, 10 U.S.C. 654, which concerns military service by persons who engage in homosexual conduct, is much narrower in scope than Colorado's Amendment 2, which this Court described as a "sweeping" and "unprecedented" measure that withdrew from homosexuals the "protections against exclusion from an almost limitless number of transactions and endeavors that constitute ordinary civic life in a free society," so much so as to "deem a class of persons a stranger to its laws." Second, *Romer* arose in the civilian context and does not affect precedents . . . holding that "Congress is permitted to legislate both with greater breadth and with greater flexibility" in the military context. Third, Colorado's Amendment 2 classified on the basis of homosexual status, while the statute at issue here classifies on the basis of past or likely future prohibited homosexual acts. Fourth and most important, the statute challenged here serves the legitimate objectives of prohibiting homosexual acts in the military, promoting unit cohesion, protecting privacy interests, and reducing sexual tensions, while this Court found that Amendment 2 had no legitimate objective.

8

RACE

The intersection between racial politics and constitutional law is as old as the Constitution itself. At the Constitutional Convention, Northern delegates agreed to slavery in order to win support from Southern delegates. As a result of this compromise, the Constitution prohibited Congress from outlawing the slave trade until 1808; counted each slave as three-fifths of a free person when apportioning legislative districts; and required states to return those "held to Service or Labour in [another] State, under the Laws thereof." One hundred years later, after a Civil War was fought over slavery, the Constitution was amended to outlaw slavery, to guarantee the right to vote irrespective of "race, color, or previous condition of servitude," and to ensure that no state "deny to any person within its jurisdiction the equal protection of the laws." Today, the battle lines are drawn over the meaning of the Constitution's cryptic demand for "equal protection of the laws." Can government ever place burdens on individuals solely on the basis of their race? Conversely, can government ever extend preferential treatment on the basis of race? Should the judiciary play an activist role in reviewing linedrawing on the basis of race? If so, what types of remedies can the courts fashion?

This chapter will consider these questions through an examination of four issues which divided (and continue to divide) the nation. Section I, through a review of the internment of Japanese-Americans during World War II, examines the limits of judicial review and the correspondingly paramount role that the elected branches play in this area. Section II reveals the instrumental role played by the elected branches in school desegregation both in making *Brown*'s repudiation of separate-but-equal education a reality and in limiting the effectiveness of court-ordered busing remedies. Section III describes the current battle over affirmative action in the context of federal governmental efforts to increase minority ownership of broadcast facilities and other business enterprises. Section IV traces the evolution of minority voting rights. This discussion reveals that the meaning and consequences of slavery still frame contemporary racial politics.

I. THE JAPANESE-AMERICAN CASES:
THE FAILURE OF CONSTITUTIONAL DEMOCRACY

The internment of Japanese-Americans during World War II represents one of the most egregious violations of constitutional principles that this nation has ever witnessed. With no evidence of disloyalty or subversive activity and without the benefit of any form of hearing,

Japanese-Americans were imprisoned solely because of their ancestry. The internment "disparaged fundamental principles—that guilt is individual; that citizens are to be treated with equal care and concern; that all Americans have the constitutional right to move about freely, to live and work where they choose, and to establish and maintain homes and families—all of which are not to be impaired except on an individual basis, and only after adequate notice, hearing, fair trial, and due process of law." Arval A. Morris, Justice, War, and the Japanese-American Evacuation and Internment, 59 Wash. L. Rev. 843, 844-45 (1984). "Even in wartime," as Chief Justice William H. Rehnquist observed, "citizens may not be rounded up to prove their loyalty." All the Laws but One 206 (1998). The internment, which was authorized by the President, advocated by the War Department, ratified by Congress, defended by the Justice Department, and approved by the Supreme Court, destroyed the right to peaceably assemble, the right of free speech, the right to vote, and the right to equal protection of the laws.

The Supreme Court's approval of the internment should not be dismissed as an historic relic. Instead, it is illustrative of the Court's practice of deferring to claims of military necessity. Consequently, the principal checks against government abuse are elected branch sensibilities and sensitivities. As Chief Justice Earl Warren wrote in 1962: "The consequence of the limitations under which the Court must sometimes operate in this area is that other agencies of government must bear the primary responsibility for determining whether specific actions they are taking are consonant with our Constitution" (document 1).

The Japanese-American experience tells a mixed story. On one hand, the internment decision and its judicial defense demonstrates an alarming failure of all three branches to exercise their responsibility as guardians of the Constitution. On the other hand, starting in 1976, elected branch efforts to remedy this injustice suggest an encouraging self-awareness and humility in popular government.

A. From War to Internment

On December 7, 1941, Japan attacked Pearl Harbor, devastating America's Pacific fleet. After the United States declared war on Japan, the persecution and intimidation of Japanese-Americans became a political possibility. Within a few weeks of the Pearl Harbor assault, the Japanese—linked by color and culture to a treacherous enemy and lacking political power—became an easy target for wartime frustration. Walter Lippmann, the nation's preeminent political columinst, called for "Washington to adopt a policy of mass evacuation and mass internment of all those who are technically enemy aliens." The Fifth Column on the Coast, Feb. 12, 1942, Wash. Post, at 9. Likewise, California's attorney general (and later Supreme Court Chief Justice) Earl Warren declared shortly after Pearl Harbor that "the Japanese situation as it exists in this state today may well be the Achilles' heel of the entire civilian defense effort" and that only the armed forces "can protect this State from the Japanese situation." G. Edward White, Earl Warren: A Public Life 69-70 (1982). For Warren, the solution to the "Japanese situation" was forcible relocation. In explaining the necessity for this draconian solution as well as the reasons to limit relocation only to the Japanese, Warren said that "when we are dealing with the Caucasian race, we have methods that will test the loyalty of them;" "when we deal with the Japanese, we are in an entirely different field and we cannot form any opinion [because of] [t]heir method of living." Id. at 71. This racial xenophobia and stereotyping came to typify federal policy to the West Coast Japanese.

The debate over evacuation began immediately after Pearl Harbor when General John L. DeWitt called for the removal to the interior of all alien suspects over fourteen years old. DeWitt, who later became Western Defense Commander, subsequently pushed for full scale evacuation. In a report to Secretary of War Henry Stimson, DeWitt explained that "[t]he Japanese race is an enemy race . . . [and it therefore] follows that along the vital Pacific Coast over 112,000 potential enemies, of Japanese extraction, are at large today." Commission on Wartime Relocation and Internment of Civilians, Personal Justice Denied 6 (1982).

DeWitt's recommendation, although originally opposed by Stimson and Attorney General Francis Biddle, met with the approval of President Franklin Delano Roosevelt. For Roosevelt, "[w]hat must be done to defend the country must be done" (document 2). Through Executive Order 9066 (issued in February 1942), Roosevelt empowered the military to "prescribe military areas" and "determine from which any or all persons may be excluded." Congress, fully aware that the policy of exclusion, removal, and detention of Japanese-Americans was based on race and would be carried out without individual hearings, supported the program by enacting legislation ratifying the executive order. 56 Stat. 173 (1942). This legislation was uniformly supported, receiving only brief debate in the House and little more in the Senate. 88 Cong. Rec. 2722-26, 2729-30 (1942). After the initial curfew and within six weeks of Congress' action, General DeWitt issued civilian exclusion orders instructing "all persons of Japanese ancestry" that they would be "evacuated" within one week of the posted notice (document 3).

The degradation felt by Japanese-Americans cannot easily be described. Gordon Hirabayashi's account of his refusal to comply with General DeWitt's initial curfew order and the litigation which ensued underscore that the only significant difference between Japanese-Americans and other citizens was race (document 4). More shocking are the stories of Japanese-Americans subject to internment. Those interned suffered a multitude of deprivations both materially and personally. These persons remember the sting of being discriminated against by their own government and countrymen and the failure of the judicial system to rectify the mistakes of political leaders. The Commission on Wartime Relocation and Internment of Civilians, in its description of the relocation camps, concluded that the "camp experience" was one of "suffering and deprivation."

B. The "Military Necessity" Justification

A decision to subject American citizens to internment for no reason other than the color of their skin seems unthinkable. In the Japanese-American cases this is precisely what occurred. Restrictions on individual liberties were not supported by military necessity. Instead, the War Department and the Department of Justice knowingly deceived the American people and the courts about the so-called "fifth column" threat of Japanese-Americans.

The War Department. Evidence concerning Japanese-Americans' loyalty was suppressed by the War Department. A report prepared by General DeWitt intentionally and incorrectly reported that ethnic Japanese in Hawaii significantly aided the Pearl Harbor attack, that West Coast Japanese were involved in shore-to-ship signaling to enemy submarines, that FBI seizures of arms and contraband supported espionage claims, and that the Japanese community was isolated and might therefore harbor pro-enemy attitudes (document 5). In direct contradiction of these claims, a May 1942 Office of Naval Intelligence Report concluded that "the entire 'Japanese Problem' has been magnified out of its true proportion, largely because of the physical characteristics of the people [and] should be handled on the basis of the *individual*, regardless of citizenship, and *not* on a racial basis." An Intelligence Officer, The Japanese in America, Harper's 489, 497 (Oct. 1942) (emphasis in original).

Assistant Secretary of War John McCloy reached this same conclusion. In a memorandum to General DeWitt, McCloy stated his belief that "social considerations rather than military ones determine the total exclusion policy." Japanese-American and Aleutian Wartime Relocation: Hearings Before the Subcomm. on Administrative Law and Governmental Relations of the House Comm. on the Judiciary, 98th Cong., 2d Sess. 42 (1984). McCloy's principal concern, however, was not the injustice of the evacuation but inconsistencies between the DeWitt Report and representations made in court by the Department of Justice. Peter Irons, Justice at War 207 (1983). The DeWitt Report, rooted in the belief that the Japanese race is an enemy race, "justified the evacuation because it was absolutely impossible to determine the loyalty of Japanese no matter how much time was taken in the process." Hirabayashi v.

United States, 627 F.Supp. 1445, 1451 (W.D. Wash. 1986). In contrast to this absolutist position, government attorneys emphasized the confluence of the need to act and the impossibility of satisfactorily determining loyalty at that time. Brief for the United States at 61-63, Hirabayashi v. United States, 320 U.S. 81 (1943) (No. 870). General DeWitt, "[having] no desire to compromise in any way [the government's] case in Supreme Court," altered his report to conform to the Department of Justice's position (document 6).

The Department of Justice. The Department of Justice was never informed of these alterations in the DeWitt Report. The War Department's purposeful misrepresentation of the risks of Japanese espionage and sabotage, however, was not lost on government attorneys. In a memorandum to Solicitor General Charles Fahy, John Burling of the Alien Enemy Control Unit wrote:

> We are now therefore in possession of substantially incontrovertible evidence that the most important statements of fact advanced by General DeWitt to justify the evacuation and detention were incorrect, and furthermore that General DeWitt had cause to know, and in all probability did know, that they were incorrect at the time he embodied them in his final report to General Marshall. Peter Irons, Justice at War 285 (1983).

Burling believed that the Justice Department had an ethical duty not to cite or rely on the DeWitt Report. He therefore placed in the final draft of the Justice Department's *Korematsu* brief a footnote clearly designed to alert the Supreme Court to the Department's repudiation of much of the DeWitt Report. The footnote alerted the Court that "[t]he Final Report of General DeWitt . . . is in several respects, particularly with reference to the use of illegal radio transmitter and to shore-to-ship signaling by persons of Japanese ancestry, in conflict with information in the possession of the Department of Justice." Korematsu v. United States, 584 F.Supp. 1406, 1417 (N.D. Cal. 1984).

The War Department requested Solicitor General Fahy to remove the footnote. Burling, along with Edward Ennis, Director of the Department's Alien Enemy Control Unit, strenuously objected to any alteration in the footnote (document 7). Assistant Attorney General Herbert Wechsler, supervisor of the *Korematsu* brief, mediated the dispute and eventually drafted a new compromise footnote acceptable to Solicitor General Fahy and the War Department. The new footnote stated: "We have specifically recited in this brief the facts relating to the justification for the evacuation, of which we ask the Court to take judicial notice and we rely upon the *Final Report* only to the extent it relates to such facts." Brief for the United States at 11 n.2, Korematsu v. United States, 323 U.S. 214 (1944) (No. 22). The footnote, which appeared on page 11 of the Supreme Court brief, provided scarcely a hint of reservation about the War Department's justification for exclusion. The forthright repudiation of the Final Report was replaced with semantic ambiguity.

The position taken in the revised Final Report and implicitly adopted by the Justice Department proved critical to the Supreme Court in upholding criminal convictions against Japanese-Americans for violating General DeWitt's curfew and evacuation orders. Using identical language in both *Hirabayashi* and *Korematsu*, the Court proclaimed:

> We cannot say that the warmaking branches of the Government did not have ground[s] for believing that in a critical hour such persons could not *readily* be isolated and separately dealt with, and constituted a menace to the national defense and safety, which demanded that prompt and adequate measures be taken to guard against it. Hirabayashi, 320 U.S. at 99; Korematsu, 323 U.S. at 218 (emphasis added).

Moreover, the Court added that "[t]he military commander's appraisal [of danger from espionage and sabotage] . . . involved the exercise of his informed judgment." Hirabayashi, 320 U.S. at 103.

C. A Nation Atones for Its Sins

Mass exclusion of American Japanese was terminated on December 17, 1944, and internees were released beginning January 2, 1945. Although the War Department and Roosevelt's Secretary of Interior Harold Ickes had recommended an earlier release date, the President deferred action until after the 1944 election. Thirty years later, a movement began both to recognize the government's egregious conduct and to provide restitution to Japanese victims of officially sanctioned racism.

On February 20, 1976, Gerald Ford issued a proclamation declaring the evacuation "wrong" and rescinding President Roosevelt's 1942 executive order. Proclamation No. 4417, 41 Fed. Reg. 7741 (1976). In 1982, the Commission on Wartime Relocation and Internment of Civilians issued a scathing report outlining government misconduct towards Japanese-Americans (document 4) and recommending the enactment of a comprehensive restitution scheme. On August 10, 1988, after four years of legislative debate, President Reagan signed the Civil Liberties Act of 1988. 102 Stat. 903 (1988). This legislation acknowledged the fundamental injustice of the evacuation, relocation and internment of Japanese-Americans during World War II (document 8). Furthermore, through an education outreach program and restitution payments to camp survivors and their families, Congress sought to discourage similar injustices and violations of civil liberties in the future. In the words of Rep. Norman Mineta, the purpose of the legislation "has been to ensure that such a tragic abrogation of civil rights never occurs again." 134 Cong. Rec. 28270 (1988).

At the signing ceremony for the legislation, Ronald Reagan remarked that "[n]o payment can make up for those lost years. So what is important in this bill has less to do with property than honor, for here, we admit a wrong. Here we reaffirm our commitment as a nation to equal justice under the law." Pub. Papers, 1988-89 (II), at 1054-55. George Bush expressed identical sentiments in a letter to Japanese-Americans receiving restitution payments:

> A monetary sum and words alone cannot restore lost years or erase painful memories; neither can they fully convey our Nation's resolve to rectify injustice and to uphold the rights of individuals. We can never fully right the wrongs of the past. But we can take a clear stand for justice and recognize that serious injustices were done to Japanese-Americans during World War II.
>
> In enacting a law calling for restitution and offering a sincere apology, your fellow Americans have, in a very real sense, renewed their traditional commitment to the ideals of freedom, equality, and justice. You and your family have our best wishes for the future.

The Civil Liberties Act, while admitting government wrongdoing, did not erase the criminal convictions of Gordon Hirabayashi, Fred Korematsu and others. That wrong was righted through the judiciary's grant of writs of error *coram nobis*, a rarely used mechanism to nullify criminal convictions due to prosecutorial misconduct. In lawsuits filed by Peter Irons on behalf of Korematsu and Hirabayashi, *coram nobis* was granted because "the failure of the government to disclose" the *actual* reasons underlying the exclusion policy "was an error of the most fundamental character and . . . petitioner was in fact very seriously prejudiced by that nondisclosure. . . ." Hirabayashi v. United States, 627 F.Supp. 1445, 1457 (W.D. Wash. 1986); see generally Peter Irons, Justice Delayed (1989).

In 1998, Latin Americans of Japanese descent also succeeded in their efforts to seek reparations from the United States. During World War II, 2,264 Japanese Latin Americans were deported to the United States and detained in internment camps. In explaining the Justice Department's decision to pay each former internee $5,000, President Bill Clinton and Attorney General Janet Reno both spoke of this "wrongful internment" and the need to "right this wrong and close the book" on this "tragic chapter in the history of our nation." Lena H. Sun, U.S. Apologizes for Internment, Wash. Post, June 13, 1998 at A4.

D. Conclusion

Governmental conduct towards Japanese-Americans and Japanese Latin Americans during the course of World War II is instructive in understanding both the frailty of the presumptive invalidity of racial classifications and the disinclination of the judiciary to combat military excess. Furthermore, this episode suggests that the safeguard for pernicious racial linedrawing does not rest exclusively with the judiciary. The failure of government here is principally the failure of the Congress, the White House, the War Department, and the Department of Justice. In recent years, the legislative and executive branches have taken the initiative in rectifying past mistakes and articulating proper standards for constitutional government. These recent efforts are a striking counterpoint to wartime failures, highlighting elected government's ability to come to grips with its awesome responsibility in using racial linedrawing.

DOCUMENTS

1. Earl Warren Argues that the Judiciary Cannot Check Military Excess

Source: Earl Warren, The Bill of Rights and the Military, 37 N.Y.U. L. Rev. 181, 182, 191-93 (1962)

Determining the proper role to be assigned to the military in a democratic society has been a troublesome problem for every nation that has aspired to a free political life. The military establishment is, of course, a necessary organ of government; but the reach of its power must be carefully limited lest the delicate

balance between freedom and order be upset. The maintenance of the balance is made more difficult by the fact that while the military serves the vital function of preserving the existence of the nation, it is, at the same time, the one element of government that exercises a type of authority not easily assimilated in a free society.

. . . .

. . . War is, of course, a pathological condition for our Nation. Military judgments sometimes breed action that, in more stable times, would be regarded as abhorrent. Judges cannot detach themselves from such judgments, although by hindsight, from the vantage point of more tranquil times, they might conclude that some actions advanced in the name of national survival had in fact overridden the strictures of due process.

. . . [S]ome have pointed to cases like the companion decisions of *Hirabayashi* v. *United States* and *Korematsu* v. *United States* as aberrational. . . . .

Whatever may be the correct view of the specific holding of those cases, their importance for present purposes lies in a more general consideration. These decisions demonstrate dramatically that there are some circumstances in which the Court will, in effect, conclude that it is simply not in a position to reject descriptions by the Executive of the degree of military necessity. Thus, in a case like *Hirabayashi*, only the Executive is qualified to determine whether, for example, an invasion is imminent. In such a situation, where time is of the essence, if the Court is to deny the asserted right of the military authorities, it must be on the theory that the claimed justification, though factually unassailable, is insufficient. Doubtless cases might arise in which such a response would be the only permissible one. After all, the truism that the end does not justify the means has at least as respectable a lineage as the dictum that the power to wage war is the power to wage war successfully. But such cases would be extraordinary indeed.

The consequence of the limitations under which the Court must sometimes operate in this area is that other agencies of government must bear the primary responsibility for determining whether specific actions they are taking are consonant with our Constitution. To put it another way, the fact that the Court rules in a case like *Hirabayashi* that a given program is constitutional, does not necessarily answer the question whether, in a broader sense, it actually is.

---

2. Attorney General Biddle Describes Roosevelt's Decision to Evacuate

Source: Francis Biddle, In Brief Authority, 218-19 (1962)

. . . On February 11 the President told the War Department to prepare a plan for wholesale evacuation, specifically including citizens. It was dictated, he concluded, by military necessity; and added, "Be as reasonable as you can." After the conference the Assistant Secretary [of War, John McCloy] reported . . . "We have *carte blanche* to do what we want to as far as the President is concerned." . . .

. . .

I do not think [Roosevelt] was much concerned with the gravity or implications of this step. He was never theoretical about things. What must be done to defend the country must be done. The decision was for his Secretary of War, not for the Attorney General, not even for J. Edgar Hoover, whose judgment as to the appropriateness of defense measures he greatly respected. The military might be wrong. But they were fighting the war. Public opinion was on their side, so that there was no question of any substantial opposition, which might tend toward the disunity that at all costs he must avoid. Nor do I think that the constitutional difficulty plagued him — the Constitution has never greatly bothered any wartime President. That was a question of law, which ultimately the Supreme Court must decide. And meanwhile — probably a long meanwhile — we must get on with the war.

---

3. General DeWitt Orders Evacuation of Japanese-Americans

Source: Commission on Wartime Relocation and Internment of Civilians: Hearings Before the Subcomm. on Administrative Law and Government Relations of the House Comm. on the Judiciary, 96th Cong., 2d Sess. 169 (1980)

Pursuant to the provisions of Civilian Exclusion Order No. 33, this Headquarters, dated May 3, 1942, all persons of Japanese ancestry, both alien and non-alien, will be evacuated from the above area by 12 o'clock noon, P.W.T., Saturday, May 9, 1942.

.   .   .

The Following Instructions Must Be Observed:

.   .   .

2.   Evacuees must carry with them on departure for the Assembly Center, the following property:
   (a) Bedding and linens (no mattress) for each member of the family;
   (b) Toilet articles for each member of the family;
   (c) Extra clothing for each member of the family;
   (d) Sufficient knives, forks, spoons, plates, bowls and cups for each member of the family;
   (e) Essential personal effects for each member of the family.
All items carried will be securely packaged, tied and plainly marked with the name of the owner and numbered in accordance with instructions obtained at the Civil Control Station. The size and number of packages is limited to that which can be carried by the individual or family group.
   3. No pets of any kind will be permitted.
   4. No personal items and no household goods will be shipped to the Assembly Center.
   5. The United States Government through its agencies will provide for the storage, at the sole risk of the owner, of the more substantial household items, such as iceboxes, washing machines, pianos and other heavy furniture. Cooking utensils and other small items will be accepted for storage if crated, packed and plainly marked with the name and address of the owner. Only one name and address will be used by a given family.

6.   Each family, and individual living alone, will be furnished transportation to the Assembly Center or will be authorized to travel by private automobile in a supervised group. All instructions pertaining to the movement will be obtained at the Civil Control Station.

---

4. Hirabayashi Describes His Personal Ordeal

Source: Peter Irons, The Courage of Their Convictions 52-53 (1988)

During the months between Pearl Harbor and the curfew order in March 1942, things were happening fast. . . . I had already been ordered to a Civilian Public Service camp in Oregon by my draft board, but the Selective Service had reclassified all draft-age persons of Japanese ancestry as aliens ineligible for conscription, so my order was canceled on the eve of my departure, after I had been treated to farewell parties with going-away gifts.

After the curfew order was announced, we knew there would be further orders to remove all persons of Japanese ancestry from the West Coast. When the exclusion orders specifying the deadline for forced removal from various districts of Seattle were posted on telephone poles, I was confronted with a dilemma: Do I stay out of trouble and succumb to the status of second-class citizen, or do I continue to live like other Americans and thus disobey the law?

When the curfew was imposed I obeyed for about a week. We had about twelve living in the Y dormitory, so it was a small group, and they all became my volunteer time-keepers. 'Hey, Gordy, it's five minutes to eight!' And I'd have to dash back from the library or from the coffee shop. One of those times, I stopped and I thought, Why the hell am I running back? Am I an American? And if I am, why am I running back and nobody else is? I think if the order said *all* civilians must obey the curfew, if it was just a nonessential restrictive move, I might not have objected. But I felt it was unfair, just to be referred to as a 'non-alien'—they never referred to me as a citizen. This was so pointedly, so obviously a violation of what the Constitution stood for, what citizenship meant. So I stopped and turned around and went back.

This shocked some of my friends. So I said, Well, *you're* here. What gives you any more right to stay here than me? And they couldn't answer that. After that, I just ignored the curfew.

---

5. Anti-Japanese Bias and the Suppression of Evidence

Source: Commission on Wartime Relocation and Internment of Civilians, Personal Justice Denied 6-8 (1982)

. . . General DeWitt's February 1942 recommendation presented the following rationale for the exclusion:

In the war in which we are now engaged racial affinities are not severed by migration. The Japanese race is an enemy race and while many second and third generation Japanese born on United States soil, possessed of United States citizenship, have become "Americanized," the racial strains are undiluted. To conclude otherwise is to expect that children born of white parents on Japanese soil sever all racial affinity and become loyal Japanese subjects, ready to fight and, if necessary, to die for Japan in a war against the nation of their parents.

. . . It, therefore, follows that along the vital Pacific Coast over 112,000 potential enemies, of Japanese extraction, are at large today. There are indications that these were organized and ready for concerted action at a favorable opportunity. The very fact that no sabotage has taken place to date is a disturbing and confirming indication that such action will be taken.

There are two unfounded justifications for exclusion expressed here: first, that ethnicity ultimately determines loyalty; second, that "indications" suggest that ethnic Japanese "are organized and ready for concerted action"—the best argument for this being the fact that it hadn't happened.

In his 1943 *Final Report*, General DeWitt cited a number of factors in support of the exclusion decision: signaling from shore to enemy submarines; arms and contraband found by the FBI during raids on ethnic Japanese homes and businesses; dangers to the ethnic Japanese from vigilantes; concentration of ethnic Japanese around or near militarily sensitive areas; the number of Japanese ethnic organizations on the coast which might shelter pro-Japanese attitudes or activities such as Emperor-worshipping Shinto; and the presence of the Kibei, who had spent some time in Japan.

The first two items point to demonstrable military danger. But the reports of shore-to-ship signaling were investigated by the Federal Communications Commission, the agency with relevant expertise, and no identifiable cases of such signaling were substantiated. The FBI did confiscate arms and contraband from some ethnic Japanese, but most were items normally in the possession of any law-abiding civilian, and the FBI concluded that these searches had uncovered no dangerous persons that "we could not otherwise know about." Thus neither of these "facts" militarily justified exclusion.

General DeWitt's remaining points are repeated in the *Hirabayashi* brief, which also emphasizes dual nationality, Japanese language schools and the high percentage of aliens (who, by law, had been barred from acquiring American citizenship) in the ethnic population. These facts represent broad social judgments of little or no military significance in themselves.

---

6. The War Department Conceals the Bases of the Japanese-American Exclusion

Source: Hirabayashi v. United States, 627 F.Supp. 1445, 1450-52 (W.D. Wash. 1986)

[In February 1986, Gordon Hirabayashi's conviction was vacated due to prior government misconduct. In the following excerpt, the court discusses that misconduct.]

On May 3, 1943, Colonel Bendetsen sent the following message to General DeWitt relative to conferences between himself and Assistant Secretary of War McCloy:

"Mr. McCloy stated that he . . . thought [the report] could be improved upon. . . .

"In brief, Mr. McCloy's . . . objection was to that portion of Chapter II which said in effect that it is absolutely impossible to determine the loyalty of Japanese no matter how much time was taken in the process. He said that he had no objection to saying that time was of the essence and that in view of the military situation and the fact *that there was no known means of making such a determination with any degree of safety* the evacuation was necessary." (Emphasis in the original.)

On June 5, 1943, General DeWitt issued a revised version of his final report on the Japanese evacuation. In that version of the report the [italicized] portions of the following statements were either deleted from or added to the original version of the Final Report:

Page iii, paragraph 2: "The security of the Pacific Coast continues to require the exclusion of Japanese from the area now prohibited to them *and will continue for the duration of the present war.*" (Deleted from the original version.)
Page iii, paragraph 2: *"More than 120,000 persons of Japanese ancestry resided in colonies adjacent to many highly sensitive installations. Their loyalties were unknown, and time was of the essence."* (Added to the original version.)
Page 9. *"It was impossible to establish the identity of the loyal and the disloyal with any degree of safety. It was not that there was insufficient time in which to make such a determination; it was simply a matter of facing the realities that a positive determination could not be made, that an exact separation of the 'sheep from the goats' was unfeasible."* (Deleted from the original version and replaced by the following sentence.)
Page 9: *"To complicate the situation, no ready means existed for determining the loyal and the disloyal with any degree of safety. It was necessary to face the realities—a positive determination could not have been made."* (Added to the original version.)

7. The Department of Justice Debates Exposing War Department Misrepresentations

Source: Korematsu v. United States,
584 F. Supp. 1406, 1421-23
app. A (N.D. Cal. 1984)

[Justice Department Memorandum from Edward Ennis to Herbert Wechsler, Sept. 30, 1944]:

I understand that the War Department is currently discussing with the Solicitor General the possibility of changing the footnote in the Korematsu brief in which it is stated that this Department is in possession of information in conflict with the statements made by General DeWitt relating to the causes of the evacuation. Mr. Burling and I feel most strongly that . . . the footnote [be kept] in its present form. . . . This Department has an ethical obligation to the Court to refrain from citing it as a source of which the Court may properly take judicial notice if the Department knows that important statements in the source are untrue and if it knows as to other statements that there is such contrariety of information that judicial notice is improper. . . .

. . .

It is entirely clear that the War Department entered into an arrangement with the Western Defense Command to rewrite demonstrably erroneous items in the report by reducing to implication and inference what had been expressed less expertly by the Western Defense Command and then contrived to publish this report without the knowledge of this Department by the use of falsehood and evasion.

. . .

RECOMMENDATION: In view of the Attorney General's personal participation in,

and final responsibility for, this Department's part in the broad administrative problem of treatment of the Japanese minority, I urge that he be consulted personally on this problem. Much more is involved than the wording of the footnote. The failure to deal adequately now with this Report cited to the Supreme Court either by the Government or other parties, will hopelessly undermine our administrative position in relation to this Japanese problem. We have proved unable to cope with the military authorities on their own ground in these matters. If we fail to act forthrightly on our own ground in the courts, the whole historical record of this matter will be as the military choose to state it. The Attorney General should not be deprived of the present, and perhaps only, chance to set the record straight.

8. Civil Liberties Act of 1988

Source: Pub. L. 100-383,
102 Stat. 903, 904 (1988)

. . .

The purposes of this Act are to—
(1) acknowledge the fundamental injustice of the evacuation, relocation, and internment of United States citizens and permanent resident aliens of Japanese ancestry during World War II;
(2) apologize on behalf of the people of the United States for the evacuation, relocation, and internment of such citizens and permanent resident aliens;
(3) provide for a public education fund to finance efforts to inform the public about the internment of such individuals so as to prevent the recurrence of any similar event;

(4) make restitution to those individuals of Japanese ancestry who were interned;

.   .   .

(6) discourage the occurrence of similar injustices and violations of civil liberties in the future; and

(7) make more credible and sincere any declaration of concern by the United States over violations of human rights committed by other nations.

.   .   .

. . . The Congress recognizes that, as described by the Commission on Wartime Relocation and Internment of Civilians, a grave injustice was done to both citizens and permanent resident aliens of Japanese ancestry by the evacuation, relocation, and internment of civilians during World War

II. As the Commission documents, these actions were carried out without adequate security reasons and without any acts of espionage or sabotage documented by the Commission, and were motivated largely by racial prejudice, wartime hysteria, and a failure of political leadership.

The excluded individuals of Japanese ancestry suffered enormous damages, both material and intangible, and there were incalculable losses in education and job training, all of which resulted in significant human suffering for which appropriate compensation has not been made. For these fundamental violations of the basic civil liberties and constitutional rights of these individuals of Japanese ancestry, the Congress apologizes on behalf of the Nation.

II. SCHOOL DESEGREGATION

Supreme Court efforts to end racial isolation in education exemplify the   reaches and limits of the judiciary's ability to transform society. *Brown* v. *Board of Education*'s declaration that "[s]eparate educational facilities are inherently unequal," 347 U.S. 483, 495 (1954), is widely applauded. The elected branches eventually rallied behind *Brown*, making tangible the *Brown* mandate through a series of 1960's legislative and regulatory initiatives. In sharp contrast, the approval of mandatory busing remedies in *Swann* v. *Charlotte-Mecklenburg*, 402 U.S. 1 (1971), is one of the Court's most criticized rulings. The elected branches also attacked the Court here, enacting legislation and adopting enforcement schemes designed to undermine mandatory busing remedies. The quite different responses to *Brown* and *Swann* offer telling evidence of the way elected branches react to Supreme Court decisions.

A. *Brown* and the Quest for Unanimity

When *Brown* was decided, segregation was so ingrained in the South that the outlawing of dual school systems promised social turmoil and massive resistance. Typifying this period are comments—revealing a near religious belief in segregation—by Southern Congressmen in response to *Sweatt* v. *Painter*, 339 U.S. 629 (1950), a 1950 decision invalidating segregation in Texas law schools (document 1). These deep feelings were not lost either on the Court or on the Department of Justice. In an effort to temper Southern hostility, Chief Justice Warren sought to craft a unanimous opinion of limited reach and the Justice Department recommended that the Court *not* specify a remedy in the case.

Chief Justice Warren's participation in *Brown* was serendipitous. The Supreme Court was set to decide *Brown* in its 1952 term with Chief Justice Vinson at the Court's helm. After briefs were filed (including an important brief filed by the Justice Department arguing that racial segregation undermined America's stature as leader of the free world (document 2) and oral arguments heard, the Court redocketed *Brown* so that it could also decide the constitutionality of segregated education in the "federal city," Washington, D.C. At this time, the Justices were sharply divided—their December 1952 conference suggested a 5-4 opinion to *uphold* segregated education). William O. Douglas, The Court Years 113 (1980).

The division among the Justices was attributable, in part, to the uncertain history of the Fourteenth Amendment. For example, at the December 1952 conference, Chief Justice Vinson observed that, although District of Columbia public schools were segregated when the Fourteenth Amendment was adopted, Congress failed to enact proposed legislation barring such segregation. In 1953, Vinson died and Warren became Chief Justice—an occurrence prompting Associate Justice Felix Frankfurter to exclaim: "[T]his is the first solid piece of evidence I've ever had that there really is a God." Phillip Elman, The Solicitor General's Office, Justice Frankfurter, and Civil Rights Litigation, 1946-1960: An Oral History, 100 Harv. L. Rev. 817, 840 (1987). By not insisting on immediate implementation of its policy, the Court was able to unanimously agree upon a brief declaration that segregation in education was unconstitutional. A year later the Court issued its remedy for *Brown*, declaring that desegregation must proceed with "all deliberate speed." Brown v. Board of Education, 349 U.S. 294, 301 (1955).

The Court's bifurcation of merits and remedies, as well as the absence of judgmental rhetoric in its segregation decisions, reveals that the Justices sought to improve the acceptability of their decision by speaking in a single moderate voice. Indeed, as Sidney Ulmer's account of internal Court deliberations in the writing of *Brown* reveals, compromises were made by all nine Justices in order to ensure unanimity. Sidney Ulmer, Earl Warren and the *Brown* Decision, 33 J. Pol. 689, 693-96 (1971).

The Court was correct in anticipating a hostile response to its opinion. After ordering desegregation, 100 Southern congressmen united to overturn *Brown*. Their Southern Manifesto called the Court's action "a clear abuse of judicial power . . . and [an] encroach[ment] upon the reserved rights of the States and the people" (document 3). Moreover, many states sought to subvert *Brown* through the replacement of public school systems (subject to equal protection demands) with state-funded private school systems. Finally, some school systems openly defied *Brown*. The most notorious example of this phenomena is Little Rock, Arkansas, where President Eisenhower was compelled to send in the National Guard to force compliance with *Brown*.

The Court's unanimity may have played a role in President Eisenhower's intervention. Initially, Eisenhower took the unusual step of amending the government's brief in *Brown* to encourage the Court to devise orderly plans that would take into consideration the fact that the segregated lifestyles of many people had been based on over fifty years of Supreme Court sanction. Elman at 842. More striking, after inviting Earl Warren to dinner at the White House, Eisenhower justified Southern resistance to school desegregation this way: "These are not bad people. All they are concerned about is to see that their sweet little girls are not required to sit alongside some big overgrown Negroes." Earl Warren, The Memoirs of Earl Warren 291 (1977). Following the *Brown* decision, the President sought to publicly distance himself from the issue. Asked whether he agreed with the Court's decision, the President responded: "[I]t makes no difference whether or not I endorse [*Brown*]. The Constitution is as the Supreme Court interprets it." Ambrose at 338. In a radio address to the nation concerning Little Rock, Eisenhower likewise pointed to his duty to "carry out proper orders from a Federal court" and not the legal or moral correctness of *Brown* (document 4). If the Court had been divided, however, Eisenhower may not have put his weak support of *Brown* into action.

B. The Road to *Swann*

Until 1964, *Brown*'s impact was principally symbolic. Without significant coercion from the federal government, Southern states were unwilling to make meaningful *Brown*'s universalistic demand that "the doctrine of 'separate but equal' has no place" in public education. Brown, 347 U.S. at 495. Indeed, in the decade following *Brown*, less actual desegregation of southern schools occurred than in 1965 *alone*. One explanation for this transformation is Congress' authorization—through Title IV of the 1964 Civil Rights Act—of Department of Justice participation in school desegregation litigation. Over objections that "[t]his proposal would convert the Department of Justice into the legal arm of the NAACP, CORE, SNCC, and similar unofficial groups," 110 Cong. Rec. 8614 (1964) (remarks of Sen. Sparkman), Congress recognized that federal action was needed to alter the snail-like pace of Southern desegregation. As Senator Paul H. Douglas remarked: "We must face the fact that the decisions of the Supreme Court are not being carried out . . . and that unless we are to make a mockery of [them] . . .

Congress must act to put the strength of the National Government behind [them]." Id. at 6814.

More significant, the implementation of the Elementary and Secondary Education Act of 1965 (ESEA), coupled with the issuance and enforcement of guidelines for Title VI of the Civil Rights Act of 1964, marked a significant shift in federal power over state education systems. Rather than playing a minimalist role in helping schools better educate their students, the federal government became a major player in pushing schools to provide equal educational opportunity to black children. With Title VI's demand that federal grant recipients be nondiscriminatory, Congress became willing to pump billions of dollars of aid for the compensatory education of educationally deprived children. Federal funds were sufficient incentive for many school systems to comply with the Office for Civil Rights' (OCR) nondiscrimination standards.

The election of Richard Nixon in 1968 signalled a change in presidential policy in this area. Nixon's presidential campaign prominently featured a "Southern Strategy" in which he promised to ease pressure on Southern school districts to end desegregative practices. The Nixon administration, for example, instructed the OCR—as well as the Department of Justice—that "they are to work with individual school districts to hold busing to the minimum required by law." James M. Naughton, Nixon Disavows HEW Policy on Busing, N.Y. Times, Aug. 4, 1971, at 15.

Although federal court decisions continued to challenge local school policies and practices on questions of race, the "rare historic moment when the President, congressional leadership, and the public all recognized that protection of the rights of black Americans was the fundamental [social and educational] issue" had passed. Gary Orfield, The Reconstruction of Southern Education 39 (1969). Increasing emphasis on numerical measures of equality by both the OCR (to measure discrimination) and the courts (to remedy discrimination) provoked a political reaction ultimately resulting in the taming of federal school desegregation enforcement efforts. Nevertheless, by the end of the 1960s, the efforts of the federal government had dramatically eroded southern school segregation. For example, between 1963 and 1968, the percentage of black children in all-black schools in the South dropped from ninety-eight percent to twenty-five percent. See id. at 5.

C. *Swann* and the Politics of Forced Busing

The elected branches' endorsement of *Brown*'s simple nondiscrimination demand was, from the start, tempered by opposition to forced busing. A provision of the ESEA prohibits the use of federal funds for "the assignment or transportation of students . . . in order to overcome racial imbalance." 80 Stat. 1191, 1209 (1966). Moreover, beginning with a limitation rider attached to the fiscal year 1969 Labor-HEW appropriations bill, Congress has prohibited the expenditure of federal funds "to force [in order to overcome racial imbalance] any student . . . to attend a particular school against the choice of his or her parents." 82 Stat. 969, 995 (1968). Adding fuel to this opposition, President Nixon formally opposed "buying buses, tires, and gasoline to transport young children miles away from their neighborhood schools." Pub. Papers, 1970, at 305, 309.

It was against this backdrop that the Supreme Court announced in 1971 that court-ordered busing was an appropriate technique to desegregate the nation's schools. Swann v. Charlotte-Mecklenburg County Bd. of Educ., 402 U.S. 1 (1971). In approving the use of black-white pupil ratios and mandatory student reassignments as "starting point[s] in the process of shaping a remedy," the Court recognized that, to eliminate all vestiges of an unconstitutional dual school system, desegregation remedies might have to be "administratively awkward, inconvenient, and even bizarre." Id. at 25, 28.

Immediately after *Swann*, several members of Congress issued strong bully pulpit statements rebuking the Court. More significant, President Nixon delivered a national address on the evils of busing (document 5) and submitted legislative proposals that, among other things, would have Congress designate a hierarchy of remedies in school desegregation lawsuits, ranging from more preferred to less preferred (where busing would only be used as a limited remedy of "last resort" for school segregation and then "only under strict limitations"). H.R. 13915, 92d Cong., 2d Sess. (1972).

Congress ultimately rejected the Nixon proposals, claiming that the Court's status as co-equal branch warranted legislative respect to its constitutional holdings. In place of the Nixon proposals, Congress enacted, as Title VII of the 1972 Education Act Amendments, restrictions on both federal financial support of mandatory busing and federal advocacy of busing "unless constitutionally required." 86 Stat. 235, 371-72 (1972). Dissatisfied with this response, President Nixon complained that "[c]onfronted with one of the burning social issues of the past decade, and an unequivocal call for action from the vast majority of the American people, the 92d Congress has apparently determined that the better part of valor is to dump the matter . . . ." Pub. Papers, 1972, at 701, 702-03.

Congress' hesitancy here is revealing. Although Congress may well possess the power to limit the Court's remedial authority under either the Exceptions Clause or Section 5 of the Fourteenth Amendment, Congress generally views those powers as too intrusive. Consequently, legislative responses to judicial excess often take the form of funding restrictions.

D. The 1972-1980 Period

Congress, from 1972 to 1980, actively debated the busing question. During this period, statutory provisions limited the use of federal funds by OCR to require busing and instructed federal courts that busing should be a remedy of last resort. Moreover, legislation forbidding pro-busing arguments by the Department of Justice was passed *but* successfully vetoed by President Carter. Finally, Congress considered (but did not approve) a proposed constitutional amendment to outlaw busing as well as legislation forbidding federal courts from ordering busing in school desegregation cases.

During this period, legislation designed to facilitate school desegregation—The Emergency School Aid Act of 1972 (ESAA)—was also enacted. 86 Stat. 235, 354-71 (1972). Although originally devised as part of Nixon's strategy to recognize the "special needs" of Southern systems subject to desegregation orders, ESAA—especially in the hands of the Carter administration—proved an extraordinarily effective device to advance school desegregation. By conditioning ESAA eligibility on school district compliance with strict nondiscrimination standards, the ESAA "carrot" prompted massive pupil reassignment. For example, during a particular two-year period, 244,000 school children were reassigned from racially isolated classes.

Carter administration support of mandatory reassignments was also accomplished through narrow interpretations of anti-busing legislation. After Congress specified in the 1976 Byrd amendment that OCR *not* enforce Title VI to require the transportation of any student to a school other than the one "nearest" the student's home, the Carter Department of Justice concluded that Congress intended the transportation limits *not* to apply to the original student assignment scheme. Under this interpretation, OCR could still order busing through such desegregation techniques as "pairing" or "clustering." Amidst allegations that the administration interpretation purposefully distorted legislative intent, Congress—through an amendment introduced by Senator Joseph Biden—specifically denied OCR authority to *administratively impose* busing orders through Title VI. 92 Stat. 1586 (1978).

The 1972-1980 experience is a telling one. First, school desegregation decisionmaking has an administrative as well as a legislative and judicial side. OCR enforcement of Title VI and ESAA reveals that non-discrimination conditions on federal largesse are a potent tool in combating segregation. Second, the administrative side of school desegregation is far more subject to elected branch scrutiny than is the judicial side. Although declaring busing a "last resort" remedy, Congress placed no meaningful restrictions on court authority. Indeed, Congress rejected outright proposals advanced by President Nixon and others which threatened to directly limit court authority to order busing. In contrast, Congress did approve limitations on both OCR and Department of Justice authority in this area. Third, elected branch support plays a critical role in the advancement of court-declared constitutional norms. The effectiveness of ESAA enforcement in addressing racial imbalance as compared to Congress' foreclosure of sweeping Title VI enforcement through the Byrd and Biden amendments makes clear elected branch power in this area. Fourth, the White House plays a critical role in interpreting congressional mandates. The Carter administration adeptly advanced a "pro-busing" policy in the face of a generally hostile Congress through its interpretations of ESAA and the Byrd amendment.

E. The Reagan Administration

The Reagan administration, by categorically opposing mandatory pupil transportation remedies, stood in sharp contrast to its predecessor. President Reagan called forced busing "reverse segregation" and his Assistant Attorney General for Civil Rights, William Bradford Reynolds, expressed concern that busing remedies "are threatening to dilute the essential consensus that racial discrimination is wrong and should not be tolerated in any form." Speech by William Bradford Reynolds, Assistant Attorney General for Civil Rights, Before the Delaware Bar Association, Feb. 1982, at 9. Reynolds also argued that involuntary busing "has failed to advance the overriding goal of equal educational opportunity." School Desegregation: Hearings Before the Subcomm. on Civil and Constitutional Rights of the House Comm. on the Judiciary, 97th Cong., 1st Sess. 618 (1982). Instead of mandatory pupil transportation, the administration advanced a remedial strategy program which included "*voluntary* student assignment program[s], magnet schools, and enhanced curriculum requirements, faculty incentives, in-service training programs for teachers and administrators, school closings, if [there is] excess capacity, or new construction." Id. at 631.

Despite Congress' apparent distaste for busing, the administration's position came under sharp attack. In House Judiciary Committee hearings, Reynolds was accused—by Congressman Harold Washington (D-Ill.)—of "giv[ing] voice to the same old separate but equal doctrine." School Desegregation: Hearings Before the Subcomm. on Civil and Constitutional Rights of the House Comm. on the Judiciary, 97th Cong., 1st Sess. 627 (1981). Furthermore, over a strong statement of opposition by Republican congressmen, a House Judiciary Committee staff report accused the administration of misstating the case against busing and advancing in its place ineffective desegregation techniques (document 6).

These criticisms of the Reagan administration should not be overstated, for Congress continued to enact funding restrictions limiting OCR enforcement. Congress also—as part of the Reagan administration's "New Federalism in Education"—repealed the ESAA program along with over two dozen separate education programs and authorized their various activities in a new education block grant. 95 Stat. 357, 441-82 (1981). Under the block grant, states would receive lump sum federal support and then establish their own priorities.

F. School Desegregation After Reagan

Reagan administration challenges to federal court control over school systems were realized in the final months of the Bush administration. In *Freeman* v. *Pitts*, 503 U.S. 467 (1992), the Bush administration argued against "prolong[ed] judicial control of hundreds of school districts" and insisted that "no single tradition in public education is more deeply rooted than local control." Brief for the United States as Amicus Curiae at 8, Freeman v. Pitts. Agreeing with this argument, Reagan and Bush Supreme Court appointees (Sandra Day O'Connor, Antonin Scalia, Anthony Kennedy, and David Souter) supplied the decisive votes in a decision that set the stage for diminishing judicial involvement in school desegregation. Upholding district court authority to relinquish jurisdiction over student assignments, *Freeman* relieved DeKalb County, Georgia, of any obligation to address racial isolation caused by changing demographics. As a result, DeKalb could make use of neighborhood school assignments, despite the fact that fifty percent of black students attended schools that were over ninety percent black.

The Bush Justice Department fared less well in *United States* v. *Fordice*, 505 U.S. 717 (1992), a decision that scrutinizes the legality of historically black colleges. Initially, Bush Solicitor General Kenneth Starr argued that increasing financial support for black colleges impermissibly perpetuated segregation by encouraging African-American students to attend such schools. Responding to complaints from black educators and Health and Human Services Secretary Louis Sullivan, Bush—feeling "that Justice's position could be harmful to historically black colleges"—personally ordered Starr to support increased state aid to black public colleges. This policy reversal, while unusual, was not altogether surprising. Although the Reagan and Bush Justice Departments vigorously supported color-blind approaches to school desegregation and opposed race-conscious affirmative action, Presidents Reagan and Bush were strong backers of historically black colleges. Indeed, immediately before his intervening in *Fordice*, Bush met with members of a presidentially appointed federal advisory board on historically black colleges.

Solicitor General Starr, following the President's directive, withdrew a brief already filed with the Court and submitted a new brief. Linda Greenhouse, Bush Reverses U.S. Stance Against Black College Aid, N.Y. Times, October 22, 1991, at B-6. The second brief spoke of state discrimination being manifested "in a deprivation of equitable and fair funding to historically black institutions" and that "[s]uggestions to the contrary in our opening brief . . . no longer reflect the position of the United States." Reply Brief for the United States, United States v. Mabus [later Fordice], 211 Landmark Briefs 425 (1992). But the Supreme Court (led by a coalition of Reagan and Bush appointees) rejected claims that historically black colleges should maintain their racial identity through the upgrading of public funding.

Reagan and Bush Supreme Court appointees also played a decisive role in *Missouri* v. *Jenkins*, 515 U.S. 70 (1995), a decision which, among other things, rejected educational achievement as an appropriate goal of a desegregation order. In so ruling, the Court turned down Clinton administration arguments that educational achievement can and should be linked to prior unlawful racial segregation. Brief for the United States as Amicus Curiae, Missouri v. Jenkins, 239 Landmark Briefs 751-55 (1995).

Following these decisions, several major school districts began phasing out their desegregation plans, including Boston, Buffalo, Charlotte, Cleveland, Denver, Las Vegas, Nashville, Seattle, and St. Louis. By 1997, nearly 70% of African American students and 75% of Latinos attended schools that are predominantly black or Latino (with one third of minority students attending schools where 90% or more of their classmates are Latino or black). Furthermore, a 1999 Gallup Poll found that 60% of both African Americans and whites opposed "stepping up efforts to integrate white students with minority students," preferring, instead, to increase "funding and other resources for minority schools." Tamara Henry, Is School Desegregation Fading?, USA Today, July 22, 1999, at 1A.

G. Conclusion

The demand that there be neither white schools nor minority schools but just schools is broadly accepted. The accomplishment of this demand is quite another matter, for there are bitter divisions over both the definition of what constitutes a segregated school system and the determination of the appropriate remedies for such segregation. One thing is clear, however. The reach and limits of this nation's commitment to eradicate dual systems is defined by the interplay between political action and judicial decision. Beginning with the simple nondiscrimination mandate established in *Brown*, the school desegregation issue has been defined by the political culture surrounding it.

DOCUMENTS

1. Southern Congressmen Attack Truman Administration and Supreme Court Rejection of Segregated Law Schools

Source: 96 Cong. Rec. A4224-25, 8346 (1950)

Mr. [Ben] GUILL [R-Tex.]

.   .   .   .

It should be apparent now to every single thinking citizen of this country living below Mason and Dixon's line that the Truman administration has declared war upon the South and intends to carry that war to a brutal and successful conclusion.

Compared to this cold war of 1950, the War Between the States was a clean and honest conflict. The War Between the States was fought in the open by men who are [sic] willing to fight and die for principles in which they believed. The cold war against the South of 1950 is one-sided and it is fought with knives in the dark. It is fought by legal ambush and sly administrative practice. It is fought by infiltration, treachery, and deceit. It is fought by nameless men in secret places and there is no mercy, little honesty, and less decency among those who fight it.

.   .   .   .

Mr. [John] WILLIAMS [D-Miss.]. . . .

.   .   .   .

For years, Congress has been under constant assault from Communists and other organized minorities to outlaw segregation and to amalgamate our people into one mongrel race. To the everlasting credit of the Congress, let it be pointed out that it has consistently repelled their onslaughts, and has resisted their efforts to degrade our civilization.

Yet, in the face of these acknowledged facts, the Supreme Court has taken it upon themselves to outlaw, by judicial fiat, a social custom which has maintained to the advantage of all races for 200 years.

2. Department of Justice Opposes School Segregation

Source: 49 Landmark Briefs 118-19, 121, 123

The constitutional right invoked in these cases is the basic right, secured to all Americans, to equal treatment before the law.
. . .

[R]acial discriminations imposed by law, or having the sanction or support of government, inevitably tend to undermine the foundations of a society dedicated to freedom, justice, and equality. The proposition that all men are created equal is not mere rhetoric. It implies a rule of law—an indispensable condition to a civilized society—under which all men stand equal and alike in the rights and opportunities secured to them by their government. Under the Constitution every agency of government, national and local, legislative, executive, and judicial, must treat each of our people as an *American*, and not as a member of a particular group classified on the basis of race or some other constitutional irrelevancy. The color of a man's skin—like his religious beliefs, or his political attachments, or the country from which he or his ancestors came to the United States—does not diminish or alter his legal status or constitutional rights. "Our Constitution is color-blind, and neither knows nor tolerates classes among citizens."

.   .   .

The existence of discrimination against minority groups in the United States has an adverse effect upon our relations with other countries. Racial discrimination furnishes grist for the Communist propaganda mills, and it raises doubts even among friendly nations as to the intensity of our devotion to the democratic faith. In response to the request of the Attorney General for an authoritative statement of the effects of racial discrimination in the United States upon the conduct of foreign relations, the Secretary of State has written as follows:

"The segregation of school children on a racial basis is one of the practices in the United States that has been singled out for hostile foreign comment in the United Nations and elsewhere. Other peoples cannot understand how such a practice can exist in a country which professes to be a staunch supporter of freedom, justice, and democracy. The sincerity of the United States in this respect will be judged by its deeds as well as by its words."

---

3. Southern Congressmen and Senators Decry *Brown*

Source: 102 Cong. Rec.
4515-16 (1956)

[Following *Brown*, 19 Senators and 81 Congressmen signed a Southern Manifesto attacking both the decision and the Court.]

.   .   .

We regard the decision of the Supreme Court in the school cases as a clear abuse of judicial power. It climaxes a trend in the Federal judiciary undertaking to legislate, in derogation of the authority of Congress, and to encroach upon the reserved rights of the States and the people.

The original Constitution does not mention education. Neither does the 14th amendment nor any other amendment. The debates preceding the submission of the 14th amendment clearly show that there was no intent that it should affect the systems of education maintained by the States.

The very Congress which proposed the amendment subsequently provided for segregated schools in the District of Columbia.

When the amendment was adopted, in 1868, there were 37 States of the Union. Every one of the 26 States that had any substantial racial differences among its people either approved the operation of segregated schools already in existence or subsequently established such schools by action of the same lawmaking body which considered the 14th amendment.

.   .   .

This unwarranted exercise of power by the Court, contrary to the Constitution, is creating chaos and confusion in the States principally affected. It is destroying the amicable relations between the white and Negro races that have been created through 90 years of patient effort by the good people of both races. It has planted hatred and suspicion where there has been heretofore friendship and understanding.

.   .   .

With the gravest concern for the explosive and dangerous condition created by this decision and inflamed by outside meddlers:

We reaffirm our reliance on the Constitution as the fundamental law of the land.

We decry the Supreme Court's encroachments on rights reserved to the States and to the people, contrary to established law and to the Constitution.

We commend the motives of those States which have declared the intention to resist forced integration by any lawful means.

. . .

In this trying period, as we all seek to right this wrong, we appeal to our people not to be provoked by the agitators and troublemakers invading our States and to scrupulously refrain from disorders and lawless acts.

---

4. President Eisenhower Sends Federal Troops to Little Rock

Source: Pub. Papers, 1957,
at 689-90, 692-94

Good Evening, My Fellow Citizens:
For a few minutes this evening I want to speak to you about the serious situation that has arisen in Little Rock. To make this talk I have come to the President's office in the White House. I could have spoke from Rhode Island, where I have been staying recently, but I felt that, in speaking from the house of Lincoln, of Jackson and of Wilson, my words would better convey both the sadness I feel in the action I was compelled today to take and the firmness with which I intend to pursue this course until the orders of the Federal Court at Little Rock can be executed without unlawful interference.

In that city, under the leadership of demagogic extremists, disorderly mobs have deliberately prevented the carrying out of proper orders from a Federal Court. Local authorities have not eliminated that violent opposition and, under the law, I yesterday issued a Proclamation calling upon the mob to disperse.

This morning the mob again gathered in front of the Central High School of Little Rock, obviously for the purpose of again preventing the carrying out of the Court's order relating to the admission of Negro children to that school.

. . . I have today issued an Executive Order directing the use of troops under Federal authority to aid in the execution of Federal law at Little Rock, Arkansas. This became necessary when my Proclamation of yesterday was not observed, and the obstruction of justice still continues.

It is important that the reasons for my action be understood by all our citizens.

As you know, the Supreme Court of the United States has decided that separate public educational facilities for the races are inherently unequal and therefore compulsory school segregation laws are unconstitutional.

Our personal opinions about the decision have no bearing on the matter of enforcement; the responsibility and authority of the Supreme Court to interpret the Constitution are very clear. . . .

. . .

The very basis of our individual rights and freedoms rests upon the certainty that the President and the Executive Branch of Government will support and insure the carrying out of the decisions of the Federal Courts, even, when necessary with all the means at the President's command.

Unless the President did so, anarchy would result.

There would be no security for any except that which each one of us could provide for himself.

The interest of the nation in the proper fulfillment of the law's requirements cannot yield to opposition and demonstrations by some few persons.

Mob rule cannot be allowed to override the decisions of our courts.

. . .

At a time when we face grave situations abroad because of the hatred that Communism bears toward a system of government based on human rights, it would be difficult to exaggerate the harm that is being done to the prestige and influence, and indeed to the safety, of our nation and the world.

Our enemies are gloating over this incident and using it everywhere to misrepresent our whole nation. We are portrayed as a violator of those standards of conduct which the peoples of the world united to proclaim in the Charter of the United Nations. There they affirmed "faith in fundamental human rights" and "in the dignity and worth of the human person" and they did so "without distinction as to race, sex, language or religion."

---

5. Nixon Addresses the Nation on the Busing Issue

Source: Pub. Papers, 1972,
at 425-28

Good evening:

Tonight I want to talk to you about one of the most difficult issues of our time—the issue of busing.

Across this Nation—in the North, East, West, and South—States, cities, and local school districts have been torn apart in debate over this issue.

. . .

There are many who believe that a constitutional amendment is the only way to deal with this problem. The constitutional amendment proposal deserves a thorough consideration by the Congress on its merits.

But as an answer to the immediate problem we face of stopping more busing now, the constitutional amendment approach has a fatal flaw: It takes too long.

. . .

. . . I want to tell you why I feel that busing for the purpose of achieving racial balance in our schools is wrong, and why the great majority of Americans are right in wanting to bring it to an end.

The purpose of such busing is to help end segregation. But experience in case after case has shown that busing is a bad means to a good end. The frank recognition of that fact does not reduce our commitment to desegregation; it simply tells us that we have to come up with a better means to that good end.

. . .

There is no escaping the fact that some people do oppose busing because of racial prejudice. But to go on from this to conclude that "antibusing" is simply a code word for prejudice is a vicious libel on millions of concerned parents who oppose busing not because they are against desegregation, but because they are for better education for their children.

They want their children educated in their own neighborhoods. Many have invested their life's savings in a home in a neighborhood they chose because it had good schools. They do not want their children bused across the city to an inferior school just to meet some social planner's concept of what is considered to be the correct racial balance or what is called "progressive" social policy.

There are right reasons for opposing busing, and there are wrong reasons—and most people, including large and increasing numbers of blacks, oppose it for reasons that have little or nothing to do with race. It would compound an injustice to persist in massive busing simply because some people oppose it for the wrong reasons.

6. House Judiciary Committee Report Criticizes Reagan Anti-busing Policies

Source: Staff of the Subcomm. on Civil and Constitutional Rights of the House Comm. on the Judiciary, 97th Cong., 2d Sess., Report on School Desegregation 18-19, 22-24, 29-30 (Comm. Print 1982)

[T]oday, for over half of the nation's children, the "neighborhood" school is no longer a reality; the distances to school are such that they ride a bus to school. Less than 7 percent of those children, or 3.6 percent of the total number of school children, are bused for the purpose of desegregation.

The amount of time spent on school buses and their costs have figured prominently in criticism directed at busing for school desegregation. But statistical studies indicate that the median travel time for elementary school students was less than 15 minutes; only 15 percent of those students traveled more than 30 minutes.

. . .

In sum, criticism of busing for desegregation must be considered in light of the following: most American children are bused for non-racial reasons without apparent educational or health harm, or parental disapproval; relative to the total costs of public schools, the costs of busing for desegregation are not great; dissatisfaction with this method is voiced more often by those fearing future orders or otherwise not presently involved, than those participating in such a plan.

. . .

1. LEGAL POSITION

Legally, the [Justice] Department appears to have taken the position that the effectiveness of a desegregation plan no longer should be assessed in terms of whether or not the deliberately-created racial isolation is reduced. Under this view, if legal barriers to free choice are eliminated, the fact that the school system remains segregated becomes virtually irrelevant. . . .

. . .

The significance of this new position is not only that the Department is failing to uphold the law; by seeking only partial relief (in only part of the school system), residential instability will be fostered, as white parents seek to enroll their children in schools not touched by desegregation. Furthermore, with only a fraction of a district involved, meaningful desegregation may not be possible.

III. AFFIRMATIVE ACTION

The affirmative action debate appears intractable. On one side, defenders of preferential treatment argue that "[i]n order to get beyond racism, we must first take account of race. There is no other way." Regents v. Bakke, 438 U.S. 265, 407 (1978) (Blackmun, J., concurring and dissenting). For these individuals, affirmative action is an equalizer—responsive to past and present discrimination. On the other side, opponents of benign racial classifications fear that substituting group identity for individual identity is a harbinger of a return to the days of "separate but equal." The first Justice Harlan's admonition that "[o]ur constitution is color-blind, and neither knows nor tolerates classes among citizens" is this group's anthem. Plessy v. Ferguson, 163 U.S. 537, 559 (1896) (Harlan, J., dissenting).

The political struggle over affirmative action is largely a battle between these competing models. While the eradication of pernicious discrimination is universally endorsed and only a handful favor a racial spoils system, proponents and opponents of race preferences are sharply divided on the question of where to draw the line separating permissible remedies from impermissible discrimination.

A. Affirmative Action Antecedents

No analysis of contemporary affirmative action battles can proceed without examining the inevitable point of reference for any discussion of affirmative action—America's approval of slavery. By allowing each of the thirteen states the right to import slaves until 1808, the Framers allowed states to exclude blacks from citizenship. With *Dred Scott* v. *Sandford*, 60 U.S. (19 How.) 393 (1857), the Supreme Court rejected congressional efforts to decree certain parts of the country free from slavery, holding that a slave owner has a right to transport his "property" as he sees fit.

One means of correcting the Constitution's defects (and providing a precursor for contemporary affirmative action debates) were race-specific measures approved by the Reconstruction Congress in an effort to assist former slaves to become "Freedmen." Remarkably, Congress' 1866 debates over these measures are strikingly similar to today's debates. Opponents called the measures "class legislation" and argued that rather than promoting "equality before the law," they "overleap the mark and land on the other side." Cong. Globe, 39th Cong., 1st Sess. 544 (1866) (remarks of Rep. Taylor). For opponents, the effect of the bill was to make minorities "superior" and give "them favors the poor white boy in the North cannot get." Id. at 401 (remarks of Sen. McDougall). Proponents argued that it would be a "cruel mockery" "not [to] provide for those among us who have been held in bondage all their lives" and that therefore the "true object of [such race-specific legislation] is the amelioration of the condition of the colored people." Id. at 588 (statement of Rep. Donnelly); id. at 939 (statement of Sen. Trumbull); id at 632 (statement of Rep. Moulton). President Andrew Johnson sided with bill opponents, vetoing the bill because "the distinction of race and color is by the bill made to operate in favor of the colored and against the white race." 8 Richardson 3611. Congress passed the bill over his veto.

B. The Johnson and Nixon Administrations

On June 4, 1965, today's affirmative action wars began with President Lyndon Johnson's Howard University commencement address. Speaking of "the devastating heritage of long years of slavery" and observing that "[m]uch of the negro community is buried under a blanket of history and circumstance," he "pledge[d]" "not . . . just to open the gates of opportunity" but to see to it that "[a]ll our citizens . . . have the ability to walk through those gates" (document 1). This speech transformed civil rights policy from a focus on individualized fair treatment objectives to an emphasis upon group claims for proportional representation. By arguing that equality of opportunity was not enough, Johnson set the stage for his administration's efforts to withhold federal contract awards from employers with inadequate minority representation. For example, pursuant to its 1965 Executive Order 11246 demand that government contractors make adequate use of minorities, Johnson's Department of Labor issued its "Philadelphia Plan"—withholding government contracts in Philadelphia and other selected cities until contractors submitted pledges to hire minority workers.

These efforts were expanded by the Nixon administration. Between March 1969 and October 1971 Nixon issued three executive orders to "help establish and promote minority business." The creation of the Office of Minority Business Enterprise within the Department of Commerce and the call for increased representation of "Minority Business Enterprises" within federal departments and agencies were the byproducts of these executive orders. For the Nixon administration, "[t]he unique historical experience of . . . disadvantaged minorities . . . cannot be ignored in shaping a national effort to produce substantial new entrepreneurial activity." President's Advisory Council of Minority Business Enterprise, Blueprint for the 70s, at 5 (1971).

The Nixon administration also strengthened the Philadelphia Plan by successfully defending the plan in court, by threatening to veto legislative efforts to rescind the plan, and by extending the plan to nineteen other cities. Although Laurence Silberman, the Nixon official in charge of these efforts (and later Reagan appointee to the D.C. Circuit), subsequently condemned these efforts as "fostering the [racial] Balkanization of America" (document 2), Nixon realized that the Philadelphia Plan created a political dilemma for the Democrats, namely, the division between two traditional Democrat constituencies: labor unions and civil rights groups.

C. Jimmy Carter v. Ronald Reagan

The Carter administration took Nixon and Johnson initiatives one step further by strengthening existing affirmative action programs and launching numerous race- and gender-conscious initiatives. Carter initiatives included efforts to demand adequate minority student representation in tax-exempt private schools, the granting of preferences to minority broadcasters, the establishment of a minority business enterprise set-aside for Department of Transportation highway programs, and Equal Employment Opportunity Commission efforts to racially balance the workplace. For the Carter administration, "[a]n effective affirmative action program is an essential component of our commitment to expanding civil rights protections." 36 Cong. Q. Almanac 91-B, 105-B (1980).

Ronald Reagan campaigned against this vision of numerical racial justice. The 1980 Republican Party Platform declared that "equal opportunity should not be jeopardized by bureaucratic regulations and decisions which rely on quotas, ratios, and numerical requirements to exclude some individuals in favor of others, thereby rendering such regulations and decisions inherently discriminatory." 36 Cong. Q. Almanac 58-B, 62-B (1980). William Bradford Reynolds, Reagan's Assistant Attorney General for Civil Rights, explained:

> [While] much racial bias sadly remains today . . . the devastating failures of today are not the civil rights causes that divided a nation and a people in years gone by. The obvious and not-so-obvious barriers that once marked blacks as inferior and second-class citizens largely have been eliminated. William Bradford Reynolds, The Reagan Administration's Civil Rights Policy: The Challenge for the Future, 42 Vand. L. Rev. 993, 1001 (1989).

This approach rejects affirmative action for groups in favor of relief for individual victims of proven discrimination. Hallmarks of Reagan's civil rights strategy include opposition to voting rights reform; attempts to grant tax breaks to discriminatory private schools; selection of appointees to the Federal Communications Commission (FCC), Department of Education, Civil Rights Commission, and Equal Employment Opportunity Commission (EEOC); and—most important—the granting of carte blanche authority to the Department of Justice to launch a frontal assault on numerical measures of equality.

Internal divisions sharply split the Carter and Reagan administrations. For example, officials in the Carter administration disagreed on the designation of sixteen slots for minority students at the University of California, Davis medical school. Solicitor General Wade McCree, although a proponent of affirmative action, opposed the plan as a racial quota. Secretary of Health, Education, and Welfare Joseph Califano supported the plan. According to Califano, his argument that affirmative action was necessary to provide opportunities to minorities at colleges and universities persuaded the President that the Department of Justice's (DOJ) legal arguments had to give way to these policy concerns. Joseph Califano, Governing America 236-40 (1981).

Inconsistencies also prevailed within the Reagan administration. In court, the administration subscribed to William Bradford Reynolds' view that *all* racial classifications are "offensive to standards of human decency" (document 3). Outside of court, however, the Reagan administration's pursuit of its equal opportunity platform proved far from clear. The administration left in place several of its predecessor's most controversial programs and policies. For example, the administration did not alter Small Business Administration and other Executive-initiated set-aside programs. More significantly, the Reagan Revolution did not bring with it changes in affirmative action requirements set forth in Executive Order 11246. DOJ speech writer Gary McDowell explained that "[Attorney General Edwin] Meese had long believed that there was a danger in 'tilting at windmills without effect'. . . . In regard to the executive order, Meese was . . . convinced that revision for the sake of revision was 'not worth the political flak.'" Gary McDowell, Affirmative Inaction: The Brock-Meese Standoff on Federal Racial Quotas, Policy Review 35 (Spring 1989).

Court opinions which alternately prod and limit federal affirmative action initiatives further complicate this mixture of principle and politics. Exemplifying this intricate constitutional dialogue and the dramatic differences between the Carter and Reagan presidencies is *Metro Broadcasting* v. *FCC*, a 1990 Supreme Court decision upholding FCC efforts to increase minority ownership and participation in broadcast management through race preferences in the granting of licenses. 497 U.S. 547 (1990). Concluding that deference is owed Congress' employment of race because of its "institutional competence as the national legislature," *Metro Broadcasting* held that "benign race-conscious measures mandated by Congress—even if those measures are not 'remedial' . . .—are constitutionally permissible to the extent that they serve important governmental objectives within the power of Congress and are substantially related to the achievement of those objectives." Metro Broadcasting, 497 U.S. at 564-65.

D. The Rise, Fall, and Resurrection of FCC Preferences

Metro Broadcasting's approval of the FCC preferences was a dramatic chapter in a decades long story of confrontational and often acrimonious exchanges between the courts, the Congress, the White House, and the FCC.

The story began in 1973 when the D.C. Circuit required the Commission to provide a comparative preference to racial minorities in order to serve program diversity objectives. TV 9, Inc. v. FCC, 495 F.2d 929 (D.C. Cir. 1973). FCC diversity preferences were expanded in 1978 at the urging of the Carter White House. Pub. Papers, 1978 (I), at 252. In May 1978, the FCC adopted, among other things, a program of tax breaks and other incentives for broadcasters who sold their stations to minority owners. With the election of Ronald Reagan, Carter-initiated diversity preferences came under sharp attack. Reagan-appointed FCC chairman Mark Fowler argued in 1983 that "[t]o diverge from a norm of color blindness is to foster racial antagonism and to denigrate individual liberty." 93 F.C.C. 2d 952, 1020 (1983). By 1986, a Reagan-dominated FCC called for a reexamination of these Carter-era initiatives. 1 F.C.C. Rec. 1315, 1316 (1986).

This reexamination outraged many lawmakers. Members of the House Committee overseeing the FCC referred to the need to draft "FCC-proof" legislation as well as the need to "fight this Commission tooth and nail" on civil rights matters (document 4). Jesse Jackson echoed these concerns. Arguing that "[m]inorities need to have a voice that speaks to them, for them and about them," Jackson thought it "no coincidence" that an FCC fashioned by President Reagan might seek to stop the growth of black-owned broadcast facilities. Minority-Owned Broadcast Stations: Hearing Before the House Comm. on Energy and Commerce, 99th Cong., 2nd Sess. 165 (1986).

On January 8, 1990, the Supreme Court entered this fray, agreeing to hear Metro Broadcasting's constitutional challenge of FCC preferences, 493 U.S. 1017. With the election of George Bush in 1988, however, the FCC was once again changing its position on race preferences.

E. Affirmative Action Under Bush

During their confirmation hearings, all of Bush's FCC appointees—Alfred Sikes, Sherrie Marshall and Andrew Barnett—expressly supported the use of preferences in the awarding of broadcast licenses. Before the Supreme Court, moreover, the Commission argued that diversity preferences served "the compelling governmental interests of promoting *diversity* in broadcast programming and *remedying* discrimination." 199 Landmark Briefs 228 (emphasis added). However, the Bush DOJ *opposed* the FCC in *Metro Broadcasting*. Characterizing the diversity preference as "precisely the type of racial stereotyping that is anathema to basic constitutional principles," the DOJ arguments in *Metro* were indistinguishable from Reagan administration attacks on race preferences. 199 Landmark Briefs 293. Nonetheless, rather than exercise his power as sole government litigator before the Supreme Court, Bush's

Solicitor General Kenneth Starr allowed the FCC to serve as the government's principal voice in the case.

Why the Bush administration presented conflicting arguments before the Supreme Court is unclear. Apparently Bush was caught between a rock and a hard place. On one hand, his desire to stabilize FCC-Congress relations necessitated formal FCC support for the program. On the other hand, his ostensible opposition to race preferences also demanded a formal repudiation of the program.

Bush's inconsistent approach to affirmative action in *Metro Broadcasting* exemplifies the Bush White House's ambiguous and often self-contradictory approach towards race and gender preferences. Like Reagan, Bush granted broad discretion to the Department of Justice to oppose affirmative action while other parts of his administration vigorously supported race and gender preferences. While declaring his unalterable opposition to quotas, Bush also emphasized his "commit[ment] to affirmative action" and, with it, his desire "to see a reinvigorated Office of Minority Business in Commerce." Pub. Papers, 1989 (I), at 21, 29. Furthermore, after the Supreme Court—agreeing with arguments made by the Reagan administration in 1988—issued five 1989 decisions making it more difficult to prove discrimination under Title VII and other statutes, Bush sought to strike a deal with civil rights interests to limit these decisions. Although an imbroglio over whether disparate racial impact proofs of discrimination would unduly pressure employers to hire by the numbers to stave off costly litigation prompted a presidential veto, Bush pressured his negotiators both to meet with civil rights leaders and to find a way for him to sign the 1991 Civil Rights Act. Ironically while dissatisfaction with the Supreme Court prompted this legislation, a key to the 1991 Civil Rights Act compromise was to delegate to the courts the specification of standards of proof governing disparate impact cases.

F. Return of the Color-Blind Constitution?

The 1991 Civil Rights Act hardly quieted the affirmative action wars. Starting with a 1993 grassroots effort to amend the California Constitution to prohibit the state from granting race and gender preferences, affirmative action remains an incendiary topic. On March 15, 1995, Senate Majority Leader and presidential candidate Robert Dole (R-Ks.) called for a comprehensive review of federal affirmative action programs, proclaiming that "fighting discrimination should never become an excuse for abandoning the color-blind ideal." 141 Cong. Rec. 7883-84 (1995). President Clinton responded by launching a government-wide review of affirmative action by saying "[w]e shouldn't be defending things we can't defend." On July 19, 1995, he "reaffirmed the need for affirmative action," declaring that "[t]he job of ending discrimination in this country is not over." Pub. Papers 1995 (II), at 1112-13. The very next day, however, the University of California Regents heeded Republican Governor and then presidential candidate Pete Wilson's claim that racial preferences "threaten to infect the nation with 'the deadly virus of tribalism'" (document 5) and voted to eliminate affirmative action hiring and admissions.

Into this caldron, the Supreme Court, on June 12, added its voice. By a 5-4 vote, the Court refused for the first time to uphold a congressionally-approved affirmative action plan. Adarand Constructors v. Pena, 515 U.S. 200 (1995). The program at issue, the Surface Transportation and Uniform Relocation Assistance Act of 1987 (STUAA), set aside "not less than 10 percent" of appropriated funds for socially and economically disadvantaged firms and then made use of race-based presumptions to help determine disadvantaged status. 101 Stat. 146. Ruling that federal affirmative action programs must be "narrowly tailored" to serve a "compelling governmental interest," *Adarand* rejected *Metro Broadcasting*'s approval of "a lenient standard . . . in assessing" the constitutionality of federal race-based action. 515 U.S. at 210. In so ruling, the Court turned down arguments by the Clinton administration (document 6) that Congress's decisions should be accorded "great weight" because of its "broad powers in matters of race" and its status as "a co-equal branch of government." At the same time, referring to the "unhappy persistence of both the practice and lingering effects of racial discrimination," *Adarand* emphasized that "government is not disqualified from acting in response to it." 515 U.S. at 237. For this reason, the Supreme Court remanded the case to the federal district court from which it originated.

For Clinton Assistant Attorney General for Civil Rights, Deval Patrick, the Court's ruling was described as "a setback, but not a disaster." Patrick Downplays Impact of Adarand, BNA Washington Insider, June 16, 1995. Along these very lines, Clinton himself argued that *Adarand* "actually reaffirmed the need for affirmative action" (document 7). By March 1998, however, the administration had eliminated or altered seventeen federal programs that grant preferences only to minorities and women. At the same time, the Clinton administration has worked hard to limit *Adarand*'s reach. Through a White House conducted affirmative action review, the administration concluded that nearly all affirmative action programs are responsive to discrimination, do not unduly burden nonminorities, and accomplish their objectives of increasing opportunities for minorities and women.

By vigorously defending affirmative action in court, the Clinton administration sought to cabin *Adarand*. One of these cases, *Hopwood v. Texas*, called into question the constitutionality of race preferences in college and law school admissions. After a federal appeals court prohibited the University of Texas Law School from taking race into account in making its admission decisions, 78 F.3d 932 (5th Cir. 1996), the Clinton Justice Department unsuccessfully sought Supreme Court review of the decision (document 8). Another setback for the administration was *Lutheran Church - Missouri Synod v. FCC*, where the D.C. Circuit rejected administration claims that racial diversity in broadcasting was a compelling governmental interest. 141 F.3d 344 (D.C. Cir. 1998).

Increasing judicial hostility to affirmative action is also revealed by the still ongoing *Adarand* litigation. After the Supreme Court remanded the case, a federal district court rejected Justice Department claims that the Transportation Department set-aside was narrowly tailored to the goal of overcoming discrimination. 965 F.Supp. 1556 (D. Colo. 1997). Following that decision, Colorado changed the rules governing its certification of disadvantaged business enterprises (DBEs). In particular, by eliminating the presumption of disadvantage for racial and ethnic minorities, the state was able to certify Adarand as a DBE. In this way, the state sought to moot the *Adarand* litigation. And while the Tenth Circuit Court of Appeals agreed that the dispute was moot, 169 F.3d 1292 (10th Cir. 1999), the Supreme Court reversed this decision and, in so doing, returned *Adarand* back to the appellate court. 120 S.Ct. 722 (2000).

Notwithstanding these judicial defeats, federal affirmative action programs continue. In 1996, for example, Republican leaders in the House of Representatives killed a proposal to ban affirmative action in federal contracting. Worried about a racially divisive election year debate, party leaders have steered clear of affirmative action. For similar reasons, many Senate Republicans joined Congress's 1998 reaffirmation of federal transportation set-asides for women and minorities. For John McCain (R-Az.), the costs of repudiating affirmative action were simply too high: "The danger exists that our [party's] aspirations and intentions will be misperceived, dividing our country and harming our party" (document 9).

G. The States Take Charge

Outside of Washington, D.C., an affirmative action counterrevolution is taking place in the states. Most significant, in 1996, the citizens of California passed a state constitutional amendment that banned affirmative action. Proposition 209 provides that the state "shall not discriminate against, or grant preferential treatment to, any individual or group on the basis of race, sex, color, ethnicity, or national origin in the operation of public employment, public education, or public contracting." Although the Clinton Justice Department argued that Proposition 209 put women and minorities who seek relief from discrimination at a disadvantage, the

Ninth Circuit approved the amendment. In a bow to the force of public opinion, the Ninth Circuit remarked: "A system which permits one judge to block with the stroke of a pen what 4,736,180 state residents voted to enact as law tests the integrity of our constitutional democracy." Coalition for Economic Equity v. Wilson, 110 F.3d 1431, 1437 (9th Cir. 1997).

California, while leading the charge in the populist revolt against affirmative action, does not stand alone. In November 1998, Washington voters approved a similar initiative. With opinion polls showing widespread support for California-like measures and with the financial support of the American Civil Rights Institute, state initiative fights—not judicial rulings—have become the focal point in the battle over preferences.

Outside of these populist efforts to bring down affirmative action, Florida, Texas, and other states have replaced some race-conscious programs with race-neutral alternatives. In November 1999, Florida's Republican governor Jeb Bush proposed doing away with affirmative action in university admissions. By guaranteeing university admission to all high school students in the top 20 percent, Bush sought to circumvent a vote on a referendum proposal to ban affirmative action. Kenneth J. Cooper, Fla. Regents Back Plan to End Affirmative Action, Wash. Post, Feb. 18, 2000 at A-12. Texas, in 1997, approved a similar plan. In seeking to limit *Hopwood*'s reach, the state now guarantees the top 10 percent of graduates from every Texas high school a spot at the public university of their choice. As a result of this program, about 300 blacks enrolled at the state's flagship public colleges in 1999-2000—a 50 percent increase over the year immediately after the *Hopwood* decision.

H. Conclusion

The affirmative action wars seem destined to continue. While Supreme Court opinions may settle the constitutionality of certain race preferences, the ultimate battles are political, not legal. Differences between the Carter and Reagan administration, President Clinton's adroit spinning of *Adarand* into a pro-affirmative action precedent, and the ongoing efforts of state lawmakers and voters to recalibrate affirmative action programs all make this point. At the same time, by defining constitutional parameters, Supreme Court decisions may well sharpen and thereby improve this debate. At this stage, it is unclear whether *Adarand's* demand that all affirmative action programs satisfy strict-scrutiny review will restrain affirmative action or simply provoke elected officials to better justify their policies.

DOCUMENTS

1. Lyndon Johnson Calls for Affirmative Action

Source: Pub. Papers, 1965 (II), at 635-36, 638

In far too many ways American Negroes have been another nation: deprived of freedom, crippled by hatred, the doors of opportunity closed to hope.

. . .

. . . Freedom is the right to share, share fully and equally, in American society—to vote, to hold a job, to enter a public place, to go to school. It is the right to be treated in every part of our national life as a person equal in dignity and promise to all others.

. . .

But freedom is not enough. You do not wipe away the scars of centuries by saying: Now you are free to go where you want, and do as you desire, and choose the leaders you please.

You do not take a person who, for years, has been hobbled by chains and liberate him, bring him up to the starting line of a race and then say, "you are free to compete with all the others," and still justly believe that you have been completely fair.

Thus it is not enough just to open the gates of opportunity. All our citizens must have the ability to walk through those gates.

This is the next and the more profound stage of the battle for civil rights. We seek not just freedom but opportunity. We seek not just legal equity but human ability, not just equality as a right and a theory but equality as a fact and equality as a result.

For the task is to give 20 million Negroes the same chance as every other American to learn and grow, to work and share in society, to develop their abilities—physical, mental and spiritual, and to pursue their individual happiness.

To this end equal opportunity is essential, but not enough, not enough. Men and women of all races are born with the same range of abilities. But ability is not just the product of birth. Ability is stretched or stunted by the family that you live with, and the neighborhood you live in—by the school you go to and the poverty or the richness of your surroundings. It is the product of a hundred unseen forces playing upon the little infant, the child, and finally the man.

. . .

For Negro poverty is not white poverty. Many of its causes and many of its cures are the same. But there are differences—deep, corrosive, obstinate differences—radiating painful roots into the community, and into the family, and the nature of the individual.

These differences are not racial differences. They are solely and simply the consequence of ancient brutality, past injustice, and present prejudice. They are anguishing to observe. For the Negro they are a constant reminder of oppression. For the white they are a constant reminder of guilt. But they must be faced and they must be dealt with and they must be overcome, if we are ever to reach the time when the only difference between Negroes and whites is the color of their skin.

2. Nixon Official Questions Affirmative Action

Source: Laurence H. Silberman, The Road to Racial Quotas, Wall Street Journal August 11, 1977, at 14

. . . While serving in the Labor Department, I helped devise minority employment goals for government contractors.

I now realize that the distinction we saw between goals and timetables on the one hand, and unconstitutional quotas on the other, was not valid. Our use of numerical standards in pursuit of equal opportunity has led ineluctably to the very quotas, guaranteeing equal results, that we initially wished to avoid.

.   .   .

In practice, employers anxious to avoid inquiry from government officials concerned only with results (rather than merely with efforts) often earmarked jobs for minorities without regard to qualifications. Influenced by government policy—this was happening, after all, under a Republican administration, unopposed on this issue by Democrats—some universities abandoned all pretense and adopted out-right quotas for minority applicants.

In hindsight, one can see this was predictable. We wished to create a generalized, firm, but gentle pressure to balance the residue of discrimination. Unfortunately, the pressure numerical standards generate cannot be generalized or gentle; it inevitably causes injustice.

Incredible as it now seems, our policy was not designed to foster proportional representation, the dangerous notion that ethnic, racial or religious groups are entitled to proportional representation in all occupations, fostering the Balkanization of America. Admittedly, it should have been clear that no other theory supports the formulation of numerical goals.

3. Assistant Attorney General Reynolds Outlines Reagan Administration Opposition to Affirmative Action

Source: Affirmative Action: Joint Hearings Before the Subcomm. on Civil and Constitutional Rights of the House Comm. on the Judiciary, and the Subcomm. on Employment Opportunities of the House Comm. on Education and Labor, 99th Cong., 1st Sess. 266-67, 273-74 (1985)

Let me now direct my attention to the new Justice Department approach in fashioning appropriate relief to correct the effects of past discrimination.

.   .   .

. . . We no longer will insist upon or in any respect support the use of quotas or any other numerical or statistical formulae designed to provide to non-victims of discrimination preferential treatment based on race, sex, national origin or religion. To pursue any other course is, in our view, unsound as a matter of law and unwise as a matter of policy. Race-conscious or sex-conscious preferences are, as history has shown, divisive techniques which go well beyond the remedy that is necessary to redress, in full measure, those injured by a particular employer's discriminatory practices. . . .

By elevating the rights of groups over the rights of individuals, racial preferences . . . are at war with the American ideal of equal opportunity for each person to achieve whatever his or her industry and talents warrant. This kind of "affirmative action" needlessly creates a caste system in which an individual is unfairly disadvantaged for each person who is preferred. A divisive influence is inevitably introduced into the workplace, the community, and the country as a whole.

Nor is there any moral justification for such an approach. Separate treatment of people in the field of employment, based on nothing more than personal characteristics of race or gender, is as offensive to standards of human decency today as it was some 84 years ago when countenanced under *Plessy* v. *Ferguson*. . . .

---

4. Congress Lambasts Reagan FCC

Source: Minority-Owned Broadcast Stations: Hearing Before the Subcomm. on Telecommunications, Consumer Protection, and Finance of the House Comm. on Energy and Commerce, 99th Cong., 2nd Sess. 17-18, 53-54 (1986)

Mr. [Mark] FOWLER [FCC Chairman]. .
. .

. . . [P]references are accompanied by so much baggage that the costs may outweigh the benefits. A primary detriment is that racial and gender classifications divide society by emphasizing the very features of people that we should be de-emphasizing: their color or gender. Rather than fostering a world in which individuals are judged on their merits, and where their race or gender is irrelevant, racial and gender preferences highlight and crystallize the precise distinctions that are at the root of discrimination.

Mr. [Al] SWIFT [D-Wash.]. . . .
I have never heard of an easy way to compensate for 200 years of systemic discrimination. I have never heard of a way that didn't involve some kind of compensatory inequities; never heard of a way that wasn't controversial; never heard of a way in which somebody couldn't raise objections as to how it was done. There isn't an easy way to do that.

The fact that you have taken the positions you have taken indicates that you don't know what is going on in this country—and haven't been paying attention for the last 30 years—in terms of the aspirations and hopes of minority American citizens.

If you care to respond, you may. . . .
(No response.)

---

5. Wilson Condemns Preferential Treatment

Source: Pete Wilson, Equal Rights, Not Special Privileges, L.A. Times, June 1, 1995 at A-11

Our state and nation are engaged in a debate that goes to the very foundation of the American dream. The question before us: Is preferential treatment based on race or gender consistent with the American Dream of equality under the law?

We are dealing with a charged issue that has been confused by emotionalism on all sides. But we cannot sidestep this issue or pretend that it doesn't exist. For this question goes to the heart and soul of the American Dream—equality under the law.

The success of the civil rights movement, against enormous odds, was based on its appeal to our heritage that this nation was founded on: the principle, as Thomas Jefferson said, of "equal rights for all, special privileges for none."

Dr. Martin Luther King invoked that principle when he described his dream that his children would one day live in a nation "where they will not be judged by the color of their skin but by the content of their character."

That principle, however, is slipping away from us when we allow affirmative action programs that grant preferential treatment based on race or gender.

. . .

Rather than uniting people around our common core, this system of preferential treatment constantly reminds us of our superficial differences. Instead of treating every American as an individual, it pits group against group, race against race. Instead of moving us forward toward a color-blind society, it is holding us back.

But worst of all, this system is eroding the American ideal that anyone who works hard and plays by the rules has an equal chance to achieve the American dream. Today, without finger-pointing at the misfired good intentions of 30 years ago, we must summon the courage to reassess the course we set.

---

6. Solicitor General Days Defends Constitutionality of Racial Set-asides

Source: 240 Landmark Briefs 604, 609-10

GENERAL DAYS: . . . The subcontracting compensation clause challenged here is a means of effectuating a national policy designed by Congress and supported by Presidents of both parties to ensure to the greatest extent possible that Federal procurement programs do not compound the continuing effects of well-documented discrimination but, rather, serve to offset their consequences.

. . .

QUESTION: General Days, why couldn't Congress have done this without a presumption, and just said that if the [contractor] can show factual economic disadvantage, it gets the benefit, but not use any presumption?

GENERAL DAYS: Mr. Chief Justice, Congress could have done that, but I think what the record reflects here is a review by Congress over a number of years, looking at the degree to which Federal contracting dollars were going to contractors who had participated in some way or reinforced discrimination against members of certain racially and economically disadvantaged groups and decided that this was the appropriate way to do it.

QUESTION: So it's really a matter of administrative convenience? They figured it would come out this way in the majority of cases?

GENERAL DAYS: Well, I wouldn't characterize it as administrative convenience. It was simply a determination that if the results that Congress wanted to have occur were to occur, they would have to be done in this way. . . .

. . .

QUESTION: General Days, what is the limit of—if there is any— of the Government's ability to use race as a—as the basis for a presumption in some of its programs?

Suppose the Government has a very important space program which just can't afford any mistakes, and it says, just looking over education statistics, whites generally have a higher level of education, and we are going to assume that any bidder that is white-owned is a more competent bidder—it's just a presumption. It can always be refuted by nonwhite bidders—and we're going to use that presumption for the program. Is that okay? A very—

GENERAL DAYS: I—

QUESTION: —very serious, critical need for perfection in this program, and the Government says, we're just going to adopt this presumption.

Of course, it's rebuttable. No problem. If you want to come in and show that even though you're not white, you're very smart and very competent, that's okay, but you can come in and show it.

GENERAL DAYS: Justice Scalia, I think that the difference between this situation and the situation that you posed is a question of whether Congress is acting for remedial purposes, and what we have here is—

QUESTION: I don't know what that means. It's a good, valid governmental purpose in both cases.

---

7. Clinton Addresses Nation on Affirmative Action

Source: Pub. Papers at 1995 (II), 1112-13

. . . [W]e must and we will comply with the Supreme Court's *Adarand* decision of last month. Now, in particular, that means focusing set-aside programs on particular regions and business sectors where the problems of discrimination or exclusion are provable and are clearly requiring affirmative action. I have directed the Attorney General and the agencies to move forward with compliance with *Adarand* expeditiously.

But I also want to emphasize that the *Adarand* decision did not dismantle affirmative action and did not dismantle set-asides. In fact, while setting stricter standards to mandate reform of affirmative action, it actually reaffirmed the need for affirmative action and reaffirmed the continuing existence of systematic discrimination in the United States. . . .

. . .

My fellow Americans, affirmative action has to be made consistent with our highest ideals of personal responsibility and merit and our urgent need to find common ground and to prepare all Americans to compete in the global economy of the next century.

Today, I am directing all our agencies to comply with the Supreme Court's *Adarand* decision, and also to apply the four standards of fairness to all our affirmative action programs that I have already articulated: No quotas in theory or practice; no illegal discrimination of any kind, including reverse discrimination; no preference for people who are not qualified for any job or other opportunity; and as soon as a program has succeeded, it must be retired. Any program that doesn't meet these four principles must be eliminated or reformed to meet them.

But let me be clear: Affirmative action has been good for America. Affirmative action has not always been perfect, and affirmative action should not go on forever.

. . .

Based on the evidence, the job is not done. So here is what I think we should do. We should reaffirm the principle of affirmative action and fix the practices. We should have a simple slogan: Mend it, but don't end it.

8. Clinton Justice Department Defends Race Conscious University Admissions

Source: Brief for the United States
as Amicus Curiae Supporting Petitioners
at 9-10, 15-16, Texas v. Hopwood,
518 U.S. 1033 (1995)

. . . By disregarding two decades of established law under *Bakke*, the decision [in *Hopwood*] has already created substantial confusion and upheaval among colleges and universities nationwide. It also calls into question the lawfulness of existing Department of Education policies and regulations, and interferes with the federal government's efforts to obtain voluntary compliance by the States with their desegregation obligations. The decision below thus raises issues of national importance that call for this Court's review.

. . . Law students cannot effectively be trained "in isolation from the individuals and institutions with which the law interacts." *Sweatt*, 339 U.S. at 634. This Court correctly concluded in *Sweatt* that a black student could not receive an effective legal education in Texas while being kept separate from "members of racial groups which number[ed] 85% of the population of the State." The predominantly white University of Texas School of Law may similarly conclude today that, absent racial diversity in its classrooms, its students will not effectively be prepared to be lawyers in Texas's (or the Nation's) racially diverse society.

The court of appeals' suggestion that the Law School may constitutionally consider non-racial factors, including economic and social background, that might be closely correlated with race ignores the Law School's compelling educational interest in maintaining a *racially* diverse student body.

9. Congress Debates Highway Set-Asides

Source: 144 Cong. Rec. S1483,
S1493 (daily ed. March 6, 1998)

Mr. [Phil] Gramm [(R-Tex.)]
There are two issues I want to address. No. 1, this provision, which the amendment of the Senator from Kentucky would strike, has been declared unconstitutional in the Adarand decision . . .

I want to remind my colleagues that whether it was 6 years ago, 4 years ago or 2 years ago, we each stood right down there in the well of the Senate, put our hand on the Bible, and swore to uphold, protect, and defend the Constitution against all enemies, foreign and domestic. Sometimes we are the enemies. The issue here is, are we going to uphold the Constitution or are we not? When it comes to the Constitution, put me down on the side of the Constitution.

The second issue is fairness. We all want to help people compete. We all want Americans to have equality of opportunity, but you cannot have equality of opportunity through a program that clearly discriminates against people. There is only one fair way to decide who gets a contract and that is competition based on merit and price.

Mr. [John] Chafee [(R-R.I.)] . . . It is not often that [Senator Gramm] is inaccurate, but I am afraid that he went overboard a little bit today when he suggested that the Supreme Court in the Adarand decision had struck down as unconstitutional the provisions of the affirmative action program. What the Supreme Court said in the 5 to 4 decision—I am talking about the Supreme Court. I like to deal with the Supreme Court. What it did is remanded that case. It did not say it was unconstitutional. Any talk of unconstitutionality came by the lower court which then examined whether the provisions in the Adarand situation conformed to the restrictions that the Supreme Court was applying.

.   .   .

Mr. [Joseph] Lieberman [(D-Conn.)]

.   .   .

I am voting against the McConnell amendment in spite of my reservations because I am convinced that discrimination persists in the transportation construction industry and in related industries, and because I believe that the DBE program is narrowly tailored to attack the ongoing practice of that discrimination. The program therefore is both justifiable as sound policy and in compliance with the Supreme Court's Adarand decision.

We have before us ample evidence of historic and more importantly ongoing discrimination in the relevant industries. . . .

In May of 1996, the Department of Justice . . . found "powerful and persuasive [evidence] that the discriminatory barriers facing minority-owned businesses are not vague and amorphous manifestations of historical and social discrimination. Rather, they are real and concrete, and reflect ongoing patterns and practices of exclusion, as well as the tangible, lingering effects of prior discriminatory conduct." . . .

In my view, this evidence of discrimination is sufficient to establish the compelling interest required by the Adarand decision. . . .

IV. VOTING RIGHTS

The right to vote would seem inherent in a representative democracy. In 1886, for example, the Supreme Court referred to voting as "a fundamental political right, because preservative of all rights." Yick Wo v. Hopkins, 118 U.S. 356, 370 (1886). Nevertheless, it took the Fifteenth Amendment, ratified in 1870, to establish the right of blacks to vote. Furthermore, it was not until 1920, with the Nineteenth Amendment, that women gained the right to vote.

Voting rights in America have been hammered out by state action, judicial decisions, congressional and executive action, and constitutional amendment. Nowhere is this more true than minority voting rights. Beginning with the drafting of the Constitution and continuing today, courts and elected officials have struggled first over the existence of and later over the appropriate protections for minority voting rights.

A. From Slavery through Reconstruction

The Constitution, as Justice Thurgood Marshall aptly remarked on the occasion of its bicentennial, "was defective from the start, requiring several amendments [and] a civil war" (document 1). In particular, the Northern delegates to the 1787 Constitutional Convention permitted the continuation of slavery to ensure that the South would join the Union. These delegates compromised by counting a slave as three-fifths of a person for determining a state's congressional representation, by requiring states to return fugitive slaves, and by allowing the importation of slaves through 1808.

The Founding Fathers also left to states the power of determining voting qualifications. At the time of the Constitutional Convention, the states had a broad spectrum of voting qualifications. While Vermont granted suffrage to every adult male, many states limited voting rights to white landholders. Indeed, the state constitutions of Connecticut, Delaware, Kentucky, Maryland, New Jersey, North Carolina, Tennessee, and Virginia excluded blacks from voting. By the time of the Civil War, only Maine, New Hampshire, Vermont, Rhode Island, and Massachusetts allowed free blacks to vote.

Following the Civil War, Congress set out to change the status of blacks in American society. Black suffrage was the subject of the Fifteenth Amendment's prohibition against denying or abridging the right to vote "on account of race, color, or previous condition of servitude." Before Congress settled on this language, Republicans who favored universal suffrage and advocated the abolition of literacy tests and property requirements encountered resistance from some Northern and Western Republicans. With eleven of the twenty-one northern states and all five border states denying blacks the rights to vote, Fifteenth Amendment supporters could not push through massive voting rights reforms. Moreover, Western Republicans wished to continue to disenfranchise the Chinese. Senator George Williams (R-Or.), for example, spoke of "the exhaustless populations of China" and warned against the nation binding itself to "the political filth and moral pollution" of the Chinese. Cong. Globe, 40th Cong., 3d Sess. 901 (1869).

With Democrats vigorously opposed to black suffrage altogether, the Amendment was narrowly worded in order to unify the Republicans. Passed by the Republican Congress on February 26, 1869 and ratified by the states on March 30, 1870, the Fifteenth Amendment granted voting rights in general but left the all-important specifics to the states.

The number of blacks voting in the South gained initially under the Fifteenth Amendment. At least one Southern black man served in every Congress from 1881 to 1901. During this time, hundreds of blacks were elected to state legislatures and thousands to local offices. Between the years 1868 and 1896, for example, Louisiana elected a black governor, 32 black state senators, and 96 black state representatives.

This brief progress was soon reversed. After the Republican party lost its majority in Congress in 1873, Northern interest in the South started to wane. In 1876, when neither Democrat Samuel J. Tilden nor Republican Rutherford B. Hayes received sufficient electoral votes to become president, a deal was struck allowing Hayes to become president in return for the withdrawal of federal troops from the South. Following this 1877 compromise, black voters were intimidated and threatened. By 1910, nearly all blacks living in the Deep South were disenfranchised by a variety of obstacles such as literacy tests, writing requirements, constitutional comprehension tests, duties of citizenship tests, poll taxes, and grandfather clauses. In stark contrast, whites were rarely subject to these tests at all. H.R. No. 4349, 89th Cong., 1st Sess. (1965).

The Supreme Court stood in the way of some state efforts to nullify the Fifteenth Amendment. Legislation extending voting rights only to those who were entitled to vote before the Fifteenth Amendment was overturned by the Court in 1915. Guinn v. United States, 238 U.S. 347 (1915); Myers v. Anderson, 238 U.S. 368 (1915). Furthermore, in the "White Primary" cases, the Supreme Court reviewed a Texas statute that barred blacks from voting in the Democratic party primary for U.S. Senators and Congressmen. A unanimous Court held that this violated the Fourteenth Amendment. Nixon v. Herndon, 273 U.S. 536 (1927). This ruling was extended in 1944, when the Court declared (8 to 1) that Texas could not exclude blacks by limiting participation in state conventions to white citizens. Smith v. Allwright, 321 U.S. 649 (1944).

B. The 1965 Voting Rights Act

Black disenfranchisement, especially in Southern states, persisted until 1965. In Mississippi, through poll taxes, intimidation, and other devices, only 6.7 percent of blacks who could vote were registered for the 1964 presidential election—prompting The United States Commission on Civil Rights to conclude that the 15th Amendment "has, in substance, been repudiated and denied in Mississippi." Voting in Mississippi 59 (1965). Matters came to a head in Selma, Alabama. On March 7, 1965, a peaceful group of 600 protesters marched against the continuing denial of black voting rights only to be teargassed and attacked "with clubs, whips, and ropes" by state troopers, as white spectators cheered. Troopers Rout Selma Marchers, Wash. Post, March 8, 1965, at A1. With television bringing pictures of this brutality into millions of homes, the Selma protest prompted a national outcry and immediate call for comprehensive voting rights legislation.

A week after the protest, on March 15, President Lyndon Johnson spoke to a joint session of Congress about the need for more effective voting rights legislation. The Emancipation Proclamation, Johnson said, was a promise of equality to black Americans: "A century has passed since the day of the promise. And the promise is unkept" (document 2). Calling for immediate action to stop state officials from circumventing the Fifteenth Amendment, Johnson introduced his voting rights bill.

The bill proposed a dramatic restructuring of the existing voting system, shifting authority away from state governments to the federal government. States could no longer use literacy tests and other methods to disenfranchise blacks. More striking, to prevent discriminatory voting practices from taking effect, most Southern states had to have changes to their voting laws "precleared" by the Department of Justice or the D.C. District Court.

In Congress, lawmakers split sharply about the bill. Supporters, like Representative Emanuel Celler (D-N.Y.), argued that "legal dodges and subterfuges" had undermined previous reform efforts. 111 Cong. Rec. 15638 (1965). Opposing members thought the bill vindictive against Southern states (document 3). By August 1965, Congress approved the measure and President Johnson signed it into law. 79 Stat. 437 (1965).

The bill dramatically increased minority registration and voting. In the targeted Southern states, the percentage of black registered voters increased from 29 percent in 1964 to over 56 percent in 1972. The number of elected black officials also increased from well under a hundred in 1964 to 963 in 1974. U.S. Commission on Civil Rights, The Voting Rights Act: Ten Years After 40, 49 (1975).

Voting rights reforms found quick support in the Supreme Court. In 1966, the Court upheld Department of Justice preclearance authority as well as the literacy test prohibition. South Carolina v. Katzenbach, 383 U.S. 301 (1966); Katzenbach v. Morgan, 386 U.S. 641 (1966). In 1969, the Court rejected Mississippi efforts to dilute minority votes by changing county elections from a single district scheme to an at-large scheme that would allow majority voters to block the election of minority candidates. Allen v. State Board of Elections, 393 U.S. 544 (1969). In 1973, the Court extended this principle, ruling that multimember districts may infringe on minority voter's constitutional right to "fair and effective" representation. White v. Regester, 412 U.S. 755 (1973).

C. Amending the Voting Rights Act

The partnership between the Supreme Court, Congress, and the Department of Justice on voting rights suffered a setback in 1980. The Court upheld Mobile's at-large election scheme for city commissioners, despite the fact that blacks constituted over 35 percent of Mobile's population and no black had ever been elected to the city's three-member commission. Mobile v. Bolden, 446 U.S. 55 (1980). Concluding that civil rights plaintiffs must show discriminatory intent, the Court rejected Carter administration arguments that the Fifteenth Amendment "forbids official maintenance of electoral schemes that enhance the effects of racial bias in voting . . . whether or not invidious racial purpose is shown." Brief for the United States as Amicus Curiae, Mobile v. Bolden, 119 Landmark Briefs at 288.

Congress responded quickly to the *Mobile* decision. Sixty-two Senators and 389 Representatives co-sponsored legislation to statutorily override the decision by allowing impact-based proofs of vote dilution. Claiming that "[t]his change [from intent to effects] is made necessary by the Supreme Court's plurality decision in Mobile against Bolden" and that "the intent test places an unacceptable burden on plaintiffs in voting discrimination cases," Act co-sponsors proclaimed that "[j]ustice demands that we pass this measure without further delay." 128 Cong. Rec. 14308 (1982) (remarks of Sen. Howard Metzenbaum (D-Ohio)); Id. at 14114 (remarks of Senator Charles Mathias (R-Md.)).

By this time, however, Ronald Reagan had been elected President. Although initially signalling his support of the bipartisan measure, Reagan backtracked after being confronted by his Attorney General William French Smith. According to Smith: "I pointed out [to Reagan] that he was dangerously close to committing himself to signing a bill that could establish the foundation for proportional representation, with the only remaining bulwark being (one hoped) the federal judiciary." William French Smith, Law and Justice in the Reagan Administration 98 (1991). Before the Senate Judiciary Committee, Smith testified that the proposed legislation "carried to its logical conclusion" would result in "proportional representation or, put another way, quotas." Bills to Amend the Voting Rights Act of 1965: Hearings Before the Subcomm. on the Constitution of the Senate Comm. On the Judiciary, 97th Cong., 2d Sess. 74 (1982). Smith, moreover, condemned the bill as "contrary to any of our basic principles of government" because its "underlying [assumption is] . . . that blacks will only vote for black candidates and whites will only vote for white candidates." Id. at 75. Yet, because of an ongoing flap over administration efforts to grant tax exemptions to racially discriminatory private schools, Smith's words rang hollow. In the midst of his testimony, a "hearing room full of civil-rights activists erupted into laughter" when Smith remarked that "the President does not have a discriminatory bone in his body." Chester E. Finn, Jr., Affirmative Action Under Reagan, Commentary, Apr. 1982 at 27.

In its report, the Judiciary Committee rejected *Mobile*'s intent test because it placed an "unacceptable burden upon plaintiffs" (document 4). At the same time, the report emphasized that "there is no right to proportional representation" under the results test. Forged by Senate

Majority Leader Robert Dole (R-Ks.), this qualification, as Reagan Solicitor General Charles Fried put it, was "so equivocal as to be incomprehensible," although it "avoided the disaster of a presidential veto and a certain subsequent override." Charles Fried, Order and Law 104 (1991). On June 29, 1982, Reagan signed the bill into law. Speaking of his "unbending commitment to voting rights," Reagan praised the measure for "securely protect[ing] the right to vote while strengthening the safeguards against representation by forced quota." Pub. Papers, 1982(I), at 822-23.

D. The Supreme Court Steps In

The Supreme Court took on the task of sorting out Congress' mixed message on race-conscious redistricting. At first, the Court broadly interpreted the 1982 amendments. In 1986, the Court upheld the statute and cleared the way for the drawing of predominantly minority districts to combat persistent minority disenfranchisement through racial block voting. Thornburgh v. Gingles, 478 U.S. 30 (1986). Following this decision, the Justice Department and some federal district courts aggressively pursued race-conscious districting in order to maximize minority representation at both the federal and state level. For example, the Bush Justice Department demanded that North Carolina, Georgia, and other states provide "black voters an equal opportunity . . . to elect candidates of their choice" by creating predominantly minority districts. Letter from John R. Dunne, Assistant Attorney General for Civil Rights to Tiare B. Smiley, Special Deputy Attorney General, North Carolina (December 18, 1991).

Support for race-conscious districting also came from the Republican National Committee. Believing that "packing blacks into a few districts means that the surrounding districts become whiter, less Democratic, and fertile soil for GOP candidates," the Committee supported civil rights groups' efforts to create predominantly minority districts by filing amicus briefs and providing technical assistance. Matthew Cooper, Beware of Republicans Bearing Voting Rights Suits, Washington Monthly, Feb. 1987 at 11. These efforts paid off. In 1992, 13 blacks and 5 Hispanics were elected from 18 newly created predominantly minority districts. By 1995, the House of Representatives had 38 black members (including 17 from the South), up from 26 in 1990 (with five from the South). Of equal significance, the 1994 Republican takeover of Congress is partially attributable to the ability of Republicans to win districts that were now more white than before.

Beyond the policy questions of which political party benefits from race-conscious districting and whether this practice ultimately serves minority interests, the constitutionality of predominantly minority districts has been called into question by an increasingly skeptical Supreme Court.

In 1993 and 1995, five of the six Reagan and Bush appointees to the Court (Kennedy, O'Connor, Rehnquist, Scalia, and Thomas) have voted to limit race-conscious districting.

In 1993, the Court called into question the constitutionality of racial gerrymandering. Shaw v. Reno, 509 U.S. 630 (1993). Rejecting Clinton administration claims "that the principle of the color-blind constitution" must yield to "the unfortunate fact that racial block voting occurs" (document 5), the Court concluded that "[r]acial classifications of any sort pose the risk of lasting harm to our society" and, consequently, racial gerrymandering is subject to the same standard of strict scrutiny review as other racial classifications. Id. at 657. Two years later, the Court struck down a Georgia redistricting plan that sought to maximize the number of majority black districts. Miller v. Johnson, 515 U.S. 900 (1995). Although prompted by Bush and Clinton Justice Department efforts to increase the likelihood of blacks being elected to Congress, the Court concluded that "[w]hen the state assigns voters on the basis of race, it engages in the offensive and demeaning assumption that voters of a particular race, because of their race, think alike, share the same political interests, and will prefer the same candidates at the polls." Id. at 911-12.

President Clinton was deeply disappointed by these decisions. Having withdrawn the nomination of Lani Guinier to head the Justice Department's Civil Rights Division because he did not agree with Guinier's calls for controversial voting rights reforms, including proportional voting and minority vetos (document 6), Clinton sought to mend fences with civil rights interests by vigorously defending the constitutionality of race-conscious districting. For Clinton, the Court's decisions in *Shaw* and *Miller* were "setback[s] in the struggle to ensure that all Americans participate fully in the electoral process." Pub. Papers, 1995 (I) at 977. Minority members of Congress were equally dismayed at the Court's rulings (document 7). Senator Carol Moseley-Braun (D-Ill.) accused the Court's "conservative majority" of doing "what conservatives used to accuse the Warren Court of doing—making law." 139 Cong. Rec. 15147 (1993). For Representative Charles Rangel (D-N.Y.), the Court was "trying to bring the United States Congress back to an old white boys' club that it used to be." Kenneth J. Cooper, Minorities in Congress Fear Loss of Diversity, Wash. Post, June 30, 1995, at A18.

Subsequent cases have left much to the ingenuity of lawmakers who are adept at drawing district lines that take account of race but also other factors, such as population equality, geographic compactness, contiguity, political boundaries, and the presence or absence of a sense of community. DeWitt v. Wilson, 515 U.S. 1170 (1995), aff'g, 856 F.Supp. 1409 (D. Cal. 1994). Also, the Court has had an increasingly difficult time in providing clear guidelines for the use of race in drawing district lines, often resorting to plurality opinions. Bush v. Vera, 517 U.S. 952 (1996); Shaw v. Hunt, 517 U.S. 899 (1996).

E. Conclusion

The struggle over voting rights remains a permanent feature of America's constitutional landscape. Congress, the Justice Department, the White House, the states, and the Supreme Court have been and will continue to be active players in this dispute. Consequently, while much of the recent fight over minority representation has been waged in the Supreme Court, it is inevitable that this issue will again return to elected government. Indeed, from 1995 to 1999, the Supreme Court has generally steered clear of voting rights disputes, leaving the implementation of its recent decisions largely in the hands of elected officials. While it seems certain that the Court will reenter this fray, it is equally inevitable that the fate of voting rights will continue to be settled by an ongoing dialogue between the courts and elected government.

DOCUMENTS

1. Thurgood Marshall
Comments on Slavery

Source: Remarks of Justice Thurgood Marshall, Annual Seminar of the San Francisco Patent and Trademark Law Association, in Maui, Hawaii
(May 6, 1987)

1987 marks the 200th anniversary of the United States Constitution. A Commission has been established to coordinate the celebration. The official meetings, essay contests, and festivities have begun. . . .

. . .

The focus of this celebration invites a complacent belief that the vision of those who debated and compromised in Philadelphia yielded the "more perfect Union" it is said we now enjoy.

I cannot accept this invitation, for I do not believe that the meaning of the Constitution was forever "fixed" at the Philadelphia Convention. Nor do I find the wisdom, foresight, and sense of justice exhibited by the Framers particularly profound. To the contrary, the government they devised was defective from the start, requiring several amendments, a civil war, and momentous social transformation to attain the system of constitutional government, and its respect for the individual freedoms and human rights, we hold as fundamental today.

. . .

No doubt it will be said, when the unpleasant truth of the history of slavery in America is mentioned during this bicentennial year, that the Constitution was a product of its times, and embodies a compromise which, under other circumstances, would not have been made. But the effects of the Framers' compromise have remained for generations. They arose from the contradiction between guaranteeing liberty and justice to all, and denying both to Negroes.

. . .

Thus, in this bicentennial year, we may not all participate in the festivities with flag-waving fervor. Some may more quietly commemorate the suffering, struggle, and sacrifice that has triumphed over much of what was wrong with the original document, and observe the anniversary with hopes not realized and promises not fulfilled. I plan to celebrate the bicentennial of the Constitution as a living document, including the Bill of Rights and the other amendments protecting individual freedoms and human rights.

---

2. Lyndon Johnson Proposes Voting Rights Legislation

Source: Pub. Papers, 1965(I), at 281-83

This was the first nation in the history of the world to be founded with a purpose. The great phrases of that purpose still sound in every American heart, North and South: "All men are created equal"—"government by consent of the governed"—"give me liberty or give me death." Those are not just clever words. Those are not just empty theories. In their name Americans have fought and died for two centuries, and tonight around the world they stand there as guardians of our liberty, risking their lives.

Those words are a promise to every citizen that he shall share in the dignity of man. This dignity cannot be found in a man's possessions. It cannot be found in his power or in his position. It really rests on his right to be treated as a man equal in opportunity to all others. It says that he shall share in freedom, he shall choose his leaders, educate his children, provide for his family according to his ability and his merits as a human being.

To apply any other test—to deny a man his hopes because of his color or race, or his religion, or the place of his birth—is not only to do injustice, it is to deny America and to dishonor the dead who gave their lives for American freedom.

Our fathers believed that if this noble view of the rights of man is to flourish, it must be rooted in democracy. The most basic right of all was the right to choose your own leaders. The history of this country in large measure is the history of expansion of that right to all of our people.

Many of the issues of civil rights are very complex and most difficult. But about this there can and should be no argument. Every American citizen must have an equal right to vote. There is no reason which can excuse the denial of that right. There is no duty which weighs more heavily on us than the duty we have to ensure that right.

Yet the harsh fact is that in many places in this country men and women are kept from voting simply because they are Negroes.

Every device of which human ingenuity is capable has been used to deny this right. The Negro citizen may go to register only to be told that the day is wrong, or the hour is late, or the official in charge is absent. And if he persists and if he manages to present himself to the registrar, he may be disqualified because he did not spell out his middle name or because he abbreviated a word on the application. And if he manages to fill out an application he is given a test. The registrar is the sole judge of whether he passes this test. He may be asked to recite the entire constitution, or explain the most complex provisions of state laws. And even a college degree cannot be used to prove that he can read and write.

For the fact is that the only way to pass these barriers is to show a white skin.

3. 1965 Voting Rights Act Debated in Congress

Source: 111 Cong. Rec. 8295,
15641-42 (1965)

[Senate]
Mr. [Mike] MANSFIELD [D-Mont.]:

What meaning was there to the promise of equal treatment when there were barriers to voting in primaries—the only meaningful election in many areas? What justice was there for citizens afforded a hopelessly inadequate education because of their race or color and then told that to vote they had to pass complicated understanding and informational tests? In the absence of Federal action, the rights promised by the 14th and 15th amendments were not only not realized, they were effectively and systematically frustrated.

But we are told that the States have sole responsibility for determining the qualifications for voting; none of us would deny that bare premise—but what a hollow and barren sound when measured against decades of abuse and contravention of the Constitution. . . .

[House]
Mr. [Howard] SMITH of Virginia [D]. Mr. Speaker, here we are again just a year after we passed the most drastic civil rights bill [the 1964 Civil Rights Act] that has ever been presented to the Congress and which we were assured by its advocates, . . . [that it] was the cure to all the difficulties under civil rights. . . .

Now, why? Is this a vendetta in order to hold certain minority votes in the grasp of Members of the Congress and the great parties? Or is it an honest effort to correct evils which have existed in the past and which are rapidly fading away, as everybody knows; there is not any doubt about that. But we must have this vengeance. We must have this vendetta against certain States of the Union. We must have a law that is going to punish a people, a part of our great Nation, for things they have done in the past. Because, under this bill, if there has ever been discrimination, the law applies and, of course, there always has been discrimination in some areas.

4. Senate Supports Effects Test

Source: S. Rep. No. 417, 97th Cong.,
1st Sess. 16-17, 193 (1982)

In our view, proof of discriminatory purpose should not be prerequisite to establishing a violation of Section 2 of the Voting Rights Act. . . .

In reaching this judgment, the Committee has made several key findings as detailed in the following parts of this section:

Requiring proof of a discriminatory purpose is inconsistent with the original legislative intent and subsequent legislative history of Section 2.

The *Bolden* litigation marked a radical departure from both Supreme Court and lower federal court precedent in voting discrimination cases.

Electoral devices, including at-large elections . . . would only be vulnerable if, in the totality of circumstances, they resulted in the denial of equal access to the electoral process. . . .

The intent test focuses on the wrong question and places an unacceptable burden upon plaintiffs in voting discrimination cases.

The proposed amendment to Section 2 is well within Congress' constitutional authority. It is not an effort to overrule a Supreme Court interpretation of the Constitution, rather it provides a statutory prohibition which the Congress finds is necessary to enforce the substantive provisions of the 14th and 15th Amendments.

.   .   .

ADDITIONAL VIEWS OF
SENATOR ROBERT DOLE

.   .   .

If a voting practice or structure operates today to exclude members of a minority group from a fair opportunity to participate in the political process, the motives behind the actions of officials which took place decades before is of the most limited relevance. Further, it places an inordinate burden of proof on plaintiffs, thus frustrating vigorous enforcement efforts. It also causes divisiveness because it inevitably involves charges that the decisions of officials were racially motivated. In short, from both a policy and legal standpoint, exclusive reliance on the [intent] test is misguided and would prevent eradication of the racial discrimination which, unfortunately, still exists in the American electoral process.

QUESTION: Is it a policy to discourage it?
Mr. KNEEDLER: Yes, although the Voting Rights Act is premised on the unfortunate fact that racial block voting occurs. And where racial block voting occurs, the result can be, as this Court has recognized, the dilution of minority votes and, to that extent, the abridgement of the right to vote that was supposed to be secured by the Fifteenth Amendment. We did, indeed, fight a civil war over these issues, but one hundred years after the Civil War, Congress determined in 1965 that the business of the Civil War was not done and that various efforts were used, either intentionally or not, to discourage blacks from registering and then to dilute their vote.
QUESTION: In this case, is it a plausible assumption that racial block voting is, A, encouraged and, B, is the explicit premise for the design of this district?
Mr. KNEEDLER: Well, . . . I think it's pretty clear that it's the premise. In fact, I think it's the premise of appellants' challenge in this case because their claim of injury as white voters must be premised on the fact that voters will vote—that there will be racially polarized voting, or otherwise the injury of which they complain wouldn't occur.

---

5. Department of Justice Defends Race-Conscious Districting

Source: Oral Arguments in
Shaw v. Reno, 1993,
221 Landmark Briefs 582-83

QUESTION: Is it the policy, Mr. Kneedler, of the Justice Department and of the United States to encourage racial block voting?
Mr. [Edwin] KNEEDLER: It is not, but as this Court has said—

6. Guinier Calls For Voting Rights Reforms

Source: Lani Guinier, Voting Rights
and Democratic Theory—Where Do
We Go From Here?, in Controversies
in Minority Voting: The Voting
Rights Act in Perspective,
289-90 (Bernard Grofman &
Chandler Davidson eds., 1992)

. . . I propose a concept, tentatively called proportionate interest representation, . . .

It begins with the proposition that a consensus model of power-sharing is preferable to a majoritarian model of centralized, winner-take-all accountability and popular sovereignty.

.   .   .

Proportionate interest representation attempts to move the process of governmental decision-making away from a majoritarian model toward one of proportional power. In particular, efforts to centralize authority in a single executive would be discouraged in favor of power-sharing alternatives that emphasize collective decision-making. Within the legislature itself, rules would be preferred that require super majorities for the enactment of certain decisions so that minority groups have an effective veto, thus forcing the majority to bargain with them and include them in any winning coalition.

---

7. Black Congressmen Decry *Shaw* and *Miller*

Source: 139 Cong. Rec. 15146 (1993);
141 Cong. Rec. 18153 (1995)

[Reaction to *Shaw*]

Ms. [Carol] MOSELEY-BRAUN [D.-Ill.].

Mr. President, on Monday, in the case of *Shaw* versus *Reno*, a bare five-member majority of the Supreme Court issued an opinion that basically said the Court does not like bizarrely shaped congressional districts when race is used to help shape them. Frankly, the Court majority behaved much like Captain Renault in "Casablanca"; having just discovered gambling is going on at Rick's. . . .

Of course, just as Captain Renault knew that gambling had been going on forever at Rick's, the Court has always known that race, like ethnic background, income status, religion, and past political voting behavior, has always entered into redistricting decisions.

.   .   .

[Reaction to *Miller*]

Mr. [Major] OWENS [D-N.Y.].

[The Voting Rights Act] has been a great success in the Congress. We now have 40 persons of African descent. . . . [I]f you had a numerical formula that every group should be represented in proportion to its size in the population, . . . you would have a little more than 40. . . . but 40 is pretty close. The act has accomplished its purpose. It goes a long way in the direction of accomplishing its purpose toward giving representation which reflects the population.

So it is a serious matter to begin to roll this act backwards. . . . [And while] the Supreme Court did not throw out the Voting Rights Act. . . . the process of strangling [it] has begun.

.   .   .

9

GENDER

Discrimination against women has remained entrenched for centuries because of tenacious cultural beliefs and practices. The movement for women's rights over the past century alleviated some of these injustices, but progress did not come through the courts. It came primarily from the legislative and executive branches, which showed a much greater capacity to recognize wrongs and to right them. Judges, at both the federal and state level, held fast to anachronous legal doctrines. Not until 1971 did the U.S. Supreme Court issue a decision striking down sex discrimination. The judicial record before 1971 was deplorable. According to one study: "Our conclusion, independently reached, but completely shared, is that by and large the performance of American judges in the area of sex discrimination can be succinctly described as ranging from poor to abominable." John D. Johnston, Jr. & Charles L. Knapp, Sex Discrimination by Law: A Study in Judicial Perspective, 46 N.Y.U. L. Rev. 675, 676 (1971).

This chapter traces the political dynamics between judges, legislators, executives, and private citizens. Section I provides a brief historical framework to identify the prevailing ideas that discriminated against women, and explains how those ideas were shaken and rejected through the legislative process, state and federal. Section II covers the struggle for equal rights. Although the Equal Rights Amendment was never ratified by the states, it laid the groundwork for major victories in the courts. Section III analyzes the issue of women in the military, a controversy of contemporary debate because of the performance of women soldiers in Panama in 1989 and in the Persian Gulf in 1991.

I. TRADITIONAL STEREOTYPES

The framers inherited British legal doctrines that subordinated women to men. William Blackstone, the great English jurist, wrote that women, once married, lost their legal existence and became "incorporated and consolidated into that of the husband: under whose wing, protection, and *cover*, she performs every thing." 2 William Blackstone, Commentaries 442. Blackstone's theory of *coverture* dominated American judicial decisions throughout the nineteenth century and most of the twentieth (document 1).

The struggle for women's rights is closely tied to the fight against slavery. One of the leaders of women's rights, Elizabeth Cady Stanton, became active in the antislavery movement. In 1840 she married Henry Brewster Stanton, an abolitionist, and accompanied him to London to attend the World's Anti-Slavery Convention. Greatly offended that women delegates were excluded from the convention, she dedicated herself to challenge traditional restrictions placed on women.

Elizabeth Cady Stanton worked with other women to change the property law in New York. Consistent with Blackstone's theory, New York had given husbands exclusive control over the real and personal property of their wives. At a 1848 women's rights convention in Seneca Falls, N.Y., Stanton helped write a Declaration of Sentiments, using the Declaration of Independence as a model to hold "these truths to be self-evident: that all men and women are created equal" (document 2). Under this pressure, New York changed its property law that year to give married women for the first time a legal basis for holding and retaining property.

A. The Right to Practice Law

This was the first of several victories in the legislatures. The record in court was more bleak. In 1869, the Supreme Court of Illinois held that Myra Bradwell could not be admitted to practice law in the state. Of her qualifications the court had "no doubt," but advised Bradwell to present her case to the state legislature if she wanted any relief. In re Bradwell, 55 Ill. 535, 540 (1869). In 1872, the Illinois legislature passed a law stating that no person "shall be precluded or debarred from any occupation, profession or employment (except military) on account of sex: *Provided*, that this act shall not be construed to affect the eligibility of any person to an elective office." Illinois Laws, 1871-72, at 578. Mrs. Bradwell drafted the bill and pushed for its passage. D. Kelly Weisberg, Barred from the Bar: Women and Legal Education in the United States, 1870-1890, 38 J. Legal Educ. 485, 502 n.61 (1977).

After that victory, Bradwell took her cause to the U.S. Supreme Court, hoping to establish as a national standard the right of women to practice law. However, the Court held that the denial to women of the right to practice law did not violate the Fourteenth Amendment guarantee of privileges and immunities. Concurring in that judgment, Justice Bradley insisted that the "paramount destiny and mission of woman are to fulfil the noble and benign offices of wife and mother. This is the law of the Creator." Bradwell v. State, 83 U.S. (16 Wall.) 130, 141 (1873). Bradley's language reflects the teachings of Blackstone:

. . . [T]he civil law, as well as nature herself, has always recognized a wide difference in the respective spheres and destinies of man and woman. Man is, or should be, woman's protector and defender. The natural and proper timidity and delicacy which belongs to the female sex evidently unfits it for many of the occupations of civil life. The constitution of the family organization, which is founded in the divine ordinance, as well as in the nature of things, indicates the domestic sphere as that which properly belongs to the domain and functions of womanhood. The harmony, not to say identity, of interests and views which belong, or should belong, to the family institution is repugnant to the idea of a woman adopting a distinct and independent career from that of her husband. Id.

Decisions at the state level reflected the same biases. In 1871, the Supreme Court of Massachusetts responded to the governor's request for an advisory opinion to two questions: (1) under state law, could a woman, if duly appointed and qualified as a justice of the peace, legally perform all acts pertaining to that office? and (2) under state law, would oaths and acknowledgments of deeds, taken before a married or unmarried woman duly appointed and qualified as a justice of the peace, be legal and valid? The court answered both questions in the negative. A woman, whether married or not, could not be appointed to a judicial office. Opinion of the Justices, 107 Mass. 604 (1871).

In Wisconsin, R. Lavinia Goodell requested permission to practice before the Wisconsin Supreme Court. The court denied her motion, arguing that the "law of nature" destines women to bear and nurture children, take care of the custody of homes, and love and honor their husbands. In re Goodell, 39 Wis. 232, 245 (1875). According to the court, the nature of woman was incompatible with courtroom conditions: "The peculiar qualities of womanhood, its gentle graces, its quick sensibility, its tender susceptibility, its purity, its delicacy, its emotional impulses, its subordination of hard reason to sympathetic feeling, are surely not qualifications for forensic strife." Id. The court identified a number of legal issues that were supposedly unsuitable for women (most of which women encountered outside the courtroom): "[A]ll the unclean issues, all the collateral questions of sodomy, incest, rape, seduction, fornication, adultery, pregnancy, bastardy, legitimacy, prostitution, lascivious cohabitation, abortion, infanticide, obscene publications, libel and slander of sex, impotence, divorce . . . . This is bad enough for men." Id. at 246.

In the face of such reasoning women had little chance in the courts, but legislative action allowed them to practice law in a number of states and territories. A rule adopted by the U.S. Supreme Court prohibited women from practicing there. In 1878, the House of Representatives began debate on a bill to overturn the Court's rule. The legislation provided that any woman who was a member of the bar of the highest court of any state or territory for at least three years, who maintained a good standing before such court, and was a person of good moral character, should be admitted to practice before the Supreme Court. The bill passed the House easily, 169 to 87. 7 Cong. Rec. 1235 (1878).

The Senate Judiciary Committee reported the bill adversely, preferring to leave the matter to the discretion of the Court. Id. at 1821. The following year, however, the Senate passed the bill. Senator Joseph McDonald (D-Ind.) said a woman, having handled a case in a state court or in the District of Columbia, should not be forced to transfer the case to a male attorney if it reached the Supreme Court. 8 Cong. Rec. 1083 (1879). Senator Aaron Sargent (R-Cal.) called attention to the progress of women in other professions and delivered a powerful argument for the bill (document 3). The bill passed the Senate, 39 to 20. Id. at 1084. Thus, an all-male legislative body provided impressive support to women's rights—rights unavailable through the judicial system. 20 Stat. 292 (1879).

Within a few weeks Belva Lockwood, who had lobbied vigorously for the bill, became the first woman admitted to practice before the U.S. Supreme Court. A few years later, when she was denied the right to practice in Virginia and appealed to the Supreme Court, the Court deferred to the lower court's ruling that state law restricted the legal profession to men. In re Lockwood, 154 U.S. 116 (1894).

In some of the new states, women were able to gain employment rights through constitutional provisions. Article XX, Section 18, of California's Constitution of 1879 provided that no person shall, "on account of sex, be disqualified from entering upon or pursuing any lawful business, vocation, or profession." Because of that provision the California judiciary declared unconstitutional a law prohibiting the employment of females in dance-cellars and bars that served alcoholic beverages. Matter of Maguire, 57 Cal. 604 (1881). That constitutional provision now appears in Article I, Section 8, of California's Constitution.

The women's movement received no support from the Supreme Court. Two years after delivering *Bradwell*, the Court decided that although women were "citizens" within the meaning of the Constitution, that status did not give them the right to vote. The Court concluded that Section 2 of the Fourteenth Amendment limited suffrage to male inhabitants. Although women were "citizens" and "persons" in the constitutional sense, that did not entitle them to vote. Children, too, noted the Court, were citizens and persons. Minor v. Happersett, 88 U.S. (21 Wall.) 162 (1875).

Not until the Nineteenth Amendment was ratified in 1920 did women gain the right to vote. Opponents tried various arguments to deny women a right that had been granted blacks by the Fifteenth Amendment. During House debate in 1915, Congressman Frank Clark (D-Fla.) said that the "Word of God inveighs against woman suffrage, and the plans of the Creator would be, in a measure, subverted by its adoption." 52 Cong. Rec. 1413 (1915). Warming to his task, Clark advised his colleagues that granting a woman the right to vote "is to unsex her and replace the tender, loving, sweet-featured mother of the past with the cold, calculating, harsh-faced street-corner scold of politics. . . who would want a 'ward heeler' for the mother of children?" Id. at 1414.

After many false starts and delays, Congress passed the Nineteenth Amendment in 1919. Ratification by the states was completed on August 18, 1920. The role of women during World War I helped the cause of woman suffrage. Also, some of the opponents of female suffrage had argued that women, armed with the vote, would advocate the prohibition of liquor. That argument evaporated on January 16, 1919, with ratification of the Eighteenth Amendment. Alan P. Grimes, Democracy and the Amendments to the Constitution 92 (1978).

B. Protective Legislation

Before ratification of the Nineteenth Amendment, women began to win some significant victories in the courts. However, the outcome often turned on a belief that women were inferior, not equal, to men. For example, in 1908 the Supreme Court upheld an Oregon law that established a ten-hour day for women but not for men. Louis D. Brandeis, serving as counsel for Oregon, defended the statute by arguing for the *inequality* of women. He believed that women were not physically able to work the same hours as men. Brandeis prepared a brief of 113 pages containing data from statutory and sociological sources to support the need for limiting working hours for women. Medical and scientific evidence supposedly proved women's incapacity for prolonged work (document 4). At that point in his life Brandeis opposed women's suffrage. Later he came to support it. Philippa Strum, Louis D. Brandeis 554-55, 128-29 (1984). Accepting the logic of Brandeis' brief, the Supreme Court upheld the ten-hour day for women while reviving the reasoning of *Bradwell*:

> Still again, history discloses the fact that woman has always been dependent upon man. He established his control at the outset by superior physical strength, and this control in various forms, with diminishing intensity, has continued to the present. . . . It is impossible to close one's eyes to the fact that she still looks to her brother and depends upon him. Even though all restrictions on political, personal and contractual rights were taken away, and she stood, so far as statistics are concerned, upon an absolutely equal plane with him, it would still be true that she is so constituted that she will rest upon and look to him for protection . . . . Muller v. Oregon, 208 U.S. 412, 421-22 (1908).

After ratification of the Nineteenth Amendment, the Court began to reconsider the justification for protective legislation for women. In 1923, it struck down a District of Columbia minimum wage law for women. Referring to recent gains by women in statutory and contractual law, the

Court rejected the D.C. statute as "simply and exclusively a price-fixing law, confined to adult women . . . who are legally as capable of contracting for themselves as men." Adkins v. Children's Hospital, 261 U.S. 525, 554 (1923). The Court continued to uphold certain types of protective legislation for women, such as a New York law that prohibited women in large cities from working between 10 pm and 6 am. Radice v. New York, 264 U.S. 292 (1924).

Still, the Court equivocated on the question of minimum wages, striking down New York's minimum wage law for women and children. A 5-4 Court saw no need for protective legislation for women when men "in need of work are as likely as women to accept the low wages offered by unscrupulous employers." Morehead v. N.Y. ex rel. Tipaldo, 298 U.S. 587, 616 (1936). A year later, in the midst of the furor over Roosevelt's court-packing plan, a 5-4 majority accepted minimum wage legislation for women. West Coast Hotel Co. v. Parrish, 300 U.S. 379, 398 (1937).

In 1948, the Court continued to give its blessing to traditional restrictions on women. A 6-3 majority upheld Michigan's law that prohibited female bartenders unless they were the wife or daughter of the male owner. Goeseart v. Cleary, 335 U.S. 464 (1948). The Court denied that the statute violated the Equal Protection Clause, remarking that the Fourteenth Amendment "did not tear history up by the roots." Id. at 465. The Constitution "does not require legislatures to reflect sociological insight, or shifting social standards . . . ." Id. at 466. Those comments strongly suggested that age-old restrictions on women could survive the Court's scrutiny. The three dissenters said that the Michigan law discriminated arbitrarily against women and denied them equal protection.

C. Conclusion

Some of the outmoded concepts began to crumble in 1960 when the Court rejected the "medieval view" that husband and wife are one person, exercising a single will, and therefore legally incapable of entering into a criminal conspiracy. United States v. Dege, 364 U.S. 51 (1960). The Court took a swipe at the "self-deluding romanticism of Blackstone." Id. at 54. Tradition prevailed in 1961 when a unanimous Court agreed that states could largely exempt women from jury service: "Despite the enlightened emancipation of women from the restrictions and protections of bygone years, and their entry into many parts of community life formerly considered to be reserved to men, woman is still regarded as the center of home and family life." Hoyt v. Florida, 368 U.S. 57, 61-62 (1961). Remnants of the law of coverture persisted until 1966. United States v. Yazell, 382 U.S. 341 (1966). It was the political pressure for equal rights that brought about widespread changes in the courts and the legislatures.

DOCUMENTS

1. Blackstone's *Coverture*

Source: 2 William Blackstone,
Commentaries on the
Laws of England
442-43 (1783)

By marriage, the husband and wife are one person in law: that is, the very being or legal existence of the woman is suspended during the marriage, or at least is incorporated and consolidated into that of the husband: under whose wing, protection, and *cover*, she performs every thing. . . For this reason, a man cannot grant any thing to his wife, or enter into covenant with her: for the grant would be to suppose her separate existence; and to covenant with her, would be only to covenant with himself: and therefore it is also generally true, that all compacts made between husband and wife, when single, are voided by the intermarriage. A woman indeed may be attorney for her husband; for that implies no separation from, but is rather a representation of, her lord. . . . If the wife be injured in her person or her property, she can bring no action for redress without her husband's concurrence, and in his name, as well as her own: neither can she be sued, without making the husband a defendant. . . .

2. Seneca Falls Resolution
(1848)

When, in the course of human events, it becomes necessary for one portion of the family of man to assume among the people of the earth a position different from that which they have hitherto occupied, but one to which the laws of nature and of nature's God entitle them, a decent respect to the opinions of mankind requires that they should declare the causes that impel them to such a course.

We hold these truths to be self-evident: that all men and women are created equal; that they are endowed by their Creator with certain inalienable rights; that among these are life, liberty, and the pursuit of happiness; that to secure these rights governments are instituted, deriving their just powers from the consent of the governed. Whenever any form of government becomes destructive of these ends, it is the right of those who suffer from it to refuse allegiance to it, and to insist upon the institution of a new government, laying its foundation on such principles, and organizing its powers in such form, as to them shall seem most likely to effect their safety and happiness. . . .

The history of mankind is a history of repeated injuries and usurpations on the part of man toward woman, having in direct object the establishment of an absolute tyranny over her. To prove this, let facts be submitted to a candid world.

He has never permitted her to exercise her inalienable right to the elective franchise.

He has compelled her to submit to laws, in the formation of which she had no voice.

He has withheld from her rights which are given to the most ignorant and degraded men—both natives and foreigners.

Having deprived her of this first right of a citizen, the elective franchise, thereby leaving her without representation in the halls of legislation, he has oppressed her on all sides.

He has made her, if married, in the eye of the law, civilly dead.

He has taken from her all right in property, even to the wages she earns.

. . .

He has monopolized nearly all the profitable employments, and from those she is permitted to follow, she receives but a scanty remuneration. He closes against her all the avenues to wealth and distinction which he considers most honorable to himself. As a teacher of theology, medicine, or law, she is not known.

He has denied her the facilities for obtaining a thorough education, all colleges being closed against her.

. . .

He has endeavored, in every way that he could, to destroy her confidence in her own powers, to lessen her self-respect, and to make her willing to lead a dependent and abject life.

Now, in view of this entire disfranchisement of one-half the people of this country, their social and religious degradation—in view of the unjust laws above mentioned, and because women do feel themselves aggrieved, oppressed, and fraudulently deprived of their most sacred rights, we insist that they have immediate admission to all the rights and privileges which belong to them as citizens of the United States.

---

3. Senator Sargent Supports Legislation Authorizing Women to Practice Before the Supreme Court

Source: 8 Cong. Rec. 1084 (1879)

Mr. [Aaron] SARGENT [R-Cal.]. . . .

It is generally recognized that women are taking to themselves a wider sphere of action and filling it well. There was a time in the history of the English people when it was looked upon as improper and degrading for a woman to appear upon the stage, and yet since that time women have made their way in that profession in spite of prejudice, in spite of the unadaptability of their sex, as it was claimed by what was called public taste, until now they have rendered the profession and themselves illustrious in it. The medical universities of the world are receiving women and instructing them in medicine and surgery, and there are many women engaged in these studies and practicing this profession. In France the universities are open to them. The prejudice in England has been gradually overcome in this direction, and the London Medical College receives them. They are admitted into the Scotch schools and into some of the best medical schools of the United States, and they are making their way in them all. There are in the various States of the Union women lawyers; and women in literature have won a very high place. No man has a right to put a limit to the exertions or the sphere of woman. That is a right which only can be possessed by that sex itself.

I say again, men have not the right, in contradiction to the intentions, the wishes, the ambition, of women, to say that their sphere shall be circumscribed, that bounds shall be set which they cannot pass. The enjoyment of liberty, the pursuit of happiness in her own way, is as much the birthright of woman as of man. In this land man has ceased to dominate over his fellow—let him cease to dominate over his sister; for he has no higher right to do the latter than the former. It is mere oppression to say to the bread-seeking woman, you shall labor only in certain narrow ways for your living, we will hedge you out by law from profitable employments, and monopolize them for ourselves.

Who fears the competition of women? Who pleads for a law to help him hold his medical or legal practice? Let him step down and out. It would be as well to enact that women should not mount the rostrum or pulpit, or engage in writing books in competition with men.

I do not imply that all who oppose this legislation fear such competition. Custom and education count for much in our opinions. Every Senator has a right to his judgment in such matters; but I have sought to show that the profession is prepared to welcome women among them, as shown by the petition I have presented.

Believing that the effect of the defeat of bills like this would be to prevent women from entering an honorable profession in which they are qualified to be useful to society and earn an honest and adequate living for themselves and those dependent on them, I am in favor of its passage, and I trust the Senate will give us a vote upon it to-day, and pass this bill as it came from the House.

---

4. Brandeis' Brief on the Capacity of Women for Prolonged Work

Source: Brief for the State of Oregon at 18-22, Muller v. Oregon, 208 U.S. 412 (1908); 16 Landmark Briefs 83-87

I. THE DANGERS OF LONG HOURS

A. *Causes*

(1) PHYSICAL DIFFERENCES BETWEEN MEN AND WOMEN

The dangers of long hours for women arise from their special physical organization taken in connection with the strain incident to factory and similar work.

Long hours of labor are dangerous for women primarily because of their special physical organization. In structure and function women are differentiated from men. Besides these anatomical and physiological differences, physicians are agreed that women are fundamentally weaker than men in all that makes for endurance: in muscular strength, in nervous energy, in the powers of persistent attention and application. Overwork, therefore, which strains endurance to the utmost, is more disastrous to the health of women than of men, and entails upon them more lasting injury.

Report of Select Committee on Shops Early Closing Bill, British House of Commons, 1895

Dr. Percy Kidd, physician in Brompton and London Hospitals:

The most common effect I have noticed of the long hours is general deterioration of health; very general symptoms which we medically attribute to over-action, and debility of the nervous system; that includes a great deal more than what is called nervous disease, such as indigestion, constipation, a general slackness, and a great many other indefinite symptoms.

Are those symptoms more marked in women than in men?

I think they are much more marked in women. I should say one sees a great many more women of this class than men. . . (Page 215.)

Report of the Maine Bureau of Industrial and Labor Statistics, 1888

Let me quote from Dr. Ely Van der Warker (1875):

Woman is badly constructed for the purposes of standing eight or ten hours upon her feet. I do not intend to bring into evidence the peculiar position and nature of the organs contained in the pelvis, but to call attention to the peculiar construction of the knee and the shallowness of the pelvis, and the delicate nature of the foot as part of a sustaining column. . . . Comparatively the foot is less able to sustain weight than that of man, owing to its shortness and the more delicate formation of the tarsus and metatarsus. (Page 142.)

Man and Woman. HAVELOCK ELLIS

In strength as well as in rapidity and precision of movement women are inferior to men. This is not a conclusion that has ever been contested. It is in harmony with all the practical experience of life. It is perhaps also in harmony with the results of those investigators (Bibra, Pagliana, etc. Arch. per l'Antrop., Vol. VI, p. 173) who have found that, as in the blood of women, so also in their muscles, there is more water than in those of men. . . . (Page 155.)

. . .

There appears to be a general agreement that women are more docile and amenable to discipline; that they can do light work equally well; that they are steadier in some respects; but that, on the other hand, they are often absent on account of slight indisposition, and they break down sooner under strain. (Page 183.)

II. THE STRUGGLE FOR EQUAL RIGHTS

Just as World War I was one factor behind passage of the Nineteenth Amendment, so did World War II elevate the status of women. During the war, women filled many jobs previously associated with "men's work": machine tools, aircraft production, shipbuilding, and munitions. "Rosie the Riveter" became the new image. Because of those efforts, federal agencies began to adopt the policy of equal pay for men and women, while some states passed equal pay laws.

Women entered a number of professions and occupations that were new to them. These achievements created tensions, legislation, and litigation. One amusing case came out of Oregon, where the legislature had excluded women from wrestling exhibitions. The Supreme Court of Oregon upheld the statute, but not without poking fun at the legislators. After taking judicial notice that the legislative assembly that enacted the statute was predominately male, the court speculated on what motivated the lawmakers:

> It seems to us that its purpose, although somewhat selfish in nature, stands out in the statute like a sore thumb. Obviously it intended that there should be at least one island on the sea of life reserved for man that would be impregnable to the assault of woman. . . . She had already invaded practically every activity formerly considered suitable and appropriate for men only. . . . In these circumstances, is it any wonder that the legislative assembly took advantage of the police power of the state in its decision to halt this ever-increasing feminine encroachment upon what for ages had been considered strictly as manly arts and privileges? State v. Hunter, 300 P.2d 455, 458 (Ore. 1956).

At the national level, the executive and legislative branches began to address many of the practices that had denied women their rights. Against the backdrop of the Equal Rights Amendment, the initial focus was on the area of employment.

A. Congressional Initiatives

In 1961, President John F. Kennedy established the President's Commission on the Status of Women. He said that the support for equality of opportunity for women in employment must be reinforced by steps "to see that the doors are really open for training, selection, advancement and equal pay." Pub. Papers, 1961, at 800. Drawing on its constitutional power to regulate commerce, Congress passed the Equal Pay Act in 1963 to prohibit employers in the private sector from discriminating on the basis of sex. 77 Stat. 56 (1963).

Title VII of the Civil Rights Act of 1964 made it illegal for any employer to discriminate against anyone with respect to "compensation, terms, conditions, or privileges of employment" because of the person's sex. 78 Stat. 255, §703 (1964). It is commonly believed that the word "sex" was added for purposes of ridiculing, and killing, the bill. No doubt the person who offered the amendment prohibiting gender discrimination, Congressman Howard Smith (D-Va.), was well-known for his opposition to civil rights. Yet he was also a supporter of the Equal Rights Amendment and had the backing of women's groups. The National Women's Party (NWP) objected to the civil rights bill because it only prohibited discrimination on the basis of race, color, religion, or national origin. The NWP said that the bill gave no protection "to a *White Woman, a Woman of the Christian Religion*, or a *Woman of United States origin*." The NWP worked with Smith on his amendment to the Civil Rights Act. Cynthia Harrison, On Account of Sex 21, 176-77 (1988).

The debate on Smith's amendment demonstrates that his motivation was more complicated than simple ridicule. If Congress only prohibited discrimination on the basis of race, Members of Congress were concerned that a white woman applying for a job would be at a legal disadvantage to black women. Employers might be inclined to hire a black woman instead of a white woman to avoid possible enforcement actions from the executive branch or litigation in the courts. It was on that basis that Congresswoman Martha Griffiths (D-Mich.) strongly supported Smith's amendment (document 1).

Several courts held that Title VII and federal supremacy took precedence over conflicting state laws ostensibly enacted to protect women. To the extent that Title VII invalidated such laws, *Muller v. Oregon* was "superseded by congressional fiat." Johnston & Knapp, Sex Discrimination by Law, 46 N.Y.U. L. Rev. at 700.

The Civil Rights Act of 1964 created the Equal Employment Opportunity Commission (EEOC) to investigate claims of discrimination. Much of the agency's workload deals with cases of sex discrimination. In some of its early actions, EEOC identified unacceptable stereotypes of women. For example, Title VII permits employers to discriminate on the basis of sex if there are "bona fide occupational qualifications" (bfoq's), such as male and female actors, male and female models, etc. Regulations issued by the EEOC restricted bfoq's to limit abuse by employers. 30 Fed. Reg. 14926 (1965).

Some of the EEOC decisions provoked fights with Congress. In 1966, EEOC permitted employers to place want ads that had "Male" or "Female" headings. 31 Fed. Reg. 6414 (1966). EEOC's decision ran counter to language in Section 704(b) of Title VII making it "an unlawful employment practice . . . to print or publish . . . any notice or advertisement relating to employment . . . indicating any preference, limitation, specification, or discrimination, based on race, color, religion, sex, or national origin," other than for bfoq's. Congresswoman Griffiths assailed the EEOC both for its "Jane Crow" policy and its attitudes about women (document 2). The next year the EEOC changed its policy to clearly oppose sex-based want ads. 32 Fed. Reg. 5999 (1967). Not until six years later did the Supreme Court agree that a city could prohibit a newspaper from printing ads that listed job opportunities under "Male Interest" and "Female Interest" headings. Pittsburgh Press Co. v. Human Rel. Comm'n, 413 U.S. 376 (1973).

In 1967, building on the policies established in the Civil Rights Act of 1964, President Lyndon B. Johnson issued an executive order that extended the government's nondiscrimination policy to include discrimination based on sex. This policy covers equal opportunity in federal employment and nondiscrimination in employment by government contractors and subcontractors. 32 Fed. Reg. 14303 (1967).

B. The Equal Rights Amendment

An equal rights amendment to the U.S. Constitution was first introduced in Congress in 1923. Progress was limited because of a major split in the women's movement. One faction, led by the Women's Bureau, objected that the amendment would jeopardize protective labor laws that had been passed to benefit women. Efforts to exclude those laws from the reach of the amendment were unsuccessful. Conservatives tended to favor the ERA, while liberals, intent on using the power of government to protect women, were more likely to oppose the amendment. Harrison, at 7-12, 17-23.

The Senate twice passed the Equal Rights Amendment, in 1950 and 1953, but only after attaching the "Hayden rider," which provided that the amendment "shall not be construed to impair any rights, benefits, or exemptions now or hereafter conferred by law upon persons of the female sex." Equal rights proponents found the rider unacceptable. It made women both equal and not equal. The House of Representatives did not act until 1970. As sent to the states in 1972, the amendment read: "Equality of rights under the law shall not be denied or abridged by the United States or by any State on account of sex." When the amendment failed to attract sufficient states by the end of the seven-year period specified in the amendment, Congress extended the deadline to June 30, 1982. Even with the extra time the amendment was never ratified.

Failure of ratification did not make the ERA ineffective. It exerted a powerful influence on attitudes within the country, including the courts. The leading advocate of the amendment, Congresswoman Griffiths, used a number of floor statements to lambast the Justices for their sorry record. Significantly, she gave more credit to state legislatures and state courts for providing enlightened leadership (document 3).

One of the states to take the lead was California, which was well positioned to play this role because of language in its constitution providing that a person "may not be disqualified because of sex, from entering or pursuing a lawful business, vocation, or profession" (currently Art. I, §8, but previously Art. XX, §18). In 1971, the California Supreme Court reviewed a state law that prohibited women from being bartenders. Although a similar statute enacted by Michigan had been upheld by the U.S. Supreme Court in *Goeseart* in 1948, the California court found the law repugnant to the state constitution, in conflict with the Civil Rights Act of 1964, and unconstitutional under the equal protection clauses of the state and federal constitutions. Sail'er Inn, Inc. v. Kirby, 485 P.2d 529 (Cal. 1971). The court noted that "mere prejudice, however ancient, common or socially acceptable," is not a justification for discriminating against female job applicants. Id. at 533. Taking aim again at stereotypical notions of women, the court observed that the "pedestal upon which women have been placed has all too often, upon closer inspection, been revealed as a cage." Id. at 541. A year earlier, the Supreme Court of New Jersey also decided to break with the *Goeseart* precedent. Paterson Tavern & G.O.A. v. Borough of Hawthorne, 270 A.2d 628 (N.J. 1970).

The struggle over the Equal Rights Amendment also affected the U.S. Supreme Court. The first case in which the Court struck down sex discrimination on constitutional grounds was *Reed v. Reed* 404 U.S. 71 (1971), voiding an Idaho law that preferred men over women in administering estates. The American Veterans' Committee and the Legal Defense and Educational Fund of the National Organization of Women (NOW) prepared a joint amicus brief signed by six parties, including Congresswoman Griffiths. The brief brought the ERA to the Court's attention: "The history of the drive for this Amendment reflects dissatisfaction with the slow pace of judicial attack on sex discriminatory laws . . . ."

In another major case during this period striking down sex discrimination, *Frontiero v. Richardson*, an amicus brief by the American Civil Liberties Union discussed the pressure for the ERA (document 4). In his opinion for a four-Justice plurality, Justice Brennan took note of Congress' "increasing sensitivity to sex-based classifications," revealed in the Equal Pay Act of 1963 and Title VII of the Civil Rights Act of 1964. 411 U.S. 677, 687 (1973). He also noted that Congress had passed the ERA and submitted it to the states for ratification: "Thus, Congress itself has concluded that classifications based upon sex are inherently invidious, and this conclusion of a coequal branch of Government is not without significance to the question presently under consideration." Id. at 687-88. Justice Powell, concurring in the Court's judgment, drew a different conclusion from the movement for an equal rights amendment. He preferred to postpone judicial action to allow the political activity to run its course. Id. at 692.

C. Conclusion

The gender cases decided by the Court, starting in 1971, seem clearly influenced by congressional action on the ERA. The decisions "have been fully compatible with arguments made by leading mainstream ERA proponents in such documents as congressional committee reports and hearings records on the ERA, and in testimony in the Congressional Record by leading ERA sponsors." Leslie Friedman Goldstein, The ERA and the U.S. Supreme Court, 1 L. & Pol. Stud. 145 (1987). Instead of behaving like a remote, independent, and counter-majoritarian institution, the Court has been "heeding quite carefully the policies endorsed by the majoritarian branches of government." Id. at 154-55. Indeed, the ultimate defeat of the ERA is sometimes attributed to the Court's adoption of the amendment's principles. Jane J. Mansbridge, Why We Lost the ERA 47 (1986).

The ERA failed for many reasons. Some women were concerned that they would lose the benefits of protective legislation. Also, *Roe v. Wade* divided the broad coalition that had mobilized behind the ERA. The strategy had been to isolate abortion as a separate issue, but *Roe* seemed to link the ERA with the pro-choice agenda. Still another emotional issue was the question of making women eligible for the draft and military combat (discussed in Section III).

DOCUMENTS

1. The Amendment to the Civil Rights Act of 1964 Prohibiting Discrimination Based on Sex

Source: 110 Cong. Rec.
2579-80, 2583 (1964)

Mrs. [Martha] GRIFFITHS [D-Mich.]. . . .
Now, Mr. Chairman, I would like to proceed to some of the arguments I have heard on this floor against adding the word "sex." In some of the arguments I have heard the comment that the chairman is making, which is, that this makes it an equal rights bill. Of course it does not even approach making it an equal rights bill. This is equal employment rights. In one field only-employment. And if you do not add sex to this bill, I really do not believe there is a reasonable person sitting here who does not by now understand perfectly that you are going to have white men in one bracket, you are going to try to take colored men and century. Before it is over, judge women as individual human beings. They, too, are entitled to the protection of the Constitution, the basic fundamental law of this country."

2. Congresswoman Griffiths Attacks EEOC Interpretations

Source: 112 Cong. Rec.
13689, 13693 (1966)

Mrs. [Martha] GRIFFITHS [D-Mich.]. Mr. Speaker, I regret that it has become necessary to tell the House about the disregard of the enforcement of the law shown by key officials of the Equal Employment Opportunity Commission toward the provisions of title VII of the Civil Rights Act of 1964, which forbid employment discrimination on the basis of sex . . . .

I charge that the officials of the Equal Employment Opportunity Commission have displayed a wholly negative attitude toward the sex provisions of title VII. I would remind them that they took an oath to uphold the law—not just the part of it that they are interested in.

In the beginning, I excused their unprofessional attitude on the assumption that these men had not ever really thought about sex discrimination.

. . .

But their negative attitude has changed for the worse. They started out by casting disrespect and ridicule on the law. At the White House Conference on Equal Opportunity in August 1965 they focused their attention on such silly issues as whether the law now requires "Playboy" clubs to hire male "bunnies."

More recently, the Executive Director of the Commission, Mr. Herman Edelsberg, speaking at New York University's Annual Conference on Labor—Labor Relations Reporter of April 25, 1966, 61 LRR 253-255—stated that the sex provision of title VII was a "fluke" and "conceived out of wedlock." This is the same Mr. Edelsberg, who in his first press conference as Executive Director of the EEOC, stated that he and others at the EEOC thought men were "entitled" to have female secretaries. The House and Senate, of course, have resisted these calls to natural rights and gone along for years with male reporters.

. . .

. . . Congress had enacted the Equal Pay for Women Act in 1963 and was thoroughly familiar with the fact that job discrimination is imposed on women and inflicts severe consequences on their earning capacity. The sex provisions in title VII were supported by the great majority of the House and Senate. I also fought vigorously for the amendment, and I have received many commendations on my fight for the adoption of the sex bias prohibition. Congressman SMITH and I have disagreed on other civil rights bills, but I certainly welcomed his support of the sex provisions in title VII to give to women—white women as well as Nego women—full and equal opportunity to seek and keep jobs to support themselves and their families.

---

3. The ERA Becomes a Platform to Rebuke the Supreme Court

Source: 116 Cong. Rec. 27999-
28000, 28004-05 (1970);
117 Cong. Rec. 35295-96,
35323 (1971)

Mrs. [Martha] GRIFFITHS [D-Mich.]. Mr. Speaker, for 47 consecutive years this amendment has been introduced into the Congress of the United States. For 26 years both parties in their political conventions have endorsed it; the Republican Party has endorsed it for 30 years. Yet it has been 22 years since the Judiciary Committee of the House has even held a hearing on it. On the eve of the 50th birthday of women suffrage, it appears reasonable to me that the proponents of this legislation, who are more than a majority of this House, have a right to have this legislation discussed. . . .

Give us a chance to show you that those so-called protective laws to aid women—however well-intentioned originally—have become in fact restraints, which keep wife, abandoned wife, and widow alike from supporting her family.

The EEOC has already ruled protective legislation invalid and cases are now headed toward the Supreme Court to test that ruling under the Civil Rights Act of 1964.

.   .   .

We will show you that the Supreme Court which has readily moved to change the boundaries of your District and the boundaries of your school district has on not one single occasion granted to women the basic protection of the fifth or 14th amendment. The only right guaranteed to women today by the Constitution of the United States is the right to vote and to hold public office.

It is time, Mr. Speaker, that in this battle with the Supreme Court, that this body and the legislatures of the States come to the aid of women by passing this amendment.

.   .   .

Mr. Speaker, this is not a battle between the sexes—nor a battle between this body and women. This body and State legislatures have supported women. This is a battle with the Supreme Court of the United States.

.   .   .

I think it is of course essential to point out, even to lawyers, that the only two rights guaranteed to women today under the Constitution of the United States is the right to vote, and the right to hold public office. No women seeking the protection of the 14th amendment has ever won a case before the Supreme Court, whether she was plaintiff or defendant.

.   .   .

Let me show you what is going to happen if we do not act. If we are not the ones that legislate—if we are not the ones that write out the discriminations—then you are going to have case after case after case brought in one district after another, in one State after another, and finally to the Supreme Court. Because we do not announce a national policy—because we do not do what we do best—we legislate.

So we are going to leave it to the Supreme Court of the United States to bring you their legislation piece by piece and bit by bit, and I would like to submit, Mr. Chairman, there are no worse legislators in this country than those sitting on the Supreme Court. The real place to legislate is with the people who know how.

. . .

Mr. Chairman, what the equal rights amendment seeks to do, and all it seeks to do, is to say to the Supreme Court of the United States, "Wake up! This is the 20th century. Before it is over, judge women as individual human beings. They, too, are entitled to the protection of the Constitution, the basic fundamental law of this country."

---

4. ACLU Amicus Brief
in *Frontiero* Case

Source: Brief of American Civil Liberties Union, Amicus Curiae, at 18-19, Frontiero v. Richardson, 411 U.S. 677 (1973); 76 Landmark Briefs 773-74

In very recent years, a new appreciation of woman's place has been generated in the United States. Activated by feminists of both sexes, legislatures and courts have begun to recognize and respond to the subordinate position of women in our society and the second-class status our institutions historically have imposed upon them. The awakening national consciousness that equal opportunity for men and women is a matter of simple justice has led to significant reform, most notably on the federal level: Title VII of the Civil Rights Act of 1964, 42 U.S.C. Section 2000e *et seq.*, the Equal Pay Act of 1963, 29 U.S.C. Section 206(d), and executive orders designed to eliminate discrimination against women in federal employment and in employment under federal contract.

The overwhelming approval of the Equal Rights Amendment to the United States Constitution confirms the dominant intent of Congress to terminate sex-based discrimination by law. In the course of the debate on the Amendment, however, Congress made plain its view that appropriate construction and application of the fifth and fourteenth amendments would amply secure equality of rights and responsibilities between the sexes. Nonetheless, Congress wishes to provide further assurances so there would not be the slightest doubt that the right of men and women to equal treatment under the law would be recognized as a fundamental constitutional principle.

III. WOMEN IN THE MILITARY

During World War II, the heavy demand for military personnel pulled large numbers of women into the armed forces. A Women's Army Auxiliary Corps, with civilian status, was created in 1942. A year later it was brought under the control of the Army and called the Women's Army Corps (WAC). Women also served in the Navy, the Marine Corps, the Coast Guard, and the Air Force. About 350,000 women served in the military during World War II. Martin Binkin & Shirley J. Bach, Women and the Military 6-9 (1977).

Congress passed legislation in 1948 to establish the Women's Army Corps in the regular army. It also authorized the enlistment and appointment of women to the regular Air Force, Navy, and Marine Corps and in the reserve components of the four services. Congress limited women to two percent of the total enlisted strength. 62 Stat. 356, 357 (1948). At the same time, Congress prohibited women in the Navy and the Air Force from being involved in combat. Women in the Navy could not be assigned to duty in aircraft "while such aircraft are engaged in combat missions nor shall they be assigned to duty on vessels of the Navy except hospital ships and naval transports." Id. at 368, §210. Women in the Air Force "shall not be assigned to duty in aircraft while such aircraft are engaged in combat missions." Id. at 373, §307(a).

A. Reforms in the 1960s and 1970s

Congress removed the two percent limit in 1967, leaving the number of women in the Navy and the Marine Corps to the discretion of the Secretary of the Navy. 81 Stat. 376 (1967). Congress also removed statutory limits that restricted promotions for women in the armed forces. Women were now eligible to be generals and admirals. Both changes resulted from the need for women to serve in the Vietnam War. In signing the legislation, President Johnson stated that there "are more than a thousand women in our Armed Forces in Vietnam today," and that the armed forces "literally could not operate effectively or efficiently without our women." Pub. Papers, 1967 (II), at 999.

The decision in 1970 to end the draft, which terminated in 1973, created new demands for women in the military. Because of insufficient male volunteers, the percentage of women in armed forces steadily climbed, passing the previous limit of two percent and eventually reaching more than ten percent. With this growth, other changes occurred. Congress passed legislation in 1975 to permit women to enter the service academies: the Military Academy at West Point, N.Y., the Naval Academy at Annapolis, Md., and the Air Force Academy at Colorado Springs, Colo. 89 Stat. 537, §803 (1975). The spirited House debate on this proposal reveals the emotional dimension of using women in the military (document 1). Nevertheless, the amendment to permit women to attend the military academies passed the House by an overwhelming margin, 303 to 96. 121 Cong. Rec. 15456 (1975).

Women now command organizations composed of both men and women. Women participate in weapons training. Job opportunities expanded. Before 1970, women could participate in about 35 percent of military jobs. Restrictions were lifted, allowing women to work in more specialized jobs. In 1989, the proportion of jobs open to women in the military were as follows: Coast Guard (100 percent), Air Force (97 percent), Navy (59 percent), Army (52 percent), and Marine Corps (20 percent). Women's Research and Education Institute, Women in the Military 1980-1990, at 2.

B. The ERA Debate

The issue of women in the military posed a severe test for advocates of the Equal Rights Amendment. Were they promoting only equal rights or also equal obligations, including the duty to serve in the military and in combat? Could women oppose military service for themselves without at the same time inviting a second-class status? As one study observed, for "large segments of the population, service is taken to prove that an individual has sacrificed for his or her country. He or she deserves to be taken seriously in return." Barbara A. Brown et al., The Equal Rights Amendment: A Constitutional Basis for Equal Rights for Women, 80 Yale L.J. 871, 968 (1971). The study concluded: "Until women are required to serve in substantial numbers, stereotypes about their inability to do so will be perpetuated." Id. at 969.

During debate on the Equal Rights Amendment in 1970, Congresswoman Shirley Chisholm (D-N.Y.) acknowledged that women seeking equal rights had an obligation to serve in the military: "Each sex, I believe, should be liable when necessary to serve and defend this country." 116 Cong. Rec. 28029 (1970). The ERA passed the House without any qualifying amendments, but the Senate accepted language proposed by Senator Sam J. Ervin, Jr. (D-N.C.) to uphold existing laws exempting women from the military draft. His amendment passed 36 to 33. Id. at 36451.

By accepting this amendment and another involving nondenominational prayers in public schools, the Senate effectively killed the ERA. A House-passed bill without amendments and a Senate-passed bill with amendments required action by a conference committee to reconcile differences between the two versions. The leader of the House conferees would have been Emanuel Celler (D-N.Y.), chairman of the Judiciary Committee. Celler had refused to hold hearings on the ERA, making it necessary for ERA supporters to discharge the ERA from his committee.

Two years later, when the ERA was again being considered, the Senate decisively rejected two of Ervin's amendments to the ERA. The first read: "This article shall not impair, however, the validity of any laws of the United States or any State which exempts women from compulsory military service." 118 Cong. Rec. 9317 (1972).

This amendment split the Senate into two camps. Some, like Senator John Stennis (D-Miss.), regarded Ervin's amendment as necessary to avoid the drafting of women and subjecting them to combat or other hazardous duty. Id. Others, like Senator Birch Bayh (D-Ind.), conceded that women would be subject to compulsory service and possible combat conditions, but emphasized the benefits of military service that flowed to men and were denied to women. In particular, he discussed educational benefits available through GI loans, low-cost loans for housing and businesses, GI life insurance, and special employment benefits available to veterans (document 2). Senator Charles Percy (R-Ill.) made the additional point that rights and duties are co-extensive: "I do feel very strongly that if women want equal rights, and I believe they do, then they should have full rights as well as responsibilities. There should be no attempt to exempt them, such as is now being proposed, from military service." 118 Cong. Rec. 9334 (1972). Ervin's amendment attracted only 18 Senators. In opposition were 73 Senators. Id. at 9336. Ervin next proposed an amendment focusing on combat:

> This article shall not impair the validity, however, of any laws of the United States or any State which exempt women from service in combat units of the Armed Forces. Id. at 9337.

The word "combat" conjured up different images in the minds of legislators. Senator Marlow Cook (R-Ky.) denied that combat necessarily meant marching across the fields in France and Germany: "Combat today may be a lady sitting at a computer at a missile site in North Dakota. Does that mean that when it says she does not have to be in combat that she can get up and walk out?" Id. at 9349. He also noted that nurses in Southeast Asia were in combat zones and were being paid combat pay. Senator Ervin rebutted Cook by saying that contemporary war was "far more brutal," including poison gas, mines, and napalm. Id. at 9350-51. The second Ervin amendment fared little better; it was rejected 18 to 71. Id. at 9351. The votes on the two Ervin amendments did not necessarily imply Senate support for women in combat. The Senate wanted to pass the ERA with the same language as the House so that the ERA could clear Congress and be sent to the states for ratification.

C. Going to Court

Several court cases challenged the selective service laws as discriminatory toward men and women. In a 1968 case growing out of the Vietnam War, a male defendant charged with violating the selective service law claimed that it was unconstitutional because it made an invidious discrimination on the basis of sex. A federal district court upheld the right of Congress to subject men, but not women, to involuntary service: "Congress followed the teachings of history that if a nation is to survive, men must provide the first line of defense while women keep the home fires burning." United States v. St. Clair, 291 F.Supp. 122, 125 (S.D. N.Y. 1968).

In 1975, a federal district judge held that legislation limiting military draft to male citizens denied them the equal protection of the law by reason of unjustified sex classification. That decision was quickly reversed on appeal. United States v. Reiser, 394 F.Supp. 1060 (D. Mont. 1975), rev'd, 532 F.2d 673 (9th Cir. 1976). Nevertheless, the district court made two key points. While recognizing that women had made "great strides" in removing the vestiges of sex discrimination, he predicted that "they will never accomplish total equality unless they are allowed to accept the concomitant obligation of citizenship [compulsory military service]." 394 F.Supp. at 1062. He also challenged the conventional belief that women were physically incapable of serving in the military:

> There is simply no basis for concluding that all or even a significant number of women are incapable of serving in the military. This is true even assuming that they would be placed in combat roles. It should be understood that the nature of combat today is highly mechanized. Id. at 1067.

In 1978, another federal district judge decided a challenge to the statutory ban on assigning female personnel to duty on navy vessels other than hospital ships and transports. A number of women in the Navy brought the suit because the statute limited their opportunities for assignments and promotions. The judge ruled that the absolute ban on assignment of female personnel to sea duty, except on certain ships, abridged the equal protection guaranty embodied in the due process clause of the Fifth Amendment. Owens v. Brown, 455 F.Supp. 291 (D.D.C. 1978).

In response to that decision, Congress made a slight alteration in the statute banning combat duty for women in the Navy. It now read: "[W]omen may not be assigned to duty on vessels or in aircraft that are engaged in combat missions nor may they be assigned to other than temporary duty on vessels of the Navy except hospital ships, transports, and vessels of a similar classification not expected to be assigned combat missions." 92 Stat. 1623, §808 (1978). The purpose was to permit women to be assigned to a greater variety of ships. S. Rep. No. 826, 95th Cong., 2d Sess. 119-21 (1978).

D. Carter Initiatives

The Soviet Union's invasion of Afghanistan in 1979 marked the first time in more than three decades that Russia had used military force against an independent nation outside Eastern Europe. This act of aggression put pressure on the Carter administration to reconsider military registration as a supplement to the volunteer force. Citizens would be registered, but not necessarily drafted. President Carter requested funds from Congress to register both men and women, explaining why women should be included (document 3). Although he recommended that women be registered, his support was lukewarm: "I don't anticipate this happening." Pub. Papers, 1979 (I), at 249. A year later he said he had "no intention of advocating to the Congress [the use of women in combat] and the Congress would never approve any legislation that would permit women to engage in actual combat." Pub. Papers, 1980 (I), at 313-14. He even gave a limp defense for registering women: "I have also asked, as a separate piece of legislation—which I think has no chance of getting through the Congress—that that registration be not only young men but women. I prefer it, but I don't think Congress will do it." Id. at 880.

During hearings in 1980, the House and Senate Armed Services Committees confronted Carter's effort to focus solely on registration and avoid the volatile issues of drafting women and using them in combat. A leadoff witness at one hearing, a mother from Alabama, testified that the three issues could not be kept separate, quoting Senator Sam Nunn (D-Ga.): "If you don't plan to draft women, there is no need to register them. If you don't plan to put them in combat, there is no need to draft them." H.R. 6569, Registration of Women: Hearings Before the House Comm. on Armed Services, 96th Cong., 2d Sess. 3 (1980). Representatives of both the Department of Defense and the military services, however, testified that military effectiveness had improved through the participation of women in the all-volunteer armed forces. Department of Defense Authorization for Appropriations for Fiscal Year 1981 (Part 3): Hearings Before the Senate Comm. on Armed Services, 96th Cong., 2d Sess. 1389 (Lt. Gen. Yerks), 1682 (Principal Deputy Ass't Sec'y for Defense Danzig) (1980).

Also at those hearings, a spokesman for the Carter administration explained that the President's decision to ask for authority to register women "is based on equity. It is a recognition of the reality that both men and women are working members of our society." House Hearings, at 7. Nevertheless, a Justice Department official invited the committee to build a strong legislative record that could be used to defend male-only registration, an issue that was pending before a three-judge district court. Apparently the Carter administration was positioning itself to prevail in the court test (document 4). The committee reports prepared by Congress carefully followed these cues from the Justice Department in justifying male-only registration. S. Rep. No. 826, 96th Cong., 2d Sess. 154-61 (1980).

The three-judge court concluded that the principal reason given by Congress for male-only registration was military flexibility, and yet flexibility was "in fact limited by the complete exclusion of women." Goldberg v. Rostker, 509 F.Supp. 586, 605 (E.D. Pa. 1980) (three-judge court). After this court held that male-only registration unconstitutionally discriminated between males and females, the Supreme Court reversed and sustained the congressional policy. The Court said that the customary deference accorded the judgments of Congress "is certainly appropriate when, as here, Congress specifically considered the question of the Act's constitutionality." Rostker v. Goldberg, 453 U.S. 57, 64 (1981). The Court agreed with Congress that it was unrealistic to divorce registration from the issues of drafting women and using them in combat. Id. at 68.

E. The Issue Resurfaces

In the late 1980s, congressional hearings prodded the military services to open additional non-combat positions for women. The U.S. invasion of Panama in December 1989 intensified the debate on using women in combat. Over 800 Army women participated in the invasion and some saw combat. When U.S. forces were sent to the Persian Gulf in August 1990, approximately 26,000 women were part of the deployment. Women flew helicopters to transport personnel, directed artillery, drove trucks, and served with Patriot missile battalions in Saudi Arabia, Israel, and Turkey. Five women were among the 123 U.S. troops killed in action. Eight other women were killed in accidents.

In 1991, the House Armed Services Committee voted to repeal the statutory limitation on assigning women to combat aircraft. In light of the record of female soldiers in the Persian Gulf, the committee said that much of the current statutory restrictions on women in combat "appears to be an anachronism." H.R. Rep. No. 60, 102d Cong., 1st Sess. 240 (1991). In contemporary and future wars, "women will be exposed to combat regardless of whether they are on the front lines" and they "deserve to be treated equally with their male compatriots." Id.

The Senate Armed Services Committee voted against any change in the statutory prohibition. Instead, it recommended study by a 15-member, presidentially-appointed commission that would report to Congress by December 15, 1992. S. Rep. No. 113, 102d Cong., 1st Sess. 216-19 (1991). The full Senate rejected that approach and voted overwhelmingly to allow women to fly combat missions. 137 Cong. Rec. 20712-34 (1991). The Senate debate shows that the most effective argument for women in combat was not gender equity but military excellence. "Flexibility," used a decade earlier to oppose the registration of women, was now used to support women in combat (document 5).

In conference, the two Houses agreed to repeal the statutory limitations on the assignment of women to combat aircraft. Moreover, Congress established a commission to assess the laws and policies restricting the assignment of women to military duties. The commission could request the Secretary of Defense to conduct test assignments of females to combat positions. 105 Stat. 2365-70 (1991).

On November 15, 1992, the Presidential Commission on the Assignment of Women in the Armed Forces released its report. By a vote of 8 to 1 the Commission concluded that "there are circumstances under which women might be assigned to combat positions," and yet by the close vote of 8 to 7 it voted to recommend the retention and codification of the Services' restrictive policies regarding the assignment of women to combat aircraft. It also stated that women should be excluded from "direct land combat units and positions" and recommended that the combatant vessel exclusion law (10 U.S.C. 6015) be repealed, with the exception of submarines and amphibious vessels.

In the Clinton administration, Defense Secretary Les Aspin ordered the military services to allow women aviators to compete for assignments to fly fighters, bombers, and armed helicopters in combat squadrons. He asked the Navy to draft a bill to repeal the law barring women from serving on combat vessels. On November 30, 1993, Congress enacted legislation to repeal the statutory restriction on the assignment of women to combat in the Navy and the Marine Corps. 107 Stat. 1659, §541 (1993). The number of women in the military continues to increase as more occupations (combat engineer, gunner's mate, etc.) are opened to them.

F. Conclusion

The constitutional issue of excluding women from military combat, followed by the decision to permit their assignment to combat aircraft, was debated and resolved almost entirely outside the courts. Legislators and executive officials examined the constitutional options under heavy pressure from interest groups that took a variety of positions on human rights, civil liberties, and gender equality. The dominant element in this debate was not the handful of decisions rendered by federal judges. The decisive factors were nonjudicial: the government's need for women to serve in the military, technological changes in the meaning of "combat," and a fundamental rethinking within American society of the opportunities that should be available to women.

DOCUMENTS

1. House Votes to Permit Women to Enter Service Academies

Source: 121 Cong. Rec. 15449, 15451, 15453-54, (1975)

Mr. [Sam] STRATTON [D-N.Y.]. Mr. Chairman, this is the women in the academies amendment. I think there has already been a great deal of attention to it, so I will not need to explain it in detail.

. . .

It is just a simple matter of equality. The services have been promoting the enlistment of women for the last several years, and with a good deal of success. Women are now in the ROTC program, and they are attending our officer candidate schools. And for the last year or more we have had women midshipmen in the U.S. Merchant Marine Academy. Therefore, it seems to me that there is no real reason why we should continue to deny women the opportunity of attending the elite defense schools, for those who wish to make the military a career and who have the qualifications to be admitted to those academies.

. . .

I think it would be well for the committee to be aware in advance of what may be proposed to sabotage this particular amendment. There may be an effort made to suggest that we ought to allow women to serve in combat. I think that is a red herring at this point. It is not necessary for women to serve in combat in order to give the country a just return for the amount of money that we might spend in educating them in the service academies.

If we should later decide we want to remove some of these combat limitations on women, we could do that at a later time. But if such an amendment should be offered now I hope the Members will vote it down.

. . .

Mr. CHARLES H. WILSON [D-Cal.]. . . .

We paid combat pay to women in the Air Force in Vietnam during the recent South Vietnamese war. We have had nurses in combat situations in every war we have had. Women have proved that they can do the things that are necessary in such a situation.

. . .

Mr. [Larry] MCDONALD [D-Ga.]. . . .

. . . What is the reason for women in the service academies other than the pursuit of some egalitarian ideal? Frankly, I can find none; going further, there are overwhelming reasons for this amendment's rejection.

. . .

After the usual 4 years of study at the service academy, there is a 5-year service obligation. Under this amendment, how will the female officer serve this obligation of 5 years if she also has three—9 month—full-term pregnancies? Further, how will this obligation of 5 years be fulfilled if this same female officer also elects to breast feed her infant over a 1-year period before her next pregnancy? It is truly difficult to visualize an effective defense force that included a portion of officers serving while 7, 8, or 9 months pregnant. Going on, can anyone seriously imagine an officer giving a lecture or leading a tank column but requiring a pause to breast feed her infant? That situation which might produce a box office triumph in a broadway comedy, has no serious parallel in the real world.

2. Senator Bayh Identifies Potential Military Benefits Available to Women

Source: 118 Cong. Rec.
9333 (1972)

Mr. [Birch] BAYH [D-Ind.]. I suggest we are not talking about just a one-way street. In passing an equal rights amendment and thus raising the possibility that some of the women of this country are going to be drafted into the armed services, we are not just talking about a pure sacrifice on the part of the women. We are talking about a sacrifice; yes. We are talking about a responsibility; yes. But we are also talking about a significant benefit to be derived as a result of this service for the country.

                    .   .   .

The GI educational bill which has provided the greatest reservoir of talent that this country has ever known, is the first example that comes to mind. This talent has been primarily limited to men, because the services have been primarily limited to men. I wonder how many young women would make the same choice that the Senator from Indiana and many other young men made. When trying to weigh whether I should volunteer or not, one of the things I considered was not only what I could do in the Army, but that if I went in the Army and served my country for a certain period of time, it would permit me, on my own self-reliance, to provide an educational opportunity for myself. Most young women in this country do not have that choice today. This amendment would give them that choice.

It would also give them the benefit of GI loans for homes, farms, and businesses. There are hundreds of thousands, in fact millions of our citizens today who finance the purchasing of a farm, a home, or a business, not because they have any unique talent, but because they have had the opportunity to serve in the U.S. Armed Forces. . . .

GI life insurance is another benefit that is gained if you serve in the Armed Forces. We would make the same benefit available to women. Veterans' mortgage insurance, up to a $30,000 guarantee on a mortgage, would be made available to young women as well as young men, as would nonservice-connected death benefits.

Perhaps the most insidious type of discrimination that results because of the way our Army is treated today is in the employment area. If you are a veteran, the Veteran's Administration seeks to assist you in seeking employment. There are a number of job opportunities, on-the-job apprentice training, and other tools provided. We know that there are certain types of employment by our U.S. Government where, if you are a man and you have been in the military, you get X number of points added to your score, to get the job over someone who may be a woman and has never been a veteran, even if that woman is smarter than you are and gets a higher score on the intellectual part of the test. By the time you add those points for service to your country, the woman goes to the bottom of the list.

What we are saying is not that this is bad. If persons serve their country, give them the extra points. They earned them. But make this opportunity available on an equal basis to the young women of this country. . . .

3. Carter Recommends Registration of Women

Source: Pub. Papers, 1980(I),
at 290-91

My decision to register women is a recognition of the reality that both women and men are working members of our society.

It confirms what is already obvious throughout our society—that women are now providing all types of skills in every profession. The military should be no exception. In fact, there are already 150,000 women serving in our Armed Forces today, in a variety of duties, up from 38,000 only 10 years ago. They are performing well, and they have improved the level of skills in every branch of the military service.

There is no distinction possible, on the basis of ability or performance, that would allow me to exclude women from an obligation to register.

I am very much aware of the concern that many Americans feel about the issue of women in combat. There are almost as many job categories in the military services as there are in civilian life, and many of these categories do not involve combat. In the All Volunteer Force, women are now successfully carrying out tasks which, in the event of hostilities, would involve deploying them in or near combat zones. But women are not assigned to units where engagement in close combat would be part of their duties,

and I have no intention of changing that policy.

---

4. The Carter Administration Urges Congress to Strengthen the Legislative History to Justify Male-Only Registration

Source: Registration of Women: Hearings Before the House Comm. on Armed Services, 96th Cong., 2d Sess. 14-15, 23-25 (1980)

Mr. [Larry] SIMMS [Department of Justice]. . . .

The Department is defending the constitutionality of the all-male registration [before a three-judge court] . . .

I believe that the most salient point upon which our analysis is based in our legal opinion is that the Supreme Court has shown a great tendency in the area of military affairs to defer to judgments made by Congress. . . .

. . . [B]ecause the Court has shown the kind of deference it has shown for the judgments made by Congress in this area, the responsibility is all the greater on Congress in considering this issue to consider it wisely and to consider it thoroughly and to make a careful judgment if it decides to either reject or accept the proposal that has been placed before it by the administration.

. . .

. . . [S]peaking solely for the Department of Justice as litigator, it should be fairly obvious to this committee that the defensibility of the all-male registration is something on which Congress perhaps should speak out clearly and formulate the kind of proposal, which will be helpful rather than hurtful in the litigation.

As a final comment, I would just make reference back to something which I understood Mrs. Holt to say during the testimony of the first witness. The issue is not in the constitutional context—as phrased by Congresswoman Holt—whether there is a military reason to register or draft women, but whether there is a military or other reason to justify not registering women. That is the burden on the Government.

The Department of Justice is under a great responsibility to defend the constitutionality of any act passed by Congress. That is the burden we will have to carry. As to whether it can be carried at this point, we believe it can if the factual basis for it is there, and I think that whether it is there is largely a matter within the jurisdiction of this committee and Mr. Pirie and his peers at the Department of Defense.

. . . [I]t is the opinion my office gave, and OMB indicates, we think the real linchpin of our country's defense is directly tied to the proposition that as a constitutional matter Congress may prohibit women from serving in combat. Everything relates back to that proposition.

---

5. The Senate Votes to Allow Women to Fly Combat Missions

Source: 137 Cong. Rec. 20710-11, 20722 (1991)

Mr. [William V.] ROTH [R-Del.]. Mr. President, the amendment which Senator KENNEDY and I will propose later is not about gender, but about excellence. It is not about women pilots flying combat missions, but about the best pilots flying combat missions.

The readiness and preparedness of our military defense is a serious matter. When our Nation's future is at stake—and the future of free nations is at stake—we want the most skilled and seasoned men and women on the job.

Make no mistake—military excellence must be our first priority. Our Secretary of Defense must have the greatest flexibility and maneuverability to marshall the forces at his command. We want the best and brightest pilots in the air, not on the ground. We want the best person in the cockpit of a Stealth fighter or a B-1 bomber—not the second best.

Mr. President, America is with us on this issue. A Newsweek poll released just this week shows that 63 percent of Americans favor allowing women to fly combat aircraft. The American people know that what is good for our military defense is also good for the country. And what is good for the country is excellence, readiness, preparedness, strength, and flexibility.

Forty years ago Congress imposed a rule which now prevents women from serving as combat pilots. The congressional restriction is as old and outdated in today's military as a World War II propeller plane.

Flexibility is impeded and excellence is shortchanged because of this artificial barrier. Our Secretary of Defense needs to have the flexibility to make intelligent decisions about who should fly these fighter aircraft.

.   .   .

For anyone who thinks we need more studies, more evidence, I say, look at the record. Women have been pulling G's in high performance aircraft for over 15 years now. Women aviators train our male combat pilots. They test the newest generation aircraft. They fly the space shuttle. Women pilots test FA-18's and C-27's, they fly transport planes and refueling planes, they fly AWACS and helicopters. In fact, women have flown just about every plane that the Pentagon has built in the past three decades. There is no question about their performance, or their experience, in this regard.

But women have proven themselves, not only in the instructor's seat and in the test pilot's seat, but in battle conditions and in the line of fire. Their aptitude and ability may have been proven here at home—but their courage and mettle were proven in the skies over Saudi Arabia, Kuwait, and Iraq.

Our women pilots showed cool thinking and competence as Army helicopter pilots, Air Force AWACS pilots, and Navy surveillance pilots in Operation Desert Storm. They flew behind enemy lines and transported troops into enemy territory. Some of them flew ahead of the ground assault into Iraq. We owe our victory, in part, to the superb performance of these women pilots.

.   .   .

What about women in ground combat? Some have raised that specter, that fear, that the Kennedy and Roth amendment will lead women down the slippery slope into the trenches of ground combat. That is an unfounded fear, and it is an unnecessary fear. Our amendment is surgical, precise, circumscribed, and only germane to the role of women combat aviators; nothing more, nothing less. We are not establishing a dangerous precedent here.

. . .

Just let me add a word or two on the question of a draft. The argument has been raised that adoption of this amendment will result in women being required to register for the draft and women being subject to the draft, if the draft were ever to be reinstated.

As Senator KENNEDY said, this simply is not true. Congress, by statute, has decreed that women are exempt from registration for the draft, and this amendment barely changes the law at all. Women are exempt from registration now, and they will continue to be, if this amendment becomes law.

I want to also refer to the Supreme Court decision in Rostker versus Goldberg. The question has been raised that if combat restrictions on women are lifted, does that mean women would have to be drafted? The answer is no. The Rostker decision does not mandate that women must be drafted on an equal basis as men for a military service in which men and women are not similarly situated.

The Supreme Court has long granted deference to Congress in military matters. If statutory combat restrictions governing assignments are lifted and the legislation makes clear, or history makes clear, the intention to leave the issue of ground combat assignments to the military, the Department of Defense could continue to close ground combat assignments to women.